THE SIGN
OF ANGELLICA

JANET TODD

THE SIGN
OF ANGELLICA

WOMEN, WRITING
AND FICTION, 1660–1800

Columbia University Press

New York

Columbia University Press

New York

Columbia © 1989 Janet Todd

Printed in the United States of America

Library of Congress Cataloging-in-Publication Data

Todd, Janet M., 1942–
The sign of Angellica.

Bibliography: p. Includes index.
1. English fiction—Women authors—History and criticism.
2. English fiction—18th century—History and criticism.
3. English fiction—Early modern, 1500–1700—History and criticism.
4. Women and literature—Great Britain—History—18th century.
5. Women and literature—Great Britain—History—17th century.
6. Women in literature. I. Title.
PR858.W6T58 1989   823.009′9287   89-9703
ISBN 0-231-07134-5

Casebound editions of Columbia University Press books are Smyth-sewn

and are printed on permanent and durable acid-free paper

CONTENTS

PART THREE

ACKNOWLEDGEMENTS

I should like to express gratitude to many people for conversations that have given or modified my ideas over the past years, especially to Marilyn Butler, Betty Rizzo, Elaine Hobby, Rosalind Ballaster, Nicola Watson, William St Clair, Clare Harris who found the cover self-portrait of Elizabeth Louise Vigée-Lebrun, and the students at the various colleges of Cambridge University who have enthusiastically elected to work on women's writing in the eighteenth century. I am also grateful to the contributors to *A Dictionary of British and American Women Writers 1660–1800* whose entries I have often consulted and to Alison Hennegan on whose library I have frequently relied. Some of the material concerning Mrs Gunning and Mary Carleton has been published as 'Marketing the Self' in *Studies in Voltaire*, 217 (1983), while a modified version of the chapter on Delarivier Manley is appearing in *Last Laughs: Perspectives on Women and Comedy* (1988), edited by Gina Barreca.

INTRODUCTION

In Aphra Behn's *The Rover* (1677), a prostitute named Angellica Bianca attracts customers by displaying an inviting and provocative sign of herself. Men hang this sign from a balcony for her and respond enthusiastically to its compliment and promise. At the end of the play, after her patrons have been merry over her 'price and picture', Angellica Bianca is denied the hero: the message of her portrait is too frank, too crude. Had she worn it close to her face as a mask, matters might have been different, but instead she chose to distance it and to draw attention to its construction. The action was conscious, blatant, unfeminine and professional.

Despite Angellica's social and moral failure within the play, Aphra Behn, the first woman writer in England known to have earned a reasonable living through creative writing, associated herself with her prostitute, whose initials she shared. Accused of pilfering from men's works, she insisted in a postscript that she had hung out 'the sign of Angellica (the only stolen object) to give notice where a great part of the wit dwellt'. Clearly she was aware of the artifice of Angellica, for the plot punishes it; the identification of the two women indicates that Behn's professional literary concern is with the portrait, with the social construction of woman, the woman in business, in activity, in story, and in history, the female persona not the unknowable person.[1]

Aphra Behn's declaration in her postscript that she had borrowed from a previous play is as resonant as her appropriation of Angellica's sign. Throughout the early period of their public authorship, women had to defend themselves against the charge that men had written their works. Both Aphra Behn and her contemporary, the prolific Duchess of Newcastle, publicly and proudly asserted their ownership of their writings and gave themselves histories and characters that could explain their unfeminine ability. In Aphra Behn's case, as in that of most dramatists

1

of the Restoration, the charge of plagiarism is partially true. Constantly plays were made out of older plays, and plots and characters travelled freely among playwrights.

For Behn, this borrowing is important since it declares to later readers what she goes on to stress herself, that the culture in which she operates is largely male. Women authors are not newborn but already part of culture and Aphra Behn's work is a clear example of borrowing, adapting and following contemporary themes and styles. The wit is in the appropriation.

In this study of fiction from the Restoration to the late eighteenth century I have followed Behn's lead and not attempted to separate female writing from the web of male- and female-authored works that form the literature of a period – although I have focused on women's achievement. Because patriarchal literary history, exemplified in Ian Watt's *Rise of the Novel*, has largely written women out of its story of eighteenth-century fiction – of Defoe, Richardson, Fielding, Sterne and Smollett – I do not believe that feminist literary history should simply reverse the faulty procedure. The novel as a genre has both fathers and mothers.[2]

The existence of Behn at the outset of my study indicates, I believe, a point often overlooked in criticism: that literature is not progressive; there is not really a *rise* of the male or of the female novel, although several women at the end of the period, like Clara Reeve or Anna Laetitia Barbauld, assessed fiction in this way. In many respects the sophisticated insights and techniques of Aphra Behn or Delarivier Manley are not repeated by later novelists, while the influence of the narrator in fiction, invoked by Aphra Behn, would only be strengthened a hundred years later in Fanny Burney and Ann Radcliffe. The mid-eighteenth-century sentimental novel expressed an inwardness and self-reflexiveness that was missing from the more moralistic and social novels of Burney or from the erotic and worldly ones of the early Behn, Manley and Eliza Haywood.

In very general terms, I see female fiction beginning with an analysis of female signs and masks, as well as the social and moral effects of sexual desire and manipulation. It then proceeds to a moralistic – later fantastic – colluding with the growing ideology of femininity, preaching and greatly rewarding self-sacrifice and restraint. But, if fiction might appear to decline as an analysis of life and increase in wish-fulfilling appeal, by the end of the century it seems to gain a new strength from an assumption of the moralist's authority. This authority is the hallmark of the novel in the later period, leading directly to the early-nineteenth-century achievement of Maria Edgeworth and Jane Austen. The limitation of restrained subject matter and obligatory ethical stance remains certainly, but the compensatory benefits are in the respectability of the woman writer and in the central position of female fiction in the culture as a whole. The role of woman as moralist exemplified by Fanny Burney is not an especially popular one today, but it is, I believe, of great importance to women's development of the novel in this early period and is related to women's general exclusion both from the empirical scientific revolution of the eighteenth century – which parallels the emphasis on realism or verisimilitude in fiction characteristic of certain strands of male writing – and from the enterprise of Romantic aesthetics with its belief in some autonomous artistic realm. Women, excelling neither in the realist novel nor in Romantic poetry, did not accept the separation of realms which both empirical science and Romantic vision implied, and they insisted on seeing the moral and educational purpose of fiction within the contemporary world.

Because of my view of the development of women's fiction I have divided my study into three parts, the first dealing with the Restoration and early eighteenth century, a period of considerable frankness in writing when the status of female fiction remained dubious; the second dealing with the mid-eighteenth century, when sentimentalism and the cult of sensibility flourished, giving a new respectable image and restricted subject matter to the woman writer; and thirdly the last two decades, in which there is in part a reaction to this restriction and in part a conscious and public embracing of it. In each section I have briefly described women's involvement in the culture, not simply as relevant background to the literature but to throw light on the achievement of female writing. I have also described as far as I can the general literary characteristics of women writers and their connection with the literary culture as a whole. Finally in each section I have chosen three or four authors to investigate in more detail, either because I find them especially skilful as writers, such as Sarah Fielding or Ann Radcliffe, or because I see them as typical of a large number of less distinguished women, as is the case with Susannah Gunning and Frances Brooke; these readings are not intended as comprehensive interpretations but as part of the ongoing argument of the book. I have not tried to weave history into literature because I feel that this would give primacy to the literature which might then appear rather simplistically to reflect historical 'facts'. Yet I hope that both the achievements of the individual women writers and the analysis of the works will gain from being juxtaposed to the more general historical chapters.

Over a hundred years after *The Rover* was performed, Mary Wollstonecraft, like Aphra Behn, implicated herself in the sign of woman, now a free-standing post needing no male support. But, perhaps because of the greater autonomy, she provoked onlookers less to merriment than to irritated mud-slinging. More theatrically than the Restoration play-wright, she wrote:

> All the world is a stage and few are there in it who do not play the part they have learnt by rote; and those who do not, seem . . . as sign-posts, which point out the road to others, whilst forced to stand still themselves amidst the mud and dust.[3]

In the revolutionary decade of the 1790s, Wollstonecraft echoed many of the insights of Aphra Behn: that, for example, femininity was a cultural construction and that writing was an act of self-assertion for women. But she suffered even more hostility than the earlier woman for her outrageous opinions and her irregular life.

Between Aphra Behn in the 1670s and Mary Wollstonecraft in the 1790s is a century of sentimental construction of femininity, a state associated with modesty, passivity, chastity, moral elevation and suffer-ing. The construction is already foreshadowed by Angellica in *The Rover*. As she falls in love and comes to desire a single relationship, she discovers her absolute exclusion from the traditional female plot of love and marriage. She becomes angry not only at the hypocrisy of men but at her own impotence, and her joking sexy prose changes to melodramatic blank verse. Her misery is uncontained by the cynical Restoration comedy of manners that easily comprehends the male libertine, caught happily at last by a virtuous wealthy wife. Angellica does not recant or reform in the play, but she does realise that there are more potent and less explicit images of womanhood than the one she chose and that she might with profit have hung out her sign more discreetly.

In the Restoration, some women could bandy wit and bawdry with the boys, and Aphra Behn flamboyantly worked with and on the desire of men who gave her grudging admiration and no pity. But, from her tarnished reputation, women of the mid-eighteenth century learned that a display of certain sorts of self was shameful. Understanding the exaggerated distinction between sexual and linguistic expectations for men and for women, they often hid themselves under pseudonyms and anonymity, writing while firmly declaring their writing transgressive. Often they became simply a 'lady' or 'One of the Fair Sex', nudged into authorship not through desire for fame like the Duchess of Newcastle but through domestic distress, financial necessity, and the urge to instruct other women in their elevated moral route. As the novelist Mary Brunton expressed it at the beginning of the nineteenth century:

I am positive that no part – no, not the smallest part – of my happiness can ever arise from the popularity of my book, further than as I think it may be useful. I would rather, as you well know, glide through the world unknown, than have (I will not call it *enjoy*) fame, however brilliant. To be pointed at – to be noticed and commented upon – to be suspected of literary airs – to be shunned as literary women are, by the more unpretending of my own sex; and abhorred as literary women are, by the pretending of the other! – My dear, I would sooner exhibit as a rope dancer –[4]

Yet despite the horror of women writers like Mary Brunton for the 'rope dancing' sort of authors – certainly she would have included both Aphra Behn and Mary Wollstonecraft in the company – and despite their subterfuges, apologies and disclaimers, such women went on writing; they declared their absolute modesty and privacy while putting their productions before the public. After understanding the clear disadvantages of her openness, a chastened Angellica living on into the eighteenth century might have continued with her trade but without hanging out her sign at all.

The femininity promoted by women writers of the mid- and late eighteenth century was presented not as a construction in the way Aphra Behn had presented Angellica's sign but as woman's natural character. Such writers might appear to collude with the cultural and economic subordination of women, since they urged their readers to be domestic and serviceable to men and children and pre-eminently to display the qualities of unselfishness, sensitivity, kindliness and asexuality. But they also created, especially in fiction, a fantastic realm in which these qualities were deeply reverenced and in which modest and passive women, unlike the victimised or scheming sexual heroines of Aphra Behn, were effortlessly dominant. The great plot of female virtue, first in distress and then rewarded by a glamorous death or an hereditary mansion, became an immensely potent myth of feminine culture.

My subject here is the entry of women into literature as a profession between 1660, the year of Charles II's Restoration, and 1800, in the period of British reaction to eighteenth-century Enlightenment and the French Revolution. I am concerned especially with fiction since this is the genre with which women were pre-eminently associated and which most influenced female consciousness; indeed fiction was often thought to be the most powerful (although also the most condemned) element in girls' education and many autobiographies indicate a tale of distress by presenting a youth devoted to the reading of fiction. But, while I am separating out fiction for especial attention, I do not find it a discrete entity. The novel expressed the self of the author as much as genres intended to be more strictly autobiographical, while the fictional influence is clear in the changing images of the self delivered in vindications and memoirs; I do not think Laetitia Pilkington's life story or Susannah Gunning's vindication are 'fiction' but without the fiction they would not have been presented as they were. The term 'novel' itself gains some coherence in this period and is a standard one by the middle of the eighteenth century, but it would take another book to define it as a genre. For the purposes of this work I will only point out the main area of its instability, its relation to 'truth'. At different periods it is interchangeable with romance and with history (these are not discrete categories and romance could at times rely heavily on documentation). In the early years the novel often claims an historical status, in the later an empirical, verifiable and general truth.

If the genre I have chosen needs no justifying, perhaps the novels themselves do. Clearly these have immense historical significance as the first large body of imaginative writing by women in English. But a problem remains of what critical tools to use on them and what aesthetic principles to judge them by. Many of them are what would later be termed popular though perhaps not mass fiction, written for an audience known to have had little formal education and limited in what it could read and should think. By traditional literary critical standards most are intrusively autobiographical, self-indulgent, and conventional in style. But what does this judgement imply? Does it occur because the novels assert outmoded values which, nonetheless, can still appear unpleasantly seductive in modern pulp literature? Or is it a reaction to a literature that constantly declares that it exists to make money? Or is it because our critical assumptions have been fashioned through a particular body of male literature and literary criticism? Is the critical privileging of the ironic and the unified literary work, as well as the assumption of a transcendental ahistorical aesthetic against which all art can be measured, historically determined? I think the answer to all these questions is a qualified yes. This fiction has never found its way into any great tradition of English literature because it does not conform to the dominant aesthetic that eschews the disparate, the sentimental and the moralistic. Yet, although it is historically conditioned, I believe that the aesthetic remains a useful category which can take in the disparate, the sentimental and the moralistic. So there can be judgement that finds the fiction of Mary Wollstonecraft, Mary Hays and Frances Brooke immensely interesting for the history of female consciousness and the novels of Sarah Fielding, Fanny Burney and Ann Radcliffe great works of literature.

When I began this study many years ago, there was little published work in the area. I planned to write a brief survey of the subject as companion to my *Dictionary of British and American Women Writers 1660–1800*. Recently there has been a heartening interest in women of this period and both general and specific studies have appeared. I believe, however, that there remains room for an overview, although it can no longer be as brief as I once intended, one that insists on historical embedding, that sees the fiction in the midst of the other genres and in relation to history, and that takes a route between the daring assumption of the recent Pandora reprint series of women's fiction – that the eighteenth-century works can be immediately and unmediatedly current – and the new scholarly investigation of individual writers and literary particulars. There is still need, I believe, to counter a common view of women's history as beginning somewhere about 1830 and consisting in an heroic struggle encapsulated in fiction, of Victorianism and feminism, repression and liberation.

I should at the outset lay out my critical assumptions. They are those of what I call feminist literary history. This largely avoids the route of psychoanalytical or deconstructionist criticism which sees feminine writing less as writing by women that as a modality open to either sex. My concern is with signature, with women writing rather than with the writing of 'woman'. In recent years there have been some illuminating studies of this female writing which have aimed to look behind the signs and signposts of literature and culture for some essential patterns of repression. I am not intending to follow this route either, although I respect it. While it might reveal great riches in nineteenth-century literature, where it has most often been deployed, it is, I think, less useful for women's literature before that period, a literature that has until recently been little studied since it owns no canonical women like George Eliot and Charlotte Brontë. Sentimental literature of the mid- and late eighteenth century in which women in large numbers first found a clear fictional voice may be 'deconstructed' but with little difficulty, for the writing openly declares its obsessions and repetitions. The early fiction of the Restoration and the later fiction of the 1790s might seem more problematic and more accessible to modern critical methods and more yielding of hidden patterns of desire and anxiety. But again I think we should not, even here, too quickly take the surface as transparent, finding, for example, identical images of madness as women's condition. There is much treatment of madness in female fiction and more implied, but in a particular decade a woman might be in a madhouse not as metaphor and symbol of some absolute and timeless psychological and literary condition, but because the laws of England allow her sometimes

7

to be shut up by her husband, as Mary Wollstonecraft asserts in *The Wrongs of Woman*, written in the late 1790s, and sometimes not, as Jane Austen shows in *Northanger Abbey*, first drafted about the same time.

In the early heady days of modern feminism, past women writers were excitedly discovered and made to yield encouraging messages for the present. So Mary Wollstonecraft became the spokeswoman for sexual liberty and female power and Aphra Behn became the supporter of the anti-slavery movement and equal rights. Yet Wollstonecraft in *A Vindication of the Rights of Woman* was a rationalist who, like most people of her day, feared the disruptive selfish effects of sexual passion; and Aphra Behn, accepting slavery for common souls, was an avid supporter of the Stuart monarchy. Through the reading of more and more of what these women write, their unique and specific voices will be heard and perhaps their differences as well as their similarities from ourselves will emerge. Inevitably reading or criticism is a dialectical encounter of past and present and inevitably the present is privileged, but I have tried to let works speak as much as possible for themselves.

When the Norton anthology of writing by women appeared it was criticised for its organisation in which female texts were prefaced first by men's political and cultural history and then by women's private history of childbirth and menstruation. I sympathise both with the editors and with their critics and have tried to avoid the dichotomy. I have done so because I believe that women are far more present in what is usually regarded as men's history than is commonly accepted. After all, the bulk of published women's writing immediately before the entry of the professional female writer in the Restoration was in political and religious pamphleteering. Women continue to be political animals in the Restoration and eighteenth century and they are as likely to comment on the public issues of the day in 1690 and 1790 as male authors.

If it is easy to prove that public political and economic history is not men's province alone, it is far less easy to say what *any* history really is and how it should interact with what we call, in distinction, fiction. For history like fiction works through narrative and selection. Its writing is as embedded in and expressive of the ideology of the times as literature itself. All historical telling is some sort of imposition on another age. Our notions that the eighteenth century was moving inexorably towards industrialism and that therefore middle-class women were becoming more and more marginalised was not much noted by the writers of the time, who were more likely to see things in political or philosophical than in economic terms. Often the perceptions of a period and our reconstructions of it are at variance. In such a morass advice books and novels are in a way as 'historical' and revealing of a time as statistical tables.

Finally, a word about the terms I have used. I have employed 'feminist' to suggest an understanding of women as a class suffering peculiar disadvantages that ought to be removed and a belief in actual or potential intellectual equality of men and women. So, although totally different in their political orientations, Mary Astell and Mary Wollstonecraft are both labelled 'feminists'. I have sometimes used the words 'liberal' and 'radical' anachronistically in the early periods, and in the final one to refer to a whole spectrum of values from old Whig notions through Dissenting ones to those reviled by conservatives as 'Jacobin'; I have retained 'conservative' to refer to a nostalgic apprehension of a hierarchical organic past, sometimes including a Christian desire to reassert traditional moral values and sometimes a yearning for external authority. I have referred mainly to England and not Britain because the works I am dealing with were mainly written in England and many of the generalisations in which I have indulged are applicable to England rather than to Britain as a whole. Marriage did not have quite the same significance in England and Scotland when eloping English couples would dash for the border; at the end of the eighteenth century when professional female writers were well established in England, the author Elizabeth Hamilton would comment on a 'dangerous distinction of authorship' in Scotland.

I have taken Aphra Behn's ambiguous and resonant remarks about Angellica as the beginning of this book to suggest my approach, one emphasising the constructed nature of female consciousness, formed in the eighteenth century to an extraordinary extent through fiction. The Restoration and eighteenth century developed the idea of patents and copyright, the making public of ideas precisely to keep them in private ownership and prevent anyone else profiting from them and appropriating them. Like the man, the woman who published could no longer be entirely appropriated and made dependent. But, since women should not be independent or self-owning, this failure to be potential property was a kind of impropriety. In the story of women's fiction, the relation of author to authorial image and to creations will vary extremely but it will never achieve the clarity of men's relation to their ideas and creations, patented, signed and alienated from themselves.

I want to look briefly at the various signs that women have hung out in their self-presentations (vindications, apologies, autobiographies and prefaces) and more lengthily in their fictional portraits of women. Aphra Behn and the other women writers lived in a culture which they affected by their writings and which affected them. They declared themselves one way or another and like Angellica they often did so with the help of men, although they usually realised less than she did the price of male aid. It is the sign of woman, not an essence of womanhood that can be studied, for Angellica, like her author, did not hang out herself, but a sexual, social, historical and artistic artefact. It may indeed have borne a great likeness to the lady – or she may have crept out to look at it in the night, so as to recreate herself more fully in its image.

PART ONE

1

THE RESTORATION AND EARLY EIGHTEENTH
CENTURY: SIGNS AND SEXUALITY

The table of contents of *The Gentlewoman's Companion* (1675) reads:

The duty and qualification of a Governess to Gentlewomen's Children
Good Instructions for a Young Gentlewoman, from the Age of Six to Sixteen
Of the Gait or Gesture
Of Speech and Complement
Rules to be observed in walking with persons of honour, and how you ought to behave your self in congratulating and condoling them
Artichoaks Fried
Beef A-la-Mode
Jellies of several Colours, for all Sorts of Souc'd Meats, and to be eaten alone
An introduction to Physick and Chyrurgery
An approved Medicine to London-Midwives to break and heal womens sore breasts
Against a stinking Breath
To Nursery-Maids in London and elsewhere
Scullery-Maids
A method of Courtship on fair and honourable terms

The incongruous effect of this list on a modern reader comes in part from its apparent heterogeneity.[1] But perhaps it is also the result of our unfamiliarity with past advice books intended to advance women's economic capability rather than what might be called their traditional femininity. If so, the effect of the later *Spectator* will be less alien:

A Woman's Character is contained in Domestick Life: she is Blameable or Praise-worthy as her carriage affects the House of her Father or her Husband. All she has to do in this world, is contained within the duties of a Daughter, a Sister, a Wife, and a Mother ... when they consider themselves, as they ought, not other than an additional part of the Species (for

13

their own Happiness and comfort, as well as that of those for whom they were born) their Ambition to excell will be directed accordingly.[2]

Although both extracts are concerned with the domestic woman, they differ in what they assume about the female role. The first suggests the still restricted but nonetheless self-reliant and socially interacting woman, while the second portrays a middle-class version of a lady, leisured and morally useful; such a lady is entirely ignorant of medicine, fair courtship and even of beef à la mode and, while she has little practical function, she has immense domestic significance.

Less than half a century separates the two extracts but they seem to express different worlds. In its ideologies and assumptions, England in 1660 is recognisably distinct from the modern period but the England of the mid-eighteenth century is far less so. Between the passages are occurring those ideological and conceptual changes that would set the country on the road towards a later middle-class democracy, prepared for industrialisation, and allow it to emerge as the wealthiest European nation, with a trading empire unmatched in history. These changes affected all men from the highest to the lowest classes; in a very different but just as profound way they also affected women. It is no coincidence that during this period they entered commercial literature as producers and consolidated their role as consumers. In Virginia Woolf's *Orlando*, the writer-hero turns into a woman in the late seventeenth century.

POLITICS AND ECONOMICS

In the Civil War of Parliament and King in the 1640s, women played a subordinate political part. For example, they gathered together to make petitions, as when in the spring of 1649 they pleaded on behalf of their imprisoned menfolk, declaring that

> since we are assured of our Creation in the image of God, and of an interest in Christ equal unto men, as also of a proportionable share in the Freedoms of this Commonwealth, we cannot but wonder and grieve that we should appear so despicable in your eyes, as to be thought unworthy to Petition or represent our Grievances to this Honourable House ... And are we Christians, and yet must we sit still and keep at home.[3]

Well, yes, they must. They had already been told that women had no place in public affairs and that they should go home and 'meddle with' their 'huswifery'.

The women's petition uses the Bible to justify a political demand for an equality entirely at odds with the usual Christian ideology of wifely obedience and subordination. It also seems to question the ideal of

14

female domesticity and privacy, placing ahead of it the Christian's duty of prophecy or speaking out. The justifying and the questioning both result from the increase in women's literacy in the seventeenth century and their inevitable assumption in a time of civil war of nontraditional social and economic roles.[4]

But, despite the questioning and women's participation in pamphleteering and demonstration, the idea of subordination was so completely accepted by both sexes that even the radical Levellers who proposed a qualified manhood suffrage did not suggest a complete female political role. Many years after the Restoration, the feminist writer Mary Astell, who did not at all approve the radical agitation, yet blamed John Milton for not noticing half of humanity:

> how much soever Arbitrary power may be dislik'd on a Throne, not *Milton* . . . wou'd cry up Liberty to poor *Female Slaves*, or plead for the Lawfulness of Resisting a private Tyranny.[5]

The new age of Charles II was very different from the old. He arrived in 1660 from leisured exile in France and quickly scandalised his Puritan predecessors by taking a succession of articulate and expensive mistresses. Tension between the aristocratic and immoral court and the more middle-class and moralistic City of London quickly arose, each in a way in the shadow of the other. Indeed the exaggerated promiscuity of the court almost seems displayed for an audience; a puritanical frame surrounds the libertine Earl of Rochester, a glamorous courtly symbol whose anxiety and seriousness in his scandalous doings and writings foreshadow his famous deathbed conversion.

Despite the flamboyance, Charles's arrival did not signal the political and cultural reversal some of his followers wished. Although an aristocratic court had succeeded Puritan government as a centre of influence, it was not all-powerful and, in the years following the Restoration, the Stuart monarchy reeled from crisis to crisis, from plot to plot, until the deposition of Charles's brother, the Catholic James, in 1688. In its reeling it dealt blows to a belief in any divinely established order and, although Stuarts reigned until 1714, the Glorious Revolution of 1688 that brought in William of Orange as co-monarch at the will of a parliamentary faction ended any residual idea of the divinity of kings.

But in spite of the political fecklessness of many of the Stuarts, there was much nostalgia for the ideal of kingship they represented, and a romantic cult grew in the 1690s around the martyred King Charles I which continued on into the eighteenth century, finding expression in the writings of both the philosopher and feminist Mary Astell and the novelist and poet Jane Barker. In less decorous women it often coexisted with a similar idealisation of the very different character of his son, whose escapades in disguise after the Battle of Worcester quickly assumed romantic form in the telling. Despite its ruler's obvious moral and political faults, Charles II's court became for the playwright Aphra Behn and the political novelist Delarivier Manley a kind of golden age of freedom and aristocratic harmony.

The political ideal expressed in the cult of the two Charleses was a strong patriarchal monarchy, theorised in Robert Filmer's *Patriarcha* of 1680, which asserted that, as Adam was commanded to rule his wife, so should a father rule his family and the king his people. This often repeated analogy, linking gender and rank, did not prevent the more outspoken women of these years, from the Duchess of Newcastle and Aphra Behn to Mary Astell, Jane Barker and the Countess of Winchilsea, from declaring themselves dedicated royalists and defenders of the Stuart cause. In their works the downfall of the Stuarts became a kind of high Christian tragedy, giving a political hopelessness perhaps but also a resigned dignity to those men and women who understood it. Aphra Behn used her final days to lament the passing of the last really legitimate Stuart, James II – a pale echo of the tragedy of Charles I's beheading – and Delarivier Manley wrote and rewrote his downfall in her fiction. The pamphleteer Elinor James accepted imprisonment for supporting him in his exile, while many years later Jane Barker was still grieving over the last Stuart king.

Royalism is not necessarily allied to women's creative writing or to feminist awareness – Puritan women were undoubtedly more socially and politically radical. But there does appear a connection between professional, nonsectarian publication and royalist views. This may simply emphasise the importance of access to print or it may have some other significance. Certainly the early Restoration was a period in which a few notorious women like the Duchess of Cleveland and Nell Gwyn could rise to open political and social eminence in a way closed to them under parliamentary or Puritan rule. Such a situation might well have appealed to Behn and Manley, who associated kingly power with a time of greater female autonomy. In one of Manley's many retellings of the story of James's downfall, the king becomes a princess and the royal succession matrilineal.

For the more respectable Astell and Barker royalism seems rather a matter of social idealism than political opportunism. They saw the court in contrast to the commercial, technological, financial and democratic tendencies of the age which they deplored and which made men more socially mobile but from which stationary women were excluded. The old hierarchical order seemed more amenable to women, however much it accepted their subordination, while a sense of class could to some extent compensate for the disadvantage of gender. Both the middle-class but genteel Mary Astell and the aristocratic Duchess of Newcastle, each in a way insecure in her status, set much store by rank.

But this is to trivialise the very intellectual attitude of the enthusiastic-ally royalist Astell who, even at this early date, saw many of the moral disadvantages of the increasing entrepreneurial spirit, the passing of power into the hands of the mercenary and corrupt. Where Addison and Steele, speaking often for the new order, saw the Stuart court as the epitome of barbarous oppression, decently replaced by new liberalism, Behn, Manley, Astell and Barker all looked back nostalgically to a gracious age before greed and selfishness became the order of the day. Astell regarded the new emphasis on money and trade as a licence for selfishness and vulgarity and an immoral reduction of human beings and their relationships to physical commodities. (The radical and anti-monarchical Mary Wollstonecraft a century later would come to share some of this view but she never expressed it as clearly and cogently as her undemocratic predecessor.)

In her political comments Mary Astell took especial exception to a man who had a great influence on the later feminism of Wollstonecraft, the Enlightenment thinker John Locke, who suggested a basic equality in humanity and saw government less as a divine mandate for kingship than as a contract between the rulers and the ruled, a voluntary association of men coming together to preserve their liberties and property and open to abolition when inadequate to its function. Like the Puritan political theorists, although he argued against monarchical authority and although his thought allowed an assumption of male and female intellec-tual equality, he yet left conjugal power intact, that 'Power that every Husband hath to order the things of private Concernment in his Family, as Proprietor of the Goods and Land there, and to have his Will take place before that of his wife in all things of their common Concern-ment'.[6] Although there may be some use of Lockean Enlightenment language by a few women in this period – in the 1690s the printer Elizabeth Johnson spoke of 'Violations on the *Liberties* of *Free-born* English *Women*' – nobody really thought of extending the notion that men had a right to depose their governors into a right of wives to depose unworthy husbands.

To the Stuart faithful the reign of the last Stuart monarch, Queen Anne, still somewhat of a usurper from her father, James II, was a peculiar period of flux and uncertainty. The process of slowly transfer-ring power to Parliament continued and government through a minis-terial cabinet was consolidated, together with the two-party system of Whigs and Tories. The two factions, the first representing parliamentary power, city interests and the importance of commerce, and the second tending to value conservatism, royal power, aristocracy and country values, grouped round or against various royal personages and powerful politicians, such as the oddly populist Protestant Duke of Monmouth, the illegitimate son of Charles II, who made an unsuccessful attempt to block the succession of his Catholic uncle, James (and who would be roundly trounced by both Aphra Behn and John Dryden for his activity); William of Orange, used successfully to oust James from the throne; and, in the early eighteenth century, the self-made Duke and Duchess of Marlborough, powerful partly through the Duke's military victories and partly through the Duchess's long-standing friendship with Queen Anne.[7] Tory opposition to the Marlboroughs meant that the formidable Duchess, Sarah, was more lambasted than praised by female pamphleteers, and there was little real enthusiasm for the Queen as a Stuart or as a woman. Nonetheless, the close relationship of Anne with the Duchess in the early years of the reign might have encouraged the glorification of female friendship, so common in drama, poetry and prose, and her existence on the throne may have dampened the misogynist tone usual in acrimonious political writing by men.

Throughout the Restoration and early eighteenth century a few women openly and conspicuously engaged in political writing, as they had done during the Commonwealth. In the troubled 1680s Elinor James earned the title 'that She-State-Politician' and for her ill-timed support of King James was briefly imprisoned in Newgate. Under Queen Anne both Mary Astell and Delarivier Manley were Tory pamphleteers, in very different modes. Astell achieved respectability with her rigorously reasoned philosophical arguments for monarchy and the established church, while Manley, for a short time following Swift as editor of a Tory journal, never quite became respectable with her satiric mingling of erotics and politics. Most of these women took on a variety of social causes as well. Elinor James employed her forthright language on the debasement of apprenticeship and the overenthusiastic use of fireworks in London streets, while the educationist Bathsua Makin wrote against the incarcerating of men in 'devouring prisons' for debt. The prolific Quaker Ann Docwra, in her numerous blasts against towns and individuals, warned against the meddling of the law in matters of faith.[8]

Yet this summary should not suggest that political writing was easy for women. It happened more conspicuously than it would at any later time in the eighteenth century, but it still required some external aid. The Quaker women had the support of their organisation, with its continued encouragement of women's participation – although this was much disputed even in the early Restoration when the leading female Quaker

18

polemicist, Margaret Fell, argued rather defensively for it. Other women had some unusual access to publishing and printing. Manley had a liaison with a London printer; Mary Astell was connected with a bookseller who must have encouraged her into the pamphlet wars of the early 1700s, so lucrative for his trade; while Elinor James was the wife of a printer.

THE ECONOMIC SCENE

As the violence of civil commotion subsided, the importance of economic factors pressed more and more on people's consciousness. Puritan values associated with the commercial City of London, such as industry, probity and self-reliance, increasingly figured as secular virtues for men in literature. The Whig writer Richard Steele, promoter of anti-courtly images for both men and women, insisted that the old hierarchy of gentry above mercantile classes should be modified. A bourgeois public space was created out of coffee houses, clubrooms and periodicals allying court, gentry and town, theoretically acceptable to all men (though excluding women) who would adopt certain urbane codes of tolerance and good manners.[9] Large commercial institutions like the Bank of England and the Stock Exchange were started and shortly came to seem as much part of the establishment as royalty and the Church of England. London swelled in size and importance. Although the hegemony of aristocracy and gentry was still assured, capitalist values associated with the middle classes were spreading upwards. The permeation is manifest in the new hero, often a younger son, worthily born yet still with his fortune to make in the world.

Except to very committed, commercially minded Whigs, the changes did not seem clear progress. Many writers, including a large proportion of women, deplored what appeared to be a new order in which financial and pragmatic considerations had usurped the role of social morality and religion. Wealth was separating itself from work and landowning, and there was much discussion of the growing luxury in some classes; the conservative uneasily viewed it as moral debasement of the nation, while the commercially minded saw it as an exciting consumerism that could generate the nation's energy. For Manley the commercial classes became corrupters of values, undermining all ties in the nation, while an innocent and trusting aristocracy remained foolishly unaware of its decline.

All the fears and hopes of early capitalism found exemplary expression in the great South Sea Bubble of 1720, when government policy, an excitement of the new idea of unearned wealth through shares, and traditional notions of the seemingly unlimited riches of the South Seas coalesced to raise the price of stock to so ridiculous a height that a crash was inevitable. So devastating was the effect on the confidence of the nation that some contemporaries likened the Bubble to the striking of the plague or divine wrath. Although women were ruined along with men – Mary Astell, for example, had some investment in the company – the disaster seemed to a few female writers quintessentially male; Jane Barker regarded it as a bungling attempt to change the traditional social and economic order. (But the genderising of economic forces could go in either direction. Defoe personified credit as feminine because of its link with unstable fortune and Swift attributed the Bubble to a coven of witches.)

The slow movement from an economic system based on household industry to something more approaching the capitalist order of external production of commodities helped obscure women's connection with productive labour. In the seventeenth century they were in guilds and trades, even it seems in accountancy since in 1653 a book called *Advice to the Women and Maidens of London* appeared with the aim of teaching the skill to women who would aid their menfolk in business – at all times the way in for women was through relationship to a man. Although arguably not as great as it was supposed to be, for the ideology of woman's confined domestic sphere was always stronger than the reality, a gradual but definite erosion of male economic influence did occur in most areas, even in those trades and functions traditionally considered women's, such as millinery. English travellers, used to female marginality in the economic sphere, commented with surprise on the involvement of women in Holland.[10] Women writers in England did not much notice the erosion but in the early 1700s the playwright and philosopher Catharine Trotter needed to urge women's right to earn a living.

One area of especial concern was midwifery. Midwives had traditionally delivered babies and been licensed to do so by the church, but over the years this licensing system had disintegrated and male writing commonly abuses midwives as ignorant and lewd, bawds as well as nurses. Repeated demands by women for their own institute of midwives were ignored; instead a battle of female midwives and male obstetricians was joined. It would continue throughout the eighteenth century until midwifery clearly became professionalised into a career for men.

But the worst of the battle was in the future and in the Restoration childbirth was still a communal female event. In 1671 there were three popular books on midwifery for the education of midwives, two by men and one, *The Midwives Book, or the whole Art of Midwifery discovered*, by a woman, Jane Sharp, the first midwife in England to publish on the subject. Written in English, appropriately the 'Mother tongue', her book has the assurance of men's and an extraordinary openness in its description of sexual organs, 'the principal Part effectually necessary for a Midwife'.[11] There was much worry about a prurient interest in the readership of books on obstetrics and gynaecology – occasionally pornography and medical handbook overlapped – and Sharp tried to avoid this problem by a sexual vocabulary heavily drawn from the respectable areas of sewing and gardening.

One of the few careers actually expanding for women was school teaching. The charity-school movement, inspired by the Society for the Promotion of Christian Knowledge, formed in the late seventeenth century to combat the moral laxity of the age, spread schools all over England and by 1729 there were 132 in London alone.[12] These taught literacy to orphans and children of the poor and prepared them for service or apprenticeship. Women were very much involved in this movement as both benefactors and teachers, and Mary Astell was among those who gained part of her living from charity-school teaching.

Women of the higher ranks were also much involved in consuming wealth. The seeming economic uselessness of some middle- and upper-class ladies but their increasing role as consumers was signalled in the court of Charles II, the frivolity of which scandalised sober moralists. Court ladies were symbols of the general fascinated anxiety about luxury, aristocratic values and hedonism. When even the poorest cloth was expensive, their elaborate dress of velvet, silk, lace, satin and embroidery must have appeared an amazingly conspicuous consumption of wealth. At the same time their exaggeratedly naughty fashions, with plunging decolletage that outrageously affronted the Puritans, elided that crucial social distinction of whore and lady, while refusing the role of woman as domestic exemplar and subordinate wife.[13]

RELIGION AND PHILOSOPHY

With the accession of Charles II the Church of England was re-established and Puritans, defined as Nonconformists or Dissenters from the Church of England after 1662, were largely left outside political influence. In 1689 the Act of Toleration slightly improved but did not mend the situation. Later in the eighteenth century the struggle of Dissenters for full political rights would fuel many other reformist causes, while their exclusion from the universities encouraged them to found their own academies and schools. In these they stressed the vernacular over Latin and emphasised self-expression for everyone, even women and the lower classes. In time these emphases would help develop female political consciousness; in this early period, however, a period still close to Puritan rule, Dissenters were usually anathema to polemical women. Aphra Behn gibed at them and Mary Astell argued against their insubordinate and disloyal tempers.

Despite the licentious image of the age of Charles II and the urbane freethinking one of the age of Queen Anne, many Stuart ladies lived pious lives, often away from London. Revulsion from the libertinage of the court is clear in the religious pamphleteering of Quaker women and in the poetry of the Countess of Winchilsea and Katherine Philips. It also emerges in the writing of the more puritanical Countess of War-wick, who saw both the plague and the Fire of London as a divine judgement on the nation's sins. In her diary she depicts the kind of life that many admired, a mixture of piety and charity, fuelled by domestic disappointments, catching the tension between the sophisticated social life in which she was expected to join and a desire for withdrawal: 'I delighted in nothing so much as being alone in the wilderness, that I might there meditate on things of everlasting concernment,' she wrote. Experiencing the agony and ecstasy of the religious life, sometimes in flames of love for Christ and sometimes trying 'to storm heaven in my importunate prayers', she also had to cope with an irascible and irreligious spouse as well as comforting and supporting the local poor.[14]

Women themselves were often conscious of an association of religion with their sex, not only in their personal experience with profane or freethinking men, but also in some more fundamental way. In the Commonwealth period, they had joined men in seeing politics in divine terms; in this sort of interpretation they had as much status as men, having equal powers of 'prophecy' and equal control through prayer. Later, although women could not be priests or ministers, they could in a libertine, freethinking and increasingly commercial age stand for the moral values of organised and traditional religion. Something of this notion may be behind Mary Astell's allegorical use of the modest woman to represent the orthodox faith she revered:

Stand off now; and make Room for Religion and Liberty of Conscience, *bring them in hand in hand! Alas Sir! Religion is left at the Door; she can't crowd in, for Liberty of Conscience has got the Start of her; Liberty of Conscience is the Goodlier Person, uses a little Art, goes Finer, has the better Address and more plausible Eloquence. Religion is a Plain Honest Matron, and this as Times go is no Recommendation. Room there for Dame Religion who has lost her Head Cloaths and is almost tore to pieces in the Croud. Help, help! let some good Christian run and intreat the* House of Commons *to send their Officers to make way for her.*[15]

Although the doctrines of religion continued to be hotly debated and many women went on living piously, a secular tendency was abroad. This de-emphasised the dogma of Christianity and stressed useful social morality, the idea of innate goodness and the need for charity. Hobbes in *Leviathan* had asserted that the spring of human action was selfishness and desire for power, but other men such as the Earl of Shaftesbury found it in benevolence. He suggested a kind of gentlemanly secular humanism, encouraging a person to interrogate his own sensations and psychological shifts. The social stress also occurs in men connected with the Kit-Kat Club, supporters of the Glorious Revolution of 1688 against James II. Both Addison and Steele were associated with this club and it was in their periodicals, *The Spectator* and *The Tatler*, that the relevance of the thinking to women could be most clearly discerned. For it was in women that the newly described social virtues and self-consciousness were or ought to be pre-eminently displayed.

A tendency away from Christian dogma and towards involvement in human nature was further reinforced by the excitement over the rational and empirical abilities of the mind. This was encouraged by the philosophy of Descartes, Bacon and Locke, and by the scientific discoveries of Isaac Newton. Neither rationalism nor science was anti-Christian in the beginning, although both tended to swerve from the more arcane aspects of dogma, and for such thinkers as Mary Astell reason and religion went absolutely in tandem, demanding an intellectual apprehension of God. Women did not play a major part in the philosophical constructions, but they were not absent from them either. Several were associated with male philosophers, as they had been when Thomas More's daughter Margaret Roper discussed problems with Erasmus. The learned aristocrat Viscountess Conway considered philosophical matters with the Platonist Henry More, while Mary Astell, Lady Masham (theological writer and pupil of Locke), and the playwright and philosopher Catharine Trotter corresponded with John Norris. In time, when Lady Masham had shifted her position, she and Mary Astell philosophically quarrelled in print, Masham accusing Astell of being visionary and abstruse and Astell accusing Masham of being materialistic.

Astell is probably the most famous of these philosophical women. She argued rigorously and repeatedly against the secular tendencies of her age epitomised by Shaftesbury and Locke. She especially deplored Locke's reduction of the importance of God in his description of the growth of human consciousness and his sense-based notion of knowledge which she felt did not really account for the moral ideas of absolute truth and goodness. The views of Locke and Shaftesbury were hedonistic in tendency, stressing the good as pleasure, and she called Shaftesbury's work poison with its shallow optimism about human nature.

Behind the arguments and assurance of a writer such as Astell is the assumption – later to be much disputed – that, although women are socially subordinate and undereducated, the intellect of both sexes remains ungendered. This assumption, as well as the strangeness of a philosophical woman at all, is caught in a letter Astell wrote to Norris:

> Sir though some morose Gentlemen wou'd remit me to the Distaff or the Kitchin, or at least to the Glass and the Needle, the proper Employments as they fancy of a woman's Life; yet expecting better things from the more Equitable and ingenious Mr Norris, who is not so narrow-Soul'd as to confine Learning to his own Sex, or to envy it in ours, I presume to beg his Attention a little to the Impertinencies of a Woman's Pen ... For though I can't pretend to a Multitude of Books, Variety of Languages, the Advantages of Academical Education or any Helps but what my own Curiosity affords; yet *Thinking* is a Stock that no Rational Creature can want.[16]

In *The New Atlantis* Francis Bacon had envisaged a utopian scientific community, disinterestedly pursuing natural philosophy, a vision partially embodied in the new Royal Society. Neither utopian nor actual community included women, but nevertheless a few exceptional ones were much inspired by the new science. This tended to be not so much the experimental sort as the conjectural and speculative, still very much an amateur pursuit, aristocratic, unpractical and nonutilitarian – and so open to women. When later in the eighteenth century science became more professionalised and utilitarian, much of this interest would diminish. The Duchess of Newcastle was enthusiastic about the recently revealed world of atoms and she wrote down her scientific deductions and observations in excited poems with such names as 'What Atomes make a Dropsie', 'Of Vacuum' and 'Quenching and Smithering out of Heat and Light, doth not change the Property, nor Shape of sharpe Atomes'. For Mary Astell the sense that the jumble of atoms created formal beauty became a religious experience revealing 'an Infinitely Perfect and Self-Existing Mind'. Jane Barker was excited by the new medical discoveries such as the circulation of the blood, while Aphra Behn helped make science accessible to a female audience by translating Bernard de Fontanelle's *Plurality of Worlds* in which a scientist philosopher explains the Copernican universe to a listening woman.

Although only the Duchess of Newcastle had the temerity to publish her scientific speculations, there was commonly much ridicule of female curiosity and participation in science. When the Duchess tried to dispute with the philosopher Henry More, he suggested that his friend, the

Viscountess Conway, reply since he did not wish to put on petticoats to do so.[17] Repeatedly in the theatre the lady scientist was made to humble herself for her encroachment on masculine territory and taught that her proper study should be the dressing-room. In 1693 the playwright Thomas Wright, following Molière's *Les femmes savantes*, ridiculed the scientific lady in his *Female Vertuoso's* and in 1730 James Miller in *The Humours of Oxford* mocked his Lady Science and forced her to confess, 'I am justly made a Fool of for aiming to . . . move into a Sphere that did not belong to me . . . I will destroy all my Globes, Quadrants, Spheres, Prisms, Microscopes . . .'[18] So widespread was the abuse aimed at controlling the intellectual woman that even the female dramatist Susanna Centlivre echoed it, although less severely, in *The Basset Table* of 1705, the heroine of which may be a dig both at the Duchess of Newcastle with her microscope and at Mary Astell with her plans for a female college. Off the stage the privately scientific Viscountess Conway felt it necessary to ridicule the openly curious Duchess.

The general dissuasion of women from empirical science, the Baconian enterprise of reforming knowledge, and the mockery of their efforts to observe the material world are linked with their exclusion from capitalist enterprise. Each is a factor in their embracing of the only authority left to them: the moral. If the natural world and its control in technology were not their concern, then manners and morals surely were; they would take to this area with enthusiasm as the eighteenth century progressed.

SOCIAL CUSTOMS

The Protestant conception of marriage had always included the possibility of spiritual equality of the partners, despite Milton's influential picture of the subordinate Eve in *Paradise Lost*. Manuals stressed wifely duty but simultaneously pointed out the superior duty to God. This double duty contained a potential for conflict wherein the transgression of the lower might be necessary for the fulfilment of the higher – the burden of many Puritan vindications of disobedient wives. Consequently, although the ideology of marriage was definite and patriarchal, some instability was implied.

There was some instability too in the process of marrying. The aristocratic union had on the whole been an arranged dynastic and financial affair, but increasingly this was under attack and the art of the period constantly assaulted mercenary marriage in favour of a tie of compatible and congenial men and women. Both Aphra Behn and Susanna Centlivre used their plays to suggest the need for affection as well as money in marriage, expressed in the age-old plot of young couples outwitting old men's desires.

When the non-domestic work of the wife was needed, as it seems to have been in the middle and lower orders during much of this period, some economic equality could obtain. But, as the country became more prosperous through its trade and technological improvements, as it moved into a capitalist kind of system, women, although they must often have continued as economic helpmates, became more *defined* by domesticity. The position of widows suggests the change: no longer seen as part of an economic unit, needing to remarry to continue the business, they came to be regarded more as appendages to men who frequently in wills enjoined them *not* to marry again. In drama in particular, the lusty widow who wanted to remarry became a stock comic figure. In life many affluent widows prized the freedom allowed to widowhood, while others, less fortunate, found themselves, after years of painful childbearing and breeding, condemned to a penurious widowhood with little chance of economic activity, despite any riches they may have brought into the marriage.[19]

It is difficult to generalise on social changes, although many scholars have tried to do so. Consequently there is much dispute about the tendencies of the changing family unit.[20] Yet there is some agreement that there *was* an increasing emphasis on the close family over extended kin − various aristocratic practices died out, such as the placing of adolescent boys in related families for training − although it should be remembered that few families would be nuclear ones of parents and children and almost all took in older generations, siblings and servants. In such circumstances the power of the father inevitably increased over the daughters and younger sons who had no other family authority to look to, while the emphasis on primogeniture in the upper orders, the right of the first-born male to inherit the estate, would lessen his control over the eldest son. In the more sentimental art of the early eighteenth century that set up the family man rather than the rake as the male ideal, there seems a new emphasis on marriage as affectionate, and on men as loving husbands and fathers. Yet the emphasis should not necessarily suggest greater freedom for women in life. If it could be argued that there was love in marriage, then it could also be argued that a wife did not need financial safeguards on entering it or indeed separate pin money (the allowance given to a woman for her private use after the bulk of her money has been ceded to her husband): 'the Yoke' will fit 'so lightly', declared the author of *The Ladies Calling* in 1673, that 'it rather pleases than galls'.[21]

As an institution marriage was never under pressure. In the troubled seventeenth century there had been some toying with unusual relationships like polygamy and free love in the more extreme sects, but such experimentation declined after the Restoration. Instead a male writer (or a male character in a work of a risqué author like Aphra Behn or Delarivier Manley) might entertain ideas of polygamy, but it was usually as part of a seduction programme for a naive young woman, to persuade her into bed while a wife was still clearly living – Manley's guardian left his seduced ward a defence of polygamy when he returned to his wife. Or he might fantasise polygamy as utopia, as Henry Nevile does in *The Isle of Pines* (1668), in which he imagines his hero shipwrecked with four 'handsome women' through whom he populates the island with 'one thousand seven hundred and eighty nine children after fifty more years'. Later on there was occasional discussion of the different marital and sexual habits of different cultures and of the incompatibility of nature and culture, but there was no serious consideration of other forms of relationship in England until the revolutionary period at the end of the eighteenth century.

If women dreamt of living with many men, on the whole they kept their dreams to themselves, although a heroine of Aphra Behn did speculate about it. Certainly they did not much fantasise about cosiness and affection within marriage. While male writers imagined a delicious polygamy or created pictures of the domestic marriage of working man and chaste, subordinate and domestic wife, women clearly remained uneasy, unwilling entirely to embrace the newer idealisations. Mary Astell accepted that marriage was the main concern of women, described as 'the dressing forth our selves to purchase a Master'; having obtained one, 'that which we very improperly term our Business, the Oeconomy of his and our own Vanity and Luxury, or Covetousness, as the humour happens, has all the application of our Minds . . .'[22]

The unmarried Astell was one among several women theorists who did not discover much emotional mitigation of the unequal state of marriage and she compared the growth of political liberties for men with the stagnation for women in wedlock. In *Some Reflections upon Marriage* in 1700 she saw marriage as potentially enslaving for women, both iniquitous and unequal, although as always with Astell one should remember that she did *not* believe that arbitrary and legitimate power within the state was wrong; she was simply pointing out absurdities in liberal thought:

> If Arbitrary Power is evil in it self, and an improper Method of Governing Rational and Free Agents, it ought not to be practis'd any where; nor is it less, but rather more mischievous in Families than in Kingdoms, by how much 100,000 Tyrants are worse than one. What though a Husband can't deprive a Wife of Life without being responsible to the Law, he may, however, do what is much more grievous to a genrous mind, render Life

miserable, for which she has no Redress, scarce Pity, which is afforded to every other Complainant, it being thought a Wife's Duty to suffer every thing without Complaint. If all Men are born Free, how is it that all Women are born Slaves?[23]

Astell's married friend, Lady Chudleigh, made the point more bitterly:

> Wife and Servant are the same,
> But only differ in the Name:
> For when that fatal Knot is ty'd,
> Which nothing, nothing can divide:
> When she the word obey has said,
> And Man by Law supreme has made,
> Then all that's kind is laid aside,
> And nothing left but State and Pride.[24]

Another of Astell's friends, the young Lady Mary Wortley Montagu, saw men desiring 'a miss for pleasure, and a wife for breed'.

Whatever the literary views, some marriages were obviously successful. One example might be the supportive union of the Duke of Newcastle and his young wife, whose eccentric pursuits and literary aspirations he encouraged, or that of the Countess of Winchilsea who saw the Earl as life's 'Crown and blessing' and 'the much lov'd husband, of a happy wife'. Both couples were childless. Very different was the violent union of the redoubtable feminist poet Sarah Fyge Egerton or the wearying marriage of the Countess of Warwick. Tied to a sickly, irascible and profane husband, the Countess tried to keep calm and control resentment with piety; yet even she was driven by his outbursts of petulant temper to 'speak passionate words softly to myself, unadvisedly with my lips'. Later she referred to her husband in her diary simply by the symbol of a cross.[25]

Marriage was assumed to be for ever and divorce was rare. But the problem of the unhappy marriage *was* aired. One stimulus was the notorious Hortense Mancini, Duchess of Mazarin, who for many women personified the decadent (or attractive) court of Charles II. She had been brought up in France where she had known the exiled Charles and when she fled from her mad and repressive husband – a man who sounds very similar to Browning's fanatically jealous Duke in 'My Last Duchess' – it was to England that she came. Charles gave her a handsome pension (stopped by the more austere King William) and she set up an eccentric household of people and pets, becoming a byword for luxury and exoticism. Aphra Behn and Delarivier Manley both much admired her as a clever, charming woman, but Mary Astell regarded her as a symbol of the decadence of the time. At the Duchess's death in 1699 the issue of separation and divorce was widely discussed: some women thought she had a right to leave such a husband, but the majority would probably have agreed with Astell that she had not, and that, while it was painful 'to have Folly and Ignorance tyrannize over Wit and Sense', nonetheless once made a marriage was indissoluble.[26]

For some women, like the Lincolnshire poet and novelist Jane Barker, spinsterhood seems to have been a choice and in her poems she wrote of its joys: 'Strong Minds, like rocks their firmness prove / Defying both the Storms of Fate and Love.'[27] For other women marriage was probably not a choice. Whether through wars, the physical weakness of male children or male emigration, there appears to have been a shortage of men in a period of generally declining population. Possibly Astell's ideal of celibacy and female friendship was a necessity for some, and there was need to make agreeable the status of the spinster. Certainly the praise of spinsterhood and celibacy, perhaps also partly a response to the extraordinary nastiness of male sexual satire, is peculiar to these years — although it takes much from the aristocratic and platonic celebration of womanhood associated with the court of Charles I's queen, Henrietta Maria. The appreciation of the single state would be much more defensively expressed by the middle of the eighteenth century.

Since the fifteenth-century dissolution of the monasteries there had been passing references to the idea of Protestant convents, but no real proposal until Astell suggested an all-female college. This would be an establishment of like-minded ladies who would pool their resources, with the richer aiding the poorer. Several women were attracted to the scheme, including the young Lady Mary Wortley Montagu, but it foundered on the Catholic tinge of such an institution; it was a particularly anti-papist time.

When the Duchess of Newcastle fantasised a community in her play *The Convent of Pleasure* she too excluded men (indeed it seems that only lower-class women with insufficient money were in need of them at all):

if you incloister your self, How will you enjoy the company of Men, whose conversation is thought the greatest Pleasure?

LADY HAPPY. Men are the only troublers of Women; for they only cross and oppose their sweet delights, and peaceable life; they cause their pains, but not their pleasures. Wherefore those Women that are poor, and have not means to buy delights, and maintain pleasures are only fit for Men; for having not means to please themselves, they must serve only to please others; but those Women, where fortune, Nature, and the gods are joined to make them happy, were made to live with Men, who make the Female sex their slaves; but I will not be so inslaved, but will live retired from their Company. Wherefore, in order thereto, I will take so many

Noble Persons of my own Sex, as my Estate will plentifully maintain, such whose Births are greater then their Fortunes, and are resolv'd to live a single life, and vow Virginity: with these I mean to live incloister'd with all the delights and pleasures that are allowable and lawful; My Cloister shall not be a Cloister of restraint, but a place of freedom, not to vex the Senses but to please them.[28]

Astell's college is rigidly chaste, although Astell herself shows some emotional attraction to other women, noting 'an agreeable Movement in my Soul towards her I love'. In the Duchess's fantasy, a budding lesbian love is cut short by the discovery that the princess is a prince. This discreet avoidance is not matched in Delarivier Manley's political fantasy, *The New Atalantis*, where love among the women in their rural retreat is clearly physical.

The open reference to lesbianism in Manley reflects the general openness about sexual matters in the Restoration. Aphra Behn addressed a poem 'To the Fair Clarinda, Who Made love to Me, imagin'd more than Woman': 'In pity to our Sex sure thou wer't sent,/ That we might Love, and yet be innocent.'[29] Lesbianism had always been a voyeuristic topic in pornographic or semi-pornographic works for men, especially those deriving from France, where the convent was synonymous with titillating forms of female sexuality – and pornography was increasing in Charles's reign.

A small measure of the public attitude to transgressive female sexuality was the fascination with transvestism, often associated with lesbianism in broadsheet or popular literature. On the stage the equivocal double transvestism of Shakespeare was no longer necessary but breeches parts for women remained popular, while in the early eighteenth century the masquerade with its possibility of cross-dressing became a common entertainment, sourly denounced by moralists as potentially transforming the 'Kingdom into a *Sodom* for Lewdness'.[30] Still widely known were the habitual transvestities like the early Moll Cutpurse who had dressed as a man and lived independently, a 'squiresse' to Dulcinea.[31] In 1717 Christiana Davis was rewarded for her bravery and impersonation of a male soldier by being made a pensioner at the Royal Hospital; a later female soldier or 'Amazon' like Hannah Snell could not have expected such public approbation, although she did manage to get a pension from an aristocratic admirer.

EDUCATION

The rationalist debate over women's intellectual ability centred on education. It was widely thought that this had declined and that women were less learned than they had been. 'Women were formerly Educated in the knowledge of Arts and Tongues, and by their education, many did rise to great height in Learning,' wrote the educationist Bathsua Makin.[32] Certainly the display of learning made by a few aristocratic women of the sixteenth century – by Queen Elizabeth, Queen Mary, Lady Jane Grey, or the Countess of Pembroke – was not matched in the Restoration, but it does not seem that women's educational standards as a whole had fallen.

The sense of deterioration was caused by the fact that male educational opportunities were improving where women's were not. At a time when a few women were apprehending the rational character of *all* humanity, and when men from the middle and lower orders were increasingly included in education, women's exclusion from all institutions of higher learning whatever their rank was especially galling.

The Dutch scholar Anna Maria van Schurman had opened the question of women's share in cultural and public life in 1641 and she provided a compelling argument for it through her own enormous scholarly achievements. Her influence was direct on Bathsua Makin who in 1673 urged that women be offered a sensible training. Avoiding claims to an education that might destabilise the new order or suggest the assumption of intellectual equality with men, she yet opposed the frivolous upbringing in refined accomplishments, a little music, dancing and fancy needlework, directed at girls of the upper ranks.[33]

Astell was tireless in countering women's trivial and faulty education which conditioned them to attend constantly and solely to the adornment of their bodies, calling it 'the enchanted Circle that Custom has plac'd us in'. Regarding female intellectual faculties as a key to the spiritual state, she put forward more rigorous and radical proposals than Makin, hoping to rescue women from a 'meanness of spirit'. Her concern was not to provide girls with a particular body of knowledge but to train them to think abstractly and systematically so that they could make the proper decisions about their lives in this world and prepare themselves for the next. Although she would not have accepted Makin's view that 'the end of your Creation, [is] to be meet helps to your Husbands', she did believe nonetheless that, *within* the world, the purpose of the education for a woman who would marry should be wifeliness.[34]

Both Makin and Astell ran schools at different times of their lives. Makin's in the 1670s was for girls from the upper classes and it combined accomplishments, domestic arts and the subjects usually restricted to boys such as Latin, astronomy and philosophy. Astell's curriculum was more vocational since her clientele were the daughters of pensioners of the Royal Hospital at Chelsea, and the aim was to teach religion, reading and writing to prepare children for work.

Obviously the education women received varied enormously according to class, geography and chance. The few extraordinary women who wrote usually had some acquaintance with the classics, and both the Duchess of Newcastle and Mary Astell liberally alluded to them despite bewailing their lack of formal education. A marked degree of learning suggested a sympathetic and learned father or brother in the background. Makin herself had been trained at home, benefiting from the company of her brother, the mathematician John Pell; Mary Astell's uncle encouraged her learning, and the Anglo-Saxon scholar Elizabeth Elstob, inspired when a girl by Astell's educational ideas, was helped in her prodigious mastering of languages by her brother. Jane Barker's beloved brother aided her in the study of medicine. But, without such family situations and without exposure to an unusual school like Makin's, most women would have been excluded from much formal study, including the learning of Latin which still formed a code of culture, a privileged discourse in which much philosophy and science was conveyed. Those women who *did* know the language well, like Jane Barker, felt self-conscious and unsexed by their knowledge.

Nonetheless modern readers should not be too impressed by the claims of ignorance made by many of the writers. Aphra Behn, who proclaimed her lack of learning, wrote intelligently on astronomy, the Bible and theories of language, while she translated from French and made copious allusions to the classics and to modern philosophers such as Descartes.[35]

Both working with and opposing the feminist intellectual aims of Astell and her female friends were the extremely influential male editors of the periodicals *The Spectator* and *The Tatler*, Addison and Steele. These men expressed the growing worry that the more leisured middle-class woman would become a copy of the frivolous and demanding court lady. Consequently they were as definite as Astell or Makin in condemning the ornamental education given to women in the upper orders. But they were not eager to replace it by the rigorous abstract and intellectual training proposed by Astell. Indeed, although many men did comment favourably on the idea of the college for women – including Defoe and Steele himself, both of whom used it in their own writings – an article in *The Tatler*, possibly by Swift, poured considerable scorn on the notion, calling it a 'Scheme of a College for young Damsels; where, instead of Scissors, Needles, and Samplers; Pens, Compasses, Quadrants, Books, Manuscripts, Greek, Latin, and Hebrew, are to take up their whole Time'. Students would grow beyond materiality, the author scoffed, and would have a touch of the 'Amazonian' about them.[36]

The education that *The Tatler* put forward was a more fitting ladylike and pious one that would prepare women to be good wives and mothers. It was a separate education aimed solely at the female sex, stressing the peculiar qualities of women and their special role in culture and society. The full flowering of this notion of the serious domestic and ladylike education, domestic in the sense not of sewing and cooking beef à la mode, but of moral and emotional service to the family, would occur as the eighteenth century progressed, but the pronouncements of Addison and Steele and their contributors were immensely influential in popularising it.

IMAGES OF WOMEN

The male control of privileged writing was commented on by the Duchess of Newcastle, the first woman in English to publish extensively, and it would be noted again at the beginning of the nineteenth century by Anne Elliot in Jane Austen's *Persuasion*. Consequently the image of woman conveyed to the modern reader from this period is overwhelmingly made by men.

In conventional literary history, this is above all the great age of English satire. Men have always hurled abuse at women but they did so with exceptional violence in these years. Women were attacked as various types – much as men were by women – but men went further in simply satirising the sex itself, railing not only against what were regarded as faults to be corrected and against a disparity between what women appeared to be and what they *should* have been, but also at what was considered women's *natural* character, their lack of a soul, their lack of personality, their narcissism and their corrupt sexual nature.[37] In addition, women were often used by men to convey an uneasy crude obsession with sex and a horror of their own impotence. The great types in male satire, embodiments of threatening and castrating female autonomy, were the Amazon, the whore and the witch; in gentler times these would be modified into the virago, the coquette and the Bluestocking.

The writing lady could be equated with the Amazon, the whore or the witch, indulging in improper verbal freedom as well as or in place of a sexual one. Verbal antics were confounded with sexual and the pen became a female instrument of lubricity. Restoration prostitutes were known for their wit, a dangerous possession for a woman, always faintly suggesting erotic impropriety. The mask or the vizard, the sign of looseness and ambiguity, was also the sign of the writer who improperly hid part of herself. Aphra Behn knew the implications of taking on the sign of the whore Angellica.[38]

Male satire delivered a sexual, aggressive image of women, a knowing Eve. Virulent in destroying Aphra Behn's reputation, the satirist Robert Gould in *Love given O're, or: A Satyr against the Pride, Lust, and Inconstancy, &c of Woman* makes Eve's creation the intention of the devil; women become cunning and 'full of lewd desires', sluices gaping for a multitude. Hell for Gould was full of women and he demanded that the muse 'Gainst the lewd Sex proclaim an endless War'. Women were, he thought, the centre of sin; they were crablike, crooked from the crookedness of the fatal rib out of which they had been formed.[39] There is some of Gould's anxious misogyny in the poetic constructions of the later satirist Jonathan Swift, whose whores stand for the corruption of their times in general and specifically for female corruption, and in whose writing women's sexuality could become synonymous with the ravages of venereal disease and of ordinary human decay and death.

The openly bisexual poet Rochester railed against the castrating and disease-giving horror of women and their narcissistic masturbatory inner world. Women cursed men with impotence according to both Rochester and Gould, in whose writing the analogy of womb and tomb became frighteningly real. The idea of male penetration into the boudoir, a common motif in literature, would in later sentimental writings serve as an excuse for heady erotic and reverential male fantasies; in the poems of Rochester and Swift, however, it was used to express male disillusion and to undress woman of her sexual allure and mystery.[40]

The overt misogyny of Gould or Rochester is distasteful but it could at least be countered with some of the crude language that would later be unusable by women. Sarah Fyge Egerton certainly gave Gould as good as she got, taking up the 'daring Pen' instead of wielding it only for 'lofty Themes of useful Houswifery'. She vigorously argued that men colluded in creating female vice and she insisted that women were more constant, more moral, and certainly more chaste than men: 'For Woman was created good, and she / Was thought the best of frail Mortality'. Men made the rhetoric of abuse and it should be returned to them.[41]

Alexander Pope used the sexual woman to express the degradation of the age. But he also felt the attraction of the domestic contingent wifely woman, the woman who must learn that beauty will fade and that narcissism will result in spinsterhood. Having bandied wit with intelligent and successful female writers such as Eliza Haywood, Delarivier Manley and Lady Mary Wortley Montagu – all existing nowadays mainly in footnotes to his work – he yet in his poetry created the clichés of the coquette, the prude and the prig, his rare feminine ideal being a retiring, affectionate woman of constant good humour and good sense, admirable in a way but not the image Pope would have wanted for himself.

The newer construction which Pope partly expresses is a reassertion of traditional 'femininity' – modesty, chastity and domesticity. It was not as easily disputed as the sexual horror attacked by Sarah Fyge Egerton. Instead of a castrating Amazon, the 'feminine' woman was a 'softer man', the passive domestic contingent lady as moral and spiritual inspiration.

Foreshadowed by the traditional *Ladies Calling* of 1673 which considered that 'the principal and distinct scenes in which a woman can be supposed to be an actor, are these three, virginity, marriage and widowhood', the feminine image was caught by the Marquess of Halifax in *The Lady's New-Years Gift: or, Advice to a Daughter* (1688), which taught female submission and advised girls to use the little reason they possessed to further their compliance.[42] The sensible woman would be constantly aware of her effect on others and would control any tendency towards learning or loquaciousness. But it was above all in the pages of Addison and Steele that the new lady was created in complete distinction to men:

> I am sure, I do not mean it an injury to women, when I say there is a sort of sex in souls. I am tender of offending them, and know it is hard not to do it on this subject; but I must go on to say, that the soul of a man and that of a woman are made very unlike, according to the employments for which they are designed . . . The virtues have respectively a masculine and a feminine cast.[43]

The Puritan *Whole Duty of Man* which taught the spiritual purpose of life to both sexes was no longer suitable for women, it seemed.

Women's 'Duties' in this world were those of 'a Daughter, a Sister, a Wife, and a Mother'. They must learn to say, 'I . . . have no other Concern but to please the Man I love: he is the End of every Care I have.' The domestic woman of Halifax or Steele was a forerunner of the 'angel in the house', still living in the twentieth century when Virginia Woolf tried to murder her.

2

THE FEMALE WITS: WOMEN WRITERS OF THE RESTORATION AND EARLY EIGHTEENTH CENTURY

When Samuel Pepys accidentally came upon his wife's diary, he found it

> so picquant, and wrote in English and most of it true, of the retirednesse of her life and how unpleasant it was, that being writ in English and so in danger of being met with and read by others, I was vexed at it and desired her and then commanded her to teare it.[1]

Pepys's command suggests one answer to the question of why there is not more surviving female writing from this period. It also highlights women's connection with the growth of literature in English that might indeed be 'read by others'.

But, even with such problems and constraints, there is a great deal of writing. Women have probably been publishing since the invention of printing and, as scholars delve deeper into history, more of this writing will be uncovered. What is especially interesting in the Restoration is the entry of women into *commercial* literature and their presence at the gradual emergence of the important new genre of the novel.

The first literary area into which women ventured *en masse* is the mingled one of politics and religion – surprisingly perhaps for those most familiar with the later idea that women should treat domestic matters. During the Commonwealth they wrote pamphlets intended to intervene in the political and religious life of the nation and they wrote clearly under their own names and printed each other's books, now inveighing against the tyrannical Cromwellian government, and now castigating the sins and high living of Oxford and Cambridge or the luxurious decadence of the restored monarchy.[2] Despite the ritual apology of pamphleteers, always pushed unaccustomedly into print by the burning issues of the times or personal grievances, and despite the added apology for their sex, these women frequently achieved an unusual assurance of tone and self-presentation by referring to divine authority,

36

which overtopped even the patriarchal one. Although a woman could call herself 'a very weake, and unworthy instrument,' nonetheless it was God who was using her and this fact gave her considerable authority. Inevitably at the Restoration much of the activity ceased with the persecution of some of the Puritan sects. In the more secular times the heirs of the prophetic women included the political pamphleteers of the various royal crises and the scandalous political novelists of Queen Anne's court such as Delarivier Manley and Eliza Haywood.

But publishing outside pamphlets, prophecies, almanacs, and a few devotional poems was still perceived as an oddity. And the few women who did proceed before the 1670s and 1680s were very much aware of their strangeness. As the poet Anne Finch, Countess of Winchilsea, remarked, 'Alas! A woman that attempts the pen,/ Such an intruder on the rights of men.'[3]

But it is not always clear in this period or in the early eighteenth century whether a work was authored by a man or by a woman. The passages with which I began Chapter One are both uncertain, the second from an anonymous magazine article though assumed to be Richard Steele's and the first from a work spuriously attributed to Hannah Wolley, presumably so as to capitalise on the name of this famous pioneer of the cookery book. By the mid-century, many reviewers believed that writing was indeed gendered and that they could detect the feminine presence in any work. But in the Restoration it was not axiomatic that women and men would write in different ways. Works attributed to Defoe may be by Manley and the authorship of the extremely popular *The Whole Duty of Man* (1658) remains disputed; largely accepted in the seventeenth and eighteenth centuries as by the well-educated and entirely capable Lady Pakington, it was more often ascribed to a male author from the nineteenth century onwards. When Mary Astell's *The Christian Religion* appeared in 1705, many thought it was written by a leading High Churchman.

The Restoration and early eighteenth century is the first period when women as a group began writing for money clearly and openly. They did so with relatively little fuss compared with the elaborate panoply of apology later thought essential for a publishing woman, although usually their sex was mentioned either to titillate or plead. They did not enter as novelists first, although this was the genre in which they were to make the most indelible mark, but as dramatists. Drama was a more lucrative form and Aphra Behn, so important for the development of fiction, was primarily thought of as a dramatist. The other major fiction writers, Delarivier Manley and Eliza Haywood, both wrote for the stage and also edited magazines.

In later years, when fiction had become more respectable, female novelists could be educators as well as fiction writers. But in the Restoration, educators who wrote were more likely to compose philosophical discourses and advice books like Bathsua Makin, Mary Astell and Hannah Wolley. The association of the early novel with the selling or at least presenting of the self and its tendency to scandalous content made education of the young an improper enterprise to combine with it.

Much of the information about women writers comes from their own accounts, which inevitably draw on the notions of women current in the period and fulfil the expectations of the various genres. But a few generalisations can be hazarded.

Women who were primarily poets, like the Countess of Winchilsea and Katherine Philips, tended to come from the upper and established middle ranks where education would be more plentiful and publication, if embraced at all, would not have been a financial necessity – though the wide dissemination of manuscripts suggests the desire for a poetic name despite all the ritual claims of modesty. The commercial writers, writing poetry, drama and fiction for money, would more likely derive from the middle and lower ranks, like Eliza Haywood, the daughter of a small shopkeeper, although they might need to fabricate more elevated backgrounds to suit their royalist tendencies. Aphra Behn was probably from yeoman stock, although there were many more elaborate accounts of her birth and breeding. Those clearly of higher status, like Delarivier Manley, the daughter of the lieutenant governor of Jersey, had often suffered a social tumble which made commercial writing a necessity. (The father as governor of a province seems to have been a common fantasy of women writers, but it appears real in Manley's case, though she did make her father die of grief at James II's deposition when history records an earlier death.) Occasionally there are slight rises through authorship. The playwright Jane Wiseman is said to have moved from a servant to a publican through her writing.

By the early eighteenth century, the ground had been prepared, although not always with decorum, and many women from the respectable middle classes could enter literature. Catharine Trotter came from a genteel but penurious background and the dramatist Mary Pix was the daughter of a clergymen. But no generalisations hold entirely and during the same period Susanna Centlivre followed Aphra Behn in tinkering with her background for public consumption. Any adjustments were almost invariably upwards in this hierarchical period, and the few writing women from poor families made little of this disadvantage – the idealisation of poverty and deprivation thought to encourage the spontaneous and artless muse was still in the future.

Manley's former patron, the Duchess of Cleveland, and Mary Astell, lampooned in the satirical *New Atalantis.*

Aphra Behn as the first successful woman playwright was the great originator, and many women consciously felt they were stepping in her footprints. But she was in many ways a difficult model. Women's lives were associated with their writings; sexual impropriety in literature indicated it in life, and a naughty writer like Aphra Behn was assumed to have a naughty life. The assumption was strengthened by scandal, which could be put to commercial use. Susanna Centlivre and Delarivier Manley both followed Behn in their manipulation of scandalous images the truth of which is difficult to gauge since most originated from male satire.

This mingling of publishing with eccentricity and licentiousness would have been disabling for women writers fifty years later, while a hundred years on, in the 1790s, it would seriously have affronted the establishment, becoming a sign of revolutionary politics. But, in the Restoration, women writers like Behn and Manley presented irregular loves and bigamous marriages as part fictional, part nonfictional, with a sparkle quite missing from the later accounts of unwedded sex and illegitimate births.

Yet, while an aura of naughtiness might sell books, it still remained scandalous, and two poles of women's writing were speedily formed: the modest and the immodest. The first was personified in the professional and flamboyant Aphra Behn as 'Astrea' (the mastering Queen Elizabeth I had also been celebrated under this name), with her bawdy plays glorifying rakes and free livers and her poems on male impotence or female passion. The second was typified by the refined, retiring poet and playwright of heroic tragedy, Katherine Philips or 'Orinda', isolated in Wales but at the centre of a network of platonic friendship 'as innocent as our Design'. Orinda's exemplary married life confronted Astrea's shady widowhood, while her retreat from publicity – she declared that she 'never writ any line in my life with an intention to have it printed' and she sickened on learning that her poems had in fact been published without her consent – rebuked Behn's hunger for financial success. The scandalous Manley elided the difference between these types by associating Catharine Trotter – about whose famous purity she was decidedly cynical – with both Behn and Philips. But Trotter's more circumspect patron Lady Piers used a poem commending *The Unhappy Penitent* to associate the playwright with the pure Orinda alone and not the tarnished Astrea:

> Thus like the morning star Orinda rose
> A champion to her sex, and wisely chose
> Conscious of female weakness, humble ways
> T'insinuate for applause, not storm the Bays.[4]

POETRY AND AUTOBIOGRAPHY

One striking theme of poetry rather more than prose was the desire for the single life, avoiding heterosexual passion, marriage and childbearing. It was an undercurrent in the verse and prose of the Duchess of Newcastle and of the poetry of the Commonwealth, which often expressed it in Christian terms as the choice of another life.

In the circle of the 'Matchless Orinda' royalist poetic ladies gave each other names of romantic heroines like Rosania and Lucasia, taming romance into female community and echoing in their platonic raptures the courtly conventions of Henrietta Maria's time. They described intense platonic friendship rather than heterosexual passion, the main staple of Behn, Manley and Haywood, finding in it much solace from lonely marriages and using it to reinforce another theme, that of retirement in nature, so much a feature of exiled royalist verse:

> No Bridegrooms nor Crown-conquerors mirth
> To mine compar'd can be:
> They have but pieces of this Earth,
> I've all the World in thee.[5]

The Countess of Winchilsea also participated in a cult of female friendship within nature, though she expressed it less possessively than the often jealous Philips:

> 'Tis to share all Joy and Grief;
> 'Tis to lend all due Relief
> From the Tongue, the Heart, the Hand.[6]

Jane Barker celebrated celibate spinsterhood for avoiding the omnipotent sexuality of men, and she frequently used her poetry to translate courtly and classical romance into simple lust.

It was not all neo-platonic raptures, however, and many women wrote witty and pointed couplets very much involved in the material world and its ridiculous ways. The energetic, unpolished Sarah Fyge Egerton and the lady or ladies writing as 'Ephelia' roundly attacked misogynists, while the royalist Anne Killigrew, disgusted with the licence of the court, urged women into a more moral virtuous role; later Lady Mary Wortley Montagu and the poet Judith Madan, writing in polished urbane couplets, expressed something of the male authority of satire in their comments on society, as well as the confidence of poetic control, rare in later women poets.

Poetry could decorously or indecorously express the self, but it was always a covert expression – the flowery romantic names suggest as much. But some women desired to reveal the self more directly in prose.

42

Early autobiographies or memoirs were often written for proper domestic reasons, like the fear of death in childbirth and the need to give the motherless girl or boy advice and information; they were not primarily intended for publication, and they arose from the exigencies of the moment rather than from a desire to promote or explain the self. The sectarian religious autobiographies were, however, often published. Although written to a formula, aiming to highlight conversion and display a particular religious belief, they could include much individual experience. The Quaker Elizabeth Hooten managed to convey her very specific sufferings at the hands of magistrates in Cambridge and other towns, at one of which she was whipped 'with a 3 corded whip 3 knotts at end, and a handful of willow rods . . . on a cold frosty morning'. Other religious autobiographies might vindicate some social or religious error. Agnes Beaumont tried at length to regain her lost reputation after she had mounted a horse behind John Bunyan as he happened to ride through her village – at least this was her version of the scandalous matter. Often such autobiographies refused to distinguish the various accents and modes, mingling inner and outer voices, God's words with human ones, and the providential with the accidental.

The secular autobiography, written to express the self for fame, probably began, as she would certainly have wished, with the Duchess of Newcastle in 1656 when she wrote of her early life, marriage and exile. Despite much mockery for the Duchess's self-glorification, her work seems to have been inspiring to many women, like the Puritans Lucy Hutchinson and the Countess of Warwick, and the royalists Lady Halkett and Lady Fanshawe, who all wrote accounts of their lives. Although they did not print them with the Duchess, they presumably expected them to be read by their posterity and perhaps by others.

DRAMA

Virginia Woolf declared that it would have been impossible for a woman to write the plays of Shakespeare. But it would not have been impossible for her to write the Restoration comedies of Etherege or Congreve. Indeed in many ways Aphra Behn's works are similar to those of her male rivals.

Almost immediately after his restoration, Charles II licensed two playhouses in London, confirming what no doubt struck many, the close association of the theatre with royalist culture – indeed his father's court had been much denounced by Puritans for its theatrical shows which often included court ladies, among them his mother Henrietta Maria, sometimes in male attire. The theatres were initially dominated by court taste, although the fare changed through the decades. Much of it at all times consisted of old plays rewritten or renewed, often with songs and dances added. But the most distinctive form of this new theatre was its urbane comedy associated with the aristocratic values of courtliness, hedonistic sophistication, wit and good manners, nurtured in exile. In this comedy sexuality and the power struggles of men and women were presented more openly and often more crudely than they would be in the elite theatre for many centuries to come.

Professional women could turn to drama because under Charles's patronage women were for the first time allowed onto the stage – indeed it was specified that women should play women's parts. Actresses like Elizabeth Barry and Nell Gwyn trod the boards, while an increasing number of women sat in the audience. Later, as the female image was sentimentalised and morally uplifted, their presence would encourage restraint and propriety in drama. But in Aphra Behn's time the courtly former exiles who dominated the theatre wished to be piquantly and wittily amused, and their unsentimental misogyny allowed an extraordinary sexual and social outspokenness to women. Meanwhile the flamboyant association of courtesan and actress, which had replaced the connection of actress and idealised lady typical of the French court of Henrietta Maria, unsettled many signs and hierarchies.

Not only Aphra Behn was involved in drama; the decorous Katherine Philips translated the heroic (and royalist) tragedy of Corneille's *Pompée* in 1663 and in 1668 her translation of *Horace* was posthumously staged in a lavish but amateur performance, the professional one following the next year; so, despite her famous reticence, she became the first woman to have her play professionally performed in London. The shadowy Frances Boothby wrote a traditional tragi-comedy, *Mercelia*, in 1669, a rather cynical play of male deceit and sexual manipulation; it was the first original drama by a woman to be commercially produced on the London stage. Elizabeth Polwhele delivered a rhymed tragedy, while Aphra Behn to no critical acclaim put on the heroic *Abdelazar* in 1676.

But there was also demand for more sensational topical fare and for light, even bawdy farces and comedies, and both Behn and Elizabeth Polwhele responded to it. Polwhele is known only for one extant play, the farcical *The Frolicks* in 1671, which had a jolly heroine called Clarabell, described by her father as 'a pert, headstrong baggage', who declares that 'Love is but a swinish thing at best'. In her preface Polwhele described herself as young and ignorant but 'haunted with poetic devils'; since little more is known of her, either marriage or death must have put an end to the haunting.[7] The case was very different with Aphra Behn, who over the next few years swamped the stage with plays, presenting lusty and witty men and women in the style of courtly Restoration comedy. She chose drama, she implied, because it required no great intellectual abilities or weight of learning and could be done as well by a woman as by a man.

A host of women dramatists followed Behn, including Delarivier Manley, who countered criticism of her erotic expression by claiming that critics would be unconcerned had it come from a man. Her defensiveness suggested what is amply documented, that the taste and tenor of the times were changing. A more sober spirit was abroad in the politically troubled decade that marked the end of the Stuart kings, and Jeremy Collier's *A Short View of the Immorality, and Profaneness of the English Stage* of 1698 well expressed it.

Echoing the old Puritan dislike of the stage, Collier blasted the Restoration theatre for its courtly privileging of libertinism, hedonism and debauchery and for its 'smuttiness of expression'. Plays, he sternly asserted, should teach virtue by rewarding it in the plot. In time indeed playwrights would, in Dr Johnson's words, make drama 'more modest' and praise virtue. In the process those female writers who had involved themselves in the taste of the former age would be denigrated, then reviled; two centuries after Aphra Behn's death Julia Kavanagh could write, in *English Women of Letters* (1862), '[Behn's] mind was tainted to the very core. Grossness was congenial to her.'

Drama responded to the changes in taste, and plays on the whole grew more sententious and moral. Prologues standardised the female apologetic mode, making a combined and massive effort to defang criticism that women were writing works, not sewing work. Rakes, who had triumphed in Behn's comedies, were led to reform and settle down into marriage. The anonymous 'Ariadne' sensibly claimed descent from both Behn and Philips when she published her comedy *She Ventures and He Wins* in 1696, a conscious effort to write in the manner of Behn but without the intrusive bawdry. Similarly careful was Mary Pix, who proclaimed that her plays were old-fashioned 'true love, and faithful friends':

> Amongst reformers of this vicious age
> Who think it duty to refine the stage,
> A woman to contribute does intend.[8]

At the turn of the century Catharine Trotter too followed Collier's advice and produced tragedies and comedies with a far more obvious moral purpose than Behn had provided. In her poem in *The Nine Muses* she insisted that a person should not write for sordid gain or fame and certainly should not aim to please without instructing. Perhaps her bent was in the end too serious for the theatre, for at the age of twenty-two, after four plays had been performed, she turned to philosophy, writing only one more drama before she married a clergyman. Later she declared that 'being married in 1708 I bid adieu to the muses'.[9] The final notable female dramatist of this period, Susanna Centlivre, in image something of an echo of the colourful Aphra Behn, also tried to divert 'without that vicious strain which usually attends the comic muse'. Yet some noted that, in the extremely popular *The Gamester* of 1705, the gambler, though indeed reformed, still ended with both riches and lady.[10]

FICTION

Ever since Caxton founded his printing press in the fifteenth century fiction had been printed in England – and condemned as escapist and vulgar by the guardians of high culture. Its vulgarity was due to its association with the vernacular but also perhaps to its connection with women. From the Middle Ages onwards, the association of romance with women and idleness was expressed in the constant male fear that a perusal of fiction would corrupt female morals.

In Elizabethan England, Lyly, Sidney and Greene assumed women among the readership for their courtly romances. Greene was described as the 'Homer of women', while Lyly announced in his *Euphues* (1579) that 'It resteth Ladies, that you take the paines to read it'.[11]

Lyly seems to have gauged his market well, for, although the complete gentleman would certainly be helped by a knowledge of romance, it was soon reported that success for ladies at court absolutely required them to use the mannered, antithetical style of Lyly's romance in much the way it required them to dress in elaborate court fashion. The use of language as a seductive screen or mask would be a feature of women's writing when they themselves entered fiction in the next century.[12]

Sir Philip Sidney declared that he wrote his prose romance *Arcadia* for his sister's entertainment and, like Lyly, he addressed 'fair ladies'. The work, which delivered exemplary figures and pathetic stories, was immensely popular throughout the seventeenth and the first part of the eighteenth centuries and was imitated and continued by many, including, most significantly, his niece.

Lady Mary Wroth published *The Countesse of Montgomeries Urania* in 1621 and it was thus the first known fictional work of a woman to be printed in English – despite the Duchess of Newcastle's claims to pre-eminence several decades later. In many ways Lady Mary is closer to the later women writers than is the privileged Duchess for, despite her aristocratic status, she may well have been writing for money, thereby anticipating scores of eighteenth-century spinsters, wives and mothers in embarrassed circumstances.

Using her relationship to the popular hero Sidney and his romance, she insisted on situating herself and her work in her uncle's shadow. But in fact the *Urania* is distinct in its foreshadowing of the later female fictional plot of what Eliza Haywood would call 'faithless Men, and ruin'd Maids'. Her emphasis is on female experience of marriage, as well as on the courtship of male romance, and, along with idealised pictures, she displays women destroyed by jealousy, rejection and lust, trapped in the code of constancy while men travel off to love again. The tone is caught in the request of one character for stories of female misfortune – a request that the later Aphra Behn or Delarivier Manley might be seen fulfilling:

> Let me but understand the choise varieties of Loue, and the mistakings, the changes, the crosses; if none of these you know, yet tell me some such fiction, it may be I shall be as luckless as the most unfortunate; shew me examples.[13]

Lady Mary Wroth's *Urania* is also distinct from the *Arcadia* in probably being a *roman à clef*, or secret history, as Sidney's work was not. It uses the romance form to comment on contemporary figures and their scandalous activities in a manner that would become common in cavalier circles in the Civil War. It would recur in the early eighteenth-century novels of women like Manley and Haywood.

Naturally such a use of romance created a furore at the court of James I and one of the victims furiously attacked Lady Mary as an 'Hermaphodite in show, in deed a monster', a form of gendered – or rather ungendering – abuse that would commonly be hurled at women writers entering the male preserve of political or social satire. Despite denying some of the apparent identifications, she had in the end to withdraw her work from sale – possibly it had originally been published without her consent.[14] The continuation she had written was not printed.

Perhaps it was her experience with the first part that caused her to create in the second a weird character called Antissia, who seems to hint at her own self-hatred as an author. Antissia is a mad writer who understands her literary activities as part of her madness: 'I was possest with poettical raptures, and fixions able to turn a world of such like womens heads into the mist of noe sense,' she declares. Her dress of veils, feathers and ruffs makes her the very image of eccentricity – as well as a precursor of the 'mad' Duchess of Newcastle who scandalised England by publishing her poetic raptures and wearing outlandish clothes.

Despite the unhappy experience, Lady Mary was not the only female imitator of Sidney. In 1651 Anne Weamys, a 'young Gentlewoman', wrote *A Continuation of Sir Philip Sidney's Arcadia* in a style far plainer than Sidney's, with the conceit that 'no other than the lively Ghost of Sydney, by a happie transmigration, speaks through the organism of this inspired Minerva', and in 1725 appeared *Sir Philip Sidney's Arcadia, Moderniz'd by Mrs Stanley*, presenting Sidney in more decorous, less exuberant language.[15]

Lady Mary Wroth and the imitators of Sidney represent a newer kind of romance, with psychological and down-to-earth elements. But, while they were writing, another heroic type from France was gaining ground, avidly read by the young gentlewoman Dorothy Osborne, who admitted she 'cryed' for a heroine 'though shee were but an imaginary person'.[16] Throughout the Civil War years and on into the eighteenth century French romance was consumed by the ladies of the court of Charles I's queen, Henrietta Maria, and by the exiled court which included the Duchess of Newcastle, although she herself was not a great reader of romance. By the time of the Restoration it was widely diffused throughout England.

French romance was leisurely, the introduction of a character always heralding a new digressive story. It was associated with, among others, Madeleine de Scudéry, whose *Clelia* ran to ten volumes, published between 1654 and 1661. She and her genre were still somewhat current in the mid-eighteenth century when Charlotte Lennox created her romance-maddened heroine in *The Female Quixote* and when the learned Bluestocking Elizabeth Carter could be taken to task for her romance-addiction.

In the seventeenth century, however, Scudéry was entirely the vogue and so sensible a girl as Dorothy Osborne, scathing about the eccentricities of the publishing Duchess of Newcastle, can sound remarkably like Lennox's satirised heroine in response, although it should be noted that Osborne swallowed the myth of the day, encouraged by Scudéry, that her brother rather than she herself was the main author of the fiction. 'Have you read Cleopatra?' Osborne excitedly asked her future husband in 1653, 'I have six Tomes on't heer . . .' The idea of six tomes of French romance would sink the heart of Charlotte Lennox's hero when he realised that the reading of them was to test his worthiness; he failed the test.

The heroic French romance was primarily concerned with love and with women as writers and readers. It was connected with the salons of the *précieuses* who aimed to speak in a refined intellectual way and to cultivate good social manners – inevitably such women were much mocked as pretentious and ignorant by men, most famously by Molière in *Les Précieuses ridicules*.[17] Through their endeavours and the fiction that grew from them, a kind of fantasy world was established in which the problems of love became the most important concerns; politics turned on private passion, and male public history became feminine romance.[18] Love was endlessly analysed and interrogated. But it was emphatically pure love not lust, love which could as well be expressed in female friendship as in heterosexual passion; it is not surprising then that these translated romances should share diction and platonic conceits with the poetry of Katherine Philips and her circle. The romances came out serially and their characters and problems were minutely discussed in England and France in much the same way that the serial *Clarissa* would be scrutinised over a century later.

Since Scudéry's famous portraits were based on figures she knew, the novels, like Wroth's *Urania*, were *romans à clef*, although women readers of England would not have responded to this element. But there the resemblance between the French romancer and the main English novelists of the Restoration ceases. For all her success and her need for money, Madeleine de Scudéry did not openly embrace professional authorship, and her sense of literature remained aristocratic. In many ways she sounds more like the ladies of the Bluestocking salons in the mid-eighteenth century, desiring authorship but needing to show reluctance. This was not the stance of the first major female novelists in England: Behn, Manley and Haywood.

By the time these women were writing, many sorts of fiction were current besides the romance, such as marvellous tales, tall tales, fantastic voyages, saints' lives and rogue biographies; all refuse the modern dichotomy of history and fiction and several make claims of historical validity buttressed by documents and records while still implying the pattern typical of romance. These different fictional varieties join romance in influencing women writers, who produced fast-paced, often political short stories and long episodic tales, opposing the huge French romances with their epic pretensions and elaborate constructions. In 1692 Congreve distinguished between romances and shorter novels 'of more familiar nature', mocking the former, while the preface to the anonymous *Adventures of Lindamira* (1702) declared that the author was turning from 'the histories of foreign amours and scenes laid beyond the seas' to 'domestic intrigues', aiming not at fabulous knight errantry but at 'real matter of fact'.[19] Manley insisted that the new bustling public was impatient with the aristocratic romance and that 'Little Histories' must be created, 'much more agreeable to the Brisk and Impetuous Humour' of the times; her own stories would not be romantic allegories, nor yet reportage, but they would be psychologically probable.[20] Yet to hide (mockingly) their connection with contemporary scandal, they too claimed to derive from manuscript sources, described as so ancient that they were written in the Land of Nod.

Behn, Manley and Haywood differed from Scudéry not only in form but in content, their roguish acceptance of sexuality. Love changes from the ceremonious code of French romance into lust with all its physical pleasures and social disadvantages for women. So it functions as disruptive desire even within the female characters, not simply as a masculine threat from without. The heroines sometimes retain the noble legitimacy of romance but gain something of the thrusting quality of the younger son who is forced to make his own fortune in the world. In women's case, however, there was only one way to do this.

But as drama was changing with the times, so was fiction. Other women writers wanted to harness its seemingly amoral power for more immediately moral ends. The secret history was called a 'growing evil' and attacked as French by Richard Steele in *The Tatler*, a form of abuse that would be used a hundred years later when women again tried to comment on the political and social scene. Jane Barker in *Exilius* (1715) firmly dissociated herself from Aphra Behn and took Orinda as her model. She opposed the 'Deluge of Libertinism which has overflow'd the Age' and saw herself reverting to the expression of virtue and honour characteristic of earlier heroic romance; in *Exilius* characters give such Scudéry-like commands as 'Go . . . conquer Lybia.' Much later Elizabeth Rowe eschewed the directly erotic by combining romantic and religious sentiment in her popular elegiac series of letters, *Friendship in Death* (1728); in time she would become the heir of Orinda as the lady writer whose example it was decorous to follow. Penelope Aubin added absolute morality and providence to her breathless romance plots, while the brisk, often satiric Mary Davys in *The Reform'd Coquet* (1724) rescued the sensational story of innocence in a villainous world, so typical of Manley and Haywood, by making it didactic. Through the figure of a male guardian the coquettish heroine is defended from the consequences of her 'head-strong' ways.

Yet, although these women differ in tone from the naughty triumvirate of Behn, Manley and Haywood, there are resemblances between the two groups. The decorous Barker's later magazine-like novel, *A Patch-Work Screen* of 1723, has an uneasy, unsettling nature reminiscent of the short tales of Aphra Behn. Each of the writers in both groups sees women constructing themselves and playing different roles; each talks self-consciously of the influence of fiction on the mind and each tries to come to terms not with some abstract humanity but with people living, in Barker's words, 'as the World now rolls'. The concern in this age is survival and existence in society, and the realisation that manners and morals are very often at odds.

Despite the romantic names and rushed schematic plots, several stories have a psychological probability that the sentimental novel will eschew. Mary Davys and Eliza Haywood show the slow ripening into love, the unromantic insistence on a basis of esteem and respect in marriage. Most of the fiction writers depict the social and psychological misery of sexual passion, the painful loss of simplicity and the self-hatred that ensues, and many display the unexplained dislike of marriage, so common though obliquely expressed in poetry. An Aphra Behn heroine runs away into great hardship from a suitor she should marry and is only brought to matrimony just before her baby is born; Jane Barker's heroine Galesia retreats from marriage, hardly knowing why she does so. Motherhood is rarely glorified as it would be in later sentimental novels; the childless Duchess of Newcastle denigrates it, while both Haywood and Manley mention the agonies of childbirth, 'the Rack of Nature'.

Like the scandalous writers, the early moral novelists tend to muddy the line of fiction and nonfiction, fantasy and autobiography, making the narrator a sincere observer, moral placer, and skilled romancist. In Manley and Haywood facts become fables and fables turn into facts with a key; the Duchess of Newcastle moves in and out of her own fantasy. In Barker the fictional patchwork screen is made of colourful scraps from her own life which are fitted into a literary artistic pattern or discarded as unsuitable. She is as likely to put herself forward in her character Galesia as the naughty Manley is to display herself as Rivella. What we might now call new journalism seems, then, to be a common form, a confronting of facts with mental constructions. The writers attempt to make meaningful patterned versions of a world that would otherwise threaten chaotically.

In all the women the didactic impulse tends to be accepted, but it is not scientific and historical fact, largely deemed unsuitable for the female pen, that is taught but worldly commonsense or morality. The ritual claims to authenticity can be mingled with romance, allowing the reader to be sceptical of both, but little scepticism is brought to bear on the message – the need for understanding the feminine predicament in the early writers and of compensating for it in the later. In spite of enormous differences among women and ages, this last characteristic will be a constant in female writing throughout the century, from Aphra Behn at the beginning to Fanny Burney at the end.

3

‘WERE I EMPRESS OF THE WORLD’:
THE ‘GERMAN PRINCESS’ AND THE
DUCHESS OF NEWCASTLE

In 1663, a princess arrived in London, hot from her escape out of Germany. She was fleeing an unwanted marriage into which her relatives were pressing her. Accompanied by a wealth of sparkling jewellery and a bundle of aristocratic letters, she established herself with noisy secrecy at an inn, where she dazzled the innkeeper and tempted him by her unprotected state to consider her a glittering catch for a relative. Speedily she was courted by a young lord, who arrived to fall in love. He was dressed resplendently and travelled in a carriage decked with liveried servants. The father was willing, the son eager, the lady decently backward, and the marriage was hastily celebrated. Only then did the bride discover that the groom was no lord but a poor law student, whose family, the Carletons, had laid out a large part of their substance on the lordly show.

But worse was to follow: a few weeks after the wedding, a letter arrived from Kent declaring the ‘German Princess’ an ‘absolute Cheat’ and revealing her humble and criminal past. She was, it seems, the daughter of a ‘jolly Fidler’ of Canterbury. She had been befriended by more affluent society, attracted by her charm and prodigious ability with languages. She had learnt to pilfer from the families that patronised her and soon grew into an accomplished thief. She married a shoemaker, tired of him, and in 1658 married again. The first husband failed to testify against her and she escaped prosecution for bigamy. The Carletons, doubly incensed by her fraud and their own failed fraud, were not so lenient and this time Mary was arrested.

The Carleton case became a sensation and Mary with it. Despite many accusations of duplicity, she stuck to her aristocratic story and was soon visited in prison by a crowd of ‘many hundreds’, among them the susceptible Samuel Pepys. He was much impressed with her charm and so declared her innocent. When the case came up, Mary Carleton proved the cleverest in a bungling court. The prosecution failed to produce witnesses or properly to question the most incriminating and she was consequently freed. She renewed her charms on John Carleton, who wavered, then, bolstered by his angry relatives, stood firm. She was financially alone, with only her sensational image by which to live. Speedily she capitalised on it by writing, or in part writing, two pamphlets in which she tried to impose on the public, as before on her husband, and to gain from them the maintenance lost from the Carletons.

Whatever the literary merits of her pamphlets, they failed to deliver affluence, for Mary Carleton's later life is in the mode of the rogue narrative rather than the noble vindication. Soon she was exploiting not the image but its sensational failure and was acting herself on the stage, representing her original presentation in a satire written about her own fraud. After this social tumble, her life is dark for seven years until rudely illuminated in a conviction of theft. Transported to Jamaica, she used her famous charm on men again and managed to escape. Re-caught the following year, she was hanged in 1673.

At each stage in her colourful created life, Mary Carleton was the subject of journalistic pamphlets, biographical writing, and scurrilous or ribald poems, but one of the most interesting of the images is contained in the second of the two works of 1663.[1] This is an adroit and stylistically proficient pamphlet, to some critics suggesting male authorship, as though a convincing female image must be man-made. But Mary Carleton's obvious cleverness and linguistic skills argue her creation of much of the work which she probably shared with a male hack; in any case, like the sign of Angellica, it might have been set out by men but the picture it displays is part of a female trade.

The Case of Madam Mary Carleton (1663) is self-promotingly dedicated to the cavalier hero, Prince Rupert, suggesting some connection with German nobility – although she admits she has a little exaggerated her rank – and some respectability in the author deemed worthy of royal patronage. For the woman, it provided the image of appealing femininity before the puissant male, the victim tinged with eroticism. The lively account that follows is the invitation, claiming history but slyly intimating romance, making a patchwork of letters, trial records and justificatory observations, mingling female images in its wit and pathos, its girlish innocence and risqué sophistication. It is a mixture in keeping with other Restoration images created by women, with men in mind.

The Case begins by comically describing two German suitors who press the author to marriage, an entertaining prelude to the more serious business of princess-presentation. This begins with an appeal to English patriotism, for her escape, she claims, is to the land of freedom. Virtue in distress should not and will not be left distressed in England. Then follows the wonderful episode of the Carleton wooing and duping, tonally various, but on the whole gravely presented. The gravity is in keeping with the dignified pose Mary Carleton generally strikes in *The Case*, of an injured innocent, 'a foreign and desolate woman'. The pose, together with the learning – the Greek, Latin, French, Italian, Spanish and 'Oriental Tongues' she claims – argues high birth in the author, as does the very skill with which she makes the argument. All combine to refute the 'vile and impertinent falsehood, that I am of a most sordid and base extraction'.[2]

The image relies a little on distress certainly, but Mary Carleton is not at all the trembling lady of sensibility of a later era but the heroic Restoration woman, strong, serious and maligned, who reveals her strength by her writing in trouble and by her general outrage at woman's oppressed situation. So she complains at being a *fem covert*, unable to act legally for herself, and she castigates English law which gives the husband power over marital property. The dignity of the heroine wears a little thin only when the other image of the rogue intrudes, of the woman with three husbands and no marital property in dispute. The same effect occurs when she bewails the lot of noble girls like herself kept passive and sedentary in genteel convents, when she has in fact had the criminal and lower-class freedom of any boy. Similarly she both uses and escapes romance – of which she claims to have been an avid reader in her youth – seeing her story as suitable for romantic treatment but also finding little precedent in a form that would reduce her to the fair damsel when she wishes to play the Lady Errant.

The dignity of her image is further eroded by her need not only to vindicate herself but also naughtily to appeal as a sexual woman of wit. So with *double entendre* she pruriently describes her exposure. She was, she recounts of her arrest, 'divested and stript of all my clothes, and plundered of all my jewels, and my money, my very bodices, and a pair of silk stockings, being also pulled from me'.[3] In another description she again sees her predicament in terms of undress before male eyes:

> See the fickleness and vanity of human things, to-day *embellished*, and adorned with all the female Arts of bravery and gallantry . . . now disrobed and disfigured in misshapen Garments, and almost left naked, and haled and pulled by Beadles and such like rude and boisterous fellows, before a Tribunal, like a lewd Criminal.[4]

The accounts of her 'undoing' are meant to titillate, hinting at rape; they are sensational and unsentimental. Allied to this slightly risqué appeal and rather at odds with the great delicacy of apprehension she professes is an occasionally coarse humour. Although her name is Maria de Wolway, she announces, the lewd will call her De Vulva, the kind of 'immodest' expression that Defoe declared he was modestly omitting from his account of his Carleton-like rogue, Moll Flanders.

In *The Case* Mary Carleton presents herself both as a distressed and a maligned lady, buffeted by the common herd and worthy of noble support, and as a witty desirable woman with masculine effrontery. (Early on she wishes she had been born a man and she mentions the slander of her cross-dressing which, at least since the days when Queen Henrietta Maria went abroad in breeches, had a royalist, foreign and naughty flavour to it.) The image of spiritedness, calculation and delicacy is complex, and the two functions of vindication and attraction not totally reconcilable. But the Restoration could accept sexual and calculating women and Mary Carleton was perhaps wise to be both appealing and alluring.[5]

Pepys, so taken with the charms of the theatrical and spurious 'German Princess', was less impressed by the theatricality of a more authentic princess, the Duchess of Newcastle. He scoffed at her admiring account of her husband, the cavalier Duke:

> in favour to my eyes staid at home, reading the ridiculous history of my Lord Newcastle, wrote by his wife, which shows her to be a mad, conceited, ridiculous woman, and he an ass to suffer her to write what she writes to him and of him.[6]

Dorothy Osborne shared Pepys's opinion of 'mad Madge', as the Duchess was called, declaring tartly that 'there are many soberer people in Bedlam.'[7]

To contemporaries, then, the Duchess of Newcastle was absurd or offensively eccentric in both her attempts at individual expression: her writing and her dress. Despite much disparagement, her unconventional actions and clothes were possible because of her husband's approbation and her exalted rank. She made much of both in the garrulous prefaces in which she justified and excused her monstrous self-expression. At the same time she anxiously fantasised about the fame that the approbation and the rank could not deliver and which she craved as much as the fiddler's daughter of Canterbury wanted to be a princess.

The extraordinary self that is expressed in the Duchess's works is not the unique private self scrutinised by Puritan diarists and it is entirely distinct from the susceptible quivering self that sentimental eighteenth-century women would later probe. In many ways it is close to Mary Carleton's image, a created self-extension, fashioned idiosyncratically and theatrically to gain attention. In life she aimed at a similar effect. To quote Pepys again:

> Met my Lady Newcastle going with her coaches and footmen all in velvet: herself, whom I never saw before, as I have heard her often described, for all the town-talk is now-a-days of her extravagancies, with her velvet-cap, her hair about her ears; many black patches, because of pimples about her mouth; naked-necked, and a black just-au-corps.[8]

In her poems and prose her mind is on display, theatrically presented in abstractions, so that psychology becomes as much a dramatic perform-ance as the progress in the black and white coach through the gaping streets of London. Her writing like her public presentation fulfils the desire for attention of an originally shy and awkward girl and is delivered in terms of gratifying and fantastic scenarios. She accepts her own mind as a distinct and definite place, a source of imaginings, observations and 'similizings' and she has no worry about identity or the treachery of the mind so typical of a diarist such as the Countess of Warwick.

'Sure the poor woman is a little distracted,' wrote the sensible Dorothy Osborne, 'she could never be so ridiculous else as to venture at writing books and in verse too.'[9] The Duchess herself accepted her vanity in publishing and tried to make it general; she began a dedication, 'To all Noble, and Worthy Ladies' with the plea:

> Condemne me not as a *dishonour* of your Sex, for setting forth this Work; for it is *harmless* and *free* from all *dishonesty*; I will not say from *Vanity*: for that is so *naturall* to our Sex, as it were unnaturall, not to be so.[10]

The Duchess wrote plays, poems, novellas, tales, moral allegories, aphorisms and scientific musings. Yet her work is not as various as this list suggests. All the genres she chose had a certain old-fashioned quality although her use of them was wonderfully innovative, and tonally they were often indistinguishable. Her plays, not for the public stage, on the whole speak in a single voice and her interest is far from dramatic characterisation; her seemingly personal poems make abstract generalis-ations and her fantastic utopias are firmly placed in her own head. Of her *Sociable Letters* (1664) she wrote: 'I have Endeavoured under the Cover of Letters to Express the Humour of Mankind.' Her reason for writing letters rather than plays on this occasion was simple, 'that I have put forth Twenty Playes already'.[11] The vigorous heroines of her fantastic tales tend like the personages of her plays to discourse on the scientific matters that form the subjects of the Duchess's own treatises and poetry.

The voice throughout is distinct, then, but the Duchess is no mistress of a range of styles. She is always cajoling, pleading, insisting, declaring, asserting at the top of her voice, always fortissimo, always vaingloriously apologetic. The voice creates a world that is animated and sensitive. Who knows the misery of the tree that is to be felled, it speculates, the terror of the hunted hare, the selfishness of the ant or the cruelty of men? Who knows why thought is located in the head, not the knee or the toe? There is a kind of Blakean excitement about all that lives and hides its special knowledge: 'Who knows, but Fishes which swim in the sea,/ Can give a Reason, why so salt it be[?]'[12] Parts of the body and mind chat of their functions and jealousies, and physical actions assume spatial bulk in 'the sweet marmalade of kisses' or in the tongue's 'Wheel, to spin words from the mind'.

It is exhilarating and exciting – in short snatches. For the Duchess, so concerned with fame, is utterly unconcerned to win approval through any ingratiating ordering of her prose or poetry. Her twelve separate volumes are rambling, repetitive, inconsistent and contradictory, each accompanied by a jumble of prefaces – ten or eleven is not an unusual number – urging and persuading the reader, justifying and excusing the work and asserting and exalting the author.

Of one thing the Duchess is quite sure, that her disordered, lively *œuvre* constitutes her claim to fame, whether or not the public likes it. However she is criticised she sees herself as the first publishing woman writer and she knows that she can only be followed; as she exults in her late fantasy, 'The Description of a New World, Called the Blazing-World' (1668), 'Though I cannot be Henry the Fifth, or Charles the 2nd; yet I will endeavour to be, Margaret the First.'[13]

That the Duchess's fantasy should be in terms of her own absolute royalty – Margaret the First – indicates a mixture of arrogance and uneasiness. She was much impressed by the royal idea and its supra-social status and much enthralled by her own aristocratic position – one of her books has on the title page that it is 'written by the Thrice Noble, Illustrious, and Excellent Princess'. At the same time the royal title excludes the last name, and she was aware of the namelessness of women who bore children who, yet, did not bear their names. Her assumed kingliness, her primacy, is a result of exultation and anxiety.

The Duchess's self-portrait in 'A True Relation of my Birth, Breeding and Life' is both unconventional and conventional. Distinct in its purpose from most previous autobiographies by women, in its desire to aggrandise and to tell the self for no domestic or religious reason, it derives from the more male genre of autobiography which sums up a public life, weighing character and temperament ponderously and balancing attributes to make an admirable composite. The form encourages the Duchess to considerably more control than she manifests in her other works. Perhaps the enormity of displaying the self for fame alone was enough to encourage unusual curbs in expression. So she sums up her temperament and stance with some succinctness, welding her eccentricities into one daring singularity:

> For I being addicted from my childhood to contemplation rather than conversation, to solitariness rather than society, to melancholy rather than mirth, to write with the pen rather than with a needle . . . I took great delight in attiring, fine dressing, and fashions, especially such fashions as I did invent my self, not taking that pleasure in such fashions as was invented by others . . . I always took delight in singularity, even in accoutrements of habits.[14]

Despite her glorying in her status, the Duchess was not born to ducal splendour and indeed much of her married life was a quite unsplendid dodging of creditors in exile. Her father was from the lower gentry, a gentleman of merit, as she asserts in her 'True Relation', who was exiled in Elizabeth's reign for duelling and pardoned by James I, a fact that might account for some of her hostility to female political power and her admiration for 'manly' activities. The youngest daughter in a large family, she was raised prudently by a mother who had herself made an imprudent slip before marriage, and 'vulgar serving-men' who might shock children with 'rude love-making' were banished from the nursery. (The first adjective is entirely typical – she had immense scorn for servants and the lower orders in general.) Given the usual haphazard education of a girl, in later life she would blame her 'ill hand' on the fact that she had been instructed by an ignorant 'decay'd gentlewoman'.

The presentation of her hierarchical somewhat isolated family in 'A True Relation' emphasises dignity through breeding as well as birth. Its members were important in her view, but not self-indulgently so and their relationships and bearing were decorous and stately. Through such a presentation she obscures the difference between her initial status and her present one and makes it clear that, although not especially well born, she deserves aristocracy.

Into the close-knit community of her immediate family crashed the 'whirlwind' of the Civil War, 'an infatuation of the kingdom to oppose and pull down their gracious King'. In the upheavals, two of her brothers were killed and her mother, long widowed, was forced from the 'cloister' of her home to suffer the ruin of many of her children. She did it patiently, rewarded by her daughter's moving tribute to her as a woman of dignity, affection, capability and courage.

Of course there is a great deal of idealisation in all this. Although mention is made of her mother's business ability – she is portrayed as 'very skillful in leases, and setting of lands, and court keeping, ordering of stewards, and the like affairs' – the obvious financial ambitions of her family are not especially stressed. In later life as duchess of large northern estates she herself would be noted for her hardness with the tenants and she always took especial care of her own financial interests – as the Duke's children would sourly note.[15] So also in the autobiography she rather underplays the necessary marital concerns of a mother of a large family when she describes her own departure for the court.

In her own account she leaves home for staunch royalist motives, to attend the unpopular Queen Henrietta Maria in Oxford, after she had heard that the maids of honour were less numerous than formerly. Indeed the Duchess claims that her family opposed her going, knowing her bashfulness and expecting her to behave improperly in a public scene. At first this seems to have been the case and she was embarrassed at the public figure she cut. In one of her plays she describes a mother rebuking her daughter, Lady Bashful, 'I am told you stand amongst Company like a stone Statue, without life, sence, or motion.'[16] This sounds like a fair representation of what she thought her impression was and of what her anxious mother might have said in consequence.

After two years of such awkwardness, however, she met and came to love 'my Lord Marquis of Newcastle', a soldier thirty years her senior, a womaniser and a widower with grown children. In her account of the courtship he 'did approve of these bashful fears which many con-demned'; in his own writings he also mentioned that he approved her shape and 'plumpe fleshe'. Despite some wariness of matrimony on the part of the Marquis, and some adroit manoeuvring and proclaimed wariness on her side, she married the man whom she would create in the pages of her lengthy *Life of William, Duke of Newcastle* (1667) as an ideal cavalier, Caesar, a heroic soldier-poet, a dignified and loyal exile and an affectionate and supportive husband. He was certainly the last of these, but the historian Clarendon was not convinced of the rest; he judged the Duke cultured and personally courageous, but limited, self-indulgent and lacking entirely in political and martial skills.[17]

Whatever the limitations he may have revealed to others, his wife would admit publicly to none in him and he in turn would see none in her, despite the barrenness over which initially she worried. The tomb-stone he erected for her after many years of marriage mentions this barrenness but speaks too of his affection, paying tribute to her as a 'wise, wittie, and learned' lady, a 'most Virtuous and a Loving and a carefull wife'.

The marriage into which she entered with her affections 'fixed' had its tribulations – mainly financial. The couple managed to live a properly aristocratic luxurious lifestyle on credit, their very extravagance somehow convincing creditors of their ability to pay. At one point she travelled with her brother-in-law, Sir Charles Cavendish, to England to try to recover some of the Newcastle estates but was unsuccessful. By the 1650s the couple had become comfortably off partly through the death of Sir Charles and partly through a repayment of a royal loan – hence the lavish publication of books by both husband and wife.

Back in England after the Restoration of Charles II, some of Newcastle's land was restored and the Marquis was made a duke in 1665. But he had lost his political influence and the couple lived a fairly retired life of literature in the country, from which the Duchess occasionally made her garish sorties into the capital – to the delight of Samuel Pepys and the London crowd. The famous one of 1667, coinciding with the publication of her biography of her husband, may have been partly to bring the now ageing Newcastle one more time to the attention of his king, since the account ends with the observation that it is easier to forget than to remember and to prefer 'present services before past'. This visit was also the occasion of her extraordinary attendance at a meeting of the all-male Royal Society. Although her words flowed so copiously onto the page, they seem to have failed her on this occasion. But nothing could detract from the memorable figure she cut; she is said to have donned a mixture of male and female attire and to have worn an immense petticoat requiring six maids for support.

The autobiography expresses part of the Duchess's craving for immortality. This craving was not fulfilled by children or by any resolute focus on the afterlife, and so, following the religious writers of the Commonwealth, she saw her work replacing babies. Her books were fruits of the mind not the body. The autobiography is one such fruit and the maternal image underscores the point that, unlike Mary Carleton, the Duchess is not writing to seduce and amuse the reader. Yet in both cases a sign of self is being made which is designed to force admiration and bring specific fame. The Duchess ends her account rather oddly and pathetically for a modern reader with the fact that she is the *second* wife of the Duke and must be distinguished from the first. This might seem to underline her repeated point of the namelessness of women and the interchangeability of wives. But it is as likely to be self-assertion, the pushing forward of an individual woman, not as an instrument of God as a Commonwealth writer might have declared, or as an anxious lady facing childbirth, but as herself, the high and mighty princess who wants significance and fears, above all, anonymity.

The Duchess seems in search of a sign for herself, now desiring exaggerated publicity, now the privacy of an anchoress, and in her search she considers herself not only as an aristocrat but as a woman, albeit an extraordinary one. In the prefaces she reiterates her husband's approval of her activity and bolsters it with his laudatory verses; here she is pre-eminent in 'wit', astounding and silencing Spenser, Shakespeare and Chaucer with her 'similizing to the Life so like'.[18] His approval is essential for, as a woman, she must justify her obsession with 'scribbling' at the expense of 'womanly duties'. The Duke never 'bid me Work, nor leave Writing', she often insists. Unusually then the Duchess can, with this approval, allow the pen to take precedence over the needle without incurring blame within the marriage.

Also she has no children and many maids and so she has little to do in the house, she insists. In any case there is an actual advantage of writing over household duties for a woman – at least of the upper orders – for such duties do not entirely engross female energies and so they leave the domestic woman time to indulge in perhaps vicious pastimes, pastimes in which the reclusive literary Duchess can have no interest.

So the excuses continue, revealing the insecurity they are designed to remove, the gap between what she wanted to do and the traditional activities of women. 'It may be said to me . . . Work Lady, Work, let writing Books alone. For surely Wiser Women ne'r writ one,' she quotes in more than one preface. The work she should have done was clear to her: 'Needle-works, Spinning-works, Preserving-works . . . Baking, and Cooking-works, as making Cakes, Pyes, Puddings, and the like, all which I am ignorant of' – although she does, she asserts, 'Understand the Keeping of Sheep . . . indifferently well'.[19] A century later an aristocratic woman would not have needed to plead ignorance of pickling but the accomplishments of embroidery, music and dancing would have taken its place.

The Duchess has other, more sophisticated excuses. Poetry is in some way equivalent to the female business of needlework. So she declares in her dedication, 'To all Noble, and Worthy Ladies':

Poetry, which is built upon *Fancy*, *Women* may claime, as a *worke* belonging most properly to themselves: for I have observ'd, that their *Braines* work usually in a *Fantasticall motion*; as in their *severall*, and *various dresses*, in their many and singular choices of *Cloaths*, and *Ribbons*, and the like, in their *curious shadowing*, and *mixing of Colours*, in their *Wrought workes*, and divers sorts of *Stitches* they imploy their *Needle*, and many *Curious* things they make, as *Flowers, Boxes, Baskets* with *beads*, Shells, *Silke*, Straw, or any thing else; besides all manner of Meats to eate: and thus their Thoughts are imployed perpetually with

Fancies. For Fancy goeth not so much by *Rule*, & *Method*, as by *Choice*: and if I have chosen my *Silke* with *fresh colours*, and *matcht* them in *good shadows*, although the *stitches* be not very true, yet it will please the Eye; so if my *Writing* please the *Readers*, though not the *Learned* it wil satisfie me . . . For all I desire, is *Fame* . . .[20]

Constantly she tries to feminise and naturalise her writing through images from needlework, as Jane Barker would do a few years later when she made her writings the patches for a screen of her life. So the Duchess spins a garment from memory or she is engaged in mental needlework. Or, to use another female activity, she is merely conversing when she writes her books. So too she seems to follow the analogy of recurring housework in her approach to literary creation, refusing to accept the static nature of writing. No preface is enough, no book is entirely finished or sufficiently revised, no introduction need be the last. Ideas and words can be repeated again and again, as social formulae are used and reused in daily conversation or as housework is done and redone, or as a seam is stitched and restitched. It is not literary revision – the Duchess like her husband was not fond of this discipline – but more a matter of simply doing the same thing over and over again. In our own time the French feminist Hélène Cixous has advocated that women break down the majesty and mystery of the closed male text by an endless seam of texts without traditional form or closure. At the beginning of women's professional involvement with literature, the Duchess seems unwittingly to have been following this plan.

Yet, despite her efforts to equate writing and needlework, the Duchess is obsessively aware that when she uses her pen she is wielding an alien instrument, that she is expressing herself without the control given by formal classical learning which she would have received if she had been a boy of her class. So in the preface to *Poems and Fancies* (1653) she apologises that she is giving only a homely 'Rye Loafe and new Butter' instead of ambrosia in golden dishes. Yet, as usual, she cannot rest in a modest posture and she goes on to boast that its homeliness may in fact be 'more savoury'.

If the Duchess will not assume the respectable role of housewife, insisting with her eighteenth-century successors that all domestic duties have been fulfilled before the pen touches the paper, neither will she take on another Restoration role: that of the seductive woman, so skilfully deployed by Mary Carleton. In the late seventeenth century a down-grading of physical passion or sexuality was conventional in decorous literature – both Katherine Philips and Mary Astell were within this tradition – but the Duchess is especially firm and repetitive in her condemnation. Her autobiography describes her dislike of men and (perhaps strategic) dread of marriage. 'It was not amorous love,' she asserts of her relationship with her husband, 'I never was infected therewith. It is a disease, or a passion, or both – I only know by relation, not by experience.' Again in the preface to *Natures Pictures Drawn by Fancies Pencil* (1656) she declares her great hatred of love and hopes that her works will 'quench Amorous passions . . . beget chast Thoughts'.[21]

Yet she is aware of the power of feminine sexuality and physical beauty over men and, since she is hungry for power, she has an ambivalent attitude to the sexual manoeuvring of women. Accepting women's political and civil impotence, she states that only their sexual attractiveness controls men, who otherwise would utterly enslave them. A speaker in 'Female Orations' claims that women are superior since their beauty makes then men's 'Saints . . . Tyrants, Destinies, and Goddesses'.[22] Yet amorous behaviour is a collusive route to partial power for women and she cannot follow it. Her refusal of this role is far more uneasy than her refusal of the domestic one. She must have known that it was not her bashfulness alone that had won the Duke.

There remains to the Duchess the sign of militant and communal chastity, a withdrawing celibacy that would constitute significance for Mary Astell or Lady Chudleigh. But, although she insists on her own purity, she does not see chastity as an absolute virtue, proper for both sexes. Unlike the Puritan writers and the later Samuel Richardson, whose hero Sir Charles Grandison was much mocked for his advocacy of male as well as female virginity, the Duchess is a woman of the Restoration and she completely accepts the double standard. Women, she thinks, must condone adultery in men, for womanising is 'no dishonour to the masculine sex'. Where later women writers see the rake, she sees the noble cavalier, and she most despises not the libertine but the man with feminine qualities, an unnatural 'vacuity' as she calls such a person. In *Sociable Letters* she declares that she would rather have 'a Debauch'd Man for a Husband.' For the Duchess, effeminacy is not simply unfortunate, but vicious.

Nor will the Duchess take refuge in a group of celibate friends, although she does in her plays imagine female communities, and in *Sociable Letters* she describes the communion of two female friends never so happy as when reading and writing to each other. Yet the communities always have a representation of herself in charge. In life, apart from her waiting maid, she seems to have had few women friends. Perhaps the account of Mary Evelyn can indicate why. After describing the Duchess's extraordinary mannerisms and airy whimsical discourse, 'aiming at science, oaths, and obscenity', she moves on to her own role:

> My part was not yet to speak, but admire; especially hearing her go on magnifying her own generous actions, stately buildings, noble fortune, her lord's prodigious losses in the war, his power, valour, wit, learning, and industry . . . Never did I see a woman so full of herself, so amazingly vain and ambitious.[23]

Although equal female communities are not the answer, the Duchess is no lover of marriage, except for her own fortunate example of it, for she sees it as inimical to the power of women. Noting that every creature strives for 'preheminency', she is amazed that only women 'Who seem to have the meanest souls of all the creatures Nature hath made' never endeavour 'to get power'. Marriage is 'at the best . . . but the womb of trouble, which cannot be avoided'.[24]

From all these opinions on women's duties, celibacy, female friendship and marriage, it becomes clear that the Duchess holds contradictory and inconsistent views on the nature of the female sex as a whole. She accepts that there are distinct male and female qualities which can, however, cross genders. She dislikes 'Masculinacy' in women, she frequently asserts, when this implies swearing, gaming, drinking and politicking, and she seems to have no great enthusiasm for masculine capacities; in 'The Discreet Virgin' she describes men as 'like Flyes bred out of a dunghill, buzzing idly about' while women are 'industrious Ants and prudent Bees'.[25] Yet she wants women to be 'masculine' in spirit and intellect, and she never suggests any glorification of those qualities which a few decades later would insistently be praised as feminine. Clearly some of the assumed masculine qualities are the ones desired: reason and robust imagination. The question is whether or not women possess these. It is a question she answers in a variety of conflicting ways, while she endeavours to display them within herself as proof either of female potential or, more often, of her monstrous distinction. Like Mary Carleton she wants to take on roles open only to men, yet she remains uneasy at intellectual and social cross-dressing.

At times – but only in an odd paragraph or two – she sounds like the rationalist Mary Astell or later Mary Wollstonecraft in *A Vindication of the Rights of Woman*, and she can write passages in which she clearly asserts the constructed nature of women's predicament:

> we are become like worms that onely live in the dull earth of ignorance, winding our selves sometimes out, by the help of some refreshing rain of good educations which seldom is given us; for we are kept like birds in cages to hop up and down in our houses, not sufferd to fly abroad to see the several changes of fortune, and the various humors, ordained and created by nature; thus wanting the experiences of nature, we must needs want the understanding and knowledge and so consequently prudence, and inven-

tion of men: thus by an opinion, which I hope is but an erronious one in men, we are shut out of all power, and Authority by reason we are never imployed either in civil nor marshall affaires, our counsels are despised, and laught at, the best of our actions are troden down with scorn, by the over-weaning conceit men have of themselves and through dispisement of us.[26]

And yet (any summary of the Duchess's thoughts on women is a succession of 'yets') although she allows the 'great complaints' of 'our Sex' to be expressed in her work — that 'men from their first Creation' usurped 'supremacy to themselves' — although she is eloquent on women's loss in English custom of their names and estates on marriage and on the attitude to daughters as 'Moveable Goods', and although she lets a speaker in 'Female Orations' try to persuade her sisters into 'Combinations amongst Our Sex, that we may unite in Prudent Counsels, to make ourselves as Free, Happy and Famous as Men' since women 'live like Batts, or Owls, labour like Beasts, and dye like Worms', nonetheless the last word is rarely given to such feminist pleadings. Far more characteristic of her prefaces is the praise of the third female orator in 'Female Orations'; she roundly declares that men protect women who are 'Witless and Strengthless, and Unprofitable Creatures' except for their bearing of children.[27]

So, the Duchess worries, is nature or nurture to blame for the stupidity of women? Probably nature to some extent for 'there is a great difference betwixt the Masculine Brain and the Feminine, the Masculine Strength and the Feminine . . . So man is made to govern Common-Wealths and Women their private Families.'[28] (Written just after the Civil War, this statement could have had some irony in it if irony without italics had ever been the Duchess's mode.) Women have clearly not been the important scientists, politicians or musicians, she insists; they invent nothing and discover nothing: 'what ever did we do but like Apes by Imitation?' But she does admit that some women are wiser than some men and that there may be women in history now forgotten who have done great things. But as ever the Duchess's immense egoism puffs out any incipient feminist feeling and she remarks that, although there may be famous women in history whom she does not know about, she does not wish to be illuminated since they might overshadow her own 'glory' and prevent her, after all, from being 'Margaret the First'. And so the arguments go on, thrashing each other, conflicting, undirected and passionate, but never complete.[29]

In all this anxiety and conflict about women's nature and her own capacities and achievements, one certainty is the Duchess's absolute desire for fame, for some sort of power over time, recognition from men and even women regardless of how stupid, how wretched or how limited they appear to be. She expresses the craving directly in her autobiography where she defensively insists that it is lawful to want 'to be the highest in Fortune's wheel and to hold the wheel from turning'. She expresses it again and again in her prefaces when she desires 'a pyramid of fame' so that she will 'live by remembrances in after-ages'.

One method was, she thought, through science. When she travelled to England for her suit during the Commonwealth period she went with her brother-in-law, Sir Charles Cavendish, an amateur mathematician and scientist, and from him she derived much of her enthusiasm for the notion of atoms. Her *Poems and Fancies*, scientific opinions in verse, came out shortly. In this she showed some excitement about the empirical work of her time and she was initially intrigued by the telescope and microscope. But she found herself silenced by the experiments of the Royal Society and, after her visit, she published little new work on scientific subjects. Her method all along had been excitedly abstract, a kind of imaginative use of Cartesian reason. In her poems she enthusiastically creates new worlds and realms from her own head rather than studying the old physical one and she uses scientific notions erratically and fantastically, endlessly contradicting and speculating anew.

In time she must have known that fame was eluding her through science and she turned her imaginative power instead to actually enacting the fame and overwhelming significance she desired. In her preface 'To all Professors of Learning and Art' in *Sociable Letters* she claims that were she 'Empress of the World' she would advance people of learning and wit. This wonderfully adolescent and naive craving for importance is best expressed in the extraordinary neo-platonic fantasies with which the Duchess beguiled herself. These fantasies enact the transfer of power from the physical and political world in which she ultimately cannot believe that women have a function to the imaginative realm over which she herself may at last have control. In this realm she gleefully creates herself as what she has only hinted at in a concessive clause in her preface, 'Empress of the World', entering into her empire with pre-Freudian gusto.

In letter XV of *Sociable Letters*, one of the correspondents, a remarkable facsimile of the Duchess herself, is said to be 'fit to be the Empress of the whole world' because 'Nature had Crown'd her Soul with a Celestial Crown, made of Poetical Flame', with 'Understanding, Judgement and Wit, also with clear Distinguishings, oriental Similizings, and sparkling Fancies'. With such gifts she should 'Reign in the memory of every Age and Nation to the world's end'. In 'The She Anchoret', the fantasy takes another tack, for fame and power merge into a celibate lady with all her

66

creator's scientific and philosophical obsessions. This noble being gives her opinions to an eager world on natural phenomena, religion, government and so on, thereby overwhelming the king of a neighbouring state who, when she refuses his hand, threatens war on her country. To avoid this national catastrophe the philosophical lady prudently poisons herself and is accorded both a huge state funeral and 'extraordinary fame'. She becomes the eighth wonder of the world.

The Duchess's most extreme empress-mongering occurs in two similar novellas or 'Fiction[s] of the Mind': 'Assaulted and Pursued Chastity' and 'The Description of a New World, Called the Blazing-World' appended to her *Observations Upon Experimental Philosophy*. It had become common in the scientific excitement of the Restoration to embed new discoveries in travel tales, for travel formed an analogy to intellectual quest, but the Duchess's use, parodying the empiricism that ultimately bored her, brings her closer to the tellers of marvellous tales. The first of her works is a philosophical story which jolts a reader familiar with later eighteenth-century fiction. When, for example, the lady might be expected to turn her weapon on herself in a crisis, like Lucretia and the chaste ladies of the sentimental novel, she shoots her assailant; when it might reasonably be anticipated that she would urge the power of her chastity and virtue, in fact she discourses on the varieties of reading matter suitable for captivity. It is not surprising that such a formidable heroine should don male attire and enter the Kingdom of Phancy to regale its inhabitants with her scientific and philosophical opinions. In time she proceeds to govern the realm as guide, warrior and empress, and she strikes all who behold her 'like an angel or some Deity'.

'The Blazing-World' is an even headier tale, but it follows a similar pattern and is related to utopian literature of the time.[30] In it the heroic lady is shipwrecked, rescued and taken to another realm of 'phancy', where she becomes empress and again entertains and instructs the natives, bear-men, bird-men, worm-men, fly-men, ant-men and parrot-men, with her opinions in science, angrily telling them to destroy their telescopes and discover truth through reason. Her intervention has upsetting effects and the worm-men, bear-men and so on are soon at odds. The Empress then decides to write her own philosophical system, and a new quixotic twist occurs when a spirit comes to her to tell her to take the Duchess of Newcastle as her scribe, since the Duchess is known to write plainly and rationally.

The two women, Duchess and Empress, or rather their souls, grow fond of each other and, when the Duchess returns to her home in Nottinghamshire, the souls of both continue their relationship as 'Platonick Lovers' – not even in fantasy does any physical sexuality intrude. At one time even the Duke is brought into a trio when the two female souls proceed to enter him. 'And then the Duke had three Souls in one Body', each of which, after a little initial jealousy on the Duchess's part, certainly inappropriate to spirits, entertain each other happily enough. The interlude allows the Duchess to lavish praise on her husband and mention once again his losses in the Civil War.

The Duchess can be second to none, even in her own fantasy. Beyond the fact that she herself has created the characters altogether, her self-created self craves within her tale her own world to rule. Candidly she admits that she will 'never be at quiet until I be one [an empress]'. So she looks around for an intellectual world to commandeer but learns that they are all already occupied and that it would be too time-consuming to try to conquer one. But then she discovers from a spirit that she can 'create . . . a Celestial World' within the 'compass of the head or scull': 'You have converted me, said the Duchess to the Spirits, from my ambitious desire; wherefore I'le take your advice, reject and despise all the worlds without me, and create a world of my own.'

This of course is precisely what the real-life Duchess was doing all along. And it is in this that her significance for women's fiction lies. She was not the first woman to publish fictional material and she was certainly not the first to publish. But she *was* the first to use published fiction to create a fantastic, wish-fulfilling, compensatory world. Such a use would become common later, but never in so naive, brazen, brilliant and self-conscious a way. 'The whole story of this Lady is a romance,' wrote Pepys, 'and all she doth is romantic.'[31]

4

❦

'AN HONOUR AND GLORY TO OUR SEX':
APHRA BEHN

The epilogue to *The Dutch Lovers* explicitly connects the entertaining deceit of Mary Carleton to the plays of Aphra Behn. Both women are seen and see themselves as in some way dissemblers – although the playwright 'swears she's the less Cheat'. Both must show themselves in finery to please a gallant male public and, if they fail to charm, the same public damns the one as hangs the other. Both the German Princess and Aphra Behn, then, try to impose on the public, and, for either to succeed, she must create an image of sexual attractiveness, whatever her age and claims to beauty and however irrelevant such appearance might seem to her professional activity. Writing, deceiving and seducing coalesce when the actor is a woman.

'All women together ought to let flowers fall upon the tomb of Aphra Behn, for it was she who earned them the right to speak their minds,' wrote Virginia Woolf in *A Room of One's Own*.[1] Aphra Behn was the earliest professional woman playwright in English and one of the earliest novel writers of either gender. Because of her fame or notoriety, her life, although uncertain and entirely dark in parts, is delivered in a variety of contemporary images, from the scurrilous one of a Carleton-like cheat, pretender to men's works and a 'lewd widow' – the egregious Robert Gould was much implicated in this creation – to the eulogistic ones of the wondrous Astrea, 'an Honour and Glory to our Sex' and the creator of 'Female Sweetness and a Manly Grace'. Her works sound all the notes between the moral-respectable and the flauntingly immodest, from serious political and literary addresses to the public through common-sensical novels to the naughty poems and plays that equal Rochester in their risqué allusions to subjects like female sexual desire, homosexuality and impotence. The images are all clearly constructed for a purpose, and

69

the facts they suggest about Aphra Behn's life are all fascinating and almost all disputed.[2]

In the late 1630s or the late 1640s she may or may not have been well born. She may not have gone but probably did go to Surinam (now Guyana) in 1663 where her father may have been appointed the 'Lieutenant-General'; if so he died on the voyage out. Perhaps she saw in this place a golden-age society of chaste and naked natives in a colourful climate of perpetual spring and autumn; perhaps she took her later descriptions in her short novel *Oroonoko* from books of marvellous travels which they much resemble; or perhaps she wrote of the real Surinam when her memory was overlaid by literary constructions and political mythologies.[3] Whatever the case, by the end of 1664 she was in London and by 1666 she was signing her name 'Behn', probably because she had married a Dutch merchant – unhappily, if her writing on marriage is any guide – who may have died in the plague. Needing money, she allowed herself in the same year to be dispatched as a spy to Antwerp (England and Holland were at war), from where she may have given true information that would significantly have helped the English had they attended to it. As it was, the government was unheeding and unappreciative and Aphra Behn was soon again in London, impecunious and briefly imprisoned for debt.

Perhaps her narrative reports from Antwerp, the fictionalised fact in which she dealt or the manipulation and cheating she must have experienced as a spy – it was intended that she would use her feminine charms in the king's service – suggested that she might work with profit on the public in the theatre. She claims, however, that she had already begun a play in Surinam. Whatever the case, she made her theatrical debut in 1670 with *The Forc'd Marriage*.

Over the next years she was acquainted with Dryden, Rochester, Otway and possibly Wycherley; her own works as well as lampoons on her suggest that she fell in and out of love with a series of witty and entertaining but unhelpful men and perhaps women. It is not possible clearly to identify these people since in her poems Behn followed Katherine Philips in hiding them under romantic and pastoral names; one with whom she seems to have had her most intense relationship may, however, have been the bisexual lawyer John Hoyle. In her works a constant theme is the power of love and the need for it to exist between people for its own sake and not be transformed into a commodity, an item to be exchanged for money, influence or selfish gratification.

One tentative image of the flirtatious Aphra Behn in love occurs in the 'Love-Letters to a Gentleman' printed on their own and then included in the posthumous eulogistic biography written by 'One of the Fair Sex' –

perhaps Aphra Behn herself. They are written to 'Lycidas' and they have the ring of letters to a real man who, like Mary Wollstonecraft's beloved Gilbert Imlay a hundred years later, is moving out as the author is moving in: 'I fancy you lessen, whilst I encrease, in Passion.'[4]

There is no closure in the letters and the writer seems at the mercy of events as the beloved pulls away, then steps forward only to retreat at each response. The constant, however, is the character of the lady, 'violent in all her Passions', loving yet appalled at what she loves and at the use of love for gain and power. Against the odds she believes that freedom and love can coexist: 'I grow desperate fond of you, and would fain be us'd well; if not, I will march off.' The pain she experiences is nonetheless subtly assuaged by the writing of it and by the expression and dramatisation of the self according to literary modes. Despite her sense of being an independent woman, she is encouraged by the sexual conventions of the time to cry out, 'I am undone, and will be free ... I am ruined, and will rail at you,' making herself the conventional betrayed victim. At the same time in her outburst she must have taken pleasure in conjuring up the unwise loving lady of Restoration drama; other passages are bombastic, presenting the writer as abandoned to love, raging at it and suffering under a fever near to madness, as if she had entered one of her own tragedies.

Self-expression like sexual desire is immodest for a woman but may be importunate:

> you bid me not dissemble; and yet you need not have caution'd me, who so naturally hate those little Arts of my sex, that may well enough bear a Censure from People so scrupulous as Lycidas. Nor dare I follow all my Inclinations neither, nor tell all the little Secrets of my Soul: why I write them, I can give no account; 'tis but fooling my self, perhaps into an undoing.[5]

It seems almost a love affair with writing. Verbal self-expression is as attractive and dangerous as sexual.

'Love-Letters to a Gentleman' is embedded in a biography that accepts the varied image it presents but also seeks to make the lampooned and notorious figure of Behn into the admired Astrea. It ends with this tribute (or self-portrait):

> She was of a generous and open Temper, something passionate, very serviceable to her Friends ... She had Wit, Honour, Good-humour, and Judgment ... She was a Woman of Sense, and by consequence a Lover of

Pleasure, as indeed all both Men and Women are; but only some wou'd be thought to be above the Conditions of Humanity, and place their chief Pleasures in a proud vain Hypocrisy. For my part, I knew her intimately, and never saw ought unbecoming the just Modesty of our Sex, tho more gay and free than the Folly of the Precise would allow. She was, I'm satisfy'd a greater Honour to our Sex than all the Canting Tribe of Dissemblers, that die with the false Reputation of Saints.[6]

The passage carefully constructs its subject as both a sexual and a gendered being, natural in the love of pleasure and cultured in becoming modesty. It sets openness, intimacy and humanity on one side and deceit, hypocrisy and censure on the other, yet tacitly admits the winding path a woman must weave to stay on the former side. At the same time, the passage accords Behn an authenticity and sincerity in life and language and connects her openness in love with her clarity and truth in literature. She may entertain, seduce, beguile, even cheat in a sophisticated mode but she does not dissemble.

The reference to the 'saints' at the end of the passage would have reminded many readers of the men who had only a few decades before ruled England under Cromwell and who were still a powerful opposition in the country. Aphra Behn lived through a decade of false and real Catholic and anti-Catholic plots, as well as through the rebellion of Charles II's illegitimate son, the Duke of Monmouth, in 1685. Although in her emphasis on physical love, she contrasts with the disapproving Duchess of Newcastle, she comes close to her in the energetic support of royal government. But for Aphra Behn the rule of Charles represented a kind of reign of love and liberation, free from puritanism and free from commerce, forming in a society that has moved far from the golden age the nearest possible image of the ideal of selflessness and ease. In keeping with her revulsion from a commercialisation of love was her distaste for the commercial classes and the parliamentary Whigs who, she felt, put a price on everything and saw politics simply as opportunism, an extension of commerce and a chance to exploit selfish interests.

Aphra Behn connected her writing with her politics and her loves. In all three spheres she felt herself to be open and sincere. She wrote to entertain or to support what she believed; she tried to tell a truth that could be told by men and women alike and to do so clearly and forthrightly. In an age of political plots and lies, of love used for secret gain and power, it became utterly important to speak as openly as one could, understanding but not exaggerating the masks and subterfuges of language. Behn enjoyed linguistic artifice and rhetoric and the play-ing of roles they allowed on and off the stage, but the enormous and frightening power of created fictions in politics made her at the same time very wary of the impositions and reprehensible manipulations of language.

She was a passionate supporter of both Charles II and James II as not simply rulers but as sacred majesties, god-kings on earth, whose private failings in no way detracted from their high office. (It was a sad end to her life that she died just as William and Mary came invited by Parliament to the throne, destroying for ever the divinity of kings in which she had so ardently believed.) For her, royalty was no patriarchal anachronism as it would be for liberated women writers a hundred years on but a mystical state. It fed the soul, so that even the ills of poverty and sickness faded into insignificance. In 'A Pindarick Poem on the Happy Coronation of His Most Sacred Majesty James II' the King becomes a god or a sun shining in the world, without whose light all would be dark. To rebel against such majesty was a kind of madness, as if in the body black bile had surfaced and ruined the constitution or as if the forces of dark hell had emerged to extinguish the light. The dedication of *Poems upon Several Occasions* (1684) refers to the 'violent storms of Sedition and Rebellion' and 'black Treason' from 'the dark Abyss of Hell'. The King was clarity, openness, like Aphra Behn herself in love and literature, while the plots and treachery were riddles, hints and disguised speaking. Public rituals and conventions of royalty and religion were, in this view, open and sincere, while danger lurked in anarchy, secretiveness and the appeal to the hidden selfish Puritan self. In *Oroonoko*, which can be read in terms of the political situation of the faltering King James, the kingly royal slave speaks truth and is vanquished by dissemblers.[7] Aphra Behn's political plays attacking Roundheads and Whigs, their modern reincarnation in her view, stress disorderly disruptive sexual and political desires, expressed in duplicitous manipulating language.

Since the playhouse audience was largely Tory in sympathy in the 1680s, royalism was not only a felt conviction but also a prudent stance for Behn, who was no doubt rewarded for her propandist efforts. At the court of Charles, morally tolerant in one view, decadent and corrupt in another, women of wit and beauty could flourish like her friend Nell Gwyn, the 'Protestant whore', the stigma of whose whoredom was much softened by new rank. Women would flourish best in an era of peace and order; under the royal system they might in addition have a little influence, like the royal mistresses and Aphra Behn through their wit. But like the Duchess of Newcastle she accepted that women were excluded from the realm of action, of war and politics.

But even in good King Charles's golden days, the situation of a playwright was precarious, Behn's theatrical political intervention terminated when she railed against the Duke of Monmouth and was briefly in custody for her imprudence. Even more threatening were actual events in the theatre. In 1682 two companies were amalgamated and new plays were for a time hardly required. The change affected all dramatists.

The position of a female playwright had difficulties beyond the political and the financial. As the tribute in the biography reveals, her image had to be defended as a woman to be supported as an author and defended as an author to be supported as a woman. Writing, like clothes, directly declared character while literary skill seemed to demand report of physical attractiveness. So the nine dedicatory poems of *Poems upon Several Occasions* enhanced her literary reputation by making the by now famous, no longer young playwright first and foremost into a beauty.

The gendering of functions and attributes entered her own mind as well, and, as for the Duchess, the literary faculty and wit must be male, although it might be completely possessed by a woman. The epilogue to *Sir Patient Fancy* asks, as many women would ask during the next century:

> What has poor Woman done, that she must be
> Debar'd from Sense and sacred Poetry?
> Why in this Age has Heaven allow'd no more,
> And Women less of Wit than heretofore?

Yet the prologue of the early play *The Forc'd Marriage* stresses female wit only when sexual attractiveness or beauty fails or becomes too cheap a commodity, and even the epilogue of *Sir Patient Fancy* subsumes female wit into an overall seductiveness of women, 'Quickest in finding all the subtlest ways / To make your Joys, why not to make you Plays?' The deployment of wit and literary skill must be for male pleasure which will be the source of gratification, money and fame for the woman.

Wit acting through language is like beauty sexually arousing, as indeed the dedicatory poems praise Aphra Behn's work for being – it was only later in the next century that wit in women would become a self-wounding instrument. In an extension of the image, witty dedications become like marriage rather than sexual invitations – men are obliged 'to receive them as they do their wives: for better, for worse; at least with feigned civility'.[8]

Although deployed for men and although associated with the masculine side, wit was in the end as much the property of women as of men, and they might therefore just as well write plays, not 'such a sturdy task', she thought. Women were, certainly, debarred from classical education and Aphra Behn much lamented the fact: it was a sad thing in itself since it confined them to the present, to the single 'Fulsom Gingle of the time'. But a classical education, however desirable in itself, was not necessary for the entertaining of the public. Her sign was comedy, according to the 'pamphlet' to the reader in *The Dutch Lover* (1673), and comic plays, despite much puffing rhetoric, were not the 'grand affair of human life', nor intended as sermons. They did not preach but divert, and they delivered not morality but 'the Picture of ridiculous mankind'. Aphra Behn would have none of the notion of transcendental art, morally efficacious and untrammelled by its age or the intention and personality of its begetter. As she noted in the preface to *Sir Patient Fancy* she was a woman 'forced to write for bread and not ashamed to own it'.

And yet, like the Duchess, as time went by, she desired fame; she wanted her name and writing to last, whatever her epitaph might declare:

> Here lies a Proof that Wit can never be
> Defence enough against Mortality.

To the published text of her late play *The Lucky Chance* (1687), as bawdy a work as ever, she appended a manifesto summarising many of her earlier prefatory vindications that squarely confronted the problem of the name, of gender and of the language suited to women. Noting the indecorous lines in many famous male plays which yet were appropriate *within* those plays, she points out that it is the added mark of her sex in her that causes her work to be especially censured:

> had the plays I have writ come forth under any Mans Name, and never known to have been mine; I appeal to all unbyast Judges . . . if they had not said that Person had made as many good Comedies, as any one Man that has writ in our Age, but a Devil on't the Woman damns the Poet.

She knew she was up against a prejudice when she insisted that her art was not her life, that if her plays followed fashion, her private activities could be perfectly decent. It was not a view of women writers that many people held.

At the end of the defence, she made it clear that her earlier view of writing simply for bread was now modified; she wanted more than transitory applause and her fee:

> All I ask, is the Priviledge for my Masculine Part the Poet in me . . . to tread in those successful Paths my Predecessors have so long thriv'd in . . . If I must not, because of my Sex, have this Freedom, but that you will usurp all to your selves; I lay down my Quill, and you shall hear no more of me, no not so much as to make Comparisons? I shall be kinder to my brothers of

the pen, than they have been to a defenceless woman; for I am not content to write for a Third day only. I value Fame as much as if I had been born a *hero*; and if you rob me of that, I can retire from the ungrateful World, and scorn its fickle Favours.

It is a mingling of modes and images, of hero and defenceless woman, of pride and petulance, of a sense of identity through public expression and of expression modified in its reception by gender. It is an androgynous image of combined male and female qualities completely expressed in a single person. It was left to her enemies to make the androgyne an hermaphrodite like Lady Mary Wroth, lacking both male wit and female modesty, unfit therefore for the privileges of either sex.[9]

When the theatrical changes came in the 1680s, the generous and extravagant Aphra Behn needed a new source of income. Being now an established literary figure, she could turn to translation, anthologies and miscellanies. Some of her activities needed skill beyond literary ability with English, but her easy and (for a woman) unusual familiarity with the educated male wits of the day must have given her some acquaintance with areas she was not taught, while translations, becoming increasingly common, could well have allowed her to educate herself. Certainly she seems to have known French – perhaps she had been educated in France as a Catholic child – and she quickly put her knowledge to use, taking on the trivial and the serious.[10]

But, for literary history, her most important new area was prose fiction, not an established form (and not yet especially lucrative). This required no more formal preparation than the writing of plays had done and it was therefore to this form that she increasingly turned in her final years, producing one long novel and several novellas and short stories.

Like the Duchess's tales, Behn's are often told in helter-skelter fashion, mingling fact and fiction; prefaces declare the stories truth but it may be a truth for entertainment. Sometimes no doubt the passing of time has hidden the topicality and a modern reader will be taking as fantasy what contemporaries saw as fact. Modes and types of writing are mingled, and characters are named from the romance, despite the contemporary and sordid nature of their predicaments. In the speedy tale 'The Adventure of the Black Lady', for example, the romantically named Bellamora is a pregnant woman alone in London, a 'fair innocent' who calls for sack to lubricate her chat with her landlady; her danger is not primarily from predatory sexual men but from the 'Overseers of the Poor' who wish to remove her to a house of correction. 'The Court of the King of Bantam' gives as much detail about the finances of the romantically named characters as a Jane Austen novel and as much description of cosy winter customs as a Dickens one. Comedy and melodrama jostle each other: the heroine of 'The Black Lady' seems in training for misery as she faces the poorhouse, but the story ends with her shopping for baubles and with the ridiculous incident of the landlady producing kittens for the bailiffs as the only newly born babies.

The narrator is all-important in this fiction, emerging as a definite character, and in a way all the tales become part of a larger fictionalised autobiography of the author. In *Oroonoko* she makes the construction of her life part of the tale: she was, she insists, the observer of events and an actor within the plot. Yet, as a narrator, she claims transparency and her story comes 'simply into the world', needing no help from invention or rhetoric. The effect is both unsettling and energetic as the narrator steps in and out of her tale as if a character had stepped from and back into the cinema screen, describing the Surinam of the setting as an idealised and literary golden-age world, from which, nonetheless, she brings back creatures for 'his Majesty's Antiquary's' and a theatrical costume of great coloured feathers.

When less obtrusive, the narrator is still a presence, older, experienced, commonsensical and knowledgeable in the ways of the world but not all-knowing of events, breezy but not insensitive. She is not authoritative – hers is only a 'female pen' – and she reconstructs, she declares, from her own experiences or from the tales of others, often presenting without comment but often placing with her wiser opinion, insisting on her authenticity, but sailing close at times to self-parody in her claims. She is too a gossip, rather like Lady Mary Wroth before her, and she can be tart in her comments. To the cliché 'the fair innocent' used in 'The Black Lady', she adds, 'I must not say foolish', and she glosses the Overseers of the Poor as those who overlook the poor. In 'The King of Bantam' she is worldly, assuming that even good men will have their cast-off mistresses, but she can also be more morally censorious as in 'The Nun', trying in the welter of facts she presents to discover a providential meaning of justice on earth.

But, despite opinions and the occasional moral effort, it is the common lack of moral placing that shocks a modern reader.[11] People perpetrate the most frightful crimes without necessarily being the worse for them. In 'Agnes de Castro' the villain fails to receive his just deserts and the rapacious heroine of 'The Fair Jilt' survives the wreck of others' lives to live penitent and happy with her husband, not the prince she had thought but still a rich gentleman. Evil is not scandalously and seductively triumphant, but it simply seems to pay. Foolish generous people who might have been loved in the sentimental period or in Dickensian fiction are gulled as mercilessly as the butts of Restoration drama, and the narrator and readers are assumed to be laughing.

Sexual matters are open and activity condoned. The pregnant Black Lady marries at the end. Yet the lower economic worth of the sexual woman is quietly accepted; in 'The King of Bantam' the pretty cast-off mistress is pliant and expendable. Quirks of behaviour are presented without disapproval. So the Black Lady, accepting society's view of her sexual fall, loathes her fallen self and transfers her loathing to her lover. In 'Agnes de Castro' the husband who uncontrollably loves another abases himself before his wife, and in the enthusiasm of his abasement 'perhaps' momentarily forgets his beloved. Heroic action is vitiated by physical weakness – just as, so often in Behn's work, high-flown romantic sexuality is terminated by disgust or impotence. So Oroonoko, the royal slave, vows vengeance but cannot rise to kill his enemy; the body of his pure and beautiful wife begins to stink. He himself dies of inward decay and mutilation. Brutality crashes through Arcadia and yawns interrupt romance.

All these elements recur in Aphra Behn's masterpiece, her long prose work *Love Letters Between a Nobleman and his Sister* (1784–7) which brings together her political and sexual themes. If the novel may be simply defined as a long prose work 'portraying characters and actions representative of real life', then this work has claim to being one of the earliest novels in English.

Despite its three-volume length it was popular and it went into sixteen editions before the end of the eighteenth century. Its existence and its popularity modify the sense one receives from standard literary histories of a progressive development in fiction, women's in particular, from the schematic and crude to the sentimental and psychologically sophisticated. *Love Letters* is indeed psychologically acute but it differs substantially from this later fiction. Sexuality not chastity is marketable and the Puritan self-scrutinising of sentiment becomes the self-conscious assessment of a self for survival and manipulation of others. Because of this content *Love Letters* moves from the epistolary mode in which it begins into a mixed one of narrative and letters, so that the narrator can point out to the reader the dissembling nature of self-expression and allow posing and posturing letters to be read by different readers and differently interpreted.

Love Letters is partly in the scandalous mode, similar to the French Gabriel de Bremond's *Hattigé* depicting the loves of Charles II and his court. It is journalistic, based, like most of the short stories claimed to be, on fact. But in this case the story is known well beyond Behn's version of it. Indeed it was unfolding as she wrote. Her book appeared in three parts over four years and perhaps some of its innovative changes in narration and conception of character are adjustments to external events. However brought about, the result is a study of the masks or signs of femaleness and of the often corrosive effect of them on the personality of the woman and of her victims.

The public story and the original texts are extraordinary enough. In September 1682 the *London Gazette* ran an advertisement for Lady Henrietta Berkeley, 'a young lady of a fair complexion, fair haired, full breasted and indifferent tall', who had run off with her brother-in-law, Lord Grey of Werke.[12] To add to the politically sensational aspect of the story, the abandoned wife was reputed to have had an involvement with the Duke of Monmouth, whose rebellious cause Lord Grey espoused. To prevent her recapture, Lady Henrietta married a servant of Lord Grey's, so removing herself from the power of her father. In due course Lord Grey was tried for rape and then for treason, but he managed to escape or evade all punishment. In Aphra Behn's novel, Lady Henrietta and Lord Grey become Sylvia and Philander, the Duke of Monmouth is Cesario and the servant-husband Brilliard.

But it is not as simple as that, for the story, especially the first part, takes on much autobiographical resonance as well. Some of the letters are similar to her seemingly autobiographical poems concerning the value of sexual love when sincere and some of her problems over respectability when sexual nature has been acknowledged are expressed in Sylvia's anxiety; these problems also inform the pattern of action, the repeated arousals and disappointments of the lovers.

Part I, written in 1682–3, is an amazing achievement in letter form, different in its delineation of the psychology (and physiology) of sexual passion from anything in French romance. It mainly tells the story leading up to the elopement, detailing the characters' growing sexual desire and their sexual fulfilment after some circumstantial and some physiological hitches. Part II opens after Philander and Sylvia have had many months of love in exile. Three new characters enter at different times, each forming with the protagonists triangles of desire in which Sylvia and Philander as central erotic objects use their attractiveness to manipulate and control. The first is Calista, young wife of an elderly nobleman, discovered by Philander during a separation from Sylvia when he was beginning to understand his own constitutional inconstancy. Calista is already desiring without an object and his appearance fulfils her fantasies – as the difficulty of access to her fulfils his need for adventure. Meanwhile, unknown to her, her brother Octavio has seen Sylvia and becomes entirely entranced by her. Sylvia finds his self-abasement before her interesting; occasionally she loves him, and she certainly finds his money useful, since this is now a commodity in short supply for the elopers.

Octavio has a rival, the third character, the servant Brilliard. In romance the faithful retainer, used by Philander to secure his pleasure by marrying his mistress, would have remained eternally a servant. But in Aphra Behn's tale he is very much a man with a mind and body of his own. The extraordinary sexual attractiveness of the haughty Sylvia is as potent with him as it once was with his master and, as her social position deteriorates, his demeanour becomes more familiar.

In its title, 'The Amours of Philander and Sylvia', Part III accepts the degeneration in the central pair from lovers to intriguers. It charts the downfall of the simply loving victims, Calista and Octavio. Calista is impregnated and escapes to a convent, not before she has been forced into shooting her husband. In her refuge she learns from Sylvia the inconstancy of the man she loves. She takes her vows and becomes a nun. Philander is left desiring, intermittently 'because he had possess'd her' and then passionately because she seems really lost to him. He amuses himself in a way that foreshadows Richardson's rake Lovelace: projecting fantastic total mastery over all the women with whom Calista is immured.

Meanwhile in parallel lives Octavio remains so smitten with Sylvia's charms that he ignores all the revelations of her mercenary, promiscuous, selfish character until he cannot endure that the wind should touch her face. For her he ruins his financial and political position, his reputation in society and his status as a grateful and deserving nephew. In due course he sinks to shooting (albeit accidentally) his elderly uncle who has also displayed a sexual passion for Sylvia, thus echoing the violence in his sister's story. After repeated signs of her infidelity he is fooled back into amorousness until even he has had enough, as Sylvia stupidly runs off again with the inconstant but ever fascinating Philander. He writes to her a moving letter marvelling at her abuse of his 'soft good nature', provides a pension for her, and enters a monastery. Sylvia is left to Brilliard, the servant, who one drunken night achieves his rights as a husband. The cynical end finds Philander resettled at court in splendour, while Sylvia is left controlling her servants with her sexual charms and preying when possible on other rich naive young men.

The novel unfolds against the political backdrop of the treasonable intrigues of Cesario against his king (here Aphra Behn could revenge herself on the Duke of Monmouth, who had endangered her theatrical career). Philander, who has embraced his cause, inevitably escapes its wreck. Politics and sex, as so often in Aphra Behn's work, come together, suggesting that inconstancy in one sphere mirrors it in another. It is not simply that treasonable activity encourages improper sexual passion but rather that it makes people inauthentic in love since it renders all the

80

names and vows by which people try to live meaningless. Philander who betrays his king may betray everyone else. When still a maid, Sylvia understands the horror of rebellion, but, as she deteriorates morally, she speaks less of her horror.

But clearly it was not its political message that kept the book in print in the Hanoverian years, but rather its sensational elements, including its sexual explicitness – although the sexual act is delivered in the elaborate language of romance. The rather lascivious dedication to the first part describes the letters as 'soft and amorous', the dedicatee as young, beautiful and made for love. Throughout the novel Philander is attracted to chastity only as a titillating mask of erotic longing; Sylvia is 'loose, wanton . . . and languishing' and there is much pornographic description in the letters intended for the arousal of the other, of beating hearts and fainting limbs.

Sylvia displays herself for conquest and each titillates the other with lascivious description: 'When entering thy apartment, I beheld thee extended on a bed of roses, in garments, which, if possible, by their wanton loose negligence and gaiety, augmented thy natural charms.'[13] But by the side of all this amorous rhetoric, the first sexual activity is a sorry disappointment, for Philander – like the men of Behn's poem 'The Disappointment' and *A Voyage to the Isle of Love* – finds that 'Excess of Love his love Betray'd', to quote the poem. But his impotence – perhaps suggesting earlier indulgence – really hardly matters to the reader, for the sexual act has occurred in expectation on paper a hundred times.

In the novel various types of sexuality are naturalised: incest, transvestite sexuality and voyeurism. In the last the readers are implicated, often represented by other watchers in the story. So Philander sees the old husband 'loll and kiss, and hang his tawny wither'd arms on her fair shoulders, and press his nauseous load upon Calista's body', anticipation of the necrophiliac love of Brilliard taking advantage of his haughty wife's fainting fits to fondle and kiss her. Sylvia dons male dress as a necessary disguise, for greater ease in travel; she then uses it for the freedom in action and attitude it allows. But later it is not a desire simply for freedom but also for the power of titillating. At first she incidentally arouses love in Octavio but she comes to use the ambiguous attraction quite consciously to interest her wealthy prey. She manipulates the erotic longing of her enamoured page, feeling and conveying the excitement of his valeting her in front of another man.

In the beginning, the sexual paradise Philander wanted with Sylvia was seen as a golden age of freedom where sex was unrestrained before 'the cold matrimonial embrace was decreed' and women became property. In the following books sexuality would simply become a commodity even more debased than marriage for women, rather as the dashing gallant rebels dwindle into traitors. The golden-age society of freedom might exist in fantasy or in Surinam, but Europe needs a king and sexuality needs sincerity and control. The danger is not primarily religious – not much is made of the incest theme – but social and psychological. The implied message is not the twentieth-century one of liberation, nor the eighteenth-century one of necessary virtue or chastity, but the Restoration one of social common sense. Free sexual activity might be pleasant, but it leads a woman to ostracism or the convent. As a heroine in *The Rover* said of the free love her cavalier offered: 'What shall I get? A cradle full of noise and mischief, with a pack of repentance at my back?'

The most extraordinary creation of the novel is of course the *femme fatale* herself, the Nana-like Sylvia representing social, sexual and political corruption, the manipulator of signs more potent than Angellica's, although just as theatrical. Initially she seems a victim of the double standard. Her sister when she first hears of the affair warns her that Philander who has been once false will be so again and will leave her 'nauseated by Use'. But her sister utterly underestimates the resources of Sylvia. Her selfishness makes her quickly look to her own interest and she uses her continuing sexual attractiveness less for mutual pleasure, as at first, than for economic gain. Her moral decline is suggested as she comes to eye Octavio's jewels as well as his person, and indeed in the end to regret his money more than his love. Desire continues, but the plots and stratagems around it become as important, and she almost plots for the sake of plotting as she almost runs off for the sake of the deceit. Her lack of control, suggested in her first sexual endeavour when she beds a man who is her sister's husband and a political traitor, wars with self-interest. Later it is expressed more in ungovernable rage than in sexual voraciousness, frequently conveyed in the repertoire of theatrical tragic language. But in the end she is fascinating because she is never simply uncontrolled or simply mercenary. The struggle for power means more to her than power. The process, the energy is everything and she 'bends like a slave for a little empire' over a man.

The narrator comes into the story once the pastoral infatuation of Part I is told and the protagonists have entered the world of social experience. In other words she is there once Sylvia is about to deteriorate and so requires placing and she gives pattern to a story otherwise made unstable by its dependence on 'news'. The narrator is not quick to judge and for a long time she finds Sylvia somewhat excusable because she is beautiful and because she 'had sense enough to know it too'. She wishes the reader to follow the progress rather than hastily judge it. She shows Sylvia both as a scheming woman and as she appears in her lover's eyes, utterly desirable even when manipulating desire. Only when the moral lines are quite clear does she make an open statement of Sylvia's character: she is insolent, vain, opinionated, obstinate, critical, sexually alluring, constant from pride and shame not inclination, and 'loving the Triumph, tho' she hated the slave'. In the end of course the narrator lines up behind sincerity, which, with all the suffering it causes its victim, is still life's best gift. The unwise Octavio is sincere and his desperate futile throwing away of all he has for love wins her admiration – and a sombre sumptuous portrayal of his entry into a monastic order, in which he overwhelms her like a lover. For him she intrudes heavily: 'Thus the best and most glorious man that ever grac'd that part of the world was undone by love.'

The creation of the narrative voice, pulling away from the letters, emphasises the constructed nature of the personalities revealed. As the narrator uses the literary code to present the tale, so the characters use masks to hide and suggest. Success as reader and actor in the world requires interpretative skill. The narrator shows characters reperusing their own letters to gauge their effect, reading between the lines of their lovers' writings. She teaches reading as energetic interpretation rather than as empathy and involvement.

Towards the end of *Love Letters* the narrator and Sylvia sit sobbing as the beautiful Octavio is erotically undressed in preparation for his monastic vows. This happens in front of the whole emotional town, in a religious ceremony which will put him out of the sexual reach of all and place his fortune in the hands of the church, not of Sylvia. It is an absurd and complex moment which the sobbing actors completely comprehend. In 'The Fair Vow-Breaker' Isabella smothers her first husband and asks the second to dispose of the body. The corpse is in a sack which she stitches to the second man's collar; so the corpse drowns the husband. In *Emperor of the Moon* an old man with much learning is fooled into believing a transparency placed at the end of his telescope is a reality, while a man who believes that laughing can cause death tickles himself as a method of suicide; but the laughing man does not die and there is 'No Moon-World'. In a way all the works of Behn together teach a kind of acceptance of the absurdity of life, its ridiculous constructions and risible sexual and intellectual infatuations. But the absurdity should only be accepted after the stratagems and follies have been interpreted and understood.

5

LIFE AFTER SEX:
DELARIVIER MANLEY

The nastiness of women for male satirists was supremely expressed in the sexual act and its aftermath: male disillusion, impotence and venereal disease. A comfort in this situation was the common narrative of female distress following defloration, a much told tale of madness, disease and death. As the eighteenth century wore on women writers would frequently glorify this female trajectory and give it an immense potency. But it was extremely rare for them to counter the narrative directly and uncover its assumptions, to demystify the sexual act that had taken on such immense porportions. Before the sentimental image of chaste, maternal, subordinate womanhood hardened into a prescription, however, Delarivier Manley was one woman who tried to give the conventional tale a subverting comic turn and provide the sexualised female writing with a cheerful rather than horrific aim.

Manley enters history primarily on the periphery of the lives of her more remembered male colleagues Swift and Steele. Her early years can be glimpsed only through her own creations. In her fictional auto-biography *The Adventures of Rivella* (1714) she tells the life of Rivella, a literary character who yet claims to have written Mrs Manley's works: *Rivella* is the *History of the Author of the New Atalantis*, a work which by 1714 everyone knew to have come from the pen of the infamous Mrs Manley.[1]

Rivella was the daughter of a gentleman whose absolute loyalty to Charles I was in due course rewarded by Charles II with the lieutenant-governorship of Jersey. Born unhandsome between two pretty sisters, plump and pockmarked, Rivella nevertheless gained a lifelong admirer who now tells her tale. She had a sheltered upbringing, one of those private virtuous educations that always spell ruin in Manley's novels; in *The New Atalantis* a similar character is infected by an imprudent aunt with French romance and its high notions of female honour and male

84

reverence. On the death of her father, Rivella was easily persuaded into marriage with her older kinsman, now her guardian. The marriage proved bigamous and Rivella was left alone, a fallen woman with an illegitimate son. Recovering her wits if not her reputation, she began writing for the stage, the most obvious outlet at the time for the woman writer.

At this point fiction needs illumination from other sources. Manley lived for a time with the Duchess of Cleveland, Charles II's former mistress, who ejected her guest after some months, suspecting a liaison with her son. Later Manley took her revenge when she created the amorous Duchess de l'Inconstant in *The New Atlantis* out of her one-time friend and benefactor. Amorous entanglements followed, including one with John Tilly, warden of the Fleet Street prison, as well as a sordid effort to gain money from another person's estate, an episode which, when fictionalised in *Rivella*, even the partisan biographer cannot make wholesome. In her later years, Manley had a rather uneasy relationship with John Barber, a printer from the City of London. Despite personal disappointments, difficulties and illnesses, she continued writing until her death in 1724 at Barber's printing house.

Early on in her career she wrote a volume of travel letters and had a modest success with one play. She then shrewdly turned to the new genre, the scandalous chronicle or secret history, already so successfully used by Aphra Behn, and, more significantly for her purposes, by a Frenchwoman, Marie d'Aulnoy, who, like Behn, had been a spy and who specialised in fictionalised scandal from the more lubricious courts of Europe. For Manley's most famous work in this line, *Secret Memoirs and Manners of Several Persons of Quality, of both sexes. From the New Atalantis* (1709), she was briefly detained by the authorities, an affair made heroic in *Rivella* where she described her spirited admission of guilt to save her publishers and sources. *The New Atalantis* became notorious in later centuries for its erotic depictions, rendered the more unsavoury by the knowledge that they were created by a woman. But, at the time, the work was considered also as political satire, especially aimed at linking Whig public corruption with private indecency.

Steele, who was already promoting the newer, modest and sentimental concept of womanhood in *The Tatler* and *The Spectator*, condemned female political activity on aesthetic grounds, considering that 'there is nothing so bad for the Face as Party-Zeal'. While she remained immune to this kind of belittling advice, in *Rivella* Manley did appear to succumb to the notion that women should avoid political affairs when she admitted that 'Politicks is not the Business of a Woman'. Considering the date, however – 1714, the year that ended Tory influence in government and concluded Stuart rule – she might just as well have written that Tory politics was not good business for anyone. In her choice of genres and subject matter, Manley did indeed make something of being a woman, but she rarely appeared hindered by the notion, expressed by Steele and rapidly gaining ground, that there was a content and mode inappropriate for the female sex.

In her works and the comments of others, Delarivier Manley's life emerged as energetic, disturbed and utterly involved. Without any sentimental views of female friendship and of romantic liaisons, she campaigned as vigorously against erstwhile friends like the Duchess of Cleveland, Richard Steele and the feminist poet Sarah Fyge Egerton – who appears as the apple-pie toting termagant in *The New Atalantis* – as against established opponents like the hated, immensely powerful Duchess of Marlborough, whose political energy, scandalously transformed into sexual appetite in the satires, Manley seemed covertly to have admired. Often morally dubious in personal, financial and literary dealings, she rarely appeared pathetic, despite the very real difficulties she faced in her life as an unprotected woman making a still unconventional literary living. Much is obviously unknowable about her activities and views, but one thing is sure, that she never achieved the elevated detachment from social and political matters that she attributed to her voyeuristic goddess in *The New Atalantis*: 'I see the World without going into it, and hear so much, that I do not desire to see it'.[2]

More even than Aphra Behn, Delarivier Manley experiments in her fiction with the narrative voice. Points of view shift in a world that is corrupt, trivial, harsh and yet vastly entertaining. In *The New Atalantis* she adopts as connecting device the story of two good but naive goddesses, Virtue and Astrea (Aphra Behn's sobriquet) or Justice, who travel through society in the worldly company of Intelligence, the purveyor of information and gossip about the English upper orders. Anecdote, allegory and social comment mingle as the feminine viewpoints vacillate; sometimes the comment is naive, sometimes condemnatory, sometimes simply cynical or resigned. The goddesses know much and learn more, but they do not and cannot act in the world they perceive; they become fitting examples of the female narrative role of gossip, storyteller, and commentator.

In *The Secret History of Queen Zarah and the Zarazians* (1705), the narrative voice is sometimes close to the voice Behn had used in *Love Letters Between a Nobleman and his Sister* to allow description but suggest distaste. Sometimes it is closer to the ingenuous voice of satire so skilfully employed by Manley's friend Jonathan Swift: faced with the enormous and preposterous expense to the country of Blenheim Palace, built by the grasping Duchess of Marlborough with public money, it comments, 'There's more in it than a few dull-sighted People are able to see through.' At other times the voice shares sophistication with the reader: 'it is a ticklish Business for a Woman to repent of a Thing that extreamly delights her.'[3] In *The New Atalantis*, Astrea is given the naive view, expecting moral principles and reality to coalesce, and language and the world to run parallel. The naivety of her expectation is heightened when a poetic account expressing pastoral virtue is set beside a prosaic worldly description of the same events in which the absolutes of morality have no place.

Beyond the satiric point in these juxtapositions of different voices, there is in Manley's work a sense of excitement at the power of language. Words can control response and make and unmake a world. Speeches within her tales do not exist in isolation, but are shown manipulating, deceiving, and enlightening their recipients, while responses and reactions are as carefully displayed as the original words themselves.

Manley was much concerned with the craft of writing, with form and genre, and with the relationship of a work to its author and readership. The foreword to *Queen Zarah*, often ascribed to her and certainly illustrating her frequent tendency to justify, excuse and boast all at once, concentrates less on the writer than on the reception of literature, whether it should improve or entertain or illuminate life by copying it. Poetic justice is now praised and now mocked with the opinion that the good are not often the happiest in life and vice need not be obviously punished in literature. Some synthesis comes through the effect on the reader, who must find the vicious worthy of punishment, even if they are not punished by the author.

The problematic relationship of commercial literature to society and its beliefs is caught by the foreword not in extended analysis but simply in the placing together of conflicting views. Distinct unexplored aims of literature and life are juxtaposed, suggesting the equivocal nature of the relationship between moral constructions and experience. At one moment fiction is discerned in strict market terms: it must please, without insisting on onerous judgements or reflections, and it must conclude in aesthetic comfort, must 'satisfie the Disquiets of the Reader'.

The moral mode that would come to dominate fiction during the 1720s and 1730s in the works of, for example, Penelope Aubin, a lay preacher as well as a novelist, and a preacher in both roles, interrupted plots to deliver moral reflections. Writing in a completely antagonistic mode, Manley mocks the habit when, in *The New Atalantis*, she allows the sententious to be interrupted by impatient listeners and when those who speak of moral matters like marriage are cut off with a yawn. A character in *Queen Zarah* begins a long general attack on the practice of duelling, an attack which would be frequently echoed in sentimental literature, but he is silenced by a bored friend who wants to hear of the specific scandal they were enjoying. The habit of making fiction express more morally elevated views than the reader usually holds or could practise in life is often satirised by Manley, who sees it as yet another bizarre construction of a culture that constantly forms ideals it cannot embody.

But at other times the purpose is conventionally moral:

> The chief End of History is to instruct and inspire into Men the Love of Virtue and Abhorrence of Vice, by the Examples propos'd to them; therefore the Conclusions of a Story ought to have some Tract of Morality which may engage Virtue.

Put more succinctly in *The New Atalantis*, fiction should show 'suffering Vertue, crown'd with just Rewards, and Vice beneath the Ax'.[4]

Many of Manley's readers must have chuckled at this statement, for by the time of *The New Atalantis* she was famous for her naughty scenes, however politically motivated and however yielding of morality. She was herself acutely aware of the objections that could be made to her scandalous and sexy subject matter. As many detractors insisted and she could not deny, her main material was gossip about the great, secrets revealed of wicked happenings that people would rather have kept hidden. Inevitably the secrets that she told appealed to the prurient desires of the reader and could titillate the sophisticate and corrupt the innocent. Sometimes she glories in what she is doing and sometimes defangs it by declaring that her revelations are innocuous for the events are all far in the past. But in the preface to the second volume of *The New Atalantis*, after she has had the measure of hostile reaction and enthusiastic consumption, she makes greater claims, setting out grandly to turn her image from a female scandal-monger into a male satirist in the line of Horace, Juvenal and Dryden; satire, she claims, was always personal or it would have had no bite, and the flailing of individual vice signified not a vicious gossip but a 'lofty stedfast Soul'.

Whatever her noble stance, what most struck readers of the time and later was the openness of both the presentation and the discussion of sexuality. In her pages women still suffer for sexual activity far beyond men, but on the whole it is a social suffering and the sexual fall, largely demystified, does not bear the immense religious and moral weight it will achieve in sentimental literature. As she had been in Aphra Behn's work, woman is often here the actual subject of desire, rather than simply the pretty object of male love or lust. Hence such frank descriptions as the following from Part I of *The New Atalantis*:

> the Dutchess softly enter'd that little Chamber of Repose, the Weather violently hot the Umbrelloes were let down from behind the Windows, the Sashes open, and the Jessimine that cover'd 'em blew in with a gentle Fragrancy; Tuberoses set in pretty Gilt and China Posts, were placed advantageously upon Stands, the Curtains of the Bed drawn back to the Canopy, made of yellow Velvet embroider'd with white Bugles, the Panels of the Chamber Looking-Glass, upon the Bed were strow'd with a lavish Profuseness, plenty of Orange and Lemon Flowers, and to compleat the Scene, the young Germanicus in a dress and posture not very decent to describe; it was he that was newly risen from the Bath, and in a lose Gown of Carnation Taffety, stain'd with Indian Figures, his beautiful long, flowing Hair, for then 'twas the Custom to wear their own tied back with a Ribbon of the same Colour, he had thrown himself upon the Bed, pretending to Sleep, with nothing on but his Shirt and Night-Gown, which he had so indecently dispos'd, that slumbring as he appear'd, his whole Person stood confess'd to the Eyes of the Amorous Dutchess, his Limbs were exactly form'd, his Skin shiningly white, and the Pleasure the Ladies graceful entrance gave him, diffus'd Joy and Desire throughout all his Form; his lovely Eyes seem'd to be closed, his Face turn'd on one side . . . was obscur'd by the Lace depending from the Pillows on which he rested . . . with an amorous sign, she gently threw her self on the Bed close to the desiring Youth.[5]

This is a portrait of the Duchess de l'Inconstant, entranced by the charms of a new lover. Much is interchangeable among erotic scenes of Behn, Manley and Haywood but what is unusual for amorous descriptions is that the gaze is female and the languorous artful seductiveness of the body is a man's. Like so many fictional women before and after him, accused of narcissism as they go about their necessarily self-interested business of attracting another, the young man has arranged himself to be seduced. The spontaneity of response is here the woman's; it is engaging to the reader in its frankness and, indeed, in its effectiveness, for the man quickly comes to answer the woman's desire and fulfil the reader's hopes.

It is, however, a kind of dream of equal sexuality. It is made possible partly through Manley's concentration, similar to that in both Behn and Haywood, not on the sexual act itself, but on its prelude and setting. In her stories, stress is on the stimulus to copulation; repeatedly there are details of the heat, flowers and gardens, opened windows, the fragrant smells, the luxurious accessories, and the dishabille of the lovers. The atmospheric details emphasise the inevitability and naturalness of sexual expression for male and female alike, while the social elements, the fashion and luxury, are those associated with women as well as men.

Yet, in the last analysis, there is the sexual act to perform, an act which is absolutely unequal in its physical and social repercussions – in Behn it is often interrupted to the woman's annoyance, in Haywood to the man's, but in Manley it usually takes place without chance or providence to prevent it. Ultimately, the Duchess's spontaneity of response must be ominous, however attractive it might initially seem; it would be so in man or woman in this dangerous, scheming society, but in the latter its result is almost inevitably bound to involve misery. Despite her active, lusty, possessive gaze, when the sexual act occurs, the Duchess becomes simply the object instead of the subject, and she dwindles from active desiring agent into a commodity: 'he got the possession of her Person'. In time her exchange value deteriorates and she sinks from acting as lover of a king to being, like Sylvia, the mistress of servants.

The New Atalantis is a dystopia beside Bacon's utopian *New Atlantis*, replacing the idea of disinterestedness with a reality of self-interest and cupidity. In Manley's works, the driving force of humanity is desire – both for money and sex, which become interchangeable. In the latter women may suffer consequences more than men but the most successful learn to manipulate sexual desire in others and to avoid being, like the Duchess, controlled by it themselves. Although a narrator might condescendingly admire the spontaneous gesture and the authentic emotion, she may also lament, with sophisticated melancholy, that the sincere and transparent are not fitted for a world in which survival means dissimulation and constant devotion to self-interest. Marriages for love may be the ideal, but marriages for financial interest are both common and appropriate, although ritually condemned. Women marry for reputation and maintenance, men marry to clear their mortgages; the success goes to the most manipulative and cunning. When equality is reached, there is an impasse, as happens in Defoe's *Moll Flanders* where the heroine fools and is fooled simultaneously, or in the life of the 'German Princess' who cheats and is cheated by her 'lord'. The answer to the rake, the male predator, who stalks through so much female fiction of this century is not the later, almost compulsory demand for his destruction or for more male protection of women from men, but the recommendation that women achieve more awareness, wit and self-control.

The world of the scandal novels is quite openly sordid and debased, its inhabitants opportunistic and self-aggrandising. Yet it is also energetic and vigorous. Luxury is appalling and attractive. There is much describing of elaborate clothes, coaches and expensive interiors, much detail of gold, lace and costly embroidery. Rich food and drink accompany the intimate bawdy talk on nights that are always oppressively hot, and they augment the sense of intricate social corruption. Sexuality is overwhelming and inevitably isolating through its expression in individual desire, but the sheer number and variety of the sexual scenes Manley describes make physical enslavement a soothingly uniting predicament. As night comes in her tales, the copulations begin and the separate sins become a comfortable communal fall.

To survive in the harsh, complicated society of *Zarah, The New Atalantis* and *Rivella* everyone must wear a mask. Social grace is wanted, not the sentimental virtues of chastity and compassion, so much preached for and to women, decorum not sincerity, good conversation and worldly sense: 'The Knowledge which teaches Men to live among People of civility and Manners'. Yet, although very much a lady as well as a goddess, one of the two onlookers of the scenes in *The New Atalantis* is nevertheless 'Virtue'. Her presence emphasises the apparent need of society to define an ideal of virtue and to try to illustrate it in life – usually, it becomes apparent, at another person's (woman's) expense.

Because of this need, education is especially problematic, although there is general unquestioning acceptance that it should be in virtue, particularly for young girls. Virtue is needed to guard a girl against premature indulgence in sex, and 'virtuous' books must keep out titillating romances that encourage her seemingly natural desire for seduction. Despite a rhetoric of admiration, the purpose of a virtuous education in moral principles, sincerity and chastity seems clearly to be the thwarting of nature, a necessity for existence in a civilised world.

Yet, repeatedly, this education is revealed as socially inept, even dangerous for girls. By suppressing sexual expression, it merely delays and heightens it; as Astrea wearily remarks at the close of yet another story of seduction and betrayal, 'we see the tender Sex, with all their Native Timorousness, Modesty and Shame-fac'd Education, when stung by Love, can trample under Foot the consideration of Virtue and Glory'.[6] For the older male seducer, a virtuous education simply renders the young girl a yet more delicious prey; it becomes a seductive attribute to femaleness, sought by men to enhance the charms of the victim and give piquancy to defloration.

As snug havens of domesticity, families do not seem to exist in the cold world of Manley's novels, and the most successful survivors are those who have learned that they are essentially alone. Society is the small group of the court and its hangers-on, and there is no sense of alternative worlds except through rustic exile or foreign escape. Communal activity may give sensation and pleasure but never security, and even associations for political purposes and financial intrigue are temporary and precarious.

There is, however, one striking example of a successful communal venture, the scandalous Cabal of upper-class women described in Book II of *The New Atalantis*. The ladies who form this group have no desire for the high-mindedness and celibacy shown in other fictional female communities, like the learning academy of Mary Astell or the philanthropic institution of Sarah Scott described in *Millenium Hall* (1762); instead they aim at pleasure and they make themselves remarkably comfortable in a country house surrounded by extensive grounds and views, and stocked with good wine. Despite the naive Astrea's initial view, that they are a defensive huddle of women trying to avoid 'that rapacious Sex', they are clearly sexual beings involved in sexual encounters 'beyond what Nature design'd'. Yet, although scandalous, the lesbianism is not especially shocking, and even Astrea, when she comes to understand its existence, opposes it more for social than for moral or religious reasons, seeing it as preventing advantageous marriages and as provoking 'obscene Laughter' in men. And the positive social and psychological side is also stressed, for in the Cabal loving women share property, if only inside relationships: 'In this little Commonwealth is no Property; whatever a Lady possesses is, sans ceremone, at the service, and for the use of her Fair Friend, without the vain nice scruple of being oblig'd.'[7] Here in the Cabal women can play men, taste their power, and reject its usual implications, that 'Woman was only created (with all her Beauty, Softness, Passions and compleat Tenderness) to adorn the Husband's Reign, perfect his Happiness, and propagate the Kind'.[8]

The seemingly feminist tone of this last statement is not a dominant one in Manley's works, although it occurs frequently. Usually, however, it has an ambiguous context that makes it yet another of the many modified tones of the tales. Certainly Manley understands that the cards are stacked against women in the sexual game and that they are therefore at an immense disadvantage in the social one. But individual women, like Aphra Behn's Sylvia in *Love Letters Between a Nobleman and his Sister*, can manipulate others and scheme their way to the top just as well as men. The unremitting pursuit of self-interest, condemned but described with gusto all the same, is a female as well as a male attribute, and this coincidence in activity gives a kind of equality to the fictional society that makes a feminist protest almost irrelevant. All power is socially desirable and morally corrupting and usurped female power is, if anything, marginally more harmful because less expected. The detested Duchess of Marlborough with her enormous power suggests this view to Manley, and Jane Austen illustrates it a century later in her satirical portraits of the haughty Mrs Ferrars and Lady Catherine de Burgh.

Manley expresses the conventional distaste for the use of sexuality by women, and she condemns them for employing their sexual desirability to trap rich men into marriage. Yet she also gives them justification by asserting that the same desire for riches and power animates both sexes; while men have many routes to attain them, women have only their sexual attractiveness.

Because of the different social effects of sexual indulgence on men and women, different narratives are inevitably provided for them. But the difference is not that men may prey on women or guard and save them according to genre, while women must enter the archetypal stories of the virgin or the whore; instead both sexes divide into the naive and the manipulative, and their stories evolve accordingly. Silly innocent women are fooled by men, who are in turn deceived by sophisticated scheming women. The female victim is always pitied at length, but she is given none of the spiritual significance she would acquire in the novels of Samuel Richardson a few years later. She suffers for her sexual activity far beyond men, but on the whole it is a social suffering and the sexual fall, largely demystified, does not bear the immense religious and moral weight it has in sentimental literature.

One sexual narrative is repeated so frequently in Manley's tales that it assumes the status of a myth. It coincides with the developing intertwined stories of virtue in distress and of love betrayed, which will come to dominate literature about women and which is already expressed in the woman-centred tragedies of Otway and Rowe. It is this story that *Rivella* will so naughtily subvert.

A young innocent girl is unprotected by a sensible mother; she finds at puberty that her male guardian or father figure is displaced by or transformed into a lusty and destructive man bent on rape or seduction. The sad account of Charlot from Part I of *The New Atalantis* is typical. In this narrative Manley has ample opportunity to repeat her worldly points about the problematic nature of education and to illustrate the difficulty of constructing a viable self amidst conflicting influences of moral instruction, ambivalent literature, overwhelming personalities and natural sexual but socially destructive drives.

In the tale, the Duke — like Manley's other villains, self-made and acquisitive despite his title — educates his ward Charlot only in virtue, banishing from her environment all novels and poetry that might provoke lascivious feelings or teach dissimulation. She thus becomes a modest, silent, sincere young woman, a correct product of the education she has experienced. Then literature wickedly intrudes into her chaste scene and all becomes heated and obscure. First Charlot simply reads instructive moral poetry, which reinforces her virtuous inclinations. But her acting-out for her guardian of scenes from the works, her assumption of roles despite her authenticity and innocence, has the effect of inflaming the Duke, whose fatherly love is rapidly transformed into an altogether less proper emotion. Meanwhile he himself is a victim of literature in his assent to the notion of the amoral political author Machiavelli that greatness may be expressed in wickedness; he therefore finds himself lusting after the person whose purity he should guard, uninhibited by any restraint on his inclinations.

Preparing to seduce his ward, the Duke excites her mind with less elevated verse. Charlot has learned to see the father where the Duke is now presenting the lover; consequently his signs of desire assume incestuous overtones for the reader. In due course, his disorder, his trembling and shortness of breath inject Charlot with 'that new and lazy Poison'. Certainly it is the birth of sexuality in her, but it is also the beginning of desire for social power, always a component of sexual feeling in Manley's works. The apparent need to please in women is, according to the author, often less the desire for sexual gratification than a claim to influence; other forms of empire seem 'to be politically deny'd them, because the way to Authority and Glory is stop'd up'.[9] Charlot is excited by a temporary sexual power that gives her social influence but which she does not adequately understand – 'ignorant of the Power of Love, that Leveller of Mankind'. So she cannot use this power to promote her own interests.

Under the influence of the seductive Ovid, Petrarch and other licentious reading, 'Books . . . abominable for Virgins . . . such as explain the Mysteries of Nature, the congregated Pleasures of Venus', her moral education melts into 'Precepts of airy Virtue', and she desires and gains sexual fulfilment. The reader becomes the voyeur of the first seduction and is delivered the scene through the eyes both of the amorous Duke and of the naive daughterly girl. But the sexual climax, coming after the expected description of excessive heat, waiting bed and dishabille, is, in literary and social terms, anticlimactic: while yet she was 'doubtful of his designs, he took advantage of her confusion to accomplish 'em . . . Thus was Charlot undone! thus ruin'd by him that ought to have been her Protector!'[10]

Entering the new category of the fallen woman, Charlot finds her virtuous education valueless. Designed to guard virginity for social or moral ends, it has no purpose outside the sexual meaning and no relevance to the fallen woman's need to gain control over herself and her environment. Indeed such an education is now actually harmful, for it simply renders Charlot sincere and without disguise. A worldly-wise countess who 'knew the Management of Mankind, and how to procure herself universal Love and Admiration', a lady who has been bred up in the 'fashionable way of making Love, wherein the Heart has little or no part', gives Charlot new role models from literature of manipulative and powerful women who have understood men and gained power and influence. At the same time she tries to teach the young girl that love must be used by a woman as a tool with which to establish herself in the world. But the good Charlot cannot so quickly learn a new lesson; she fails to fix the Duke in marriage and watches her own passion grow as his declines, not understanding that 'the same unaccountable thing that cools the Swain, more warms the Nymph'. The end is inevitable. Giving up the role of educator, the Countess concentrates on herself and her interest; she sets up the seductive sexual scene, and swiftly catches the Duke in marriage. Charlot is left to 'Horror, Sorrow, and Repentance'. 'She dy'd a true Landmark: to warn all believing Virgins from shipwracking their Honour upon . . . the Vows and pretended Passion of Mankind.'[11]

But of course the moral is not as clear as this. The repentance has few religious overtones, and the honour and virtue obtain no transcendental meaning. Astrea comments at the end of Charlot's story:

> Men may regain their Reputations, tho' after a Complication of Vices, Cowardice, Robbery, Adultery, Bribery, and Murder, but a Woman once departed from the Road of Virtue, is made incapable of a return; Sorrow and Scorn overtake her, and . . . the World suffers her to perish loath'd, and unlamented.

Vice is translated into sexual activity for a woman, and into murder, robbery and bribery for a man, and both translations are given social not moral significance. Indeed chastity for a woman is not really a virtue at all, but simply good social sense in the absence of consummate ability.

The story of Charlot gains some resonance in Manley's works from its equivocal use of the theme of virtue in distress or love betrayed, and it adds more through the autobiographical content. For a version of the tale of Charlot is so often told that, even without a knowledge of *Rivella*, it would be difficult not to discern that it held some special fascination for the author. Sometimes the story trails off into sorrow and exile, as it did in the narrative of Charlot and the Duke; sometimes it ends in the woman's suicide and the man's unperturbed re-entry into society. But it can also continue in the less dramatic sadness and sordidness of a woman's life outside respectable society. It is into the last narrative that Manley herself most clearly enters. In *Rivella*, the narrator claims that the story of Delia in *The New Atalantis* is actually the life story of the author of that work. Rivella, the famous writer, becomes the result of the sexual victimisation of Delia, an innocent young orphan; Delia and Rivella unite in Delarivier.

95

Like so many of her predecessors in Manley's works, Delia is poisoned by romantic tales. She is persuaded into marriage with her guardian, a man twenty-three years her senior. The marriage is simply a variation of seduction, since it proves bigamous. The effect is the usual social isolation of the woman and her realisation at last that virtue is specific to gender. Men may sin and sin and be socially reclaimed, but women, even if only guilty in appearance, are irretrievably lost and cannot be reconciled to society: 'Is it not this Inhospitality that brings so many unhappy Wretches to Distruction? dispairing of Redemption, from one vile degree to another, they plunge themselves down to the lowest ebb of Infamy!'[12]

In its use of the narrative of virtue in distress, the story of Delia highlights many of the difficulties Manley had encountered in the presentation of a public female image. The teller of Delia's story, aiming to rouse as much sympathy as possible in the reader, insists that the young girl is innocent of sexual longing despite her unwise perusal of romance and that she is precipitated into marriage through illness; her guardian cares for her and she is grateful. Such a timely collapse would come to many later heroines who find themselves married or compromised not through sexual desire but through physical weakness. Meanwhile the guardian, like the Duke, is tinged with incest, for he is associated with her father and was present at her birth. Yet, Astrea, goddess of justice, will have none of this special pleading and, in her critical comments, the narrative of virtue in distress becomes a less elevated tale of foolish love betrayed, and the heroine is transformed from a pure child into a silly sexual woman.

The usual narrative ending is withdrawal and death for distressed innocence, and suicide for betrayed passion. But of course Delarivier Manley does not kill herself or pine and die. Instead, she becomes a writer and she uses her infamy to her advantage. The sad story of Delia is continued in the robust *Rivella*, where the reader learns that a woman without reputation and honour may be freed for economic activity. In time she transforms herself from the deceived and confused object of desire into its subject. But, although Rivella is sometimes described as a looker, an amorous gazer on others, far more strikingly she uses herself as a writing subject to create in her inflaming works an elusive and suggestive image of herself as object of male desire. It is, after all, female desirability, not desire itself, that has social currency and gains social power in a patriarchal world.

Manley's view of herself as a young woman in her fictional auto-biography, 'Sweet, Clean, Witty, Friendly, Serviceable', is relayed through the medium of a male admirer, whom she created to tell her story. The same useful gentleman is given a quick justification for the older Manley's notorious public life with its sexual irregularities, political scandals and shady legal and financial dealings:

> Her Vertues are her own, her Vices occasion'd by her Misfortunes; and yet as I have often heard her say, If she had been a Man, she had been without Fault: But the Charter of that Sex being much more confin'd than ours, what is not a Crime in Men is scandalous and unpardonable in Woman.[13]

In the work of Manley, as in that of Behn, many signs of woman are hung out. Some follow Behn's fictional narrators in suggesting an older worldly gossip, like Phoebe Crackenthorpe of *The Female Tatler* or Intelligence in *The New Atalantis*. Some, feeding on her reputation as depicter of improper sexual encounters, resemble the signs of Angellica and Mary Carleton and emphasise physical and verbal seductiveness. Others follow the Duchess of Newcastle and the later Aphra Behn in asserting the writer and her fame. Still others merge the two and use the image of the literary lady for a verbal erotic seduction, the prose forming a kind of boudoir into which the reader must expectantly penetrate. As can be discerned, the prude and the ingenu(e) have no place in Mrs Manley's audience.

In *Rivella* the author displays herself for her purchasing male reader-ship and makes a direct link between authorship and seduction, literary consumption and sexual gratification. Her words dissolve her fatness, smooth her pock marks, light up her expressive eyes and give an 'establish'd Reputation' to her neck and breasts. The final scene of the autobiography, echoing the many sexual and scandalous encounters in Manley's books, invites the fictional listener, with the reader, to hear the author's seductive conversation, sit at her well-furnished table, and to repose with her 'during the Heat of the Day' on her bed, 'nicely sheeted and strow'd with Roses, Jessamines or Orange-Flowers . . . her Pillows neatly trim'd with Lace or Muslin, stuck round with Junquils, or other natural Garden Sweets'.[14]

Despite the amorous build-up and the many precedents in her tales, this scene will – just this once – not give way to the narrative of love betrayed, for, even beyond sexual cunning, it hints at a new power of women through their manipulation of literary language. The lady here is a writing woman who has weathered sexual and social disasters and has learned the power of words. No sexual act that might objectify and victimise the female is written into her account, although sexual activity may be implied, and the end is not the rushed retreat of the satisfied man and the sorrow of the abandoned woman. Instead there is a companion-able airing in the park or on the water when the heat of the day is gone.

Here in this ending of Manley's fictional autobiography, a mixture of imaginative history and scandalous exposure, desire is controlled and contained, and the reader is made to agree with the listener whom the author has created for herself, that she, a fallen woman who does not die, a maker of wicked romances, is the 'only Person of her sex that knows how to Live'.

Rivella is well aware of the identification of woman writer and whore in male writing and she comically plays with the convention. She uses the image of the literary lady for a verbal erotic seduction brought about through the special female ability of the author to please with scenes of love. In her prose there is a sense of excitement at the power of language, a new social power to set beside or, indeed, to manipulate and direct sexual power. Words can control response and make and unmake desire. They alone can construct the meaning of the sexual act and they alone can create sex without pregnancy, venereal disease or lifelong misery.

In *The New Atalantis*, Manley diffuses the criticism that she is corrupting the mind of the reader with the rather lame excuse that only vicious activity can harm, not the mere hearing of scandal. Yet she does not rest with such simplicity and, in common with the writers throughout the eighteenth century, she is both appalled and excited by the obvious and feared effect of literature on the mind. While declaring that stories of sexual excitement cannot by themselves corrupt and incite to sexual activity, she provides example after example of young girls inflamed into love by the rash perusal of romantic tales. But in *Rivella* she avoids this whole troubling nexus by moving her story into the sophisticated world of the older woman and the always privileged men. Rivella presents an image of herself as consummate mistress of the titillating effect and there need be no pretence that literature does not often and deliciously nudge life: 'After perusing her Inchanting Descriptions, which of us have not gone in Search of Raptures which she every where tells us, as happy Mortals, we are capable of tasting,' remarks the obliging male.[15] Men's often dangerous desire ends, where it ought, in the author herself; female desire need not result in distress but instead it yields delight and money through its representation. The whore becomes storyteller of men's lust and recorder of the comic history of virtue in distress made entertaining and profitable.

PART TWO

6

THE MID-EIGHTEENTH CENTURY: SENTIMENT AND SINCERITY

> As women are, in polished society, weak and incapable of self-defence, the laws of this country have supplied this defect, and formed a kind of barrier around them, by rendering their persons so sacred and inviolable, that even death is, in several cases, the consequence of taking improper advantages of that weakness.[1]

It would be hard to imagine such a condescending and complacent opinion being directed at the Duchess of Newcastle, Aphra Behn or Delarivier Manley; they might be – indeed were – the objects of misogyny and scorn but never of such belittling idealisation. The England that could afford such a construction of womanhood, the England of the middle years of the eighteenth century, was not the politically unstable, shifting society of the Restoration but one that had clear political achievements to its credit and a distinct national pride in its economic and social accomplishments. It could envisage keeping women of the higher ranks idle and leisured, and could use such weak and sacred figures to embody some of its economically less convenient values.

POLITICS AND RELIGION

With the procession of the Hanoverian Georges, England achieved considerable political solidity, and the danger of violent civil strife was lessened. Party conflict was kept in check by a series of strong if turbulent ministries which stretched from the 1720s to the 1780s. The country remained broadly monarchical, but it seemed impossible to be enthusiastic about the hardly legitimate, German-speaking Georges, although in 1760 with the accession of George III the nation had once again a king more or less accepted by all. In the 1720s and 1730s there was still some hope of re-establishing the ill-fated Stuarts through James's grandson Charles but, after the failure of the rebellion in 1745, the possibility of a

101

Stuart restoration very much diminished. By the middle of the century the Jacobite rebels had been romanticised into folk heroes, suitable subjects for Scottish ballad writers.

Woman were much involved in both rebellion and romanticisation, rather as they had been in the earlier Stuart cults. The Jacobite Lady Grizel Baillie had aided the cause in her youth; later she wrote a series of popular Scottish songs and by the beginning of the next century she was featuring in Joanna Baillie's *Metrical Legends of Exalted Characters* (1821) as the very type of the romantic heroine. The progress seems similar even if the songwriter had been on the government side; Alicia Cockburn and Jean Elliot were both Hanoverians, but both later wrote Scottish laments which derived some of their popularity from the nostalgic emotionalism in which the Jacobite cause had been wrapped.

At the same time the wilder areas of Scotland and Wales were being transformed from breeding grounds for civil upheavals into mental and physical tourist areas. Mountains and desolate places became interesting and English readers enjoyed stories set in a Celtic fringe, dreaded as exile a generation or two before. As England, Wales and Scotland were fashioned into Britain, much effort was expended on creating a mythic British past of poetic druids and mead-drinking warriors. So great was the enthusiasm for such a heritage that it was easy for Macpherson (inventing ancient Scottish poetry for his bard Ossian), Chatterton (inventing medieval verse for his monk) and Iolo Morganwg (inventing Celtic rituals and Welsh druids) to impose on the nation with their forgeries.[2] Women were quick to exploit the vogue and the sentimental values of the mid-eighteenth century were discovered in a host of melancholic Edwins, Eldreds and Eltrudas.

In the 1730s the prime minister Robert Walpole kept England out of major European conflicts and so allowed a concentration on economic development and consolidation. The period of relative calm was interrupted in 1756 by the Seven Years' War, a large-scale imperial conflict with France, the final result of which was an immense trading empire for England, which added much of India among other territories to its colonial North American possessions.

For women the subcontinent was the place of last resort for husbands. Mariana Starke, daughter of a governor of Madras, mocked vulgar indolent English ladies who travelled to India in search of rich colonialists to provide them with a life of ease and unwarranted importance. She also pointed to another aspect of imperial possession: limited and not especially popular wars. In a poem of 1789 she told the sorry story of a loyalist soldier from the former American colonies, persecuted in the new United States and treated as a beggar in England.[3]

Although the empire had come from desire for 'customers not colonies', there was, after the event, some political rationale for it derived from a sense of political superiority. The English of the mid-eighteenth century thought of themselves as peculiarly free from despotism, despite the continued struggle of Dissenters for political rights, and peculiarly just in their laws, despite the obvious inadequacy of a class-bound judicial system and peculiarly egalitarian despite their participation in the iniquity of the slave trade. The Protestant parliamentary victory of 1688 was commonly interpreted as a victory for freedom. It was made palatable to most moderate conservatives by the fiction of James II's abdication and it became the symbol of the English compromise, which sometimes was, and certainly ought to have been, the envy of less enlightened nations. The idealisation of English liberty, together with a belief in the gradual and inevitable progress of political development, was especially a Whig phenomenon. Nonetheless, it is not easy to separate the parties distinctly since both by mid-century accepted the ideals of 1688.

The linking of outspoken and activist women with the court and with the Tory party seems to have been broken in this period and on the whole women, like men, were moderate, middle of the road. The novelist and playwright Frances Brooke was typical, expressing a patriotic viewpoint in her magazine in the 1750s and mocking opinions that appeared at odds with the English common sense of the majority, like, for example, the Dissenters' view of the massive Lisbon earthquake as a divine punishment for moral and political sins.

Enthusiasm was left for marginal groups such as the followers of John Wilkes, a Member of Parliament expelled from the House of Commons, who became for a time a focus of political reform. Wilkes was helped by several women, including the pamphleteer Charlotte Forman, herself the daughter of a Jacobite pamphleteer, and the historian Catherine Macaulay, whose writings made an important political link between the new reforming agitation and its Puritan Commonwealth antecedents. Macaulay was politically active throughout her life, especially as the scourge of Burke, later to be Mary Wollstonecraft's opponent; in the 1770s in an attack on Burke she proposed frequent elections and an extension of the suffrage; in 1775 she took issue with his views on America, and just before she died she argued against his conservative opposition to the French Revolution.[4]

Presumably women played some role in parliamentary elections, since they crowd into Hogarth's 'The Election'. In the 1780s, several well-born ladies, like the Duchess of Devonshire and her sister Lady Duncannon, as well as the novelist Anne Damer, campaigned for the moderate Whig reformer Charles James Fox. The Duchess in particular was much abused and she and her sister were said to have gained votes by kissing the voters. Inevitably vilification took a sexual tone:

> The girl condemn'd to walk the streets,
> And pick up each blackguard she meets,
>   And get him in her clutches;
> Has lost her trade – for they despise
> Her wanton arms, her leering eyes –
>   Now they can kiss a Duchess.[5]

This desire to silence women's endeavour with sexual abuse, common throughout the period, was especially effective in the second half of the eighteenth century when femininity and the domestic sphere for women were so much part of the prevailing ideology. The Duchess did not repeat her electioneering activities although she remained a firm supporter of Fox. (A man's reputation could, however, only be enhanced by knowledge of his sexual exploits and both Wilkes and Fox gained popularity from their notorious philandering.)

Some decades before, Lady Mary Wortley Montagu, born early enough to be aware of the open political activities of such writers as Delarivier Manley, helped her husband in an election of 1714. Later, in 1738, she supported Walpole in a series of journal articles attacking his enemies and in 1739 she described the attempts of a group of women to avoid being excluded from the Gallery of the House of Lords, calling them 'Amazons' and 'the boldest assertors, and most resigned sufferers for liberty, I ever read of'. The ladies, mainly aristocratic, tried many stratagems to gain entry, as, for example, pulling rank – 'The Duchess of Queensbury, as head of the squadron, pished at the ill-breeding of a mere lawyer' – and they laid lengthy siege to the building. But when they finally gained admittance all they could do, according to Lady Mary, was applaud and jeer.[6]

In more traditional areas of power female influence possibly declined. Court patronage certainly continued in mistresses and queens, although there is no equivalent to the court of Queen Anne and the Duchess of Marlborough, but it lessened as the domestic image of woman strengthened. Lady Mary was active in politics, but her daughter, Lady Bute, who was the wife of the prime minister (and who regarded her mother's political and publishing activity as unseemly) had little influence; Queen Caroline, wife of George II, had considerable although always covert power, while her successor Queen Charlotte, wife of George III, kept aloof from politics.

In the middle decades of the eighteenth century the Anglican church settled down into a comfortable stability. Pluralism was common and younger sons of the gentry expected to move easily into the Church, now very much seen as part of the social establishment. So it had limited relevance to the lower orders who were also less catered for by some of the Dissenting sects tending, as the century progressed, towards a more intellectual than emotional understanding of religious doctrine. The emotional gap was filled by enthusiastic forms of Christianity within the Church of England, especially the Methodists who sought to move religion out into the fields and to bring people to Christ through exuberant conversion and congregational experience rather than ritual and argument.

Although Methodism, like Anglicanism in general, kept to the Pauline view that women should be silent at religious services and did not allow the political participation so typical of the Quakers, the emphasis on emotionality and authenticity, attributes increasingly associated with femininity, meant that women in fact played a very definite part in the movement. Most dominant was the Countess of Huntingdon – called the 'most precious saint of God' by the hymn writer Augustus Toplady – a forerunner of the formidable ladies of charity so common at the end of the century. In the 1740s she made her house into an exemplary place of piety which inspired this exclamation from her chaplain, the famous Methodist preacher George Whitefield: 'We have the Sacrament every morning, heavenly consolation all day, and preaching at night. This is to live at Court indeed.' She used her social position to further the Methodist cause and tried to mediate between the varieties of Methodism as well as between Dissent and the Church of England. At the same time she wrote scores of encouraging letters exhorting others to piety and faith and describing and analysing her own spiritual progress. The emotional extremes she finds in herself are typical of Methodist autobiographies and resemble those of the Puritan Countess of Warwick, at one minute feeling the most holy ardour of desire, at the next falling low in the dust lamenting her unfaithfulness, unprofitableness and unfruitfulness.[7]

THE ECONOMY

There were some rumblings in religion and politics, but government remained largely in aristocratic hands and the dominant values were those of the upper orders and their supporters, people who through birth or education regarded themselves as a notch above the city merchant and the industrialist – although the growing sense of 'class' itself suggests some social instability. In the new sentimental drama rich merchants might be treated reverentially, although even there they tended to be used to expedite the plot, and their worth was usually shown not by further acquisition of money but by retirement to the country and a gentrified way of life. On the whole the person in trade continued to be mocked, and money was not felt to confer status unless it was combined with patronage of the arts or with a style of living associated with the educated classes. Addison's notion of gentility united gentry and aspiring middle class in its de-emphasis on land and title as the only source of status. But the ideal in most literature remained self-consciously that expressed in the country house. Although the inventions on which much industrial technology would be based were being made in the middle years of the century, new patents were taken out in large numbers mainly after 1790; large-scale industrialisation was still in the future and England remained an agricultural country.

Yet, despite the opposition in much literature to capitalist advance and trade, sometimes snobbish and sometimes morally acute, landed men did in fact participate in the new wealth, especially through agricultural reforms. These expanded meat production and vastly increased the amount of food available, making it possible for the population to swell by almost a quarter through the first half of the century, although the great increases came at the end. But there was a price to pay, for the land in the new agricultural system, especially from the 1760s onwards, was enclosed land which had before supported the poor in some sort of independence. Advantages were only belatedly felt since bad harvests made progress impossible through much of the 1760s at least.

Through all this time, activity to support the family in the home declined and domestic goods like candles and cloth were increasingly made outside. Poor women would have continued to work in farms, usually owned by a family member, although they may also have acted as seasonal farm labourers.[8] In towns they might have sold and traded items or worked as domestic servants, much in demand by the wealthier classes; more and more it was women who entered service and consequently the expensive manservant grew into something of a status symbol, often idle and bedecked while the real physical work was done by women.[9]

Whether in country or town, however, women would have added domestic chores to their outside labour. Mary Collier, the 'Washer-Woman' poet, rebuked Stephen Duck, the thresher, another poet from the lower orders, when he complained of his lot. She pointed out that women worked a great deal harder than men since they added domestic drudgery to their labour outside the house: 'when we Home are come / Alas! we find our Work has just begun.'

Among the more affluent classes, the need for female labour continued to decline – although women probably played a more active economic role than was described – and leisure became the usual state of the wife. (It was of course very often the state of the man as well away from his land although this was less commented on.) The new leisure and luxury brought about by successful trade were much feared by moralists who inveighed against the frivolity and triviality of the idle lady, but the situation was eagerly exploited by entrepreneurs, and a 'commercialisation of leisure' continued apace. A large consumer industry flourished, providing everything from fashionable carriages and china to novels, magazines and scientific instruments to entertain people at home or in public.

Fashion of the upper classes became increasingly elaborate – although never as extreme as in France, since in England it remained influenced by the middle classes and the gentry who prized more practical clothes. Hooped skirts, stiffened with whalebone over petticoats, gave a dome-shaped appearance to the fashionable lady; this was flattened towards the end of the period when skirts were so tremendous that the well-dressed found it necessary to go sideways through double doors. Meanwhile coiffures grew so tall that they could catch fire from the candles in chandeliers, and the décolletage fell so deeply that white fichus were needed by respectable ladies to cover the space. Stays were tight and there was much shaping of the female figure, with back boards and weights for the head to ensure correct posture; female toes were forcibly encouraged to turn out. Frequently the whole concoction of the fashionably patched, peached and plumped lady seemed a defiance of the female body.

In general dress for both sexes in the upper echelons of society was elaborate and stately, and male and female fashions were closer than they would ever be again. Both sexes used patches, wigs, powder for the hair and heavy make-up. But transvestism remained a fascination and breeches parts for women were as popular with theatre audiences as they had been in the Restoration – the actress Peg Woffington was described in the 1740s as 'A creature uncommon / Who's both man and woman'.[10] Hannah Snell joined the army as a soldier and fought in India; later she returned to play herself on the stage in London and Bath – rather in the manner of Mary Carleton many decades before. At the end of the century this kind of crudity seems to have been less popular and a more typical figure was the curious Chevalier D'Eon, the transvestite ambassador from France, believed by some to be a girl brought up as a boy; he fascinated the age with a real suggestion of gender confusion. At the same time what might be called functional transvestism continued. Charlotte Charke, the daughter of the playwright and poet laureate, Colley Cibber, played breeches parts and dressed as a man off the stage to make a living and avoid creditors, while Lady Wallace donned male clothes to attend debates in the House of Lords in the 1780s.

Leisure demanded pleasures. Drinking and gambling were rife and the affluent but unintellectual could fill the rest of their time – at least in London – with a round of entertainments, such as shows, dancing and freak exhibitions. The pleasure gardens of Vauxhall and Ranelagh with their public masquerades mingling sexes and classes catered for many tastes, including those of men and women simply seeking assignations. Sexuality for men and lower-class women was remarkably free – though remarkably restrained for respectable middle-class women – and porno-graphic books and prints were openly advertised and sold in London. As John Shebbeare noted in the mid-century, 'every print-shop has its windows stuck full with indecent prints to inflame desire through the eye, and singers in the streets charm your ears with lascivious songs to waken you to the same employment'.[11]

Among the promoters of leisure women figured quite prominently. For example, a Mrs Cornelys organised lavish masquerades and the entre-preneurial Mrs Salmon of Fleet Street displayed her waxworks including royal personages and famous contemporaries like Samuel Johnson and the Methodist John Wesley; Mrs Goldsmith set up her effigies in a crypt in Westminster Abbey and Mrs Mills boasted that she opened her show 'from 9 in the Morn, till 9 at Night' and at Christmas.[12] More spectacular shows were catered for by Mrs Mynns from a booth on the side of Smithfield fairground; she is said to have spent ten months preparing one spectacular entitled 'The Siege of Troy'. The more questionable Mrs Hayes declared in her advertisement that 'at 7 o'clock precisely 12 beautiful nymphs, spotless virgins, will carry out the famous Feast of Venus, as it is celebrated in Tahiti, under the instruction and leadership of Queen Oberea (which role will be taken by Mrs Hayes herself) . . .' Even further down the scale of propriety was the notorious bawd Mother Needham, occasionally impersonated by masqueraders, no doubt in ironic reference to the view that such entertainments were invitations to wantonness.[13] In the novels of the period some of these public events functioned as promoters of plot, often allowing encounters that could not otherwise have taken place. But a lady at such shows always risked being interpreted as a provider as well as a patron of pleasures.

MARRIAGE, MOTHERHOOD AND ITS ALTERNATIVES

In mid-eighteenth-century England the social and sexual hierarchy was firmly in place and there was less challenge to it than there had been fifty or a hundred years before. Over the aristocratic raciness of the Restoration, at least as it was filtered through literature, the new propriety encouraged by Addison and Steele was prevailing – at first for women and later for men as well. Decorum was stressed and the differences rather than the similarities between men and women came to the fore. The family, woman's proper milieu, was the unit of society, and paintings and novels emphasised the domestic affections that could be encouraged in its bosom.[14] The bonds of the immediate or nuclear family were strengthened, and a sense of individual autonomy pushed against the old identification with church or king. The architecture of the period with its stress on separate rooms suggested a growing desire for physical privacy. At the same time people were immensely curious to know what went on in private places; hence the interest in gossip and home lives, the fascination with letters and facial expressions. A symbol of the age might be the 'jealousy glass' developed in France which allowed a person to look surreptitiously at another without seeming to be looking.

Child rearing became emotionally important – possibly because slightly more children were living, although infant mortality remained high and few families would have escaped the death of a child. Despite the increase, it was generally thought that the population was declining and breeding was encouraged in families of the better orders. A barrage of books fell on insecure parents, preaching on all family matters from begetting to breast-feeding.

In 1760 the first two squabbling Georges has been replaced by the young George III, who prized the domestic virtues; he hoped to be commencing a reign of virtue and a week after his accession he issued a royal proclamation, 'For the encouragement of piety and virtue, and for preventing and punishing of vice, profaneness, and immorality'.[15]

The centre of the home was the woman. By the middle years of the century it was accepted that women should be bound by a superior – or stricter – morality and that some version of the double standard was natural and necessary. Occasionally there were doubts raised and an acknowledgement that this distinction was socially constructed rather than natural. For example in 1754 an anonymous critic of Samuel Richardson distinguished between political and religious chastity. The first type, for women alone, was accepted as a male social need, politically necessary to keep families intact, inheritance clear and distinctions of rank in order – necessary in short to avoid what Dr Johnson called with his usual directness 'confusion of progeny'. This double standard could not be justified on moral grounds: what should 'bring the greatest disgrace and ruin, the utmost shame and infamy on the woman, should not at all affect the man, though the most guilty'. The other type of chastity, the religious was specifically Christian and suitable for both sexes, but not then much regarded, the author declared. What he clearly did not accept was the newer and increasingly dominant notion, supported by Richardson in *Pamela* and *Clarissa*, that might be called sentimental chastity. This gave spiritual significance specifically to chaste women, while turning firmly away from the idea of political chastity. This sentimental sort was embraced wholeheartedly by many women, at least in public, and few in the mid-eighteenth century would have agreed with the critic's mockery of the exemplary Richardsonian heroine for making such a 'a rout and a pother' about her 'virtue'.[16] As male honour became less clearly located in aristocracy and breeding in an increasingly mercantile culture, it tended to be relocated in the body of the woman, and the medieval plot of gentlewoman in love with pure commoner was replaced by that of pure woman pursued by corrupt aristocrat. If men's honour and credit were becoming financial, women's were growing wholly sexual.

But the institution of marriage was the cornerstone of society for both men and women. Increasingly even in the upper orders the choice of spouse was left to children, although it was still assumed that a girl would not marry against her parents' wishes. It was simply considered absurd for *anyone* to marry without being assured of a 'competence'. Although a few amused foreigners pretended to think otherwise, in England the man alone could make the first move in courtship and this fact was reflected in the assumed motives for marriage. John Gregory, later one of the men attacked for trivialising women in Mary Wollstonecraft's *Vindication of the Rights of Woman*, puts the point clearly:

> A man of taste and delicacy marries a woman because he loves her more than any other. A woman of equal taste and delicacy marries him because she esteems him, and because he gives her that preference.[17]

Such an assumption makes much funnier Jane Austen's *Northanger Abbey*, where Catherine Morland marries for love while Henry Tilney marries from gratitude at being admired by her.

Because of increased choice, novels and books of advice on courtship and marriage abounded. The older misogynist attacks on marriage declined and were replaced by a literature surrounding the married state with quasi-religious significance – this mainly consisted of fiction and poetry since advice books were often fairly practical. Real-life courtships fascinated the reading public and the sprightly letters between the novelist and playwright Elizabeth Griffith and her future husband Richard which reveal the lady's persuasion of the gentleman out of seduction into marriage were extremely popular. So fascinating was the topic that there was even a journal called the *Matrimonial Magazine* in 1775.[18]

Lord Hardwicke's initially rather unpopular Marriage Act of 1753 overhauled the loose marriage laws and made the tie stricter; parental consent was required for persons under twenty-one to marry and clandestine marriages and easy bigamy were prevented. In the end the act probably improved things for young women since they could not so obviously be exploited by fortune hunters, but it also clarified the economic nature of the transaction of marriage.

This was made even clearer in the immensely influential *Commentaries on the Laws of England* by William Blackstone, professor of law at Oxford, which dominated legal thinking for many years to come. In Blackstone, men and women were not equal and so neither was marriage. Men were called by ancient law 'the worthiest of the blood' and they always inherited over daughters, while there is much mention of 'the empire of the father'. Yet men's nature was untrustworthy and it was assumed that women needed protection from their fickleness and licentiousness. In marriage a woman became legally a kind of property of the man, subject to the same sort of laws as ordinary property.[19] To steal or defile an heiress was equivalent to theft on a large scale and should carry severe punishment.

Blackstone clearly describes the notion of the *fem covert*, the woman hidden in marriage:

> By marriage, the husband and wife are one person in law: that is, the very being or legal existence of the woman is suspended during the marriage, or at least is incorporated and consolidated into that of the husband: under whose wing, protection, and *cover*, she performs every thing; and is therefore called in our law-french a *fem-covert*.[20]

In rare cases courts of equity could uphold the rights of rich women whose property had been settled on them by their families – although this was more for the sake of the families than the women – but mostly the common-law notion that all property travelled to the husband on marriage prevailed.

Despite much idealisation of marriage, the inequitable laws and the widespread belief that, in the words of the moral essayist and poet Hester Mulso Chapone, a husband had 'a divine right to the absolute obedience of his wife', meant that many women, instead of protesting, expressed pessimistic views about the state and its trials.[21] For example, although she carefully presented conventional opinions on marriage in *An Unfortunate Mother's Advice to Her Absent Daughters* (1761), Lady Pennington expatiated on the situation of a woman tied to an unworthy man:

May Heaven, in mercy, guard you from this fatal error! Such a companion is the worst of all temporal ills; a deadly potion, that imbitters every social scene of life, damps every rising joy, and banishes that chearful temper which alone can give a true relish to the blessings of mortality . . . Should the painful task of dealing with a morose tyrannical temper be assigned you, there is little more to be recommended than a patient submission to an evil which admits not of a remedy.[22]

Lady Pennington had fallen out of matrimony and much of her life was spent in vindicating her conduct. Separations were fairly common among writing women such as Laetitia Pilkington and Charlotte Lennox and no doubt spurred their literary activity, but they were less common in the population as a whole. They could of course occur by desertion in the lower orders where it was quite easy for a man to leave his wife and even marry elsewhere; besides, middle-class strictness in marriage may not have reached into the very lowest classes. In the upper strata legal separations could occur where women had managed to hold on to some property and divorce was occasionally obtained, although it was an expensive process. A man could sue for one on account of adultery alone, but a woman had to prove adultery together with cruelty or desertion, unless she could claim impotence.

In practice mainly men sued for divorce and the event was rare, usually accompanied by a spate of justificatory and titillating pamphlets. Only in the highest orders, where in any case adultery was still often condoned, would there be any re-entry into social life for a woman after divorce or separation. In general, however dreadful the domestic situation had been, she was beyond respectable society and her daughters would become less marriageable.

Illegitimacy, common in all classes, was greatly increasing, and Foundling Hospitals were established to cater to the need. The law required a man to support his illegitimate child, but only if fatherhood could be proved – obviously a very difficult enterprise. Unmarried mothers were caught by two laws: all illegitimate births had to be declared, while the murder of an illegitimate child by a mother was punishable with death. In practice the upper classes with their greater mobility often managed to hide such births in provincial country towns or in foreign parts. Lady Elizabeth Foster's children by the Duke of Devonshire were born on the Continent, while his Duchess's were born at home.

Because of the obvious disadvantages of marriage (these were not confined to women, for many men complained of being responsible for their wives' debts), many widows with adequate financial resources did not choose to marry again. There was little equivalent now to the mockery of predatory sexual widows in the Restoration. If women did make a second marriage, they sometimes chose men who were younger than they were or socially or financially below them. Mrs Thrale scandalised her friend Dr Johnson by marrying an Italian musician, Gabriel Piozzi; she had, she declared, 'married the first Time to please my Mother', and was pleasing herself on the second occasion. After having been married to a man of almost fifty when in her early twenties, the widowed Countess of Carlisle, now in her late thirties, married a man of twenty-four, while the Duchess of Leinster was married for the second time to her children's tutor. These ladies did not escape censure, as Dr Johnson's harsh reaction to Mrs Thrale's marriage indicates, and often it was their own children who were most disapproving. Mrs Thrale had tearfully confessed her affection for Piozzi to her eldest daughter only to meet with a violent response, while the Duchess of Leinster felt it wise to stay abroad to avoid the censure of her family. Catherine Macaulay, the historian, at the age of forty-seven married for the first time; because her husband was twenty-six years her junior, her reputation, literary as well as personal, was destroyed.

The great function of woman was motherhood, the basis of which was cruelly spelled out by Blackstone when he asserted 'the legal power of a father, (for a mother, as such, is entitled to no power, but only to reverence and respect)'.[23] Although she had no legal rights over her children, either when the husband was alive or when he was dead, unless he chose to give them to her, a woman's function in bearing and raising children was greatly emphasised. Indeed it would probably have filled most of her time since there was little contraception (condoms were used primarily with prostitutes in the hope of avoiding venereal disease). In addition wet-nursing was common, so that the contraceptive effect of breast-feeding – there was also the notion that women should not indulge sexually during lactation – was lost, and women of the higher ranks were enormously fecund.[24]

Wet-nursing was not confined to the upper orders and often poor women sent their children out to even poorer women so that they could work outside the home. The campaign for breast-feeding, associated with the natural philosophy of Jean-Jacques Rousseau, an immensely influential thinker in all areas during this period, would have touched only a fraction of women in the upper orders. But many women too seem to have supported breast-feeding, such as the French Madame Le Rebours who published the news that her breast-fed child had lived when the others had perished. Male opinion was still usually on the other side, and Richardson's exemplary Pamela had to defer to her husband on this subject, as on most others. Medical advice was divided (it would largely support breast-feeding at the end of the century) and the muddled notions must have confused young parents who were told, for example, that a mother, despite much discomfort, should wait several days before giving the breast. While maternal milk might be considered good for an infant on emotional grounds, the milk of a big-breasted peasant woman from the country was often thought to be more nourishing.

On the whole books of advice on child-getting and -rearing, even those by men, tended in this period to cite the ancients less than earlier ones had done and to make increasing claims to scientific knowledge, although, as in all areas, scientific notions were held together with a residue of superstitious and folkloric beliefs. By the middle years of the century the earlier physiological discoveries had permeated the culture and the seventeenth-century religious vocabulary had given way to a mechanistic one that considered the body as a complicated machine with related but distinct parts. Often human and animal mothers were compared by male authors and, against all evidence to the contrary, there was a widespread idea that animals became mild when they became mothers. The view was common that marriage and motherhood would tame an otherwise unmanageable woman and make her more feminine.

Other, even more extraordinary notions abounded; there was, for example, much speculation about generation without the help of men through some sort of electromagnetic force, about the genesis of the child in either the sperm or the egg, but rarely both, and about how to beget a male baby through lying on the right side and binding up the man's left testicle. Curious folk opinions lived on, such as that which connected the sizes of the male nose and the penis or the female mouth and the vagina – perhaps another source of the decorous silence enjoined on women.

Obstetrics remained rudimentary despite men's scientific claims and there was much discussion over the use of medical instruments to deliver a child or to dismember it to save a mother. The controversy of the Restoration period continued between male obstetricians and female midwives, who were still denied any incorporation and much ridiculed as ignorant and superstitious. Elizabeth Nihell followed the example of Jane Sharp in publishing a treatise *On the Art of Midwifery* (1760), in which she attacked as arrogant and derogatory to women the views of the influential medical writer Dr William Smellie and other 'Instrumentarians' who 'cut their Way in with iron and steel'. (For her pains she was much mocked by the novelist Tobias Smollett and indeed is still belittled by male writers. For example the critic Arthur Cash recently wrote, 'The prolonged attack of this ignorant group of women upon the practitioners of the new science was reprehensible, but effective. The woman who made the most noise of all was Mrs Elizabeth Nihell .·.' and he goes on to describe her 'campaign of fright'.[25] As male physicians and surgeons, backed by their institutions, professionalised midwifery, women were increasingly ejected from childbirth in the upper orders, despite Nihell's efforts to suggest the unseemly nature of men's attendance at such a time.

Because of the prestige of marriage and motherhood, spinsterhood was not as flamboyantly embraced as in the reign of Queen Anne, and the militant celibacy of Mary Astell and Lady Chudleigh was a thing of the past. By the eighteenth century the spinster was considered not as an unmarried woman with an occupation but as an unoccupied woman unlikely to marry. Yet the novelist and playwright Frances Brooke for one created an appealing portrait of a rather crusty, self-reliant spinster, Mary Singleton, a far robuster figure than the marriageable heroines of her novels.[26] Hester Mulso Chapone, knowing the cultivated society of other women, declared that the single life should not be feared and that an unhappy marriage was far worse than spinsterhood. But few outside fiction suggested that a single life should actually be embraced. Single women were usually dependent on male relatives and 'old maid' was a term of abuse that frightened many into unrewarding matrimony.

On the other side, the immense pressures of the new pious ideology on daughters to put the interests of parents before their own meant that many women had to choose spinsterhood to fulfil their duties. Lugubrious prefaces tell of daughters propping up aged parents and writing to support them in comfort. The freedom that spinsterhood represented to earlier writers seemed in these stricter times illusory; the Bluestocking writer Catherine Talbot complained that a spinster had only the appearance not the reality of freedom.

Lesbianism, described so openly by Aphra Behn and Delarivier Manley in the Restoration, disappeared from female writing as the century progressed, although it continued to exist intermittently in male pornography and reportage. The fictional separatist communities tinged with lesbianism and hedonism in Manley's works or the outspokenly celibate and intellectual one imagined by Astell gave way to gentler communities of victimised women coming together to perform charitable functions. In Sarah Scott's *Millenium Hall* (1762), based a little on her life with Lady Barbara Montagu after she had separated from her husband, a group of women create a feminine utopia caring for the elderly, the poor, the sick and the handicapped. The community is mainly made up of women who have suffered from men and it is more sentimental, less intellectual than Astell's proposed college. The same is true of the female community in Clara Reeve's *The School for Widows* (1791), while the Protestant convents suggested for single women by Samuel Richardson in his novels have a defensive rather than aggressive quality.

For women without fortune or husbands to support them and with insufficient knowledge or reputation to become governesses, teachers, companions or domestic servants, prostitution was a common method of making a living. Although their numbers were often widely exaggerated, there were obviously very many plying their trade, especially in London, where Harris's Lists describing the skills and health of various ladies of the night helped prospective customers to make an informed choice. As the image of the lady became more genteel and sexless, the difference between her and the prostitute widened until by the end of the century a respectable lady could busy herself with reforming the fallen without fear of contamination. As humanitarian sentiment increased, there was a desire to see prostitutes – a group which often included simply 'fallen' women or women living with men outside matrimony – not as professional women but as victims of society in need of help and encouragement to reform. So the Magdalen Hospital for Penitent Prostitutes was set up as a refuge and it soon became a visiting place for Londoners much like Bedlam Hospital for the insane. Although many praised the hospital as liberal and enlightened, others criticised it as simply a convenient place for men to deposit their cast-off mistresses. And in fiction at least there continued some warning that sentimental sympathy for the fallen might be misplaced. In Frances Sheridan's *Memoirs of Miss Sidney Bidulph* (1761) the heroine comes to grief because she persists in seeing a promiscuous woman as a victim.

Many women must have been forced into prostitution by rape. This was a crime and theoretically took the death penalty, but there is not much evidence that this deterred the exploitation of lower-class women by upper- and middle-class men. One famous case was that of Anne Bond who in 1729 accused her master, Francis Charteris, of rape. Charteris, it seems, had raped several others as well and he was sentenced to death, although there was much murmuring at the trial that rape of servants was not an uncommon event. In the end, perhaps inevitably, he was pardoned.[27] When in Richardson's *Pamela* a cynical neighbour learns that Mr B is simply trying to seduce or rape a servant girl, however virtuous, he is surprised that any fuss at all is being made over the fact. In addition there was some idea that a man alone could not easily rape a woman without her collusion; consequently, in fiction, an actual rape often demanded fainting or drugs, as was the case in the most famous rape of all in *Clarissa*. The notion also persisted, along with the idea that women rarely had sexual pleasure, that, although they might be sexless before intercourse, they could well become insatiable after it; consequently an act of copulation, wanted or not, was often seen as the inexorable prelude to a life of prostitution unless the woman speedily died.

116

EDUCATION

Locke thought a child could be moulded by early training; Rousseau considered that a natural upbringing should bring out the natural goodness supposed to be within the pre-cultured child. The ideas of both men were much discussed during these years, although education would become a burning issue mainly in the 1790s.

Because Rousseau believed in a clear demarcation between men and women, the education he suggested for the girl in his *Emile* differed radically from that given to the boy. Where the latter should be trained and developed in isolation from the corruptions of society and taught to be autonomous and self-reliant, the girl, Sophie, was to be educated to solace, please and minister to men: 'woman is expressly formed to please the man'; her learning should be just enough to make her companionable. By the 1790s this feminine education in dependence and contingency, in which the girl was taught always to consider the gaze of the man, would seem appalling to almost all serious women writers, but in the mid-eighteenth century the conception of woman it suggested often appeared an advance on the frivolous image that had descended from the Restoration. For women in Rousseau's view were, in the end, not inferior to men although they were created to minister to them; they were, instead, a distinct group with different duties and needs. Consequently both their education and their peculiar contribution to culture and society could be stressed. Yet, despite much positive appreciation from women, even at the time there was the occasional effort to modify the picture of *Emile* and Rousseau's friend Madame d'Epinay accepted women's primary domestic material role but refused to limit the boundaries of female learning; women were, she thought, potentially if not actually equal to men in intellect.[28]

Obviously the new image of the lady needed constant construction even though, when constructed, it was regarded as entirely natural. The middle classes, especially from the 1770s onwards, seemed avid for advice on how to bring up daughters or on how to comport themselves as ladies. On the whole this advice when given by other women accepted the prevailing gendered psychology that made of men and women distinct intellectual and emotional creatures and commonsensically set about showing women how to conform to it to best advantage. Hester Mulso Chapone considered that 'the mind in each sex has some natural kind of bias, which constitutes a distinction of character, and that the happiness of both depends, in a great measure, on the preservation and observance of this distinction'. Women have 'exquisite perceptions', men have 'strength of intellect'.[29]

But the extreme image of the passive daughterly girl was left to male advice books for women, such as *Sermons to Young Women* by the Reverend James Fordyce – later termed 'sentimental rant' by Wollstonecraft and interrupted by the Bennet girls when the pompous Mr Collins tries to edify them with it in *Pride and Prejudice*. The book descended in a clear line from the Marquess of Halifax's *Advice to his Daughters* of 1688, which was still being read in the mid-eighteenth century.

Fordyce presented a dramatic scheme of sentiment, opposing the fluttering timid lady ('the gentle trusting creature') to the violating ruffian man; female chastity became a woman's 'treasure' which it was her main business to guard and her education should therefore be a moral one in self-control. She needed constantly to please the man and even her religious devotion was described as giving her 'dignity and new graces' in the eyes of the watching male. Another popular advice book, Dr John Gregory's *A Father's Legacy to his Daughters* (1774), advised a girl to hide the ways in which she might deviate from the passive ideal of femininity, for example in spiritedness, gaiety, physical power and affection. This last was too much for Hester Mulso Chapone, who suggested that, instead of denying her love for a husband, a woman might simply try being sincere.

Much of the sentimental religiosity of Fordyce's portrait found its way into the sentimental novel of the period and it was against this novel that many of the female authors of advice regarded themselves as writing, fearing that the heady fantasies that responded to the gendered psychology – that timid passive ladies could somehow have immense significance and power – would be believed by romantic girls. Such girls would then wrongly imagine that the submissiveness of a man in courtship would be carried over into marriage – which, the advice givers declared, was emphatically not the case.

In the middle classes more women than ever before were receiving an education, although much of it was in accomplishments aimed at procuring them a husband, and there seems to have been little overall improvement of standards. Inevitably so since it was accepted by most that a woman's life would simply be domestic. Boarding schools sprang up to cater for the demand; a few of these were undoubtedly worthy – several were run by women with a serious interest in education – but many were greatly criticised for their frivolity. Undoubtedly this criticism was justified in most cases, but it is also likely that the real cause of dissatisfaction was the social mobility such institutions suggested; girls from the lower middle class might learn ladylike behaviour and acquire ideas above their station.[30]

Given the equation of men with reason and activity and women with emotion and passivity, there was great debate over the female intellect and whether or not it was suitable for higher learning of any sort. The next problem was whether learning was compatible with women's primary domestic role and with femininity – the hatred of the pedantic woman continued. Thinking always of the marriage market, Dr Gregory characteristically suggested that, if a woman happened 'to have any learning, [she should] keep it a profound secret, especially from the men'.[31] William Kenrick, speaking in the biblical tones that still often inflicted discussions about women and their place in society, warned the 'daughter of Britain' to avoid improper knowledge and curiousity about the ways of men, lest she provoke the pointed finger and end by dropping the 'tear of misery'.[32] Even Hester Mulso Chapone, who wanted history and poetry taught to girls, worried about the effect:

> The danger of pedantry and presumption in a woman – of her exciting envy in one sex, and jealousy in the other – of her exchanging the graces of imagination for the severity and preciseness of a scholar, would be, I own, sufficient to frighten me from the ambition of seeing my girl remarkable for learning. Such objections are, perhaps, still stronger with regard to the abstruse sciences.[33]

Lady Pennington was more robust, believing that most forms of study might be beneficial to girls. Although 'the management of all domestic affairs is certainly the proper business of women', she considered, the neglect of them has come more from frivolity and vanity than from 'too great an attachment to mental improvements.'[34]

Since all institutions of higher learning were closed to women – Elizabeth Montagu, described as the 'Queen of the Blues' for her activities as a hostess and patron, resurrected Mary Astell's idea of a women's college, but the idea met with little support – any rigorous education had to be found at home, usually with the help of a paternal library. The classical scholar Elizabeth Carter was taught languages by her father and Catherine Macaulay learned history from hers. Hannah More's dominating and domineering father instructed his daughters enough to allow them to teach for a living in the absence of adequate dowries, but he found the gifted Hannah altogether too quick for a girl at Latin and mathematics and he stopped her lessons. The novelist Sarah Fielding attended a school but her considerable linguistic knowledge came from studying on her own – it is typical of the times that, despite her learning, her brother Henry Fielding should praise her for her good heart rather than for her extensive knowledge.

As in the earlier period, the great dividing line was Latin, in which many works were still written, although the number was fast decreasing. Latin was regarded as a male preserve, a code that separated the sexes, and which enshrined the masculine civic and heroic virtues unattainable by women. Even though women often learned it, they still felt a painful inferiority because they had not received it within formal education; others were encouraged to read primarily in translation. When they translated themselves, which they often did, it was usually from the modern languages of French and, later, German.

The general moderate view was that women could study but not too much and that domestic duties must always come before intellectual pursuits. Sarah Fielding may have been calling on experience when she gave this speech to a character in her novel *David Simple*:

> I loved reading, and had a great Desire of attaining Knowledge; but whenever I asked Questions of any kind whatsoever, I was always told, *Such Things were not proper for Girls of my Age to know: If I was pleased with any Book above the most silly Story or Romance, it was taken from me. For Miss must not enquire too far into Things, it would turn her Brain; she had better mind her Needle-work, and such Things as were useful for Women; reading and poring in Books, would never get me a Husband.*[35]

The weight of opinion can be seen pressing even on an immensely gifted woman like Lady Mary Wortley Montagu, who was well aware of the miseries of would-be women scholars:

> We are permitted no Books but such as tend to the weakening and Effeminateing the Mind, our Natural Deffects are every way indulg'd, and tis look'd upon as in a degree Criminal to improve our Reason, or fancy we have any.[36]

Yet she too felt the need to mock the learned lady. Meanwhile Lady Hervey earned the commendation of the fastidious Earl of Chesterfield for discreetly hiding her knowledge of Latin altogether.

IMAGES OF WOMEN

The prevailing view of women was constructed from a hotch-potch of scriptural beliefs, cultural myths, social observations and seemingly scientific or medical opinions, each of these containing quite overt contradictions. In *Emile* there is a startling vision of the sexual woman hounding men to death next to the portrait of the girl assumed to be *naturally* modest. In physiological treatises, 'genius' or intellectual ability was connected with male virility – great works really were thought to be seminal – and since there was no corresponding ovular theory, learning and creation appeared unsuitable and even impossible for a woman. At the same time, genius was thought to have an effeminising effect on men, for in learning and creation blood travelled to the head and the seminal fluids were deprived of their force. The normal female was, then, rather like a man who had been effeminised by study.[37]

However contradictory and absurd the notions, men generally agreed that women, with their wet, cold composition and their tendency to vapours because of their wandering or at least troublesome womb, were not suited to high intellectual endeavour, and ambitious women must have suffered from this agreement. Throughout the middle decades of the eighteenth century there was a low grumbling at their social and cultural status; advice books hint at resentment, novels detail specific injustices, but there is little general and overt protest. The poet Elizabeth Tollet, who looked back to the earlier women writers for inspiration, simply let her fictional Hypatia lament that she was born female in a masculine world, and Elizabeth Griffith complained of the need always to flatter men. In the early decades Lady Mary Wortley Montagu wrote ironically, 'I am glad [women] can find, in the imaginary Empire of Beauty, a consolation for being excluded every part of Government in the State.'[38]

The real consolation was the new status accorded women in the sentimental movement, triumphing in the middle years of the eighteenth century. Beginning in the manner of the Earl of Shaftesbury by emphasising sentiment or moral reflection, it rapidly moved to stressing sensibility, the sensitive response to the pathetic or affecting in life or art; virtue from good feelings was more important than a rationally inspired and calculated goodness, and physical manifestations such as tears and blushes became signs of virtuous sympathy and modesty. While the typical individual consciousness was much in focus, there was equal emphasis on family and community, depicted less in political or economic than in emotional terms – indeed sentiment, though so often associated with the middle classes, seemed to turn from its predominant economic concerns and yearn for a semi-feudal, vaguely aristocratic world in which loyalty and affection rather than cash formed the bonds.

Women were especially associated with the emotional, affective and familial qualities. So they achieved an extraordinary centrality in the culture as a whole. Their subjectivity, partly as women and partly as examples of extreme sentimental vulnerability – they were considered to be better at suffering – fascinated both men and women. At the same time the sentimental construction with which they were identified prevented them from claiming any political, economic or intellectual status and the rationalist claims of the Restoration period seemed as

121

inappropriate in these decades as the later revolutionary assertion of political rights. Women became what Steele had called them, 'the fair sex', allowed influence only through manipulating men with their winning combination of beauty, domestic virtue and passivity; or, as Fordyce expressed it in his *Sermons*: 'It is thine, thou fair form, to command by obeying, and by yielding to conquer.'[39]

Given the emphasis on female vulnerability and contingency, overt misogyny of the Restoration kind now seemed churlish, and a veritable furore met the publication of the cynical letters of the Earl of Chesterfield who regarded women as children of a larger growth, worthy only of aiding in the sexual education of young men and unworthy of serious male confidence. (Lord Chesterfield moved in aristocratic circles where the sentimental ideology was in any case less prevailing than further down the social scale.) Women were more irrational, emotional and intuitive than men, and also more naturally virtuous. Although, with the exaggerated emphasis on chastity, virtue for women often diminished into simply a synonym for virginity, virtue in the culture as a whole, which included benevolence, generosity, modesty, and sympathy, could also be enshrined in women, now firmly associated with the caring and serving functions. Providing they curbed their tendency to frivolity and accepted the new sexlessness assumed for them, they could become refiners of society, a role in which they were given much male encouragement. Often men compiled volumes of worthy ladies as suitable role models: for example, the Reverend John Duncombe's *Feminiad* and George Ballard's *Memoirs of Several Ladies of Great Britain*, inspired in part by the ageing Anglo-Saxon scholar Elizabeth Elstob, herself inspired by Mary Astell.

Advice books, including those on education, express the ideal image of meritorious modesty: 'True female Merit strives, to be conceal'd / And only by its blushes is reveal'd.'[40] Fordyce thought 'Meekness . . . the proper consummation of Female Excellence' and praised as charming 'a constitutional Softness'. While he mocked the idea that women should be simply a sort of better servant, he made them entirely contingent beings, claiming with that mixture of biblical and 'commonsensical' rhetoric so typical of the period that they were 'manifestly intended' as mothers and helpmates: 'to be a kind of softer companions, who, by nameless delightful sympathies and endearments, might improve our pleasures and soothe our pains; to lighten the load of domestic care, and thereby leave us the more at leisure for rougher labours or severer studies; and finally to spread a certain grace and embellishment over human life'. (It was quite clear to the outraged Mary Wollstonecraft in 1792 whose life this referred to.[41])

The contingency accepted by Fordyce marks almost all male books on women. When the critic Hugh Blair discusses elocution, he considers that a woman's voice ought to be well modulated not so that she can communicate but so that she can please and entertain. Rousseau's Sophie dresses modestly not to express her own self-respect or avoid rape but to excite men, since her dress is torn from her body in the imagination of the watching male. Delicacy of body betokens the delicacy of mind prized by men and so women are encouraged to exaggerate weakness to make themselves more marriageable; as Burke wrote in 1757: 'The beauty of women is considerably owing to their weakness and delicacy, and is even enhanced by their timidity, a quality of mind analogous to it.'[42] In short, woman had moved from being Eve, the sexual temptress, to being Eve, the gullible mother of mankind, needing protection and condemned for ever to give service.

Most of the images so far described have been created by men. Certainly women accepted these images, but they could also force them to serve their own purposes in quite striking ways. One example is that of the female novelists and another that of the Bluestockings.

Male writers had stressed the passivity and virtuous influence of women; female novelists in particular formed this combination into a fantasy of specifically female power, very different from the power of Behn's and Manley's knowing and manipulating women, but nonetheless a sentimental equivalent. The popular novels that embodied this fantasy appalled the educated elite but greatly appealed to domestic women, for whom they were clearly written. And they could also function as a kind of analogy to femininity in life. In women writers physical assault seemed less often a threat than linguistic assault, the loss of reputation or name through 'perverse interpretations' or slander of 'spiteful and malicious tongues' as Sarah Fielding and Jane Collier put it in The Cry (1754). The novel too was language and it replaced physical with mental adventure for the female reader. It was as important that virtue triumph in literature as in life, but 'perverse interpretations' might still thrill and unsettle before being firmly rejected.

The Bluestockings, a network of wealthy ladies and their friends, who in their houses provided a sober and decorous equivalent of the seventeenth-century French courtly salons, shied away from the sentimental extreme and had little sympathy for the heady fantasies delivered in the novels. Instead they took the sentimental notion of women as refining agents of coarse masculinity and set about purifying the manners of actual society. Accepting much of the ideology of womanhood and impeccably chaste in their private lives, these ladies could encourage considerable intellectual activity in women without disturbing the hierarchies of gender and class.

Despite conforming to the age's ideology of female chastity and decorum, the Bluestocking ideal was not a saccharine one, and in 1782 Elizabeth Montagu wrote to Elizabeth Carter about a friend:

> I really believe she was just like Eve before she eat the apple, at least she answers to Milton's description of her. She would have preferred her husband's discourse to the angels. I am afraid you and I my dear friend should have entered into some metaphysical disquisitions with the angel, we are not so perfectly the rib of man as woman ought to be.[43]

7

THE MODEST MUSE: WOMEN WRITERS
OF THE MID-EIGHTEENTH CENTURY

> The modest Muse a veil with pity throws
> O'er Vice's friends and Virtue's female foes;
> Abash'd she views the bold unblushing mien
> Of modern Manley, Centlivre and Behn . . .
> (John Duncombe, *The Feminiad*, 1754)

'There is a line, far on this side of indecency, which female gentleness
should not step beyond.'
(*Critical Review*, 62, 1786)

In the middle years of the eighteenth century, women entered literature in
strength. The phenomenon provoked much comment from male writers.
'In former times, the pen, like the sword, was considered as consigned by
nature to the hands of men,' wrote Samuel Johnson in 1753 '. . . the
revolution of years has now produced a generation of Amazons of the
pen, who with the spirit of their predecessors have set masculine tyranny
at defiance.' In case this seems admirably assertive, it should be remembered that Johnson, like most men of the time including Swift, disliked
and feared Amazons – indeed he exaggerated their man-hating horror in
an account he translated of them – while a sword in the hands of women
must be self-destructive. Laetitia Pilkington, who, through her association with Jonathan Swift, seems something of a relic from the more
robust age of Queen Anne, will be seen wielding the pen as sword, so
irreparably wounding her reputation. But such women as Charlotte
Lennox, Frances Sheridan, Frances Brooke and Hester Mulso Chapone,
all ladies approved by the Doctor, will never openly handle a weapon or
in any way defy 'masculine tyranny'.

What women created in the mid-eighteenth century was not simply
writing but *feminine* writing. Prose and poetry were considered firmly
gendered, and sensitive readers could immediately tell the sex of the

THE SIGN OF ANGELLICA

author. A woman writer was expected not simply to express her sex but also to call attention to her femininity, her delicacy and sensitivity. Oliver Goldsmith claimed that he could tell the gender of a writer by the style and 'a nameless somewhat in the manner', while the *Monthly Review* in a piece possibly by John Cleland of *Fanny Hill* fame declared that a discerning reader could always judge when '*femality*' was present. Review after review stated what women should write and how they did write, ringing the changes on the abstract terms denoting female author-ship: elegance, delicacy, modesty, spontaneity and artlessness.

Clearly the image of the woman writer has changed since the days when Aphra Behn exchanged wit with Restoration rakes and gave the audiences the bawdy farces she saw they wanted. The new woman writer often needed money as surely as Behn and was as thoroughly a professional writer in the way she gauged the market and understood its wants. But these wants had changed and the image the woman needed to convey had changed as well. The new writer was probably as present in her works as Manley, Behn or Barker, but the sign under which she now sold herself was very differently constructed from theirs and indeed it was denied that the sign was actually constructed at all. The presentation of the woman writer, always part of the product, was thought to be the presentation of the essential woman, woman as she innately and absolutely was and should be.

The new writer had to conform to the age's ideal of womanhood, whatever the individual reality seemed to be. She had to be virtuous and domestic, writing either from financial necessity, unsupported by the proper guardians of femininity such as husband or father, or from a desire to teach virtue to the unformed. The work she wrote was not presented aggressively to the public as an artful piece desiring to overwhelm the reader and give fame to the author. Instead it was a response to misfortune which had thrown the woman into the unusual necessity of providing financially for herself and her dependants. She would write and earn money while filling as before every possible domestic duty.

Preface after preface finds the female author writing at the bedside of a dying husband or parent or rocking the cradle of a fatherless child. Elizabeth Boyd published her novel to provide for her 'ancient' mother and Sarah Fielding wrote because of a 'Distress in her Circumstances'. The learning she had acquired was not at the expense of domestic duties, she assured her readership, 'nor was the leisure which she found for such acquirements produced by neglecting anything necessary or useful for the family'.[1] Her brother Henry also wrote for money and no doubt had other duties, but he felt no need to alert the public to the fact so frequently.

Women writers were now rarely puffed because of their art. They were not compared with Shakespeare or Ben Jonson as the Duchess of Newcastle or Delarivier Manley might have been but, instead, apologised for appearing in so unfeminine a way on the public scene. If financial need could not absolutely be asserted, then a reluctant appearance had to be made. Friends were needed to press the retiring lady into publication – the case with many Bluestocking ladies – or even force the issue by publishing her 'effusions' without her initial consent.

The image and stance of women writers were inevitably connected with the content of their writing. For a man the value of his work might lie in its independence from its creator – as the strengthening notion of copyrights and patents indicated – but for women the creation remained part of the creator, and linguistic and physical purity coalesced. The audience, especially for sentimental fiction, was considered by mid-century to be mainly female, but the judgements that mattered often remained male. The lavish praise that famous men like Johnson, Fielding and Richardson bestowed on young women just beginning in literature was supportive and no doubt encouraging, but it was also restricting, and inevitably the women so singled out would be aware of the terms of this admiration and necessarily eager to write within them. Since critics were clear about what and how women should write, the pressure to conform must have been immense. Women too kept up the pressure and the Bluestocking ladies were as sure as male critics about what was proper and improper for women to discuss. Decorously repudiating the literary mantle of Manley, Behn and Haywood, the classical scholar Elizabeth Carter placed herself in the pious retiring tradition of the Dissenting poet and fiction writer Elizabeth Rowe; in her poem 'On the Death of Mrs Rowe' she firmly dissociated herself from those without 'modest grace' who in their writings took 'lawless freedoms' which made the muses blush.

Synonymous with sentiment and sensibility, women must write moral didactic or sentimental works suitable, above all, for the perusal of other women. The lively, resourceful Elizabeth Griffith, friend of flamboyant actresses like Kitty Clive and Peg Woffington, yet saw that the needed money was in morality; so she set up as a female moralist and adviser of young girls, showing them how to submit to society and use their virtuous superiority to best advantage. Frances Brooke's translation of the French sentimental novelist Madame Riccoboni was considered appropriate for delicate women but less so for a male readership. Satire might intrude in the episodes in female fiction but should not be the whole mode since satire was essentially masculine. The separation of modes did not result in a separate-but-equal situation, for the masculine

127

satiric vehicle was ultimately superior to the feminine sentimental one. Standards were assumed to be lower for women writers and critics were expected to be more lenient to female productions. There was widespread fear that men were taking advantage of this gallant leniency and one critic complained that 'By a Lady' on the title page of a novel could well signify a male hack, one of the 'dirty-shirted dunces', instead of one of the 'fair sex'.

The pressure towards respectability in life and literature can be measured in those who resisted. Unwilling or unable entirely to adapt themselves to the changed ideology, these women often desired to express themselves in the semi-fictional mode popularised by Delarivier Manley, harnessing some of the literary power she had shown women how to use. But they failed to appreciate the need for different, more subtle and secretive strategies and the little adaptation they did make opened them to a charge of duplicity that would have been inappropriate for Mary Carleton, Aphra Behn or Delarivier Manley. Meanwhile their nonconformity prevented them from creating a culturally potent image in accordance with the times.

Some of these writing women were scandalous actresses or known courtesans like Colley Cibber's daughter, Charlotte Charke, who tried to extract money from her father through her autobiography describing a life of transvestism and marital irregularities. Another was the courtesan Con Phillips, who published *An Apology* with great éclat in 1748 – her declaration of her life as 'Sorrow, Misery, and Infamy' is neither sincere nor false, simply inappropriate to the wonderfully extravagant career of multiple marriages, pleasures and 'Adventures', all given in what Lady Mary Wortley Montagu called 'rapturous description'. Then there was Viscountess Vane, like Con Phillips notorious for her extravagance and scandalous conduct – or a little lax 'in point of prudentials' in her own words. In 1751 she may have written or simply inspired the story of her life which was inserted into Smollett's novel *Peregrine Pickle*. As bizarrely nonconformist as Con Phillips, Lady Vane yet felt the force of the ladylike image to which she could not adhere, while she tended both towards vindication and display – admitting, however, that the 'killing edge' of her charms was a little blunted by time.

The by now elderly Lady Mary Wortley Montagu, who had lived in Italy for many years and was out of step with the cultural changes in England, saw refreshing honesty in the likes of Phillips and Vane. She wrote to her daughter that Con Phillips, although profligate, was 'superior in virtue' to her male lovers and that Lady Vane's memoir had 'more truth and less malice than any I ever read in my life' – despite her comparison of the lady to a spendthrift highwayman who can only pride himself on his generosity since honesty is out of the question. But her enjoyment of the spirit of adventurers was not openly shared by her contemporaries, and the Bluestocking Elizabeth Carter, for example, judged Con Phillips 'a very bad woman'.[2]

Also out of step with the age was Lady Mary's belief, illustrated by her response to Lady Vane's memoir, that literature to do good should be cautionary by implication rather than directly edifying:

> Her history, rightly considered, would be more instructive to young women than any sermon I know. They may see there what mortifications and variety of misery are the unavoidable consequences of gallantries. I think there is no rational creature that would not prefer the life of the strictest Carmelite to the round of hurry and misfortune she has gone through.[3]

Sadder than any of these notorious women, Laetitia Pilkington failed to conform by having not beauty but wit, which she came to learn was no longer a suitable attribute for a woman. In the Restoration and reign of Queen Anne she might have been as wittily notorious as Aphra Behn or Delarivier Manley, but in the more sentimentally gendered society of the mid-century, when the border of respectability was closer to home, she became a byword for malice and unfemininity. Like Manley she was a friend of Jonathan Swift, but of a different era and not even born when *The New Atalantis* was being celebrated. Unlike her predecessors, she could not in the changed ideological climate ebulliently display the contradictions of her position as feminine object and writing subject or enjoy with Behn and Manley discovering the gap between the sign and face of woman.

After Manley and the early Haywood, Laetitia Pilkington is a disturbing writer to read. Although the earlier women were much vilified, they were mocked by both men and women as equals, as simply other human beings. There was a gusto about the abuse and about the response that makes the reader sometimes sympathise with them and sometimes condemn but rarely pity or worry over their possible moral corruption or inability to cope. With Laetitia Pilkington, the gusto gives way to obvious pain and malice, and the reader is often made to feel not sympathy and occasional anger but pity and contempt.

Laetitia Pilkington – a divorced woman with children to support or, in Jonathan Swift's unkind phrase, 'the most profligate whore in either Kingdom' – used her *Memoirs* (1748–54) to make money. In them she followed Aphra Behn and Delarivier Manley in investigating psychological pressures within a social context, probing the shifting personality of woman constructed according to certain moral and ideological principles quite at odds with the harsh social reality. She had a desire to uncover the awkward unassimilable feelings of a woman below the clichés of gender characteristics and activities, the extraordinary history that did not conform to ordinary stereotype.

Pilkington's main literary merchandise was the famous satirist Jonathan Swift from whom she derived her unconventional and uncomfortable role as chastener of her age. But the role was not really open to a woman, and, when she took up the Swiftian pen, she tended to write not satire – not even scandalous satire like Delarivier Manley's – but invective and abuse. Pilkington's anger and bewilderment at this transformation became a covert motif of the *Memoirs*.

What Pilkington revealed was that women did not have power over language but language had power over women. Calumny murdered since for women reputation was identity. A woman became 'even such a one' as she was represented and there was no possibility of change; representation was the reality. Pilkington's reputation was destroyed. She concluded that she had no social identity, and then assumed that she could exist in her writings as a genderless voice, an impersonal calumniator, beyond conventional and gendered morality. Her self-image swelled with her mistaken power and became outrageous: 'I, the Cream of Historians, Mirror of Poets, worthy not only the bays but the laurel made for mighty conquerors from my signal victories, proceed in my true history . . .'[4] She was only slightly in jest.

But in her role as historian she found she could not convey the corruption of the age but only her own: 'There are many strange ways of getting into the favour of the great – pimping, lying, flattering,' she claimed and she intended to take all three routes. In fact the *Memoirs* speedily declined into vituperation and menace for money. Married men refusing to subscribe to her volumes were threatened with exposure of their peccadilloes and ladies with exhumation of their base ancestors: 'Oh my dear ladies, why are you so frightened?' she sneered. She threatened all her enemies together: 'A pen is mine – let them take up another, and may-hap they will meet their match.'[5]

The exemplary Mrs Montagu, Queen of the Bluestockings, delivered an epitaph on Laetitia Pilkington, once praised for her wit by Jonathan Swift. She again used the metaphor of the sword, inevitably exposing her own prejudices, but, more significantly, revealing the truth that women, if they wished to achieve literary power in this age, had to avoid the masculine role of wit and satirist and create instead the image of modest and suffering femininity:

Wit in women is apt to have bad consequences; like a sword without a scabbard it wounds the wearer and provokes assailants. I am sorry to say the generality of women who have excelled in wit have failed in chastity; perhaps it inspires too much confidence in the possessor, and raises an inclination in the men towards them without inspiring an esteem so that they are more attacked and less guarded than other women.[6]

Samuel Richardson expressed a more common disgust:

Mrs Pilkington, Constantia Phillips, Lady V— . . . what a Set of Wretches, wishing to perpetuate their infamy, have we – to make the Behn's, the Manley's, and the Haywood's look white. From the same injur'd, disgraced, profaned Sex, let us be favoured with the Antidote to these Womens Poison![7]

The antidote would come from the sentimental author who led a proper private life and showed its effects in her virtuous writings.

THE PROFESSIONAL WOMAN WRITER

Given the growing stress on untrained spontaneity in writing and the association of women and sensibility, it is not surprising that many women from the lower class should begin publishing during these years and that they should form a significant part of the group which Southey called 'Our Uneducated Poets'. For success they needed patronage. Elizabeth Bentley, the daughter of a cooper, was patronised by many in the social ranks above her, including Elizabeth Carter and Hester Mulso Chapone, and she managed to earn sufficient to provide herself with a small annuity; the middle-class friends of Mary Leapor, a cook and housemaid, were raising a subscription for her when her short life ended; while Jean Glover, a strolling tambourine player, owed her brief poetic fame to Robert Burns. Such women knew that they were famous because they were curiosities and they tended to stress their lowliness. Janet Little, the Scottish milkmaid, insisted on calling attention to her humble condition as a 'crazy scribbling lass', as did Mary Collier, the washerwoman, who was well aware of how she should present herself both as the domestic woman writer and as the peasant:

I think it no Reproach to the Author, whose life is toilsome, and her Wages inconsiderable, to confess honestly, that the view of putting a small Sum of Money in her Pocket, as well as the Reader's Enjoyment, had its Share of Influence upon this Publication.[8]

Although some of these lower-class women writers managed to make a living through literature or use their patrons to advance themselves, generally their lives make sorry reading. Ann Candler of Ipswich found that her literary achievements and interests only served to embitter her days in the workhouse when in time she sank back into the class from which she had come:

> Within these dreary walls confin'd,
> A lone recluse I live,
> And, with the dregs of human kind,
> A niggard alms receive.[9]

In contrast to poets and letter writers, most novelists came from the middle ranks and the lower reaches of the gentry; they tended to have more elevated backgrounds than Eliza Haywood's and to have experienced more respectable upbringings than Aphra Behn or Delarivier Manley. The novelist Charlotte Lennox, probably the daughter of a captain, was something of a throwback to Behn and Manley in her dubious claim to a governor for a father, but in any case her life did not quite conform to the new image since she grumbled vociferously about her husband and seems in the end to have separated from him. Another novelist, Sarah Fielding, came from a landed family, and the playwright and novelist Elizabeth Griffith's ancestors were churchmen and her father a theatre manager. Like the few scholarly women, many novelists came from clerical backgrounds. Frances Brooke was the daughter and wife of clergymen and she became the friend of such establishment figures as Johnson and Richardson. The father of Frances Sheridan was an archdeacon. Presumably such girls were given quite literary educations at home and then thrown onto the world with insufficient money to support a genteel leisured existence. Aristocrats rarely turned to the novel except under some idiosyncratic compulsion; the obsessively gambling Duchess of Devonshire squandered a fortune at cards and was probably the author of a fantasy about gambling entitled *The Sylph* (1780) in which, as in Mary Davys's *Reform'd Coquet*, an attentive male lover helps save a woman from herself. But this, like the size of the Duchess's debts, was unusual.

Although London was still the centre for women making their way in the theatre and in periodicals, literature, especially fiction, could be and was pursued in the provinces as well. In later decades substantial groups of writing and reading women existed in towns like York, Bristol, Norwich or Ipswich. (Wales and Scotland provided scenery for novels but not many novelists.) Increasingly there was a sense of a nonmetropolitan personality and existence and many women – especially poets – introduced admiring descriptions of their favourite haunts into their work.

In the earlier period a handful of women were involved in general magazines, as well as those few aimed at the female sex, but now, with the increase in the female readership, they clearly favoured periodicals specifically for women. In the later decades women would again enter general publishing but, despite Lady Mary Wortley Montagu's anonymous and uncommercial involvement in political journalism with her *Nonsense of Common-Sense*, in the middle years women mainly published magazines for other women (men were horrified that Isabella Griffiths might be involved in reviewing for her husband's general *Monthly Review*).

Most of the women's magazines were modelled on the earlier *Tatler* and *Spectator*, also aimed in part at a female readership, and they differed widely from the early scandal and gossip sheets. They ran sentimental stories which advised on marriage and courtship and printed and answered readers' letters like modern agony columns. A much reformed Eliza Haywood, who published several magazines in the 1740s and 1750s, among them *The Female Spectator* (1744–6), provided a refined version of the scandalous novels of her youth, stressing the moral and social messages of her anecdotes. Other women tried a format of edifying essays combined with titbits of news and information. Frances Brooke's *The Old Maid* in the 1750s included literary and theatrical reviews as well as gossip, while Charlotte Lennox's *Lady's Museum* in 1760 was interesting mainly because it helped pioneer the serialising of novels before publication.[10] The magazines were immensely important for women writers, pulling them into a community of shared culture and allowing them outlets for their work. In the 1760s *The Lady's Magazine* printed the work of the adolescent Charlotte Smith and it is hard to see how she would have launched herself as a poet without such encouragement.

In several magazines there was need for a writing persona, a female equivalent of the personas of Addison and Steele, a respectable Phoebe Crackenthorpe. Frances Brooke created Miss Singleton, the old maid, while Eliza Haywood in *The Female Spectator* constructed a wise older woman reformed after a youth of 'vanity and Folly'; although carefully moral, she still sounds rather like the earlier Haywood in the way she berates the artificial constructed innocence of young girls.

Since women could not easily make a good living from writing alone, literature was often joined to another occupation. In the early years, this might have been the theatre. In the mid-eighteenth century the stage still beckoned but the association of actress and whore was still somewhat in force and such an association could not help the decorous writer.

As they achieved more respectable standing in the community, women writers could decently combine literature with educating the young. Many women were both authors of advice books and governesses or teachers in schools, although the pattern was less common than in the late eighteenth century. The Anglo-Saxon scholar Elizabeth Elstob, whose success occurred in the early years, later tried to struggle out of debt by starting a school; she was rescued from its failure by several philanthropic ladies who found her a refuge as a governess. On the edge of literature women augmented their incomes in several bizarre ways. Laetitia Pilkington sold prints and pamphlets after she had spent some time in prison for debt; later she became a ghostwriter for other people's letters and poems. Others insisted that writing only served another function: 'I am no writer,' declared the aggrieved spy Mary Tonkin – whose experiences in the employ of her country were even more dismal than Aphra Behn's – but she needed the power of writing to vindicate herself.[11] Whatever else writing women did to keep themselves, very few indeed achieved real affluence and complete respectability. None reached the heights of Samuel Richardson, the well-to-do printer, or of Henry Fielding, the justice of the peace.

The Bluestocking hostesses and their friends provided a network of support for thinking women and a safety net of patronage for those needing to publish to live. Where Elizabeth Elstob had struggled along on her own until the last part of her life, Elizabeth Carter received an annuity from the wealthy Mrs Montagu, who took her role of women's supporter so seriously that she sounds at times as if she were running a modern grant-giving foundation for women. With Bluestocking patronage, Carter even managed to earn a considerable sum from her translation of Epictetus. There was a sense of solidarity that made Carter appear a credit to all of them, and her friend Catherine Talbot wrote that her work was an honour to England and 'womankind'.

Mostly the Bluestockings patronised poetry, translation and other types of nonfiction, published through subscription. They sought to encourage women, even of the lower classes, but they did not intend to change the hierarchical structure in any way. Mrs Montagu, an early patron of the milkwoman poet Ann Yearsley, did not aim at raising her station or at allowing her 'to devote her time to the idleness of Poetry'. Women, especially middle-class ones of irreproachable private lives, could be aided in entering culture by conforming to certain expectations; so they would help destroy the frivolous and lewd image of the female writer or talker and generally raise the status of their sex. Inevitably the Bluestockings must have functioned at times to censor as well as support. Although much chastened, the novel was still a slightly suspect genre and its sentimental vision often seemed to these ladies little better than the erotic fantasy of Manley and Haywood. So on the whole the Blues did not patronise the novel – and the novel was perhaps the one genre that did not especially need their help.

Women continued to enter all genres, although the modes of satire and scandal fiction inevitably declined, as the melancholy experience of Laetitia Pilkington indicates. In drama they had less success than in the earlier period, perhaps because the novel now seemed the obvious route for the impecunious woman and perhaps because the theatre was less in flux than before and so less open to women. Nonetheless they were still a force here and they wrote far more plays than they would in the nineteenth century. Elizabeth Griffith, Frances Brooke and Frances Sheridan, whose work influenced her son, Richard Brinsley Sheridan, had some success mainly with mannered comedies and musicals, although a drunken actor ruined one of Griffith's plays and rowdy audiences were often a trial. (Each of these women was also a novelist.) The court was no longer an important patron and a writer must know and please certain powerful theatrical men like David Garrick and Frances Sheridan's husband, Thomas. Few women ever had this sort of influence but in the 1770s Frances Brooke co-managed the Haymarket Opera House. In later decades Hannah Cowley made a moderate living out of drama, tempering comedy to the sentimental and patriotic times, praising good hearts, marriage and England, while Sophia Lee managed to make enough from a comedy to set herself up with a school in Bath.

In poetry the earlier Augustan mode of the witty and condensed heroic couplet, used so successfully by Lady Mary Wortley Montagu and Judith Madan, grew less popular and women conformed to the taste for the sentimentally effusive, the melancholy and the brooding. Lady Mary had by this time left the country and Judith Madan, converted to Methodism, turned like her friend the Countess of Huntingdon to hymns and religious musing.

The association of women with spontaneity meant that women primitive poets such as Mary Collier and Mary Leapor were as welcomed as men, although there was little effort to create ancient female primitives. These modern women, from Mary Collier, born about 1689, through Mary Leapor, Ann Candler and others to Ann Yearsley who died in 1806, tended to try to conform to the popular taste in poetry, but they often used the muse to express what their patrons must have regarded as quite unpoetic and bitter sentiments:

> Alas! what can you have
> From her, who ever was, and's still a Slave?
> No Learning ever was bestow'd on me;
> My Life was always spent in Drudgery.[12]

More comfortably placed women were, however, very much influenced by the kind of writing attributed to ancient poets and they created a mass of elegiac and wistful verse lamenting the pains of affection and the inevitable waning of life. They celebrated the communal familial side of sensibility, bemoaned the disruptive horrors of war, the evils of the slave trade and the misery of dying relatives, repeatedly depicting the correct sentimental response of the flowing eyes or the single tear. Their poems crystallised into tableaux of sentiment in which a family group took up the different postures of piety, sensitivity and affection.

At the same time they wrote poems about sensibility itself, not yet complaining of its belittling association with woman but lamenting rather complacently its tendency to bring suffering. Probably the most famous poem in this line was Frances Greville's 'A Prayer for Indifference':

> Nor ease nor peace that heart can know,
>   That, like the needle true,
> Turns at the touch of joy or woe,
>   But, turning, trembles too.

On the surface such a poem expressed desire for insensitivity, but its readers knew that it was not really questioning the worth of sensibility, now seen as woman's glory. The young poet Helen Maria Williams, much beloved of Dr Johnson and the Bluestocking ladies, was perhaps more honest when she replied to Mrs Greville:

> No cold exemption from her pain
>   I ever wish'd to know;
> Cheer'd with her transport, I sustain
>   Without complaint or woe.[13]

Hannah More, not yet the stern anti-sentimentalist she would become in the 1790s, made another response to Greville in 1782 by associating sensitivity with an elite of feeling: 'Where glow exalted sense and taste refin'd,/ There keener anguish rankles in the mind.'[14]

The mid-eighteenth century was a remarkable period of women's letter writing. The brilliant, colloquial, witty and sentimental correspondence, often published or at least much circulated, inevitably influenced fiction and was in turn clearly influenced by it. The most striking examples come from Bluestocking and aristocratic ladies with the leisure and social subjects for lengthy and entertaining relationships by post.

In the early decades two former ladies of the bedchamber to Queen Caroline, the Countesses of Hertford and Pomfret, chatted in letters about literature and the goings-on at the still indecorous court of George II:

Our forest [of Windsor] rings with the gallantries of his royal highness the duke; and the kind assistance that lord Harry Beauclerk has lent him in managing an interview with the daughter of a yeoman . . .

wrote Hertford; but she did not repeat *all* the scandal, she insisted, since her letters might be opened by someone other than her friend. The Countess of Pomfret in France had less scandal to offer but she filled out her letters with comments on the fashions in Paris, where dresses for balls were trimmed with different-coloured furs.[15]

Throughout the century the correspondence of upper-class women had a licence foreign to published writing, and often a letter of one of the notorious daughters of the Duke of Richmond or of Lady Mary Coke will almost catch the tone of Haywood or Manley from many years before:

Miss Chudleigh is going to wash herself in the Bathes of Bohemia. They will be very famous if they can cleanse her from all her disorders. She sets out in february, and has, as the Town says, left the Duke of Kingston a Milliner that she found in Cranbourn Alley to supply her place during her Absence.[16]

The less elevated in society eschewed such flippancy and developed a style very close in its intimacy and almost erotic language to that used for female friendship in sentimental epistolary fiction. Still others adopted an informal supple style that could accommodate bits of gossip and general reflection:

There are times when even the magnificence of the sky, the fair extensions of a flowery lawn, the verdure of the groves, the harmony of rural sounds, and the universal fragrance of the balmy air, strike us with no agreeable sensations . . . nothing surely but the ungrateful perverseness of one's own humour. This reflection throws human happiness in a most mortifying light.[17]

Many women could employ a variety of styles for different occasions and there was clear consciousness of the letter as an art form. Lady Mary Wortley Montagu read the correspondence of the famous French writer Madame de Sévigné – as did the Countesses of Hertford and Pomfret – and she was inspired to emulate her, while she herself became a model and standard for others with the publication of her letters from Turkey. Elizabeth Carter took inspiration from the letters of Katherine Philips and Elizabeth Rowe, on both of whom she commented admiringly in her correspondence with Catherine Talbot.

Given the desire of the middle classes for advice, an obvious growth area was didactic and informative literature. As many mothers in the later decades beccame uneasy at the sentimental values displayed to girls in novels, they sought out books preaching obedience and submission to children. Ann Murry's *Mentoria* in the 1770s was written originally for the pupils in her school, but its mixture of anecdote, biblical story, moral poetry, factual information and instruction in etiquette, set out in the catechistic question and answer form popularised by Rousseau, proved appealing to a wider public. Hannah Woolley had been successful with her cookery book in the 1660s but she achieved less fame than an eighteenth-century cookery writer like Hannah Glasse, who also taught the servant (and presumably her middle-class employer) how to set a table, make eel stew for consumptives, and 'hysterical water' from millipedes.

But it was above all fiction that was associated with women and the image of femininity, and it was here that the greatest increase in production occurred. Circulating libraries, depending heavily on novels, had begun in the early decades but they grew in size and number in the middle ones. Literary societies mushroomed and it was socially acceptable to be well read in modern productions; subscription lists printed in books played on the desire of men and women to be seen as literary consumers. With all this commercial support the demand for novels grew through the 1750s and sixties, slackening at the end of the seventies but accelerating again in the eighties. The commercial importance can be gauged from the increase in pirates who capitalised on popular writers and published books quickly at reduced prices.

But the diffusion of fiction should not be exaggerated. Reviewing magazines and journals remained relatively expensive – about half a guinea a year – and, although there was much uneasiness that servants were apparently reading sentimental novels, there is little evidence that this fiction moved into other sections of the lower class, where chapbooks were still most common. Few writers in the middle years could live entirely off fiction as they could do later; even an extremely popular author like Samuel Richardson only made much out of his novels when he was already a successful printer and of course he printed his own work. Henry Fielding gained large sums only towards the end of his life when he was established and a justice of the peace. Sterne made a good sum from fiction but not enough to support himself, and he was also a clergyman, while the medical Smollett gained more from his history writing than from fiction. Both Hume and Gibbon as historians were more flourishing than most novelists. For women at this stage, when there were quite large numbers but no overwhelmingly successful practitioners, it must have been extremely hard to make a living from authorship, and impossible from fiction alone.

THE NOVEL

By the middle of the eighteenth century sentimental tendencies were in all genres, but in the novel they were predominant. Literary history has not privileged the sentimental, resolutely seeing the eighteenth century as the age of Pope and Swift giving way to the age of Johnson, three men who regarded themslves as upholding a classical tradition of heroic, satiric and intellectual art. Yet such men represent only a part of the literary scene, influential indeed but by no means overwhelming in their effect. The novel that comes closest to this tradition is again the most privileged in literary history, that which leans towards satire and intellectual play on the one hand and to realism or verisimilitude on the other: the novel of Fielding, Smollett, Sterne. (Richardson, once considered lubricious, has come in for close study only very recently.) No woman is represented in the group. Yet, in the period itself there was much discussion of the feminising of culture and a common notion, or fear, that the novel had become a feminine genre.

The novel that women wrote and should be writing was the sentimental one, romantic in many ways while taking in some realistic elements. It did not pursue verisimilitude for its own sake or put the empirical before the ethical and it declared loudly that it had a particular moral aim − although opponents simply found duplicitous the protestations of morality in the later novel of self-regarding sensibility. It was not a direct development from those aspects of the early novel which a straightforward progressive history of fiction would see as prophetic − individual psychological realism of the sort hinted at in Aphra Behn and Jane Barker, frankness about physical matters in the manner of Behn, the early Haywood or Manley, acceptance and indeed investigation of the fictional project itself in the manner of all these writers. Consequently, in its apparent conventionality and its clichéd language, the mid-eighteenth-century novel often seems tiresome to the modern reader with other expectations. This generalisation is true of both types of sentimental fiction, types which overlap and which cannot be entirely separated, but which it is helpful to distinguish at this stage: the novel of sentiment or generalised moral reflection predominantly written in the 1740s and

139

1750s and the novel of sensibility concentrating on sensitive response and the fluctuating moods of the susceptible body, more commonly written in the 1760s and 1770s.

Convention and cliché are essential to both sorts of novel. Because virtue can be discerned in everyone and because the emphasis is on emotional sensitivity not intellectual analysis, conventional situations and stock characters are appropriate. So this fiction is peopled with such stereotypes as the weak father with the self-sacrificing daughter, the noble slave, the melancholy generous youth, the faithful retainer and the pure and suffering maiden, and its stories vary the common familial predicaments of virtue in distress. To bring out the virtue in the reader, the emotional response the work demands must be heightened; distress must be less tragic than deeply pathetic and instead of being displayed in one overpowering event it must occur again and again in the episode. The aesthetic unity of fiction, desired by discriminating readers from the end of the nineteenth century onwards, is uncommon; pathetic action may be repeated to what now appears a ridiculous degree and then followed by farcical episodes seemingly quite at odds with what went before. In the theatre melodramatic scenes often served as preludes to an act of juggling. The novel plot can be interrupted by lengthy melancholic verses or comic scenes only tangentially connected with the action.

Like the situations and characters, the language is conventional. Adjectives and nouns gain resonance as counters for common emotion and are constantly repeated. Hearts are overflowing and tears sympathetic. The tone is always hyperbolic; people are the best of brothers, the purest of sisters or the worst of villains. There is no room for great subtlety in depiction of individual characters, but there is space, at least in the earlier novel of sentiment, for the deep probing of emotional states on a generalised level, similar in effect to the soul-searchings in Puritan spiritual journals and, more recently, in Methodist autobiographies. Often works pull towards allegory and folk tale, uncovering the general below the particular, the moral character below accident, appearance and manner.

In the later novel of sensibility the emotional message is carried in sentimental tableaux which stop the action rather as the lengthy moral generalisations had done in the novels of sentiment. So the viewer can learn sympathy and respond tearfully. Although this habit was later much condemned as self-indulgent, the initial theory behind the convention was communicative and altruistic.[18]

The fascination with sensitivity and sensation in the novel was connected with the age's mechanistic understanding of psychology. Especially in the 1750s and '60s many books described the physical workings of sympathy, the transmission of emotion in physical terms. Every part of the body was thought to feel, and the mind and body became a single unit.[19] There was great excitement that the passions could be categorised, and several followed Le Brun in thinking that every idea had a corresponding physical expression. A language of gesture was formed and illustrated in books for actors, and physiognomy became all the rage — for a while there seemed really to be an art of reading the mind's construction in the face.

Psychology was assumed to be universal, and fictional characters were quite properly clichés. Physical beauty was not primarily an erotic stimulus but an indicator of moral worth, so that beauty in the wicked became an affront to morality and a snare for the benevolent. Many of the heroines of the feminine novel were interchangeable, like their names, endless variants on Julia, Isabella and Emily, all beautiful because immaculate and undifferentiated in their bodies which spoke purely of their minds' purity.

Although the sentimental representative could be man or woman and indeed the most famous examples in English are perhaps Sterne's Yorick and Mackenzie's Man of Feeling, the most sentimental situation is certainly woman's and, even in the novels that convey the male sentimentalist, the pathetic scenes into which he enters and to which he responds usually display women in postures of distress: mad, ill, seduced, raped or dying.

The most influential male novelist of women's sentimental fiction of both sorts was undoubtedly Samuel Richardson. Together with Henry Fielding, he conferred a status on the novel form which, together with the increasing propriety of expression, made the genre a far more respectable one for women than it had been a few decades before. Very quickly reviewers made Richardson and Fielding into the twin poles of fiction, genderised in a way so typical of the times. Thus Richardson's domesticated romance became the feminine mode of writing, as no woman's work could claim to be in these modest times. Fielding's ironic history the masculine, both consciously innovative forms such as no woman could claim for herself in these modest times.

Richardson represented the subjective, personal, domestic and internal, where Fielding stood for the objective, impersonal, public and external. While Richardson in his didactic mode made no claims to authorial power, Fielding emphasised the manipulative power of the author with his narrator, the maestro, the human creator, in a way foreign even to the early women writers. His works represented a new literary realism, superseding the cruder claims of historical truth of early travel narratives and rogue biographies. As women such as Behn,

Manley, Haywood and Barker were only partially involved in the empirical, epistemological changes in the earlier period, so in the later one women were largely absent from this development, insisting still, in complex or simplistic ways, on fiction's access to psychological and moral truths. With this continuing concern, their conventional insistence on artistic unskilfulness precisely drew attention to their rejection of the largely male belief that fiction's reality lay in art itself and not in its intervention in life.

Although Richardson was obviously not a woman writer, his early pretence in his epistolary novels that he was merely editing female texts, as well as the apparent autonomy he gave to the letters of women, made it seem that a female voice was actually present, while his centralising of female subjectivity, his concern for the problems of seduction, marriage and moral discrimination were typical of women writers. Where Fielding seemed to embrace a notion of poetic justice, a sort of literary providence taking over from the divine, Richardson recoiled from this supplanting of God's justice. Women tended to agree with Richardson, again refusing any sense that literature's autonomy could provide its value.[20]

The importance of Richardson for the feminine novel cannot be exaggerated although his isolation from what went before certainly can and has. The moral purpose he gave to fiction was already there in Elizabeth Rowe whom he printed and Penelope Aubin for whom he may have contributed a preface on the need for purity in the novel, while the centralising of female consciousness was in Behn and Manley, the exploitation of the epistolary form in Haywood, and the archetypal plot of virtue in distress in all these women. But the combination was new, as was the Puritan moral seriousness of the endeavour which, in the case of *Clarissa*, lifted the common story out of the merely entertaining into the almost mythic. Pulling away from the investigation of psychological idiosyncracy towards which Behn and Barker in particular sometimes appeared to be tending, he concentrated thoroughly on an inner life made representative and archetypal. In addition he made the epistolary mode into the sentimental vehicle *par excellence*, a tool for probing not only morality but, later, consciousness and sensation. Richardson gave an immense significance to female chastity, raising it from a physical condition to a spiritual state. The situations in which he displayed this chastity became current in the culture and all writing women must have felt to some extent the pressure of his first two novels: *Pamela* (1740–1), the story of a chaste servant whose virtue is rewarded in marriage to her erstwhile seducing master, and *Clarissa* (1747–8), the story of unfair parental pressure on a supremely virtuous girl who leaves her father's house only to be raped by Lovelace, the man in whom she had put her trust.

Dr Johnson declared that anyone who read Richardson for the plot would hang himself before reaching the end. But in fact the plots of these novels were immensely powerful and their meanings endlessly brooded over and debated. Only an incorrigible anti-sentimentalist like the aristocratic Lady Mary Wortley Montagu could sneer at the *social* stupidity of Clarissa. Yet, although women writers found them greatly inspirational, most stopped short of the ultimate outrage in the rape. Possibly they lacked Richardson's religious faith that made such an appalling act possible to accept if heaven were truly there to console; possibly they felt the latent male sadism in the portrayal. Lady Echlin in particular, one of Richardson's many female correspondents, could not bear it, felt faint and disordered when she read it, and set about composing a more suitable ending. Above all she revolted against the message that the heroine's virtuous passivity was in the end socially and politically impotent.[21]

Both the wish fulfilment of *Pamela*, where virtue seemed to be materially rewarded, and the myth of *Clarissa*, where female physical and social weakness had immense moral and religious power, were adopted by women in serious novels of female suffering as well as in escapist fantasies of feminine significance. In later sentimental works, a release from the progress to death could come through female friendship, defence and comfort in a hostile male world – the French novelist Madame Riccoboni, widely read in England, pictured heroines emotionally sacrificing lovers to their female friends.[22] More frequently it came through a relationship in which the man was feminised out of the aggressively sexual and into the domestic sphere. In this last fantasy, women, who in life made no claims to property, yet managed to hold on to it in fiction, and a frequent ending was the entry of a younger son of the nobility into the female estate. Richardson had tried to make a sentimental hero in Sir Charles Grandison in his final novel, but Sir Charles's mixture of social power and familial virtue did not, it seems, much appeal to women. The feminised man, however, neither a seducing aristocrat like the glamorous Lovelace nor the inconstant upstart of earlier fiction, had little of Sir Charles's overpowering social effect and his customary posture was at the feet of his beloved. In the novels of Frances Brooke, Elizabeth Griffith and the Minifie sisters, heroes are timid, living only to please women – the absolute antithesis of the situation described as marriage in the conduct books and a complete contrast in fantasy to the Duchess of Newcastle's enthusiasm for the mastering rake.

By the 1760s and 1770s, although the influence of Richardson continues, especially in the favouring of the epistolary style, there is further pressure from Laurence Sterne who tried to catch the fluctuating movements of a sensibility that was simultaneously physical and mental. His habit of sexual innuendo was quite out of the question for women writers but his self-conscious shifting style was appealing. By 1789 an impatient Mary Wollstonecraft could find the manner of his hero Yorick ubiquitous in the feminine novel:

> Nothing but sentiment! the finely fashioned nerves vibrate to every touch – Alas poor Yorick! If an earthly wight could punish thee . . . thou wouldst be condemned to reviewing all the sentimental wire-drawn imitations . . .[23]

Other tendencies derived from the French. The subversive effect of Rousseau's *La Nouvelle Héloïse* was felt by women more towards the end of the century, but already the emphasis on sentimental reactions and the reverential treatment of motherhood were having an effect. Rousseau added to the fetishisation already present in Richardson, whose Lovelace dreamt of gazing on the full breasts of a suppliant Clarissa feeding his twin bastards, but he also promoted a maternal image more attractive to women, of the powerful controlling mother, freed from some of the constraints of the virginal girl.

The full-blown novel of sensibility took some time to construct. In the 1740s and '50s Sarah Fielding could still combine a picaresque plot, associated with her brother Henry, with a sentimental message of vulnerable goodness, while she scattered moral sentiments throughout her work in a way which would have had Manley's characters yawning. Her novels still distance events with a third-person narrator; consequently she can touch on such potentially explosive themes as adultery in the central characters (see *The Countess of Dellwyn*, 1759) which would be inappropriate some years later. As sympathy grew for victims of society, including fallen women, and as sensibility more clearly came to encompass a measure of sexual desire, the adulteress could no longer easily be a central character and she was kept for the margins. Real exemplary sensibility would lead to misery before adultery. So Fielding's Countess of Dellwyn, who fell from vanity not lust, is replaced by Elizabeth Griffith's Lady Barton (*The History of Lady Barton*, 1771), an unhappily married woman who is allowed the reader's sympathy and who in the end remains faithful. Only in the shocking 1790s would the pattern be subverted in Mary Wollstonecraft's *The Wrongs of Woman* where the heroine with whom we sympathise is an adulteress – but by then the notion of adultery itself was being questioned.

If women made much of motherhood in fiction, especially in the period of high sensibility, they made less of the long-suffering wife, so much beloved of male writers like Henry Fielding, perhaps in part because so many women wrote from miserable domestic situations and found it difficult to glamorise the figure. But above all readers appeared to want to read of the young heroine, of virtue in distress made potent, of the chaste passive feminine woman humbling partiarchy. A fantasy of aristocracy conveyed the dream as women, always aristocrats in feeling, became aristocrats in society as well.

Many who derived from or identified with the upper orders and their educated classical culture were made uneasy by the novel. It had of course been attacked since its inception, but in this period its peculiar effect on women was even more frequently stressed for it was now assumed that women formed the largest part of its public. Since they were more susceptible, the effect of any literature on them would be greater than on men. Indeed their tendency to nervous diseases could only be exacerbated by their continual exposure to an imaginative realm: 'perhaps of all causes that have harmed women's health, the principal one has been the unfortunate multiplication of novels in the last hundred years . . .'[24] As ever, the main fear was of the loss of mental and physical chastity which would ruin marriage chances or prevent the proper fulfilment of domestic duties:

> Miss reads – she melts – she sighs – Love steals upon her –
> And then – Alas, poor Girl! – good night, poor Honour![25]

In 1778 Vicessimus Knox in his *Essays Moral and Literary* blasted the novel for giving an amiable name to vice and a gracefulness to moral deformity.

Yet, despite some mockery, the sentimental novel flourished in the middle years of the century and most women seem to have accepted it – at least openly – as a vehicle of feminine morality rather than deformity. In it the role-playing of the woman author typical of Barker, Manley and Haywood was no longer proper and it was believed that the femininity conveyed in the writer and the heroine was the natural state of woman; the novel that delivered it, however crafted, was artless, modest and sincere.

RE-FORMERS:
ELIZA HAYWOOD AND CHARLOTTE LENNOX

According to the critic and sentimental novelist Clara Reeve in 1785, Eliza Haywood managed to atone for her early wicked fantasies and to become in the middle years of the eighteenth century a force for the moral improvement of young girls. She 'repented of her faults, and employed the latter part of her life in expiating the offenses of the former'. The critic went on to wish piously, 'May her first writings be forgotten, and the last survive to do her honour!' In Clara Reeve's presentation, Eliza Haywood becomes a Magdalen figure who reforms into sentiment; certainly she adapted to the market and adjusted her image.[1]

By the middle of the eighteenth century the woman writer who wanted to please the public understood that she must describe sentiment, not sex. Although a few years later women would make a fantasy world of sensibility as heady in its way as the erotic one of Manley and the early Haywood, in the 1740s and 1750s they did not often sensationalise their subject. Female characters could be sentimentally presented as passive and victimised, but their passive victim status was not yet delicious; titillation should not return by the back door. A possible way of signalling a moral purpose was to enact the replacement of the power-seeking woman with the new feminine one, to transform the coquettish into the sentimental sign. And, in different ways, the older Eliza Haywood and Charlotte Lennox did just this.

When Haywood's *The History of Miss Betsy Thoughtless* (1751) was first published, a reviewer sniffed at its seemingly pedestrian story – the reforming of an ordinary girl:

> the history of a young inconsiderate girl, whose little foibles, without any natural vices of the mind, involve her in difficulties and distresses, which, by correcting, make her wiser, and deservedly happy in the end. A heroine like this, cannot but lay an author under much disadvantage . . .[2]

It was, the reviewer declared, 'a barren foundation' for a novel. In time such a plot, taking on the male mentor as reforming agent, would make the literary glory of Jane Austen.[3] Emma Woodhouse and Elizabeth Bennet are, after all, corrected out of their 'little foibles' before becoming 'deservedly happy', while, in the style of Lennox's *The Female Quixote* of 1752, Catherine Morland in *Northanger Abbey* is cured (rather more speedily than Lennox's tiresome heroine) of her addiction to a later form of romance, the gothic novel.

The moral plot of the reformed coquette already existed in the 1690s; in the early eighteenth century, along with Mary Davys, Pope took it up in *The Rape of the Lock*, which tells of the chastening of a beautiful, narcissistic girl who learns through the simulacrum of a rape – the cutting of her most artfully placed lock of hair – that a woman's destiny is not self-contemplation and significance but contingency and marriage. What seems new in the 1740s and 1750s is the seriousness of the treatment, the sense that the coquette must not simply be taught different ways but actually be humbled and re-formed.

Pope attacked the early Eliza Haywood in *The Dunciad*, depicting her as a kept mistress with a bevy of bastards (real or literary), a prize in a urinating contest between men. For many years she went silent as a novelist. Probably this silence had little to do with Pope's character assassination – but such adverse publicity cannot have helped her in the increasingly moral years. By the time she returned to fiction in the more decorous 1740s, she took the precaution of writing anonymously and in the new mode of sentiment and propriety. Fittingly her novel *Miss Betsy Thoughtless* delivers a similar moral message to Pope's *Rape of the Lock*.

After her past of scandalous and erotic novel writing, Eliza Haywood could not set up with quite the sternness of Penelope Aubin and Elizabeth Rowe, but she obviously did understand that the publication of *Pamela* had given great prestige to the didactic form of the novel, one combining entertaining and convincing event with total moral commitment to the ideology of femininity: 'Who could have dreamt, he should find, under the modest Disguise of a *Novel*, all the Soul of Religion, Good-breeding, Discretion, Good-nature, Wit, Fancy, Fine Thought, and Morality?'[4] In *Betsy Thoughtless* she clearly accepted the new mask of the woman writer and hung up her sign as teacher and chaste author, turning the cautionary element that had always marked her fiction into a moral one.[5] The novel *Betsy Thoughtless* avoids the first-person narrations which allowed so much self-indulgence and narcissistic self display – and would do so again in the later novel of sensibility. But, unlike that in Aphra Behn's short fiction, the method here does not provide the kind of detachment which risks different interpretations in the reader.

The female novel had usually offered a (perfunctory) statement about its usefulness, but in this work the statement is loudly made:

> Though it is certain that few young handsome ladies are without some share of the vanity here described, yet it is to be hoped, there are not many who are possessed of it in that immoderate degree Miss Betsy was. It is, however, for the sake of those who are so, that these pages are wrote, to the end they may use their utmost endeavours to correct that error, as they will find it so fatal to the happiness of one who had scarce any other blameable propensity in her whole composition.[6]

It begins in a sentimental generalisation: 'It was always my opinion, that fewer women were undone by love, than vanity.' Others follow: 'Love, when real, seldom fails of inspiring the breast that harbours it with an equal share of timidity' and 'Nature may be moderated, but never can be wholly changed.' Characterisation is subordinated to these moral and social generalisations and the names of the actors indicate quality: Thoughtless, Forward, Goodman and Trueworth. With such names no psychological suspense is possible. The interest is in the analysis and moral generalisation, not in developing individual psychological insight.

In *Betsy Thoughtless*, the narrator is a man among men, following the fiction that the author and the readership are male. The narrator is wise, older and pedagogic, pointing out the stupidity of certain actions and underlining the basic goodness of the heroine despite her naivety and social foolishness. There is a little authorial fun in the manner of Henry Fielding rather than Manley, a stress not on the social and erotic power of the writer but on the power of narration: 'I will not anticipate that gratification, which ought to be the reward of a long curiosity.'

The most extraordinary effect of Haywood's novel – looking back at it from later years – is, however, of a kind of freedom. The book is moral, quite different from her earlier *Love in Excess* or Manley's *Rivella*; yet there is an openness in the writing and indeed in the activity described – even though this activity is often censured – that would be out of place a decade or two later. It is true that the heroine learns that she must be careful of her conduct and not enjoy power over suitors in the robust way of early eighteenth-century women, but in the process of learning she takes considerable liberties and she scandalously hints at a distinction between the woman and the image of femininity.

The novel focuses not only on woman but on the reputation or the sign of womanhood acting in society. A woman who sullies her reputation brings disgrace on her whole family; so Betsy must learn, as Laetitia Pilkington could not, that she is a public commodity. One mentor figure even tries to persuade her to adopt a dubious morality: 'a woman brings less dishonour upon a family by twenty private sins, than by one publick indiscretion.'[7] Although she rightly balks at the debasement, there is some truth in the idea – the public indiscretion has worse *social* consequence than the private sins. Neither of course should be countenanced by a good woman.

Because Betsy values herself on the quantity and quality of her lovers, with no real sense that her emotions should be engaged, the story is a series of episodes, in which she walks abroad, flirts with whomsoever she meets and learns her error time and time again. She must understand that 'the honour of a young maid' is 'a flower of so tender and delicate a nature, that the least breath of scandal withers and destroys it'. She does, however, have a great ally and advantage in the narrator, who constantly asserts that the heroine is all right really, despite often appalling actions and considerable carelessness about other people's feelings. In this special pleading the reader may discern something of the old Haywood. Nonetheless the narrator's partiality does not interfere with the main moral, which is clearly and repeatedly expressed.

That the double standard, so unsettled by Behn and Manley, is firmly in place is not doubted by the narrator or the heroine, and even a man with the name of Trueworth can have his fling in a way unthinkable for Betsy. Virtue in a woman may be more than chastity, but it certainly demands chastity first and foremost.

There is a down-to-earth atmosphere about the novel. Ordinary middle-class families squabble over trifles and note the stuff and price of dress. Improper behaviour is not just hinted at in vague abstractions like 'familiarity', 'debauchery' or 'dissipation' or in the language of religiosity so often used to titillate, but simply shown as romping about, pulling onto the bed, and kissing on the lips in dark recesses.

There is still the sense, as in the old Haywood, of girls at the mercy of men and there are some vulgar suggestions of sexuality in those who have already fallen, but sexuality is not now the main driving force of the heroine. Instead Betsy's problem is the desire for power before marriage: ' "Whether I marry him or not," ' said she to herself, ' "the addresses of a man of his rank will make me of some consideration in the world." ' Her mistake is the idea that she can have the adoration which the peculiar construction of the confined lady allows, as well as the freedom of action taken by the Restoration kind of woman. She must learn that it may be 'strange' but is nonetheless true that a young woman cannot 'indulge herself in the liberty of conversing freely with a man, without being persuaded by him to do every thing he would have her'.[8]

Betsy aims to postpone marriage. She does not want to become 'a matron at my years' and her idea of matrimony is at the outset resolutely unsentimental: 'to be cooped up like a tame dove, only to coo, – and bill, – and breed'. In her aim she seems to accept the obedience that marriage implies for a woman and, unlike the wicked women of the sentimental novel, she never decides to marry for the sake of the freedom she can have as a wife. She knows that it is more fun to be 'courted, complimented, admired, and addressed by a number than be confined to one, who from a slave becomes a master, and, perhaps, uses his authority in a manner disagreeable enough'. She assumes that a lover will be obedient and assiduous, although she knows that a husband has all the rights. But she has yet to learn that, given this inexorable progress, it is foolish to tyrannise over those who in the end will have all the power.

At the same time she holds a contrary view of marriage as simply social consequence:

> if ever I do become a wife, I should like to be a woman of quality: they may say what they will, but a title has prodigious charms in it; the name Fineer also becomes it. 'Lady Fineer's servants there! Lady Fineer's coach to the door!' would sound vastly agreeable at the play or opera.[9]

She does not consider the sexual return in courtship or the social subordination in marriage which immediately tilt the balance of power towards man.

In the event marriage is worse than she had supposed. Since she had no awareness of sexuality or of passion, she had seen the state on the one hand as mild confinement and on the other as the attractive acquisition of social power and gratification, equipage and consequence. She soon finds she has married a man who considers a

> wife no more than an upper servant, bound to study and obey, in all things, the will of him to whom she had given her hand; – and how obsequious and submissive soever he appeared when a lover, had fixed his resolution to render himself absolute master when he became a husband.

The quarrels are mundane and unheroic, related to the financial power of the husband in modern marriage:

> [she] produced an account to what uses every single shilling she had received from him had been converted since the last dispute they had with each other on this score.
>
> In presenting these papers to him, 'Read these bills, said she, 'and be convinced how little I deserve such treatment from you; you will find that there are no items inserted of coffee, tea, or chocolate; articles,' continued she, with an air a little disdainfully, 'which you seemed to grumble at, though yourself and friends had the same share in, as well as me and mine.'
>
> 'Rot your accounts!' cried he, tearing the papers she had given him into a thousand pieces; 'have you the folly to imagine I will be troubled with such stuff?'[10]

Although there is realistic detail in the texture of the novel, the characters are not given much complexity and are mainly comprised by their names. But in Betsy there is some development after she has entered marriage, when her inner life is conveyed as a change in understanding. In this union we watch her inability to 'dwindle into a wife' at once and to learn to practise those 'softening arts she had been advised to win her lordly tyrant into temper'. She does, however, come to understand that her flirting days are over and that the 'pride of subduing hearts is mine no more':

> she now saw herself, and the errors of her past conduct, in their true light. 'How strange a creature have I been!' cried she, 'how inconsistent with myself! I knew the character of a coquet both silly and insignificant, yet did everything in my power to acquire it: – I aimed to inspire awe and reverence in the men, yet by my imprudence emboldened them to the most unbecoming freedoms with me.'[11]

She reviews marriage with similar clarity and then takes the socially momentous step of leaving her husband – as Eliza Haywood and Charlotte Lennox seem actually to have done in life. She does so while wondering whether anything justifies breaking the marriage vow.

Whether or not she is justified in this act, all the suffering she has undergone has wrought the right change in her and she turns from being a flirtatious, power-seeking woman into the sentimental lady. In this role she is seen by the worthy man she should have married, in the country she had once despised, sighing, pensive, and tearful – in other words utterly appealing in the new sentimental mode. On cue her husband dies, so that the reformed lady and worthy man may be married. Presumably her name is changed from Thoughtless to Trueworth. Virtues are rewarded in the end, says the narrator. Certainly the social and sentimental ones are.

Charlotte Lennox achieved extraordinary approval from famous and respectable literary men. Samuel Richardson printed her work while Dr Johnson wrote proposals for her, supplied dedications, perhaps helped with parts of her novels, and was tireless in promoting her writing. Johnson gave a party to celebrate the publication of her first novel, *The Life of Harriot Stuart*, in 1750 and complimented her publicly: of Fanny Burney, Elizabeth Carter and the young Hannah More, he declared, 'Three such women are not to be found: I know not where I could find a fourth, except Mrs Lennox, who is superior to them all.'[12]

Yet Lennox did not quite conform to the proper feminine image of the writer. There is a slender link with the indecorous Behn and Manley in the flamboyant claim of a governor for a father rather than the more usual clergyman, while her later life, like Laetitia Pilkington's, was simply too harsh not to be deeply resented. She had married a shiftless and reputedly unkind man and was spending her married years in chronic debt, trying to relieve the family's poverty through a little (unsuccessful) acting, more translation and, in time, novel-writing. Her final years were unrelievedly dismal. Probably separated from her husband, whom she termed 'a most unnatural man', she lost her daughter, while her son had to flee to America. She suffered a long illness and died almost destitute.

Many commented, rather vaguely, on her 'unhappy' and 'distressed' existence, but she did not evoke much pity. Poverty, unhappiness and struggle had obviously soured her and she did not in her last years command much affection from anyone. She was never really part of the respectable and influential Bluestocking circle and, as Mrs Thrale remarked, although her books are approved, 'nobody likes her'. In time she alienated the ladies who had patronised her by making them fear to become the butts of satire in her novels.

Many of the heroines Lennox created were thoroughgoing ladies of sensibility, fainting and falling ill for love and conducting themselves with exemplary decorum and piety; others, however, were tougher, occasionally unlikeable, while their situations sometimes had a nasty complexity, at odds with the simple sentimental message. This is especially so in her last novel, *Euphemia*, published in 1790, where the heroine as female friend and coping woman is emphasised over the heroine as wife and mother, while the ending is not the death of the inadequate spouse, nor a marriage to end all impropriety but simply the coming together of the two friends and the hope of a reasonable future life in the circumstances of unchangeable marriage. Presumably Lennox's own unfortunate experience has intruded and, although the tone remains sentimental, the modification of the plot is not.

Her most famous novel, *The Female Quixote*, was, however, published nearly forty years before *Euphemia*, when Lennox was still the toast of Dr Johnson and his circle. It is one of the parodic novels based on Cervantes and his idea of the fiction-maddened imagination, a form of which the eighteenth century appeared very fond. The novel is not the story of the reformed coquette, but it is very close to it since, in a woman, false activity in the world can only concern her relations with men – she cannot ride abroad like the Don or even tumble in inns like the quixotic Tom Jones. Her mistake is like the coquette's, the assumption of too great female significance and social power.

The story concerns Arabella, the daughter of a disillusioned and reclusive Marquis who raises her in magnificent isolation. In the castle she becomes addicted to old French romances of the type written by Mademoiselle de Scudéry. Knowing nothing of society, she expects to find the characters of these fictions in real life and she fashions herself and her appearance to conform to romantic expectations. Entirely under the influence of heroic romance, she constantly misjudges the people she meets, especially when, after her father dies, she is taken into the social world of Bath and London, and she causes immense embarrassment to her cousin who loves her and whom her father wished her to marry. Her response is bizarre for the mid-eighteenth century, but her reaction to heroic romance is pretty close to Dorothy Osborne's a century before, concerned that her lover have precisely the right attitude to the heroines' dilemmas.

Arabella has the facility of reconstructing all events and people to fit into her romantic world, a facility clearly aided by her social status and her much praised beauty; she resembles nothing so much as the Duchess of Newcastle in full fantasy and antique dress. But in time, like Betsy before her, she is cured of her delusions, although not until she has repeatedly erred and until she has understood through experience the incompatibility of ancient morals and manners with the laws and values of modern Christian England.

For the future of the reformed-coquette plot, it is significant that a male agent causes her reformation. Betsy Thoughtless had had mentors, although none had been effective, and in the end experience and common sense brought about her change. Arabella, however, needs the help of an older clergyman (perhaps Lennox originally thought of vesting authority in a woman, a sensible countess who begins Arabella's re-education but suddenly disappears from the plot). Interestingly the use of the male mentor – different from his use as lover in Mary Davys's *The Reform'd Coquet* – allows a firm statement of patriarchal and sentimental doctrine combined, while at the same time leaving to the lover figure some of the appeal of weakness.

Mademoiselle de Scudéry was no doubt still read when Lennox was writing, but the more recent naughty novels of Manley and the early Haywood may well have been closer to many readers. Much is made of Arabella's isolation which has put her out of touch with the modes of her time. (Indeed this must be extreme since she states, when searching her memory for literary precedent for her intended act of leaving the castle, that 'she did not remember to have read of any heroine that voluntarily left her father's house' – this at a time when no ordinary reader of fiction could possibly have escaped knowledge of Clarissa's momentous act a few years before.) Certainly there is play on the contrasts among the different forms of fiction, especially in the use of the loaded word 'adventure'.

From her reading, Arabella expects the heroic adventure of French romance. Yet, when she enquires about them in other girls, she learns only malicious gossip and naughty doings. Delarivier Manley had called her fictional autobiography *The Adventures of Rivella* and the word had become associated with amorous escapades rather than with medieval derring-do. As the monitory Countess primly asserts:

> the word adventure carries in it so free and licentious a sound in the apprehensions of people at this period of time, that it can hardly with propriety be applied to those few and natural incidents which comprise the history of a woman of honour.[13]

In Manley and the early Haywood, the effect on young girls of reading any romantic fiction, heroic or erotic, had been the arousing of sexuality, so that, in complete contrast to the heroic romance itself, their danger had come from a development within more than from plots and stratagems outside. And they had faced the seducer rather than the abductor, not the unknown knight on horseback but the father, the uncle or the brother. In *The Female Quixote* there is no parallel, but there is a sense that Arabella is in the end freed both from the erotic naughtiness of the English writers and from the heroic absurdity of the French. Although she allows none of it to her heroine, Lennox in her dedication shows that she at least knows of the 'subtle sophistry of desire'.

What Arabella will read in the future is obviously Samuel Richardson. 'Truth is not always injured by fiction,' declares the mentor. 'An admirable writer of our own time, has found the way to convey the most solid instructions, the noblest sentiments, and the most exalted piety in the pleasing dress of a novel.' It is also the future programme for feminine fiction.

Before she is directed towards the author of *Clarissa* with its heroine of 'exalted piety', Arabella makes the mistake of believing with her literary predecessors that a woman can fashion her own sign. She sets about it in many different ways. First she looks much in her mirror and finds there an appearance that conforms to the expectations of beauty. From her aristocratic father she has learned artfulness. As he improved his grounds – 'the most laborious endeavours of art had been used to make it appear like the beautiful product of wild uncultivated nature' – so his daughter dresses unfashionably but artfully:

> All the beauties of her neck and shape were set off to the greatest advantage by the fashion of her gown, which, in the manner of a robe, was made to fit tight to her body ... Her fine black hair hung upon her neck in curls, which had so much appearance of being artless, that all but her maid, whose employment it was to give them that form, imagined they were so.[14]

Secondly she strikes self-conscious attitudes and demands that others play parts in her elaborate world, rather like Lovelace in his creation of a false world for Clarissa. Only Arabella is more trapped in the illusion than anyone else, although others suffer through her, and she has no knowledge that it is the straightforward power of rank and wealth that allows all the deception. Her demands on others are eccentric and ridiculous, but they are also improper in the importance they give to the young girl. Like the coquette who wants significance from men and like Betsy who thinks that her consequence must be increased by the ardour of titled lovers, Arabella believes that 'the blood that is shed for a lady enhances the value of her charms'.

Along with her appearance, she fashions her language. She wishes to speak with authority, which for a woman can only come from the code of high female heroics, the kind of bombastic abstract language which was used in the (bad) translations of the French romances she reads. (The syntax too seems the result of bad translation from the French and it makes people into grammatical entities dependent on the speaker; so for example Arabella's maid becomes 'her on whose fidelity I relied'.) This language was also employed by the passionate and betrayed heroines of Behn, Manley and the early Haywood: 'Grief, Rage, Jealousy, and Despair' is a typical utterance. It would later be modified and elaborated in the self-indulgent and self-regarding fiction of sensibility which would in time come to worry critics as much as the wicked heroics of the early writers. But in its original form it seems incompatible with sentiment, suitable instead for use by coquetting girls for whom 'adventure' means sexual indulgence and 'favours' fondling and kissing.

Arabella knows that one tool of self-creation is literary depiction. She wishes to be the heroine of a romantic history, the subject of a narrative of which she can be the auditor – this wonderful narcissistic pleasure is allowed to Mr B in *Pamela* who avidly listens to the recounting of his wicked deeds. But Arabella has only her down-to-earth maid Lucy to function as romantic historian, and Lucy understandably finds her instructions daunting. She is at one stage told that she must

not only . . . recount all my words and actions, even the smallest and most inconsiderable, but also all my thoughts, however instantaneous; relate exactly every change of my countenance; number all my smiles, half-smiles, blushes, turnings pale, glances, pauses, full-stops, interruptions; the rise and falling of my voice; every motion of my eyes; and every gesture which I have used for these ten years past; nor omit the smallest circumstance that relates to me . . . You may proceed to tell them, how a noble unknown saw me at church; how prodigiously he was struck with my appearance; the tumultuous thoughts that his first view of me occasioned in his mind.[15]

This is made especially ridiculous because Arabella not only demands an utter centrality no maid ever gave her mistress, but also desires a fictional biography conceived by the subject beyond the powers of the historian. Had she written her own detailed account, she might have turned novelist herself.

Finally Arabella wants to replace law and religion, both of which systems seem to assign lesser status to women, with heroic romance in which women have vast significance. So, like a lawyer, she searches her romances for precedent for an action or judgement and she accepts the morality of her books although she knows in theory that the pre-Christian characters are ignorant of proper charity and forgiveness. When it is pointed out to her that she is condoning some decidedly illegal and unchristian activity in her romantic enthusiasm, she remarks loftily: 'The law has no power over heroes.'

Because her law is the heroic one, she has no concept of the modern legal codes of England in which heiress-hunting and rape are criminal offences. Indeed real male sexual violence or cunning are unthinkable in her scheme of things. She has no idea of her real position in society as a 'good match' because of her wealth and beauty, and she has no notion of what 'possession' means; consequently she rides off alone in a coach with a man (that common location of dastardly deeds in the woman-centred novel) with only trust and the purest of thoughts.

What Arabella must be reformed and redeemed into is sentiment, the ideology of femininity. And first of all she must learn of her own insignificance. This is not easy, for some of her vainglorious ideas have derived from her very real importance. Her father was privileged, noble and immensely rich, so that he could isolate her from society and yet educate her to a high degree. When he sees something of the absurdity her romantic addiction has caused in her, he overlooks it because of its consonance with his own aristocratic haughtiness of demeanour.

The romances that have so damaged Arabella are, it is interesting to note, the legacy of her dead mother, the insignificant woman who, married in a sentence, was inferior to her husband in rank, but who was chosen as a wife for her beauty and good sense – in that order. The Marquis's plan of magnificent isolation for himself did not accord with his wife's desires, but these were never consulted, and she managed to alleviate the 'very disagreeable' solitude into which she was forced with the reading of compensatory romance. Considering that she was already very much an inferior wife, such reading could have no adverse effect on her, but on her more nobly born and unmarried daughter it certainly could.

Arabella has to learn that she cannot have the absurd centrality depicted in French romance. She must understand that she will not make the rhetoric that contains her but live instead in the rhetoric of others, the creators of her social reputation. Following the example in heroic romance, she is horrified at being gazed on by men, feeling their appropriating look the ultimate indignity; yet she will have to comprehend that she must indeed be the object of male gaze, since this is the reality of a woman in society and it comprises the only influence she can properly have over men, one of whom must choose her if she is to become a wife.

In the end Arabella is redeemable because, with all her faults, she already has many of the attributes of the new sentimental heroine. For a start she entirely eschews female sexual desire; she is not a heroine of Behn, Manley or the early Haywood, not even a heroine like Richardson's Pamela who unaccountably stays with her master when she should leave his house. The heroine she aspires to be is desirable and adored; she is abducted and rescued by men, but she does not actually desire herself. The women she admires are passive; they 'do not give their consent' to all this amorous activity of abduction, 'but for all that, they are, doubtless, run away with many times; for truly, there are some men, whose passions are so unbridled, that they will have recourse to the most violent methods to possess themselves of the object they love.' When transposed into sentimental diction this is a proper view for a woman to take, made ridiculous only by the assumption of repeated violent action. What would be unthinkable for Arabella is the unbridled passion of the woman herself.

In the earlier novels, Arabella's kind of desire for importance and heroine status was often coupled with sexual ability; the woman used her attractiveness, desire and allure to manipulate men. But no one in this story finds Arabella at all attractive when she is deluded by romance and demanding significance. Her main suitor and later husband Glanville is first of all smitten with her because of her beauty; when he thinks of marriage to her as she is, he finds it unacceptable because it would affect his standing in society and cause him endless embarrassment: 'he could propose nothing to himself but eternal shame and disquiet, in the possession of a woman, for whom he must always blush, and be in pain.' The concern is not really for Arabella herself since she is oblivious to the embarrassment she causes and quite content in her delusions. In the end it is he who wishes to manipulate her, not the reverse: 'his happiness depended upon curing her of her romantic notions.'

What is palpably real is, then, Arabella's beauty, powerful only when gazed on by men. So when for a moment she seems to be imposing her view of herself on society and constructing a successful persona, the narrator tells the reader that it is actually her absolute physical beauty that is working. She comes to a ball robed as an heroic princess and people

157

do in fact treat her with the exaggerated respect she expects, but it is in spite of not because of her play-acting and dress: 'the astonishment her beauty occasioned, left them no room to descant on the absurdity of her dress.' What she herself aims to create never prevails. Arabella is beautiful and therefore desirable to men until her beauty fades. She must be brought to reality and disillusionment so that she can be married before this fading occurs.

Arabella also has other sentimental traits. In church – where despite her stated piety most of her encounters commence – she conforms to the image so beguilingly described by Fordyce in his *Sermons*: 'She blushed with a very becoming modesty.' She has, we are told, 'great sensibility and softness' and she derives pleasing satisfaction from a benevolent act however absurd it may appear. Above all she attracts the hero most strongly when participating in a sentimental tableau, the daughter at the bedside of the dying father; there she is all tenderness and pious care.

And she has, along with beauty and tenderness, the true feminine and sensitive body, much given to blushing, crying and fainting – indeed she faints all day after her father's death and is even suspected of being dead herself – while a soft languor appears in her eyes when she is sorrowful. Her voice, despite her heroics, can become 'enchantingly sweet'. Although she has been caught artfully adorning her body in heroic style, she can also be negligent and sincere and she is described as dressing in a fraction of the time it takes the fashionable woman to prepare herself.

In other words, despite her admiration for the Amazonian Thalestris, there is nothing 'masculine' about her. She has none of the appalling health of the corpulent Miss Grove, who was given to outdoor exercises in her youth and has thereby contracted 'a masculine and robust air not becoming her sex', a health which allows her to engage lustily in sexual encounters in her adulthood and withstand the frequent lyings-in her activity demands. Instead Arabella has the delicacy, even weakness, of proper femininity, finding it difficult to walk two miles outside the castle and swooning when she stumbles. So her final repudiation of the heroic Thalestris who cut men in pieces is entirely in keeping – after all, as the trivial Miss Glanville remarks, for such extraordinary deeds she must have had 'very masculine hands'.

The foreshadowing of Arabella's translation into the scheme of sentiment is in her actual effect on men. Her antique clothes serve to make her not a heroic princess but a more sexually alluring woman, especially when also draped in sentiment. So her posture of grief after her father's death and her elaborate mourning combine into one riveting effect:

[Glanville and his father, Sir Charles, entered] Arabella's chamber, who was lying negligently upon her bed.

Her deep mourning, and the black gauze, which covered part of her fair face, was so advantageous to her shape and complexion, that Sir Charles, who had not seen her since she grew up, was struck with an extreme surprise at her beauty, while his son was gazing on her so passionately, that he never thought of introducing his father to her, who contemplated her with as much admiration as his son, though with less passion.[16]

The final phrase here becomes necessary in the context of Arabella's later suspicion that her uncle desires her as well as her cousin. The suggestion is improper in the novel of sentiment, which indicates how large is the gap between the new novel and the fictive world of Delarivier Manley, in which no woman would have been safe displaying her shape to advantage before an avuncular gaze.

The actual change in Arabella occurs after a kind of new baptism. She has imagined an abduction which she intends to counter 'in manner truly heroick' with sublime virtue and grand courage. In reality she jumps into the Thames, a commonplace river which happens to be at hand, and in doing so mocks the suicides that followed the successful abductions or attempted rapes in heroic romance. She is rescued but, in keeping with her delicacy, falls ill from her immersion. So she comes under the influence of the wise divine who teaches her the Johnsonian message of common sense: books are not 'copies of life and models of conduct' but 'empty fictions'. She could in fact have learned much of this from the works of Behn, Haywood and Manley, had she read them.

The Doctor – image of the real-life patriarchal moralist Dr Johnson, called within the novel 'the greatest genius in the present age' – takes a stern line on heroic romance:

Every page of these volumes is filled with such extravagance of praise, and expressions of obedience, as one human being ought not to hear from another; or with accounts of battles, in which thousands are slaughtered, for no other purpose than to gain a smile from the haughty beauty, who sits a calm spectatress of the ruin and desolation, bloodshed and misery, incited by herself. It is impossible to read these tales without lessening part of that humility, which, by preserving in us a sense of our alliance with all human nature, keeps us awake to tenderness and sympathy, or without impairing that compassion which is implanted in us as an incentive of acts of kindness'.[17]

Through his words Arabella learns humility instead of absurd heroic significance; she will in future be looked at as an object in society and will at last understand social embarrassment, the controlling fear of 'contempt and ridicule'. She marries and ends her romance and adventure.

She is ready to be a wife because she has learned that what romance teaches is false: men do not exist to serve women.

The plot of the reformation of the heroine, replacing a sexual fall with social error, had a future glory in the Great Tradition of fiction set out by F.R. Leavis, in which Jane Austen serves as a sort of mother. It had an equally serious use in the earlier novelists such as Fanny Burney at the end of the eighteenth century who reacted against many aspects of sentimental fiction. But it was not a plot that greatly appealed to the female reading public in the decades following 1750 and it serves rather as overture to the full sentimental opera to come.

In literary terms what Charlotte Lennox enacts is, then, the changing of the female novel. The implied audience will not be arousable men but malleable women. No longer will it be an investigation of female masks, the construction of woman by education and society, and the workings of desire as sexual passion and hunger for significance. Instead it will serve as conduct book, colluding with the new ideology of femininity and teaching the sentimental image of womanhood. The message will not be self-knowledge and limited self-fulfilment within society, as in Manley, but self-sacrifice and the understanding of constraint.

9

NOVELISTS OF SENTIMENT:
SARAH FIELDING AND FRANCES SHERIDAN

The task of providing Richardson's 'Antidote to . . . Womens Poison', begun by Lennox and a reformed Haywood, was completed by the novelists of sentiment, Sarah Fielding and Frances Sheridan. Each fulfils his demand and indeed writes in his shadow. Frances Sheridan dedicated her most famous work *The Memoirs of Miss Sidney Bidulph* (1761) to the author of *Clarissa* and *Sir Charles Grandison*, while Sarah Fielding, who met Richardson between the writing of the first and second parts of her novel, *The Adventures of David Simple* (1744 and 1753), soon became his 'much-esteemed Sally Fielding'. Richardson helped her publish her works, encouraged people to subscribe to them, and printed many of them himself, including *The Governess* (1749) and *The History of the Countess of Dellwyn* (1759). Further, he told Sarah that a famous critic, probably Samuel Johnson, had praised her delineation of human emotions at the expense of her brother's: 'His was but as the knowledge of the outside of a clock-work machine, while your's was that of all the finer springs and movements of the inside.'[1]

Yet, despite the close connection between these novelists and Richardson and despite the certain influence of his work, both Sarah Fielding and Frances Sheridan subtly questioned some of the Richardsonian assumptions. Both authors examined the implications of sentimental principles and beliefs, and the problems of their expression in society; both investigated the sentimental obsession with female chastity and probed the implications of an altruism and familial piety that could so easily become self-destructive masochism.

Sarah Fielding and Frances Sheridan are sentimental novelists who deal with serious moral problems: how much is owed to others and how much to the self, to what extent the mental constructions of morality and religion should weigh against the desire for fulfilment and gratification. The sentimental philosophy here is politically and socially significant and

161

psychologically complicated, far from the apolitical self-indulgence associated with the Cult of Sensibility. The romantic novels which simply elevated feminine sensibility without investigating what sort of world it could flourish in served an important escapist function for many women, but the novels of sentiment written by Fielding and Sheridan disturb the reader into confronting the price as well as the charms of sentimental virtue and femininity.

Both women share their names with more famous male relatives, the novelist Henry Fielding, Sarah's brother, and Richard Brinsley Sheridan, Frances's son. This is simply a coincidence, but it is a symbolic one. For both women would have defined themselves in familial terms, as sister and mother. There has been much emphasis on the help Henry gave to Sarah – literary history often ascribes the best passages of female writing to men – less on what both women gave to their men.[2] But what Henry certainly helped provide for his sister was the acceptable image of the woman writer. In the preface he wrote to the second edition of her *David Simple* he stressed her lack of learning and literary experience but he extolled her feeling heart: 'Sex and Age entitle her to the gentlest Criticism,' he declared. The Sarah Fielding he created (with her assistance) appealed to male readers and literary promoters through the humility and gratitude of the stance, as well as through subject matter and style.

Perhaps as attractive to female readers like Elizabeth Carter and Catherine Talbot, both of whom admired her, was her modest admission that she was not writing for fame but from financial necessity – she remained unmarried and had only a small income with which to support herself. Such a motive suited the retiring feminine image. Again out of step with English taste, as she had been in her admiration of Con Phillips, Lady Mary Wortley Montagu in Italy found such middle-class excuses tiresome and she pitied Sarah Fielding for being 'constrained in her circumstances to seek her bread by a method I do not doubt she despises'.[3]

Frances Sheridan was also admired by Johnson and Richardson and she too conformed to the image of the virtuous woman writer. Married to Thomas Sheridan, a respectable but sometimes impecunious theatre manager and man of letters, she was seen by many as primarily a wife and mother. And, despite her success in many literary genres, unlike the hapless Laetitia Pilkington she 'never forgot, that though wit may dazzle, yet esteem is only due to benevolence of heart and purity of mind'.

These pious words were written by Mrs Sheridan's granddaughter, Alicia Lefanu, whose biography of 1824 portrays an exemplary figure.

Like many of the prefaces of the mid-eighteenth century, as well as Victorian biographies of other female authors – Mrs Gaskell's life of Charlotte Brontë, for example – the main concern is that the woman should appear domestic. Frances Sheridan is described as combining literary ability with 'every domestic virtue that most endears and distinguishes a woman'; her mind was pure, her character 'modest, diffident, and gentle'. When fortune smiled on her, she 'sacrificed the gratifications of vanity . . . to the duties and vocations' of wife and mother, while popularity never superseded 'the virtues which are peculiar to her sex, and which rendered her a model, whether considered as a wife, a mother, or a friend'.[4]

Even her husband is forced into the portrait by Lefanu. Although Frances admired him as a literary man and became acquainted with him by writing on his behalf in one of the pamphlet wars in which he was frequently involved in Dublin, her granddaughter yet sees the attraction in domestic terms: 'It was his exemplary conduct as a son, a brother, and a friend, that riveted her esteem.' Needless to say Frances made an exemplary wife and died in particularly wifely fashion:

> She never omitted, during the course of this, her last illness . . . to issue daily, from her sick bed, the necessary domestic orders, evincing the same anxiety to procure the articles which he particularly liked, and in every point great or small to study his welfare and comfort, which had made her, in her days of health, as valuable as a directress of his household, as she was charming in the light of a friend and companion.[5]

Truly an exemplary end.

Alicia Lefanu has more difficulty with Frances as daughter than as wife. Her father, an Anglican clergyman in Ireland, thought that writing was 'perfectly superfluous in the education of a female . . . The Doctor considered the possession of this art as tending to nothing but the multiplication of love-letters, or the scarcely less dangerous interchange of sentiment in the confidential effusions of female correspondence.'[6] This parental opposition does not disturb the sentimental presentation because its quaintness rather than its threat is underlined; the father is an eccentric 'oddity' who, by the time his daughter reaches adulthood, is humbled into 'mental imbecility'.

When Frances Sheridan writes seriously, she does so, like Sarah Fielding, for money; she publishes only when her husband is in financial difficulties, for only then is the cultivation of literature truly compatible 'with the duties more exclusively appropriated to the female sex'. As Alicia Lefanu ringingly concludes: 'The authoress of some of the most admired productions of her time was also acknowledged to excel in every

163

branch of domestic economy.' Her most famous novel, *The Memoirs of Miss Sidney Bidulph*, becomes an expression of its author's wifely image; it is praised by Lefanu: 'Love was reduced to his subordinate place, and made subservient to the triumph of wedded constancy, and the exercise of domestic duties and affections.'

Given their support by respected literary men and women, as well as the exemplary pattern of their lives, it would be easy to see Sarah Fielding and Frances Sheridan as examples of collusion with the eighteenth-century ideology of femininity. Certainly neither woman makes the open protest of Laetitia Pilkington or slightly shocks with her down-to-earth detail in the manner of Lennox and Haywood. (There do, however, remain a few unsettling episodes in Sheridan, a disapproved lover tending the diseased breast of his lady for instance.) Yet there are advantages to their conformity and their constriction in subject matter. Both characteristics allow the authors to concentrate on and investigate the limited material of consciousness, existing within social constraints, as well as the ideology of Christian sentimentalism. In addition, not needing to seduce, outrage or threaten, these women can use the autobiographical impulse, so strong in female writing, to present the material with commitment but also with some distance.

Yet, despite the obvious aesthetic achievement of their best work and despite their approval by literary men revered in the twentieth as well as the eighteenth century as arbiters of culture, Frances Sheridan and Sarah Fielding fell out of the cultural memory as thoroughly as the scandalous Delarivier Manley or Laetitia Pilkington, and indeed all women writers before Jane Austen. The disappearance suggests that they may have had literary faults beyond their sex.

One might of course be found in their image as writers. Here the very construction of them as devoted wives and domestic women, so seductive to the eighteenth century, was probably their downfall. In a post-Romantic culture that values art as antagonistic to domesticity and its virtues and the artist as self-asserting rather than self-sacrificing, more of a selfish child than a devoted mother, such ladies as Sheridan and Fielding would be deemed incapable of producing high art.

And there is a problem too with their mode, or, perhaps one should say, with our traditional manner of regarding their mode. In the 'rise of the novel' view, it is assumed that fiction is primarily the realistic novel and that the nineteenth-century version is the object to which every fiction writer in the eighteenth century is struggling, with more or less success. But this version of literary history was obviously unknown to writers in the period and it seems that no two practitioners of the art of the 'novel' would have agreed on its definition or progress.[7] Certainly the novel of sentiment such as Frances Sheridan and Sarah Fielding wrote is not aiming at surface realism – in one case the characters are allegorically named, as they are in *Betsy Thoughtless*, in the other the events are schematic and exemplary, as they are in *The Female Quixote*. Henry Fielding claimed of his sister's fiction:

> the Merit of this Work consists in a vast Penetration into human Nature, a deep and profound Discernment of all the Mazes, Windings and Labyrinths, which perplex the Heart of Man to such a degree, that he is himself often incapable of seeing through them.[8]

More than the 'novels' of Manley and Behn, then, the kind of fiction Fielding and Sheridan wrote delivers moral generalisation and it tries in sentimental fashion to teach assent to its morality through an emotional appeal to the reader. The aim is social and psychological analysis, not verisimilitude and the catching of *individual* personality.

David Simple and *Sidney Bidulph* are both deeply concerned with sentimental philosophy. They ask how a person should live in society and investigate the ultimate limitations of any route through the world. In this respect they are a cross between the wayfaring quest of romance and its religious counterpart such as *Pilgrim's Progress* which, allegorising and spiritualising the quest, in the end proves its inadequacy in the world. In concern they are close to Richardson, but although the women writers clearly feel the power of his myth, they avoid some of its implications in much the same way as Richardson's correspondent Lady Echlin had recoiled from the ultimate expression of *Clarissa*. By so doing they can no longer avail themselves of its comforting message of power from powerlessness, the almost magical quality of the dying feminine victim. Sarah Fielding makes her protagonist a man although his predicament remains quintessentially female, while in *Sidney Bidulph* the heroine can suffer extremely but does not die to obtain reverence.[9] The morality both novels teach is shown as painful and ineffective in worldly terms. The shadow of the afterlife – without which such pain would be impossible to enjoy in art or endure in life according to Richardson – is far more discernible than in the fiction of high sensibility, but the sense of it is less able than in *Clarissa* to compensate for the generalised ills in this world.

David Simple recounts the life of a male ingenu, the choice of gender allowing a picaresque plot without turning the hero into a knowing rogue or predator like Aphra Behn's Sylvia. With a male character as victim, the progress becomes an analogue of the human predicament, not simply the female one. A man who takes on feminine qualities avoids rape and abandonment, but he can suffer most of the other ills society inflicts on the gentle and the caring. The action of the first part is the search for a friend, 'a little Community as it were of two, to the Happiness of which all the Action of both should tend with an absolute disregard of any selfish and separate Interest'. By the end David has formed a fellowship of four souls with which he travels into the miseries of the second part.

Sidney Bidulph is a rather different novel. Although it seems in some ways the typical sentimental one of female virtue in distress and has a recognised social world of decorum, marriage markets, drawing-room embarrassment and inadequate mothers, it is really a female equivalent of *David Simple*. The heroine is not seduced and abandoned or tested beyond endurance, but is simply caught like David in the sentimental beliefs in delicacy and honour which cause pain but for which there is yet no decent alternative. Set in the past with its future therefore known, it expresses an almost elegiac sense that the compassion and benevolence so necessary for human life, like the femininity that best expresses them, inevitably form social victims – victims who are powerful only in the fact that they can entail their misery on those who love them.

Written as a series of long letters to an absent female friend, it tells the mournful story of Sidney Bidulph who loves and is beloved by a passionate man, Faulkland, who has been tricked into a single sexual slip with the niece of the villainous Mrs Gerrarde, described – ominously from a friend of Samuel Johnson – as an 'Amazon'. When Sidney's loving but unimaginative mother discovers this slip, she opposes the match, and the obedient Sidney miserably concurs. She is persuaded to marry another man and finds some happiness in domestic duty and in her children. But again Mrs Gerrarde intervenes and alienates the affections of the husband, who is persuaded into jealousy of Faulkland. Taking on the role of guardian, so common a feature of female novels, Faulkland pretends love to Mrs Gerrarde to carry her off and gallantly save Sidney. Husband and wife are reconciled and the husband dies. But, still inspired by notions of propriety, duty and absolute chastity, Sidney persuades Faulkland to marry his first mistress. Unfortunately she has been deceived by the girl's parade of herself as virtue in distress and the marriage soon dishonours Faulkland. When he believes that he has accidentally killed his wife in adultery, he flees England, having first persuaded Sidney at last to marry him. When both learn his wife is alive, he despairs and seems to will himself to die, while she, with resignation, heads into a life which a narrator informs us will be a series of deep misfortunes. The ending is a confusion of disastrous and pathetic events, the telling of which is aimed at 'involuntary tears' in the reader.

General moral sentiments form the core of *David Simple* and they are scattered through *Sidney Bidulph*. Through maxims and anecdotes, right thinking and responding are taught; benevolence comes from empathy, not rational sympathy. Extremes inevitably and repeatedly demand their opposites; happiness must lead to misery, poverty to wealth. Characters are duplicated and stories repeated, the repetition suggesting that experiences are general and typical, and moral predicaments common and unavoidable. Characters themselves understand the stereotypes and plots they represent and occasionally draw attention to the way the mind is conditioned or blinkered by experience. A kind of Lockean claustrophobic association that both determines and limits, makes them see others as constructed like themselves: when David, who has been fooled and cheated by his brother, 'first set out, he had but half a Crown in his Pocket, a shilling of which he gave away in his Walk to a Beggar, who told him a Story of having been turned out of doors by an unnatural Brother'.

In *Sidney Bidulph* there is similar claustrophobic conditioning of the mind, but the point is less obviously made, for here it derives from sentiment itself and may simply represent a moral necessity. Through painful experience Sidney in particular becomes aware of the power and construction of mental images. A sense of honour and female reputation changes with changing circumstances, as Laetitia Pilkington had bitterly discovered, and with the change goes a change in attitude. Sidney has moments when she is aware of the transition from one state of mind to another, following a new mental image. So when she suddenly understands the whore where she had constructed virtue in distress and sees Faulkland 'in a light in which I had never before viewed him; overwhelmed by misfortunes, of which I accused myself as being the author', she admits, 'Shall I own it to you . . . I think I never loved him as I did at that moment.'[10] Yet she cannot completely embrace her new sense of her own constructing power and responsibility, and in the end she reiterates the doctrine of sentiment. Bitterly Faulkland notes that, after all the collapses, she can still control herself, and it is this feminine stoicism, this Christian resignation in her, that finally maddens him; it is he who dies, possibly by his own will.

In these portraits of hero and heroine there is an unsentimental sense of the mind constructing the world. But, as in *David Simple*, there ultimately remains a belief in the sentimental values. So this fiction gives a very different impression from the fiction of Behn, Haywood and Manley, whose sense of the constructing power of the mind was as acute but who allowed this sense to overwhelm morality.

The novel of sentiment includes readers, male or female, as principal characters to be educated in feeling. To help them learn, a hierarchy of responses is posited. After an affecting episode when a destitute man is aided in *David Simple*, two stances are decent: an ordinary person, a middling materialist, might see how pleased such a man would be to receive clothes, but the sensitive reader should understand the more poignant emotion available to a sick man who accepts sudden kindness. Again at a play the trivial mock the action but Lady True-Wit 'bursts into a Flood of Tears' when friends are reconciled. True wit is not clever repartee and innuendo, but a right alignment of the heart.

It is especially through the narrator that *David Simple* demands specific responses. The presence is consequently strong, by turns cajoling, berating, mocking and encouraging. For example, the narrator shows both in practice and in described response the proper limits of language, delineating the space where feeling is decently inarticulate, where patriarchal linguistic codes should be silenced by feminine feeling. Occasionally the refusal to write or describe indicates the typicality of the material: 'his Behaviour and Thoughts were so much like what is common on such Occasions, that to dwell long upon them, would be only a Repetition of what has been said a thousand times.' On other occasions the silences draw attention to the artifice of telling, the refusal of the novel to form a fantasy world. But the most important gap comes from the reluctance to articulate deep feeling, the insistence on its sacredness as unlogical and pre-linguistic. Before fundamental emotion the narrator, like Jane Austen seventy years later, offers the tact and propriety of silence: 'Tenderness, when it comes to the height, is not to be described.'

Another exemplary response is the appropriate weeping. Copious public tears for oneself are not indicated, being a sign of the self-centred and trivial person. An arrogant rich woman 'for want of Words to vent her Rage . . . burst into Tears'. In the good person tears flow publicly only for another as a sign of empathy. Real suffering of the self requires either silence or the single tear, that sure mark of the sentimental soul. When friends part, the reader must cry but the characters should not, for fear of inflicting misery on others. When a beloved dies, the horror is 'too great to find Vent in tears'. The worthless and malicious rave, scream and faint at suffering; the good know such manners self-indulgent and self-centred.

In *Sidney Bidulph* too the true moments of emotion are silent, as in the reunion of husband and wife: 'we neither of us spoke; there was no language but tears, which we both shed plentifully. Mr Arnold sobbed as I pressed him to my bosom.'[11] Characters *do* work themselves up into emotional states of mind, like Sidney's mother, who exclaims, 'My poor, forsaken, virtuous child'. But the emotional manipulation is understood or the emotion itself is justified. When Faulkland's tears fall silently on

Sidney's hands, they are not self-indulgent tears of high sensibility, but the result of overwhelming events.

A passage towards the end of the last part of *David Simple* catches the pedagogy of silence and tears and the complicated relationship of characters, reader and author in the fiction of sentiment:

> Day after Day with Fear and Trembling to enter those very Chambers we used to fly to for Comfort, and to fly from them with bleeding Hearts that can contain no longer without the Vent of Sighs and Tears – to wake from every short Sleep (obtained only by long watching) dreading even to ask for our Friends, and to receive the continual Answer, that they spent the Night in Pain – to have each Day bring the same mournful Prospect of being again Witness of that Pain – to have our Minds so weakened by the continual Daggers that pierce it, that our Judgement is lost, and we hourly accuse ourselves for something we have done, or something we have omitted, condemning ourselves for what we cannot account for – this is a Scene of Misery, that, I believe, whoever has experienced, will think nothing in this World can equal; and a Scene I purposely chuse to mention in general Terms, lest if any gentle Reader has conceived an Affection for *David*, and his *Camilla*, should I say, thus *David*, and thus *Camilla* felt, it might too much wring and grieve the tender Heart. But by passing quickly over all the Sorrows that affected *David* and his *Camilla*, I would not be understood as if they felt not the paternal Concern for such Children being torn from them. The true Reason why I dwell not on that Concern, is, that Words cannot reach it – the sympathizing Heart must imagine it – and the Heart that has no sympathy, is not capable of receiving it. *David* was, on every tender Occasion, motionless with Grief; and *Camilla*, although her Mind was too humble to distort her Countenance, yet did the Tears flow in Streams from her Eyes, and she was at once a Picture of the highest Sorrow and the highest Resignation; for Clamour is rather a Proof of Affectation than of a Mind truly afflicted; and tender Sorrow neither seeks nor wants Language to express itself.[12]

Here narrator, character, and reader are joined in a common experience so miserable that pure emotion not its description is needed.

Full detail like full physical response would be self-indulgent and overmanipulative. The sympathetic heart beats silently. The sentimental novel directs a blow at the passionate female and her bombastic expression, the self-assertive characters of Behn and Manley who would have railed against fate as well as the female condition, and would certainly have distorted their far from humble countenances. In a way the whole enterprise of sentimental fiction aims at its own silencing. Yet it *has* spoken at length.

Sidney Bidulph is as exemplary as *David Simple*, although the first-person narrative obscures this at the outset. There are devices to heighten the significance of the heroine, who presents herself initially as a lady of some intelligence and satiric wit. So when grief disorganises her pen, a doctor takes over and forms Sidney into an aesthetically pleasing and spiritually significant tableau: 'Surely nothing ever appeared so graceful . . . For my part, I looked on her with such reverence, that she appeared to me like an angel, interceding for us poor mortal sinners.' In the fiction of high sensibility such reverence would be demanded simply for the idea of femininity; here, however, suffering explains the attitudes.

Sidney excels not simply in feeling but in the fineness of her moral response. An example is her second refusal of Faulkland, brought about in part by her demand that a man have the same high standards of morality as a woman and in part by her sense of self-esteem:

> what should I now bring to your arms? A person faded by grief; a reputation (though undeservedly) once called into question; a little helpless family without fortune; a widowed heart, dead to love, and incapable of pleasure. Oh, Sir! could I bear to be your wife in such conditions? Indebted to you as I am, past a possibility of my ever making you a return, to what a mighty sum would you raise the obligation? How poor would you make me in my own eyes? Humbled as I am by adversity, my soul has still too much pride, or let me call it delicacy, to submit to this.[13]

Because in *David Simple* the hero takes on the role of the female, the sentimental female character seems to duplicate him, but Cynthia, the friend rather than simply the exemplary wife, is allowed a little astringency, a pale shadow of the antagonism of Manley's women. The identification of woman and sentiment is so complete that she can, as David cannot with propriety, criticise the social order in a way always implicit in sentimental writing but impossible to express directly in sentimental terms. Like many secondary women in female novels, then, those of Fanny Burney later for example, she can articulate a kind of feminism that encourages moral judgements in the reader; here it comes through description of the mercenary unions of patriarchy, so often obscured by codes of chivalry. This is how she renders a proposal of marriage:

> I like your Person, hear you have had a sober Education, think it time to have an Heir to my Estate, and am willing, if you consent to it, to make you my Wife; notwithstanding your Father tells me, he can't lay you down above two thousand Pounds. I am none of those nonsensical Fools that can whine and make romantick Love, I leave that to younger Brothers, let my Estate speak for me; I shall expect nothing from you, but that you will retire into the Country with me, and take care of my Family, I must inform you, I shall desire to have every thing in order; for I love good Eating and Drinking, and have been used to have my own Humour from my Youth,

which, if you will observe and comply with, I shall be very kind to you, and take care of the main Chance for you and your Children. I made him a low Court'sey, and thanked him for the Honour he intended me; but told him, I had no kind of Ambition to be his upper Servant . . .[14]

The Aphra Behn type of views held here by Cynthia are not undercut, but she herself is undermined by her less than exemplary feelings for her persecutors. Assertion of rights precludes the victim, and this kind of feminism moves towards the rationalism of the ultimately poisonous character, Mr Orgueil, and seems oddly masculine in the gender economy of the novel.[15]

The summary of sentimental philosophy in *David Simple* is tenderness, that supreme social virtue according to David Hume.[16] Occasionally one might suspect that the simple tender David is being treated ironically but it would be an improper suspicion. Tenderness must always be reverenced. David requires strong proofs of ill will but quickly discerns signs of tenderness; only lack of tenderness really risks his condemnation: 'to see another in Misery, and be insensible of it, would be a Proof of the want of that tenderness I so much admire.'

Tenderness acts most strongly within domestic relationships and consequently the family is much valued. Father and daughter form an especially emotive tie, or brother and sister, these heterosexual domestic pairs assuming more resonance than the romantic coupling of lovers. Inevitably the sexual passion is played down. The heroine Camilla wishes to live with her father; when she does so, marriage is of no further concern to her: 'It was impossible for me to change my Situation for a happier, for, in my Opinion, to live with any one we love, and find that every Action we do is pleasing to them is the Height of human Felicity.' (In *Emma* Jane Austen would comment rather wryly on this sentimental opinion when the heroine declares she is entirely happy with her father until it rushes through her with the speed of an arrow that she wants to marry her neighbour.) In bad characters, sexual passion has often destroyed tenderness, for passion is a frenzy that distorts more than the face; it kills friendship by substituting jealousy for generosity. The sentimentalist understands that great affection can exist without appetite, but the hard-hearted find the two inextricably joined. True sentimental ties form relatives not lovers.

In *Sidney Bidulph*, too, domesticity is good, 'a scene of still life' as the heroine calls it. Love in Faulkland goes beyond sentimental affection and is wonderful, but dangerous to ordinary existence. Constantly Sidney retreats from his fiery passion. She loves him from the beginning but only marries him when he is brought down and humbled. At crucial moments there is always a reason not to take him and put herself in his power.

Sentimental relationships are caught in female friendship, such as the tie between the correspondents of the novel, too distant to be of any practical help to each other – 'We can have but *one friend* to share our heart, to whom we have no reserve, and whose loss is irreparable' – in the unfinancial ties of service, of mistress and maid who unthreateningly shift their social status, and, above all, in the filial bond. 'How delightful are the sensations . . . that I feel hourly springing in my heart!' exclaims Sidney, 'Surely the tenderness of a mother can never be sufficiently repaid – I never see my dear little girl, but I think such were the tender sentiments, the sweet anxieties, that my honoured and beloved mother felt . . .'[17] But filial sentiment exists within society and its rules, and, when she is turned out of her husband's house, she cannot take her children for she has no claim to them. More overwhelmingly, it is her sentimental respect for her tender mother that precipitates all her unhappiness in society.

People of sentiment will not work to improve their living standard or give themselves consequence over others. If disasters befall them – usually through no fault of their own but rather through impersonal social misfortunes of the law or, what is perhaps the favourite device, being surety for a friend – they simply consume less. Sometimes they find something unprofitable to do, like digging a little garden; this will certainly not breed turnips for livestock, in accordance with new agricultural theory, often not even potatoes, but usually flowers. Or they may sew a little for a small fee. Sidney Bidulph is found by her future husband reading Horace and is lightly rebuked by him for ignoring her sewing; she is hurt but not affronted and years later when she is poor it is, as she wryly notes, her sewing not her Horace that she needs.

Most commonly the person of true sentiment suddenly and unexpectedly receives support from someone else. This is not earned but is more like grace from above, although the reader does have the sense that it is a just reward for a kind of personality. Feeling and money, cash and compassion become weirdly interchangeable. The device, which will be much used in the novels of sensibility, is a fantastic one turning on the notion of a benefactor with no authoritarian threat to the benefited, only infinite benevolence.

The problem of sentiment in both *David Simple* and *Sidney Bidulph* is the problem of the isolated nuclear family: its precariousness in a malicious world and its reliance on the benevolence of others. There is no legislation or external revolution that can bring about the sentimental order, and rectitude on principle or the rationalism embraced by the early feminists is rigorously opposed through the frightening depiction of Mr Orgueil:

> I look upon Compassion, Sir, to be a very great Weakness, the real Love of *Rectitude* is the Motive of all my Actions. If I could be moved by Compassion in my Temper to relieve another, the *Merit* of it would be entirely lost, because it would be done chiefly to please myself. But when I do for any one, what they have a Right to demand from me, by the Laws of Society and right Reason, then it becomes *real Virtue*, and *sound Wisdom*.[18]

To act correctly owing to correct principle is to find no use for the sentimental qualities of compassion and tenderness. The principled person easily becomes complacent and priggish; in time, more importantly, he can grow cruel, as Part II strikingly reveals. With principle and rationalism denied there is no systematic and general way forward into a better world.

At the end of *Sidney Bidulph* and in Part II of *David Simple* sentiment suffers its logical worldly defeat. The characters are forced into the immobility or contingency of the family and dependants. The sentimental domestic reunions and the tableaux of affection, so movingly presented in sentimental art, give way to scenes of separation and death, and benevolent hearts become prey to predators. In Part I, David Simple thought that he had found a true sentimental community on earth among his relatives and friends, a pale analogue of the heavenly community. But he discovers in Part II, as Sidney Bidulph would also do, that earth is absolutely distinct from heaven. The unchristian presumptuous nature of the sentimental enterprise when confined to earth grows clear, as well as its dependence in defeat on the Christian narrative.

Happiness, which seemed possible within the family of benevolent people in isolated country places, is destroyed when these are put into a wider context. The sentimentalist must sometimes leave the family, and the country like the town is full of other people. Selfishness and malice are as strong as compassion and altruism, and the law can kill benevolence. The family weighs down both David and Sidney and entangles them 'in the snare of [their] love for others'. David in particular, while caring for his family, grows afraid and inactive. Only faith can help at this juncture, and the pessimistic Christian takes over from the optimistic sentimentalist:

> I thought myself at home in this World, and attached my Heart to the Enjoyment of it, as strongly, though in different Ways, as does the Miser or Ambitious – . . . when Poverty broke in upon us, I found my mind in such Chains as are much worse than any Slavery of the Body . . . my Eyes were

forced wide open, to discover the Fallacy of fancying any real or lasting Happiness can arise from an Attachment to Objects subject to infirmities, Diseases, and to certain Death; and I would not, for any Thing this World can give, lead over again the last Twelve-month of my Life.[19]

In both *David Simple* and *Sidney Bidulph* there are slight modifications of this pessimism. In the former it occurs through a nod towards the Richardsonian solution of redemptive female death and an improved community. Camilla, David's wife, dies like Clarissa in an exemplary scene. The only two good characters left alive are Cynthia and the daughter of David and Camilla, another Camilla, both cared for by an unknown patron. This ending of providentially supported female community – echoing to a completely different effect the exhausted female communities of Manley and Haywood – moves towards the escapism of noneconomic, nonpolitical female bonding, characteristic of the novel of sensibility. Power through sentimental struggle in an evil world has been denied, but the extreme impotence of women promises a quasi-magical power entirely outside the bourgeois economy in which the rest of the novel has functioned.

Richardson had declared that the sufferings of Clarissa would be intolerable to read if it were not for an afterlife. The same could be said of *Sidney Bidulph*, of which Johnson remarked: 'I know not, Madam! that you have a right, upon moral principles, to make your readers suffer so much.'[20] In the novel Frances Sheridan follows Richardson's Christian scheme and sees the conclusion of the sentimental way in heaven which validates and justifies earthly sufferings. Its preface discusses the issue of whether virtue should be rewarded in literature and points out that, because there is a Christian afterlife, there is no need to impose a happy ending. So in *Sidney Bidulph* she can show that her heroine 'tho' a woman of most exemplary virtue, was, thro' the course of her whole life, persecuted by a variety of strange misfortunes'. Since Sidney's portion is so absolutely 'affliction', if one is not to arraign providence, there must be a belief in justice hereafter.

Yet, as in *David Simple*, a point is reached in the novel where the moral value of religious belief and sentiment is almost questioned:

> When I reflect on the past, when I survey the present, and my foreboding heart whispers to me the future sufferings of our dear unhappy Mr Faulkland, all my philosophy forsakes me. I have borne up under my own sorrows – his quite subdue me.[21]

Sentiment seems to be destroying the self and itself, with only partial help needed from the villains. As Sidney's brother remarks, it is all 'a series of fatal events, each of which was occasioned by motives in themselves laudable . . .'[22]

174

David Simple clearly displays the sentimental predicament. A resolute anti-sentimentalist like Lady Mary Wortley Montagu can remark tartly of the novel that the actual moral was 'the ill consequences of not providing against casual losses', but the more sympathetic reader who accepts the sentimental values of kindness, generosity and benevolence must find satisfaction only in the clarity of the vision if it seems that the shadowy afterlife provides insufficient.[23]

With *Sidney Bidulph*, however, there is a kind of psychological comfort which links the novel to the extremes of the period – to Aphra Behn with Angellica's flaunted sign and to Mary Wollstonecraft with her mud-bespattered one. Richardson had given immense reverence to the female victim, turned almost into a Christ figure in her redemptive ability in death. But Frances Sheridan avoids this route for her self-conscious heroine and gives her instead the power of self-dramatisation which the writing act has always implied and which had been especially apparent from the inception of the novel. With this power, Sidney Bidulph can in a way accept her sentimental role without necessarily having any hope of changing it: 'I was born to sacrifice my own peace to that of other people.' This resignation is somehow not pathetic but almost self-assertive – the heroine becomes that approved biblical character, the peculiarly afflicted of the Lord. When Mary Wollstonecraft declared herself a sign for others, she had lost the sense of the Christian scheme, and gratification had to come in this life, in the idea of a female future. With Sidney there is a similar self-dramatisation in affliction although the consolation in sentiment remains resolutely Christian:

> I have been set up as a mark . . . let me fulfil the intention of my Maker, by shewing a perfect resignation to His will. I hope my task is almost finished, and that He will soon permit me to return to the dust from which I came.[24]

When at the end her voice is silenced, her friend takes up the narration and accepts Sidney's self-created image:

> Many and bitter were the sufferings she had already endured; but she was, to use her own words, *Set up as a mark*; and the deep afflictions that still pursued her, and clouded even her latter days with misfortunes, may serve to shew, that it is not *here* that true virtue is to look for its reward . . . this reflection . . . had been her chief, so was it her last and only consolation.[25]

But all these hints and hopes make cold comfort, lacking the warmth of desire in the early work of Manley, Haywood and Behn and even of the Duchess of Newcastle. It is no wonder that other women writers fled from the austere logic of sentiment into the self-indulgence of a far more gratifying sensibility.

10

THE FANTASY OF SENSIBILITY:
FRANCES BROOKE AND SUSANNAH GUNNING

As written by Sarah Fielding and Frances Sheridan, the moral novel of sentiment elevated femininity and feminine values, but it placed them in an awkward and hostile environment. Whatever sly gratification in self-dramatisation there might have been, the overt reward in this world was only in the blissful domestic groupings, groupings which proved as transitory as the sentimental displays that expressed them. The main reward was in the next world, where alone sentimental values could be permanently established. In the novel of sensibility, however, the moral lessons of sentiment continued in passing, but they were far less stressed than the emotional responses of the characters and reader. The implications of sentimental philosophy were not tested and sentimental values were allowed to flourish unopposed – except by coarse, mercenary people in trade, whose habits and standards were easily snubbed. Virtue was clearly manifested as sensitivity of response, exquisite sensibility, even more than as active benevolence. If such 'virtue' proved fatal to the heroine, it usually resulted in a warm glow of melancholy in the onlookers; if the ending was happy, it commonly included an addition of material possessions. 'But why,' exclaimed Mary Wollstonecraft in exasperation at this fiction, 'is virtue to be always rewarded with a coach and six?'[1]

Frances Brooke and the Minifie sisters, Margaret and Susannah, were popular writers of the mid-eighteenth century, composing novels of sensibility primarily for a female audience, although Frances Brooke, with Charlotte Lennox, Sarah Fielding and Frances Sheridan, was much appreciated by Johnson and Richardson. The *Monthly Review* added Brooke 'to the number of learned and ingenious Ladies whom we have had the honour of celebrating', although the praise was for her tragedy rather than for her novels, and John Duncombe included her in the second edition of his *Feminiad* (1757).[2] Despite the independent attitude that propelled Frances Brooke to London to try her literary fortune, then, her public image – she was the daughter and later wife of clergymen – was typical of the new woman novelist and was utterly respectable. Such an image would not in any way have been modified by the publication of her novel *The History of Lady Julia Mandeville* in 1763.[3]

The 'Miss Minifies of Fairwater in Somersetshire' also came before the public with propriety, printing by subscription *The Histories of Lady Frances S— and Lady Caroline S—* in 1763. They made sure of their respectable image by asserting in the dedication that the novel was written 'with the warmest sentiments of virtue and honour' and by delivering a pious version of the sentimental story of virtue in distress: 'a helpless Orphan, conducted by the hand of Providence'. There is 'something sacred' in the display of 'suffering innocency' asserted the Miss Minifies, quoting Addison. Twenty-seven pages of subscribers followed the dedication, many of whom declared they would buy two or three sets of the work.

The Minifie sisters were a successful partnership, and they went to press again in 1766. After the first novel, subsequent ones were printed by publishers, obviously impressed by their subscription efforts. By 1780, however, Margaret Minifie was publishing alone, although the content of her novels – virtuous orphans marrying into the aristocracy – had not changed since her days in tandem. Her more prolific sister Susannah, meanwhile, seemed to have entered her own fiction with a most advantageous marriage. Five years after the publication of her first novel in 1763, she married Captain Gunning, soon to be elevated to Lieutenant-General Gunning, brother to the beautiful Gunning sisters, who were famous for their remarkably aristocratic marriages. Her 'adventures' real and fictional should have been over.

Yet, after fifteen years of marriage, Susannah Gunning returned to the novel with *Coombe Wood* (1783). More than ever sentimental in its main characters, the work suggested in its subsidiary ones that Mrs Gunning had possibly experienced some modification of her own sentimental depiction of marriage.

The three novels, *Lady Julia Mandeville*, *Lady Frances S—* and *Coombe Wood*, all popular with the public, are not great works but they are representative of the women's novel in the mid-eighteenth century in both content and technique. Tissues of clichés and influences, artificial in language and characterisation, they purvey a common fantasy: of passive femininity sometimes made powerful through death but more usually through the extreme reverential attitude of others towards it. An ironic or mocking voice is often incorporated in them, in memory of Manley's

Intelligence, Richardson's Anna Howe or even Frances Brooke's magazine character Mary Singleton, but like Anna Howe's it is ultimately overwhelmed by the sentimental tone and there is no real alternative to the sentimental construction of femininity, no modification or subversion of its pieties.

In *Lady Julia Mandeville* the noble, cultured but apparently poor Harry is staying at the house of the rich and benevolent Lord Belmont and his daughter Julia. Friendship glides into love, but Harry fears to declare himself to Lord Belmont because of his poverty. Leaving the house out of delicacy, he grows convinced that Julia is about to marry Lord Melvin, although in fact the preparations of which he learns are for his own wedding – it transpires that he is Lord Belmont's heir, kept in ignorance of his expectations so that his character can be improved and tested through poverty (the sentimental hero usually has a period as poor man). Owing to his kindness to a friend, however, the letter revealing all is delayed. Consumed with jealousy, Harry forces Lord Melvin to a duel. He is mortally wounded and Julia's death from grief follows. The only happiness is left to the subsidiary pairs.

This story is less typical than those of the Minifies in the sad rather than rewarded ending of virtue in distress, but other elements are more conforming: the sublime sensibility of the hero and heroine, and the inconsequentiality of the plot compared with the substantial horrors of *David Simple* and *Sidney Bidulph*. There is no real villainy, only a delayed letter, and distress seems in the nature of things rather than specifically caused; it appears almost demanded by the superlative sensitivity of the heroine.

The story of *Lady Julia Mandeville* is told through two correspondents who write what seems more like two journals than a series of letters, since what they describe requires no reply or comment. The first correspondent is the sentimental Harry, hero of the tale, and the second is the lively widow Lady Anne Wilmot, allowed sprightliness rather than pathos because of her marital status (her marriage had not been a love match). Through these two writers, the sentimental heroine Julia can be painted without any activity on her own part; consequently she can avoid the narcissistic effect that so often marks the writing sentimental girl, especially in novels by men – Richardson's *Pamela* is an obvious example.

In *Lady Frances S—* the heroine is, like Julia Mandeville, all quivering sensibility and kindess, but her main depicter is less elevated, given as she is to detailed descriptions of the heroine's elaborate dress, her 'negligently becoming' style. The constant awareness of flounces and fringes helps make the writer less worthy of being a heroine than Lady Frances and should add some complexity to the picture of femininity conveyed by the heroine. But in this novel the effect is more of contradiction than of complexity, for plot and diction are firmly on the side of literary sensibility. In *Coombe Wood* the position of writer-foil is given to a supremely trivial aristocratic woman, Lady Lucy, whose irreverent and racy prose is much more extreme, bitchy and snobbish than any in the earlier Minifie novels. But she has been largely relieved of the task of depicting the sensitive heroine.

Each of the works provides the sentimental community. In *Lady Julia Mandeville* Lord Belmont's estate is the kind of society that David Simple was trying to create for himself. It is the domestic ideal combined with an aristocratic way of life and with effortless privilege and ease. It is 'magnificence without profusion', the smiling face of 'patriarchal government'. In some ways indeed it inherits the societal ideals of Manley and Behn, the idealisation of the courtly reign of Charles II, for justice in this model is benevolent and personal, quite distinct from abstract impersonal law. But the ideal is far more familial than the utopias described in the Restoration and much is made of the 'tender pleasing duties of husband and of father'.[4]

The sense of hierarchy in this community is absolute but clothed in sentiment. All ranks, for example, enjoy the rustic dance but then the higher ones retire for conversation 'amongst those of the first sense and politeness'. The ideal is 'health, peace, content, and soft domestic tenderness', as well as a stance of each to each of 'warm beneficence and ardent gratitude'. All appear interdependent and caring; ties are sentimental and uncommercial.

The society is also reclusive, in flight from the 'world' which it finds threatening. The sentimental domestic values flourish away from the city and fashionable society and they are expressed in opposition to trade, seen as mercenary, luxurious and vulgarly snobbish. In *Lady Julia Mandeville* a daughter of commerce, all pert, brown and oozing with 'city vivacity', is pitted against the languishing country aristocrat. But the influence of the commercial and grasping world cannot be entirely avoided and Harry's desire to rise exposes him to its incivilities.

Lady Frances S— also presents country houses as seats of harmony, and the work begins with the resounding cliché of contrast: 'Charming delightful Ashley! how reluctantly did I quit thy peaceful solitude for the noise and hurry of London.' In *Coombe Wood* the ideal is embodied in the old ancestral home properly inhabited by its owners, the gentry, rather than by dissipated aristocratic tenants. Response to virtuous gentlefolk is emotional and uncommercial and the good Miss Altham provokes a 'deluge of tears' from the eyes of faithful retainers and grateful peasants alike. But again, response is hierarchical, and the single tear of refined sensibility is confined to those of more exalted rank. The ideal here is like the one in *Lady Julia Mandeville*: domesticity with affluence, the trappings of aristocracy – including its titles – without its morality.

Coombe Wood was written in the 1780s and shows some sign of the sensationalising of the sentimental novel that was occurring towards the end of the century. So the utopia of Coombe Wood is delivered less in the familial descriptions so common in the earlier novels than in extreme almost gothic contrasts. The house as ideal home is blighted when the owner dies:

> What a change does death make, even in the appearance of the outside of a house? Not a blink of light to be seen from either of the windows – *no* chearful fire – Darkness, silence, and sorrow *now* succeeded to this *once* happy spot.[5]

A second contrast is the surprisingly powerful dystopia that occurs when the house is rented by frivolous, disorderly aristocrats from London and their riotous entourage. The new community lacks all civility, hierarchy and prudence, and under this management the garden goes to ruin, the stables fall apart and all the neighbourhood becomes demoralised. The antagonistic picture of aristocracy is as typical of the sentimental novel as its distaste for trade; the cynical worldly-wise values of the Restoration have degenerated into stupid dissipation and unthinking hedonism, and their degeneration helps the fictional consummation: the marriage of aristocracy with the virtuous lower ranks to form deliciously titled virtue.

The great message of the novels, even beyond sentimental community, is female sensibility, a sensibility that has wonderful powers and allure, with none of the strains of moral seriousness. A subsidiary female character of *Lady Julia Mandeville* is praised for being helpless, weak and exquisitely feminine, timid despite her beauty and inspiring love because she is unthreatening. Lady Julia herself personifies 'female softness' and 'exquisite sensibility'; she is 'artless, gentle, timid, soft, sincere, compassionate; awake to all the finer impressions of tenderness, and melting with pity for every human woe'.[6] Her body is the sentimental organ to perfection, expressing authentically her character and the feelings she cannot suppress; her soul is in her eyes. In a later novel of Frances Brooke, *The History of Emily Montague* (1769), the susceptible hero, who loves the heroine for her 'languishing eyes' and because 'she seems made to feel to a trembling excess the passion she cannot fail of inspiring', summarises the sentimental idea:

> What a charm, my dear Lucy, is there in sensibility! 'Tis the magnet which attracts all to itself: virtue may command esteem, understanding and talents admiration, beauty a transient desire: but 'tis sensibility alone can inspire love.[7]

Sarah Fielding would not have separated virtue from sensibility, and Manley and Haywood would not have separated it from beauty, nor desire from love. We are here clearly in the centre of the Cult of Sensibility.

In the first letter of *Coombe Wood*, the heroine is 'the charming innocent sufferer', passive and domestic – even when she is painted the portrait places her within a family group. When she leaves her home, she immediately enters another domestic community and the happy ending occurs when, her father having died, a new man accepts her as daughter and nurse. The oppositional woman is, however, the devil incarnate, a monster in human shape whom it would be 'an abuse to the sex' to call woman, so high is now the notion of femininity.

The extraordinary elevation of femininity is especially caught in the pictures within *Lady Frances S—*. Of Lady Frances herself, her friend writes, 'Wherever she moved, that part of the room was like the temple of some favourite saint.'[8] So pure are women that they become angels while still on earth. The good, dying Sophy dreams of her benevolent friend in heaven:

> She held the mirror to my face, bidding me look in it. I obeyed; but was so transformed, as to have no idea of myself, till the angelic form assured me, I saw no other. The reflection was more beautiful than fancy can paint . . .

Here the motif of the mirror, so often deplored when it reveals her charms to the narcissistic young girl like Lennox's Arabella, is used to elevate the woman into the angel. When Sophy actually dies, she does so, like so many sentimental heroines, with onlookers who are united and improved by her death. The watching man is inspired to 'a fervency near to devotion'.

In *Lady Julia Mandeville* Lady Anne in the beginning lightly mocks the heroine's excessive sensibility, her 'tear of tender sympathy'. She wonders at the unnecessary catastrophe in which the hero dies 'for having [inevitably] alleviated the distresses of his friend, for having sympathized in the afflictions of others' and the heroine because of her 'exquisitely tender heart', but she concludes with a pious question, 'Shall presumptuous man dare to arraign the ways of Heaven?' Ultimately she does not doubt the value of sensibility and her sprightly voice becomes the chronicler of the sentimental fate of the main characters and the interpreter of the rituals of female death.

181

Equally contained but potentially more disruptive is the voice of the resolutely unsentimental Lady Lucy of *Coombe Wood*, who energetically conveys her economic sense of marriage, far beyond that of the originally naughty Betty Thoughtless:

> What is a woman at five-and-twenty without her *town-house* – her *equipage* – her *jewels* – her *own* parties – and the consequence which all married women have with the *pretty* young men . . . I must marry; and, if *next* winter does not prove propitious, that awkward, unfashioned, conceited *thing*, swaddled in callicoe and lace, *must* be the man: a fortune of *two* hundred thousand pounds sounds *well*, and what are the *nabobs* to me? I have a title to *tag* on to their *mean* extraction.[9]

Unlike Lady Anne, she is not taken into the scheme of the book, although her values never represent an alternative, and she ends in the same mind as she began, planning to marry for money and having only momentarily, like *Mansfield Park*'s Mary Crawford, fancied a good, grave man. Like another character from Jane Austen, the vulgar Mrs Elton of *Emma*, she concludes the tale by mocking the provinciality of the heroine's appearance.

The heroes in these novels of sensibility are exaggeratedly feminised. With the women, they have tender sensibility and their creators are concerned, like early sentimental writers, to make the quality feminine, while insisting on its compatibility with manliness. 'If tenderness is a degradation to man, how was the most worthy then degraded!' The tears are 'manly' and are shed at stories of misery. What is distinct from earlier writers, however, is the stance of these heroes before their ladies: diffidence and awe. Perhaps *Emily Montague* most entirely catches the change, swerving quite clearly from the notion of man-as-monster, so marked in the Richardsonian novel and in the early women writers, and insisting instead on a hero with the 'tenderness of a woman', a man who will enter marriage as a subordinate, not as the master envisaged in Mr B's stern contract with Pamela.

The older sentimental man is a source of unthreatening and benevolent power. He is rarely a father, since the patriarchal power of the father in this society is too extreme for him to be easily feminised, unless he is made old, poor, or ill. Often this power will be in a grandfather, made safe by his advanced years, or in an uncle who can give money and protection without overwhelming with his authority. Such a man will have the status of the father but the sensibility of the hero, usually tinged with melancholy because of lost love; he will have 'womanish softness' combined with financial resources.

In *Lady Julia Mandeville* the aesthetic quality of the sentimental scheme is underlined. The ending is the public death of the heroine accompanied by general grief, so that her death and burial form a ritual of community, a reaffirmation of common domestic virtue. The beauty that is revealed becomes the compensation for the endless worldly defeats of sensibility, necessary to the scheme since virtuous sensibility requires distress to display itself. The spectators share in this beauty in their grief for the dead, and the rustic folk gain stature from their part in the mourning. As at a sentimental play all are improved by the demonstration of grief in others.

The rituals of feminine death are also necessary to prevent the overflowing of sensibility into hysteria and madness. They allow the violence of sorrow – of the kind from which the supremely sensitive Julia dies – to subside and give way to 'that pleasing melancholy, that tender regret, which, however strange it may appear, is one of the most charming sensations of the human heart'.[10] It is the pleasure of art in life, the confusion of fiction and living. Tragedy is pleasing because it taps grief only to a certain extent, and regulated grief is 'in the highest degree delightful'. Sentimental grief which results in tears is not devastating or disquieting but gently self-indulgent.

In *Sidney Bidulph* and *David Simple*, the emphasis was on the Christian scheme, on the fact that misery was not explained if one looked only at earthly life and that virtue was not financially or even emotionally rewarded. The display of unrelenting misery could only be justified by the idea that it encouraged a belief in an afterlife as compensation for the trials and miseries in this. In Frances Brooke's novel, however, the misery is described primarily for the sensation of misery itself and for the emotional gratification of spectators and readers. A kind of sensuality of distress is appearing, 'the voluptuousness of sorrow', very different from the generalised but acutely analysed pain of *David Simple*.

As can be discerned from the short quotations, the books do not aim at originality of expression any more than they aim at originality of situation and plot. *Lady Julia Mandeville* employs the artificial language of sensibility. Its dialogue is bombastic and theatrical and its descriptions hyperbolic and adjectival. 'Esteem' is inevitably qualified by 'sincere' and 'friendship' with 'tender'. It is written 'to the moment' in the exclamatory style Richardson had popularised and which to the modern reader often appears embarrassingly bathetic: 'But behold a more charming object than nature herself! the sweet, the young, the blooming Lady Julia, who is this instant stepping into her post-chaise with Lady Anne Wilmot! how unspeakably lovely!'

In the Minifies' *Lady Frances S—* and *Coombe Wood*, the clichés continue. Meetings are wet with tears and cheeks are flushed. The technicolour emotional moments are rendered in the conventional senti-

183

mental vocabulary, helped by an array of interrupted sentences, italics, dashes and exclamation marks, which are splattered over the pages and which aim to convey the wordless feeling the sentimental novel so much prized: 'Lady Frances fell at his *generous* feet, to thank him. And, O sweet, but awful sight! down by her side, dropped the venerable Mrs Worthley ... both at once ... lifted her from the ground. – This, Madam, said he, is too much; you have distress'd me.'[11] Characters express their psychological conflicts in absurdly elevated abstractions: 'Reason having deserted the steerage of my bosom, and hurried away by the violence of my passions, I suffered them to drive me with wild fury, over dreadful rocks and quick sands.' The heroine of *Coombe Wood* falls into 'an agony of tears' when her father speaks of stinting himself for her benefit and, when he dies, she is *too* tender, *too* delicate, and her mind replete with *too* much refinement to admit of any consolation but what she 'immediately receives from heaven'. Events are conveyed in the sensational, increasingly gothic language that does duty for analysis and even at times for narrative: 'bloated with imagined success, methinks I see him just ready to seize the victim of his revenge, when behold she is miraculously delivered by the force of her own virtue.' Although not different in essence from that of other contemporary novelists, the Minifies' style of fiction writing was so hyperbolic that the term 'minific' was coined for it.

The diction favoured by the Minifies is a variant of the bombastic theatrical style. Unlike an earlier writer like Manley, however, they convey no sense that their characters are meant to be conscious of role-playing. 'For Heaven's sake! most amiable of women, forbear the melancholy subject,' declares a character who is intended to be taken quite seriously, while the heroine refers to herself as 'the deserted Orphan'.

The most extreme style is kept for the expression of the man towards the woman. In Manley the erotic gaze was sometimes woman's, or woman could visualise and create herself as the erotic object of the man and so control his response. In this fiction, the sentimental gaze is frequently the lady's and it effeminises her object, the man, caught in the kind of detail usually reserved only for depictions of women: in *Coombe Wood*, Lord Edwin is on his knees before the heroine, who is half fainting, but who has sufficient consciousness to note that 'his graceful form' received 'additional grace from the disorder of his hair'.

The man's love is so reverential that he can hardly express himself coherently before his lady:

'My *Life*! my soul! (said he, as he threw himself at my feet) you have blasted my *hopes* – you have blasted my *reason* – you have blasted my youth – you have' –
  'Stop, my lord ... '[12]

When confronted by the sentimental heroine, even his male friend throws himself into extreme postures and expresses his feelings in the reverentially hyperbolic language which the lady seems always to command:

> The door opened — it was opened by herself, and I was admitted to the presence of an *Angel*; one hand, whiter than snow, she condescended to offer me; the other covered her eyes with her handkerchief. Be not angry I *only* lifted her hand towards my lips; she was *too* much of a *deity* for more; a *touch* would have been sacrilegious. I presumed *no* farther than to breathe a blessing. *Innocence* how great thy powers! How surpassing every human excellence! . . . Here I fell again at her feet: I begged, I prayed, I wept, and when I exclaimed, For God's sake! Madam, permit Lord Edwin *one* short interview, her reply was 'No, no, no, never, never, *never*,' The picture still lay on her lap; I looked at it, then at her: she sighed deep, shook her head, and signified by one of her white hands I should no longer kneel; and, whilst I was obeying her commands, I observed she cast a look at the picture, as if it was to be the *last*.[13]

It is undoubtedly silly, but it nonetheless represents a potent fantasy in the eighteenth century. Men instantly respond to the female gesture or 'motion' and 'involuntarily' drop down on their knees at displays of femininity, now far more powerful than the imagined heroics of the demanding heroines of Lennox's Arabella. Richardson's Clarissa had achieved this devotion but only when she was dying or dead; the Minifie heroines are 'soul-inspiring' at first glance and the heroine of *Coombe Wood* is given devotion without any effort beyond a posture of distress. Even the older women, at least those who have been mothers, are treated to this elaborate respect and are reverenced for simply existing; between entering a room and sitting down, Lady Margaret manages to give an impression of graciousness, quietness, ease, condescension, courtesy, sweetness and mildness.

Men have no chance in this world, and the common resolution of the sentimental novel is the domestification of the male, both rake and aristocrat; all learn 'the infinite blessing of a virtuous domestic education'. As for the sentimental heroines, if they are still alive, they are usually rewarded richly with property. The trivial aristocrat Lady Lucy, of *Coombe Wood*, is much mocked for her dreams of marriage for money: 'I will hang myself before I will marry, till I am certain of a fine sum for pin-money, and a prospect, at *least*, of a comfortable separate maintenance.'[14] Yet the virtuous heroine herself catches a man who arrives in a splendid equipage with numerous servants and fine white horses fleet as the wind, while her moment of bliss occurs when one man agrees to marry her as another presses into her hand a deed of gift of the house he had inherited. The racy vulgarity of Lady Lucy by no means mitigates the sentimental vulgarity of this consummation.

It is impossible to know how many young girls were overwhelmed by the fictional fantasy of the mid-eighteenth century and were made to expect not the derring-do of French romances as Lennox's Arabella had done but the equally unlikely devotion of men in marriage. Certainly many women wrote to their female friends in the hyperbolic style of fiction or used it to convey the refined sensibility they cultivated. Certainly, too, many moralists feared the power of the fantasy, and advice books to women throughout the period preach the danger of trusting in novels as a guide for conduct or of expecting their heady pictures to be realised in life.

In *The Histories of Lady Frances S— and Lady Caroline S—* a character at one point exclaims, 'Can nature produce such blot, in all its works, as a parent looking with envy on her own daughter!' If the sex of the parent is changed, this represents a collision of life and fiction, for it wonderfully foreshadows events in the life of Susannah Minifie Gunning, whose 'adventures' failed to terminate as they should have done, in marriage and sacred motherhood. For in the early 1790s Mrs Gunning found herself beyond the protection of her spouse and thrown into a world in which only her pen could save her. Her activity clarified the limitations of the sentimental vision while at the same time indicating how completely women had to convey themselves in its terms. Mrs Gunning has only the image of suffering feminine passivity and motherhood to assert, although she has ample evidence that some men at least refuse to enter the fantasy.

Named the 'Gunningiad' by Horace Walpole, the furore in the family of General and Mrs Gunning is not easy to disentangle at this distance but the documents are fascinating in the way they indicate Mrs Gunning's acceptance of the codes of the woman writer and the conventions of the novel she was writing, as well as the way in which the ideology of femininity tangles with the laws and habits of patriarchal England. The singular events provoked a spate of affidavits, true narratives and anonymous pamphlets, including two presumably written by men: *A Narrative of the Incidents which form the mystery in the family of General Gunning* and *A Friendly Letter to the Marquis of Lorn* by 'a Knight of Chivalry'. Like Susannah's *A Letter from Mrs Gunning addressed to His Grace, the Duke of Argyll*, her brother-in-law, they are all dated 1791. Not surprisingly, however, the female image is best created in Mrs Gunning's *Letter*, but it can be illuminated by the response in the other two accounts as well. In *Coombe Wood*, the heroine omits to fall in love with her worthy cousin who yet agrees to give her all his estate. Nothing quite like this happens in life.

The anonymous *Narrative* catches the popular taste in scandals that has not abated since the days of Manley and Pilkington. It also catches the rhetoric needed to justify it:

> No circumstance has occurred in the variegated circle of Fashion, for a long series of years, that has excited public attention, in so high degree, as the recent dissentions which have prevailed in the family of General Gunning. – To see a young lady, in the bloom of youth and beauty, banished from the house of him whom Nature had designed for her protector – to see the parent become the accuser of his child – the husband, of his wife – was to witness a spectacle of so strange and singular an aspect, as could not fail to work, in either sex, on every passion of the mind. The malignant sneer of Revenge has been excited – the benevolent tear of Pity has been moved – and the rancorous smile has been raised on the distorted features of Envy.[15]

As the *Morning Post* put it more pithily, the Gunning events were the 'public conversation of the town'.

General Gunning and his novelist wife had an unhappy marriage, which produced one daughter, Elizabeth, a lady of 'substantial excellence' according to the *Narrative*. She was well connected through the aristocratic marriages achieved by her father's sisters. Possibly she was courted both by the Marquis of Blandford and by her cousin, the Marquis of Lorn. According to the General's side of things, she was lovesick for the reluctant Lorn (the maiden all for-lorn, as a contemporary ballad inevitably put it); to nudge him towards matrimony, Elizabeth is supposed, either with her mother's help or with that of the Bowens, hangers-on of her father, to have forged not only love letters but also notes to and from the Duke of Marlborough, releasing herself from the Marquis of Blandford. This naming of the rival was, in the General's view, to have acted 'as a stimulus' to Lorn's love. In the opposing version, however, the General, caring nothing for his wife and daughter and wishing to spare himself the expense of their maintenance and of the inevitably large dowry, framed Elizabeth with the help of his creatures, the Bowens, so that he could eject both women. Although this explanation seems rather ingenious, the author of the *Narrative* clearly, if negatively, favours it: the question, 'What *interest* can a parent *possibly* have in impeding the felicity of his child?' is ponderously answered,

> It is *possible* that a parent – we must not be understood to allude to any existing or even probable case – whose daughter's attractive charms have procured her the offer of an union with a man of her choice – may, from motives of *avarice*, object to the connection, and, though opulent himself, may seek to impede her felicity that he may not open his purse.

187

Whatever the case, letters were forged and affixed with seals not usually used by the Duke of Marlborough, but obtained from his house, while the name Lorn took on an 'e', which, as Elizabeth pointed out, she was unlikely to have given her cousin. Messengers were bribed by one side or the other, and the Bowens implicated by each. They accused Elizabeth, 'this vile daughter of your's', of bribing them to forge letters, so fooling her mother, who in turn accused the Bowens of colluding with the General in his daughter's undoing. To complete the circle, an anonymous letter allied Elizabeth and her father. Certainly the General took a high moral and convenient tone over the affair, and his wife and daughter speedily left his house. (His tone was made discordant by his payment of a large fine shortly after for 'criminal conversation' with his tailor's wife.) Elizabeth fell ill and Susannah set about writing her vindication.

Each of the three writers on the Gunning mystery presents a careful self-image. The author of the *Narrative* is impartial and judicious, investigating on behalf of the public and its right to know; the Knight of Chivalry enters as the honest man, a mingling of rough and rude Miller of Dee – 'I want no man's fortune, I court no man's interest' – and the Sternean sentimentalist, the whimsical champion of distressed virtue – 'I will be thy friend, dear girl: I will protect thee, said I . . .' The most elaborately painted sign is, however, of Susannah Gunning, the former novel-writing Miss Minifie, and her 'angel' daughter.

The hyperbolic nature of Susannah Gunning's prose has not changed since she described the angelic Lady Frances and Miss Altham. With an abundance of italicising, even beyond that deployed in the novels, Elizabeth is 'my *innocent*, . . . my glorious child', 'my *proud heart's* darling', the 'beloved object', the '*suffering angel*', 'the innocent darling of my heart', 'my soul's treasure', 'the rich gem', 'an *angel* child', 'the *glory* of her family, *beloved* by her friends, *revered* by her acquaintance, *adored* by the children of poverty, and the sweet soother of distress'.

The superhuman portrait of Elizabeth grates on the Knight of Chivalry, her supporter, who calls Mrs Gunning a 'foolish mother' and a 'nonsensical woman'. Yet the portrait is not altogether foisted on the daughter, whose words as quoted in the *Letter* confirm the assumption of heroic sentimental virtue; her answer to the General's one conciliatory approach has the unwise ring of her mother's hyperbole and would be suitable for the heroine of sensibility: 'Turn'd from your doors defenceless, pennyless and robb'd by you of what is and ever will be dearer than my life – my character'; it ends pertinently though not ingratiatingly, 'You call me unfortunate, I am unfortunate; who has made so so?' As a proper heroine of sensibility, Elizabeth does not scandalously act herself on the stage like Mary Carleton or start to blackmail those she could incriminate like Laetitia Pilkington; instead she falls ill.

Susannah Gunning in her turn sometimes assumes the mask of the wronged wife, alluding – improperly according to the *Narrative* – to the General's frequent infidelities. Mainly, however, she is a mother, and her work, appealing to the heart of the reader, is replete with sentimental tableaux of sacred motherhood. Since her daughter did not die, as might have been sentimentally expected, Mrs Gunning is forced to imagine the death. She would, she claims, have 'grieved like a *mother*', but pleasurably so since she could have anticipated a heavenly reunion. To describe herself, she forsakes the italics of her daughter's description for capitals. She is 'A HAPPY MOTHER'. Susceptibility to these domestic images becomes the test of sensibility in the reader. 'Terrific is the picture I am *forced* to exhibit – it must be a *mere* body indeed who can look upon it *unmoved*.'

As the *Narrative* truly comments, Mrs Gunning's is not 'a simple narrative of plain facts', for she brings to her creation all the arts of her fiction. Gothic elements abound as they were beginning to do in *Lady Julia Mandeville* and *Coombe Wood*: the plot is a 'horrid mystery', the General a gothic villain, and dialogue is darkly menacing: ' "then," exclaimed he, "she will be ruined for ever" ' or 'by whom have you been imposed on to believe her guilty? My blood freezes with horror!!!' This last speech ends with Mrs Gunning's favourite emphatic device after italics, the triple exclamation mark.

The writing is novelettish, with much direct speech. The allegedly hypocritical Mrs Bowen, constructing herself as confidante, wails, 'Oh, my dearest Mrs Gunning! *you* have been *deceived*! you are *cheated*! you are abused! . . . your daughter is a wretch!' Susannah in turn takes the dramatic line: 'Bold wicked woman!' she addresses Mrs Bowen, 'how dare you enter my house.' Often the act is realised by that combination of description and interpretation so common in the epistolary sentimental novel. When Mrs Bowen kisses Mrs Gunning's hand, 'I did *not immediately* withdraw it, but felt as if it had been *fastened on* by a serpent.'[16] Writing itself becomes high drama: 'I even *tremble* with horror when I reflect on the *irresistible* power that *now* bids me retrace them [the events] on paper.'

The appearance of fiction is heightened by the habits which the accounts shares with the romantic sentimental novel – and with vindications like those of Mary Carleton and Laetitia Pilkington. It quotes from memoranda written at the time and mingles hindsight with partial sight, story with opposing story. Minute particulars of the crucial days are given and the pen moves among characters to give multiple points of view, each commenting on the account of the other. Letters and documents are quoted to inform, but they also act in the plot: correspondence is forged and pens appropriated. Yet Mrs Gunning must avoid letting her narrative acquire the tinge of fiction masquerading as fact; she is after all selling not only the work but herself and must seem authentic.

So she tries to dissociate her writing from her novels, especially when she is indulging most heavily in their sentimental techniques. By so doing, she emphasises the truth of her narrative and heightens its appeal. The reader's heart must bleed the more because the truth is presented and because the writer is not a novelist here but rather a sufferer within the tale:

> Heretofore, when *fiction* has guided my pen, my heart has been softened by compassion, and my tears have flowed over distresses of my *own* creating; but *Nature* has appointed me to a task which I am totally incapable of performing – as a mother I cannot hold *her* pencil – the *colours* alone *blind* me, to lay them *on* is impossible! *one* expression, though I die in the *repetition* of it shall not be withheld, and *may* it touch with *agonising repentance* the heart of *him* to *whom* it was addressed – 'O! papa! papa! it is *you* who *falsely* accuse me?' – and to her *own heaven* her eyes were directed, streaming with the bitter tears of anguish . . .[17]

And so on, for the word 'mother' has opened Mrs Gunning's most flamboyantly baroque vein and the appeal to truth censors any reticence of fiction that might have closed it.

Like her predecessors in vindication, including Carleton, Manley and Pilkington, Susannah Gunning is creating her female mask of truth to cover the male-imposed one of fraud. As Miss Minifie's novels powerfully press against Mrs Gunning's life, so the image of her life is pressed into the modes of fiction, especially those current in the 1760s and 1770s when her style was fixed. As with each of the previous vindicators, she must appeal to the public through constructing a sign which she knew from her fiction that society would applaud, for vindicators cannot be innovators; they must aim to be not original artists but bestsellers.

In the 1660s it was clear that the eye that looked and the money that bought were male. Mary Carleton and Delarivier Manley knew they must sell themselves as heroic or romantic females but they could spice their portraits with sexuality. Their scandalous self-display was not allowed to Laetitia Pilkington, who misjudged the image and her power completely. Realising that she had a largely female fiction audience to call on, Susannah Gunning abolishes the risqué woman and the straightforwardly powerful writer altogether and capitalises the mother. Energy, suppressed power and spiritedness fall before self-pity and passivity. Yet she is as fully aware of actively using female strategies as her predecessors, for she, like them, is going to market in and for herself. If the coin she uses is conventional, it is so because the coin she wants in return is conventional too. In the Victorian era motherhood would clearly triumph over spirited nobility and virtue in distress as women's most saleable and justificatory image to other women. Writers of the type of Susannah Gunning helped to hasten the process.

The fantasy world of powerful feminine passivity, created by writers such as Frances Brooke and the Minifie sisters, and used in the self-image of women in prefaces or vindications, would be much mocked by anti-sentimentalist rationalists or religious female authors at the turn of the nineteenth century. Nonetheless it played a very significant part in the history of women's writing, since it appealed deeply to female readers. To some extent the construction of the fantasy and the signs of femininity that went with it broke down when they were intellectually battered by such writers as Mary Wollstonecraft (in her later years), Fanny Burney and Jane Austen. But by the time these women came to write they were inevitably heiresses of the centrality which the sentimental modes and signs had given to women. And even they, with all their mockery, could not entirely escape the fantasy.

For, despite the absurdity of its dream of feminine significance and its anodyne escapism, this fiction was delivering an enduring fantasy to women. Although the vision enters, in a modified way, the novels of the Brontës, it was not on the whole in culturally privileged art that it continued, but rather in the popular novel of the nineteenth and twentieth centuries – in sensational fiction and in the romances of Mills and Boon.[18] By this time there were clearly two cultures, the elite and the popular, and the vulgarity, commodification and escapism of the latter were accepted without question by the arbiters of higher taste. What remains interesting in the eighteenth century, which fashioned the form and the fantasy, is the centrality of this fiction to the culture as a whole. Although repeatedly mocked, the books were noticed in the major literary organs in a way that would be unthinkable for Barbara Cartland's work in our time. A sense of a primarily feminine culture was delivered, however collusive with ideology it now appears, through a community of readers. When the inevitable reaction came from serious-minded women writers, this achievement would most often be ignored.

PART THREE

11

THE LATE EIGHTEENTH CENTURY:
THE DECADES OF REVOLUTION

Fashion then, by one of her sudden and rapid turns, instantaneously struck out both real sensibility, and affectation from the standing list of female perfections; and, by a quick touch of her magic wand, shifted the scene, and at once produced the bold and independent beauty, the intrepid female, the hoyden, the huntress, and the archer; the swinging arms, the confident address, the regimental, and the four-in-hand. These self-complacent heroines made us ready to regret their softer predecessors, who had aimed only at pleasing the other sex, while these aspiring fair ones struggled for the bolder renown of rivalling them. The project failed; for, whereas the former had sued for admiration, the latter challenged, seized, compelled it; but the men, as was natural, continued to prefer the modest claimant to the sturdy competitor.

It would be well if we, who have the advantage of contemplating the errors of the two extremes, were to look for truth where she is commonly to be found, in the plain and obvious middle path, equally remote from each excess . . .[1]

So in 1799 Hannah More, once playwright and poet, now evangelical and reformer of the poor, summed up the female history of the late eighteenth century.

In almost all commentaries there is a sense that something has happened: that there has been a challenge to the image of woman accepted or refused. Hannah More's dismissive catalogue may refer to Helen Maria Williams, chronicler of the French Revolution, who in the 1790s was converted in the popular mind from a young heroine of sensibility into the militant supporter of blood-soaked France, or to Mary Hays, the outspoken usurper of the male prerogative of choice in love, but it certainly refers to their friend, the recently dead Mary Wollstonecraft, author in 1792 of *A Vindication of the Rights of Woman*.

Reactions to this book by supporters and enemies over the half-decade since it was written bear out the reading of women's history that More provides. They indicate the extraordinary significance of the 1790s, an era when women writers of whatever political persuasion became conscious of the many strands of feminist thinking, from the moral and religious to the secular political, and when the establishment of the woman writer was completed under the sign of the professional and moral woman.

REVOLUTION AND REACTION

The French Revolution of 1789 was a major event in the life of both England and France. As its moderate goals become more radical and bloody under Jacobin rule in the mid-1790s and as it turned from defence to imperialist aggression in the later years, Britain, once priding itself on being the most politically enlightened and liberal state in Europe, came to define itself in increasingly conservative, patriotic and anti-French terms.

The early Revolution had been welcomed by many groups: aristocratic liberals, middle-class reformers, sentimental ladies, and young poets; William Wordsworth described it as 'heaven' to be young and alive at such a dawn. It was also welcomed by provincial merchants, artisans and tradesmen, who made up the Constitutional and Corresponding Societies for discussion and promotion of reform, as well as by political thinkers like Thomas Paine, William Godwin and Mary Wollstonecraft, all inspired to radical vision by its promise.

It was especially appreciated by Dissenting men, still excluded from many civil rights in England – indeed it was only in 1789 that they had once again failed to gain the repeal of the acts that barred them from public office. Although increasingly rationalistic in doctrine as the century progressed, some Dissenters still retained the Puritan dream of a biblical millenium, a future time of heaven on earth. Wollstonecraft's friend the Dissenting minister Richard Price in 1790 commemorated the English Revolution of 1688 which had meant so much to Dissenters by preaching a sermon in praise of the new French one and by sending a message of support to the revolutionaries in France. Anna Laetitia Barbauld thought the connection of Dissenters and radical politics due to their tendency to discuss rather than reverence the doctrines of religion.

It is no accident that it should be a middle-class Dissenting woman who made this political comment, for Dissent nurtured many radical women during these final years of the century. In the Restoration those women most disturbed by female degradation had been staunchly royalist, but by the 1790s it seemed that Dissent especially allowed a political voice to women – rather as the early Quakers had encouraged them to find a religious one. Mary Wollstonecraft, Mary Hays, Helen Maria Williams, Anna Laetitia Barbauld, Elizabeth Inchbald and Charlotte Smith were all nurtured in Dissenting circles, whatever their original religious background.

It was fortunate that such an influence existed, since secular Enlightenment thinking did not promise a great deal for women. Most of the major thinkers had associated the female with reaction and benightedness – Mozart's opera *The Magic Flute* is the paradigm, with its triumph of male rationality over the darkness of the Queen of the Night. But the ideas of the actual French Revolution did seem to galvanise some women into radical and practical protest. It was in the context of this event that the French radical Olympe de Gouges annotated the new declaration of the rights of man to show women's exclusion from consideration and that Mary Wollstonecraft, arguing for the rights of women in the Enlightenment terms of the rights of all humanity, addressed her call for female education to the minister in charge of educational reform in revolutionary France.

But the political Wollstonecraft of the 1790s derived even more from the intellectual debates of London and she was most specifically turned into a polemicist by an event which came to have more and more significance in England as the situation deteriorated in France: the publication in 1790 of Edmund Burke's *Reflections on the Revolution in France*. Burke, an old-style liberal, one-time opponent of the more radical Catherine Macaulay, had been appalled both by English blindness to the significance of events in France and by the millenarian rhetoric of Dr Price. He responded by articulating a conservative British position which had, until then, lacked clear formulation. Employing the power of sentimental rhetoric with its nostalgic vision of community, he argued vehemently against the new revolutionary notions of the equality of all individuals and the perfectibility of human nature. Since humanity is in fact weak and flawed, it is immensely dangerous to ignore tradition and the hard-won wisdom of experience, he argued. People need trappings, ritual and mystery – in religion, kingship and gender – and he mocked the equalising tendency that destroyed the status both of a queen and of a woman:

> On this scheme of things, a king is but a man; a queen is but a woman; a woman is but an animal; and an animal not of the highest order. All homage paid to the sex in general as such, and without distinct views, is to be regarded as romance and folly.[2]

197

Equality cannot be reconciled with liberty and the abolition of hierarchy will lead only to anarchy and autocracy.

Initially Burke's book provoked little popular excitement, since its anti-French views were unfashionable at a time when even the prime minister William Pitt thought that the French upheavals would soon settle into order and harmony. But its powerful expression of conservative opinion gained significance as the Revolution became more radical and violent; many men such as Wordsworth and Coleridge who would come to dominate British culture in the minds of literary critics moved by the end of the decade from qualified enthusiasm for the Revolution to a position almost indistinguishable from Burke's. His book gave rise to a spate of replies, including the great radical works of Paine and Godwin which helped to stimulate for a few years a new kind of radicalism in England, one that fundamentally criticised British constitutional and social institutions. But the first of all the responses was Wollstonecraft's *A Vindication of the Rights of Men* (1790).

Wollstonecraft argued against a blind following of tradition. She pointed out the rottenness in the British social and political system. Human nature could be improved with political change, she insisted; individuals were essentially equal and each had a rational right to determine his or her own destiny. What stood in the way of improvement was tyrannical custom and law, as well as the muddy sentimental thinking which Burke displayed – at this revolutionary moment Wollstonecraft was in her most rationalistic mood and conveniently forgot that she had composed paeans to sensibility only a couple of years before. Sensibility was growing unfashionable and effeminate and her aim was to associate it with a womanish Burke, all tears and no sympathy; it was a manoeuvre that the reactionary writers would use against the radicals, including Wollstonecraft, at the end of the decade.

In December 1792 Wollstonecraft set off for France and her initial reaction of appalled rejection was typical of the new period. The revolutionary moment had been short in Britain and the swinging pendulum of philosophical and political fashion made utopian rationalism as a political philosophy seem a crazy misconception of the relation of mental ideal and material reality. By 1793 Britain and France were at war, a war which the government under William Pitt seems to have entered with fairly limited political and economic aims but which, as the years went by, increasingly assumed the ideological overtones of a crusade. The new conservatism prevailing in Britain was not the old-fashioned nostalgic sentimental one that had shared its communal vision with forms of radicalism, but a much more aggressive and philosophical kind. Meanwhile 'Church and King' clubs were established to support the status quo and the relatively tolerant attitude of the government to reforming groups and radical agitators in the early 1790s, when radical pamphlets and editions were circulating, was replaced by a repressive witch-hunt of traitors and seditious books. War hysteria grew and French agents were suspected under every bed; it became unpatriotic and unwise to criticise the government or praise the French or any part of their Revolution.

Wollstonecraft, Williams, Hays, Paine and Godwin had all become linked in the popular mind as 'Jacobins', despite the final detestation of most of them for Robespierre who led this faction in France. They were associated with sensibility and with rationalism, both regarded as ridiculous extremes in an England increasingly devoted to 'common sense'. Although, as Wollstonecraft had pointed out, nothing could be more sentimental than the tableau of the humbled French queen in Burke's *Reflections*, the new conservatives managed to impose sensibility on radicalism and suggest that both were somehow French. Gillray produced a cartoon of Sensibility as a woman crying over a dead bird with a foot carelessly resting on the French king's head, while in the *Anti-Jacobin*, the new organ founded to combat radicalism in the final years of the century, George Canning poetically lambasted it as 'Sweet Child of sickly fancy ... False by degrees, and delicately wrong'.[3] Sensibility became in Canning's poem a combination of effeminacy, Frenchness – despite the fact that England above all had been associated with its cult – Rousseau, dramatic nature description, selfishness and self-obsession, autobiography, and sympathy with guilt. The combination should be remembered when assessing the reaction to writers such as the gothic Ann Radcliffe with her lengthy descriptions of exotic un-English scenery, as well as the autobiographical novelists like Wollstonecraft and Mary Hays who might seem to the modern reader to be attackers of sensibility. Along with Helen Maria Williams and other women writers, Wollstonecraft and Hays became both effeminately sentimental *and* indecorously masculine, the 'Unsex'd Females' of the Reverend Richard Polwhele.

ECONOMIC CHANGES

After a long period of peace at home, war with its needs and shortages hastened those industrial economic changes in Britain which would in time reshape the world. Since the death rate was falling, the population in the country was increasing, so enlarging the demand for food at a time when it was difficult to import it from outside. Technological inventions allowed the beginnings of an industrial system and the acceleration of land enclosure meant a sharp increase in agricultural production; both sets of changes increased the wealth of the country but at a cost of much social disruption and, although there was more money around, not much of it reached the poorer classes, whose real wages began to increase only in the next century. Bad harvests and wet cold summers in 1794 and 1795 led to social disorder and, more significantly, fear of social disorder in the governing classes.[4] Although industry was expanding, trade was made difficult first by the American and then by the French wars and there were shortages of many foodstuffs. The cities, especially London, exerted an economic pull on the country, which had an unsettling effect on the dissatisfied young. There was much mockery of the servants' dream of the metropolis as a place where all distinctions of class could be eroded and men and women make of themselves what they would.

The increased wealth of the country showed itself in a restless and eclectic consumerism well caught in the specificities of fabric, furnishings and carriages described in the women's novels of the time. Female fashion was changing rapidly, sometimes demanding huge turbans and feathers, even for everyday wear, sometimes assuming a risqué simplicity, pulling away from the stylised elaborate elegance of the earlier, more stable years. In the late eighteenth century simpler English styles moved out into the rest of Europe; meanwhile the French Revolution, stressing classical civic virtues, encouraged a flowing Greek style of dress in women and a democratisation of fashion. Old-style petticoats and corsets were still worn by many in England, although stays and lacing were decreasing, and by the end of the decade the flowing chemise-dress was in fashion. A hundred years before, Locke had argued against stays, at least for young children, but the late eighteenth century provoked a whole literature that makes clear the symbolic value of the objects: because of the erect posture they promoted, they tended to signify correct behaviour, self-control and even chastity. By the beginning of the nineteenth century several writers commented on the decline of fainting owing to the decreasing use of stays; certainly the heroines of Ann Radcliffe in the mid-1790s faint a great deal more than those of Jane Austen a few years later.

Although much of the new wealth was in the hands of the middle class, whose flourishing could be gauged by the new villas springing up in the suburbs, there was no sense that high political power might be passing from the old aristocracy of land and finance to a middle class of industry and trade, although there was far more scope for middle-class civic activity than there had been. A notion of the specialness of privileged aristocracy was under siege and the middle class was no longer necessarily bound to the gentry by shared values of gentility; instead classes were becoming clearer and the middle ranks, an amalgam of London merchants, provincial manufacturers and country tradesmen, were separating themselves out in values and lifestyle both from those below and those above them. The new ideal was found in independence and work, underpinned by a strong evangelical religion.

The new work ideal was firmly masculine – set against the passivity of the domestic woman and the effeminacy of the idle aristocracy. It was thought that wives and adolescent daughters in the upper orders had very little to do except be ornamental; Mary Hays spoke of the 'Perpetual Babyism' of such women and Mary Wollstonecraft never tired of mocking ladies who, like Jane Austen's Lady Bertram, thought the end of existence was a comfortable life on a sofa with a pug dog. Yet, paradoxically, the masculine ideal was rooted in seemingly feminine spheres. The family and home alone justified the masculine devotion to work, and the independence was in the end a curious matter of dependence, not obsequiously on the orders above as formerly, but instead on servants, workers and of course the wife, whose labour underpinning the husband's somehow did not qualify as work but was delivered as service.[5]

Under Queen Victoria a middle-class morality of work, independence, respectability, piety and domesticity would come to permeate most classes outside the poorest, but in the eighteenth century it was already pushing against the extravagance and often libertine morality of the upper orders where kept women were often the leaders of fashion. The ménage of the Duke of Devonshire in which both present and future Duchesses simultaneously bore children to the Duke, who raised the legitimate and illegitimate in the same nursery, would not have been condoned in the middle ranks, if it could have been afforded, while the first Duchess's huge gambling debts would not have been tolerated on moral or economic grounds. At court George III's sons were much criticised for flouting middle-class morality with their extramarital liaisons and illegitimate offspring.

At the same time there was fear that aristocratic habits of confounding types of woman, classes and genders would seep into the families of the wealthy middle class. Consequently the masquerade, so popular in the mid-century, declined in the serious decades when the destabilising of class and sex took on a more menacing quality. By the time of the Revolution, masquerades were out of fashion and Vauxhall and Ranelagh were falling into disrepair. The impresario of the lavish mid-century masquerade, Mrs Cornelys, died bankrupt in 1797.[6]

The immense nature of the economic changes occurring in the country was appreciated by none of the economic theorists of the day, not even by Adam Smith and Jeremy Bentham, although their entrepreneurial and individualistic views helped to make an atmosphere conducive to capitalist growth. In this atmosphere sentimental philosophy was stripped of its ethical component and allied to the radical notion of the perfectibility of humanity to become a kind of political utilitarianism in economic terms. Political and economic action should be guided by the principle of material happiness for the majority. Bentham, Smith, Malthus and Ricardo all helped to define basic facts of society as economic and to form a climate in which financial capitalist considerations could become paramount. But in most men economics was not clearly separated from morality, and the piety and reverence for family life usually went hand in hand with capitalist enterprise.

In the nineteenth century Harriet Martineau would provide the common reader with a moral basis for the secular side of the individualistic economic philosophy. But on the whole its theory and practice did not appeal to women writers in the late eighteenth century. The economic commentators of the period were almost entirely male, and the inventing and exploiting activity of early capitalism hardly touched women. They were barred from much entrepreneurial activity by the marital laws that gave financial power to the husband and they were urged away from the principles of economic philosophy by an education that stressed their sentimental importance within the family, not their potential position within society.

The economic changes dimly but definitely apprehended meant that women were, according to the ideology of the times, more than ever marginalised into the unproductive vessels of morality – although in reality many continued to help husbands and fathers in business, still often located in the home. In *A Vindication of the Rights of Woman* Wollstonecraft made an unusual attempt to associate the new self-reliant woman she envisaged with the entrepreneurial self-made man of the middle class, the man who owed nothing to the privilege of birth and who made wealth rather than consumed it. But this idealisation of the thrusting mercantile personality was untypical of women, whose utopias tended to follow the model of the conservative communal *Millenium Hall* rather than the individualistic *Wealth of Nations*. Indeed it was untypical of Wollstonecraft herself who quickly came to see that, in a world where financial or economic considerations dominated or even coexisted in equality with moral ones, women and the poor would surely become commodities.

In the last half of the 1790s, women settled down to a subordinate but serious role as modifiers of the masculine individualistic principles of free enterprise. They constantly attacked an excessive emphasis on commerce, trade and financial concerns. Clearly this extends the sentimental dislike of trade as inharmonious and vulgar – there is much snobbishness in the distaste for commerce in the novels of Charlotte Smith and Fanny Burney – but there is an added urgency and specificity to the attacks on a mentality that replaced ethical with financial considerations. In her history of the early French Revolution written two years after *The Rights of Woman* Mary Wollstonecraft succinctly put the case against trade in a capitalist environment:

> The destructive influence of commerce . . . carried on by men who are eager by overgrown riches to partake of the respect paid to nobility, is felt in a variety of ways. The most pernicious, perhaps, is its producing an aristocracy of wealth, which degrades mankind, by making them only exchange savageness for tame servility, instead of acquiring the urbanity of improved reason. Commerce also, overstocking a country with people, obliges the majority to become manufacturers rather than husbandmen; and then the division of labour, solely to enrich the proprietor, renders the mind entirely inactive. The time which, a celebrated writer says, is sauntered away, in going from one part of an employment to another, is the very time which preserves the man from degenerating into a brute.[7]

Wollstonecraft is here referring to men and she has relatively little to say about independent women wanting to earn a living in the new economic order. Yet, earlier in her life, she had referred to her own experience as a middle-class woman trying most of the traditional routes open to her. In *Thoughts on the Education of Daughters* (1787) she gave an embittered account of the female job market:

> Few are the modes of earning a subsistence, and those very humiliating. Perhaps to be an humble companion to some rich old cousin, or what is still worse to live with strangers, who are so intolerably tyrannical, that none of their own relations can bear to live with them, though they should even expect a fortune in reversion. It is impossible to enumerate the many hours of anguish such a person must spend. Above the servants, yet considered by them as a spy . . . she is alone, shut out from equality and confidence . . . The being dependant on the caprice of a fellow-creature, though certainly very necessary in this state of discipline, is yet a very bitter corrective . . .[8]

In passing Wollstonecraft mentioned the decline of female trades, a theme that was common in other women writers. In France for a brief period under the Jacobins, women agitated for the exclusion of men from certain markets and functions and in Britain a similar demand came from Mary Ann Radcliffe, who explains in her memoirs how she had suffered from the lack of female opportunities. Others, like Mary Hays and the Quaker Priscilla Wakefield, mixed feminine and economic motives in their plea that men should be excluded from activities like midwifery and hairdressing and trades like millinery and mantua-making. Radcliffe urged the government to intervene on behalf of women in areas where they had traditionally been strong, while Wakefield demanded that it tax 'such she-he gentry to the teeth'. Both Radcliffe and Wakefield begged ladies from the upper orders to patronise women and to refuse service from men in shops dealing in feminine requirements – a sense yet untheorised of the economic power of women. Priscilla Wakefield echoed the mockery of male shop assistants in Rousseau's *Emile* and Fanny Burney's *Evelina*, couching her plea in terms of a protest against the impropriety of men servers and servants being close to women – she also felt that dancing masters should be female, since the 'persons of girls advancing towards maturity' should not be exposed to the wanton eyes of men, and that female corpses should be attended to only by women.[9] (Wakefield's tone may seem prurient and absurd today, but her suggestions are unusual for the time in being remarkably practical, and all the comments imply an uneasiness both at the collusion of men in feminine narcissism and at the male economic function of women's vanity and display.) In general the main growth industry was domestic service, the biggest employer of women outside the home; it was not always a welcome or suitable function for spirited girls or women with dependants.

In almost all the pleas for more work opportunities for women there is the fear that lack of jobs will lead directly to prostitution; interestingly this prostitution, since it includes both streetwalking and cohabitation with a man without marriage, is most frequently seen as a resort not of the lower but of the lower middle class – Wollstonecraft's sympathetic depiction of the working-class prostitute Jemima in *The Wrongs of Woman* is an exception – and the genteel education of girls with insufficient means to support their pretensions is constantly blamed for the sexual fall. In general the middle-class basis of the writing on employment is quite apparent and the complaints about the restrictions on women are mainly applicable to this class. Despite the ideology of femininity, Mary Robinson noted that lower-class women did heavier work than men, and she pitted the scouring, scrubbing drudge against the powdered male lackey: 'If woman be the weaker sex, why is she employed in laborious avocations? why compelled to endure the fatigue of household drudgery [?]' she asked.[10]

The exclusion of women from the economic bustle was especially felt by those who sensed that the country was progressing economically for men. Few of the liberal and radical men who criticised female dependence bothered to think up alternatives – Thomas Christie suggested only that the family fortune should be left to the girls rather than the boys since the former were regarded as helpless – and it was women writers of both conservative and radical persuasion who considered possibilities. Assuming something of the economic principles of Adam Smith, who insisted that all people should contribute to the good of society, Wakefield felt that women should not be excluded from the claim of public usefulness. (Once the hostilities with France had started, it could also be argued that employing women released men for the war effort.)

Throughout the eighteenth century there had been intermittent expressions of women's desire for a college, but this had on the whole been intended for well-placed ladies; Wakefield, however, suggested practical colleges for girls with training appropriate to each class. Mary Hays thought that women could become doctors for their own sex and she considered them intellectually suitable to divinity and the law, although she admitted the inappropriateness of their participating in public assemblies. Wollstonecraft suggested that 'women of a superior cast' *might* be politicians, but they could certainly run businesses and enter some professions.

Yet independence in a woman was almost always viewed as a sad necessity, the result of the failure of the man to provide for her, or of the woman to procure a husband. It was noticed in the last years of the century that the number of spinsters was greatly increasing, for the decline in infant mortality favoured girls. Many grumbled at the refusal of some men to marry – this is not a marrying age, declared Hays sourly in 1793. Providing they had sufficient means, however, both spinsters and married women could participate in one clear growth area of female economic involvement: philanthropy and charity, which, masquerading as service, could give women all the dignity that men were deriving from their ideals of work and independence.

Christian charity had always been preached for women and a vague benevolence had been enjoined on them at least from the middle of the century. But in the 1790s philanthropy became a profession, given a certain assertiveness by Sarah Trimmer's book *Oeconomy of Charity* (1787). Usually it was aimed at the poor and at spectacularly disadvantaged groups like slaves, who were romanticized into objects of humanitarian zeal in the late 1780s. But it was also frequently aimed at other women. Priscilla Wakefield established a Female Benefit Club and a Penny Bank for children; together these formed the 'frugality bank', the first savings banks for the lower classses. Sarah Trimmer gathered poor girls into Sunday schools and Hannah More supported Friendly Societies, a sort of insurance for women. The polemical dramatist, and poet, Maria Barrell took up the issue raised a century and a half before by

Bathsua Makin, the imprisonment of men for debt; only she concentrated less on the possibility of injustice and victimisation than on the horror of the effects on the family, the corruption of a father and the separation of spouses.

The tendency of this philanthropic activity was by no means radical. It shored up the status quo, preaching a mixture of self-help and resignation to the poor, and benevolence and individual charity to the rich. The poor were given education but it should be insufficient for them to grow restive; they should not necessarily write and they should confine their reading to such literature as Hannah More's *Cheap Repository Tracts*, which urged duties on all ranks of society while keeping hierarchy intact.

Some later historians have put immense weight on this female philanthropic activity, crediting More's efforts at teaching, reading, and preaching Christian resignation with helping to avert a British revolution, a constant fear of the upper orders throughout the period. Others have pointed out that those who could read the *Tracts* could also read the inflammatory rhetoric of Paine's *Rights of Man* or indeed of Wollstonecraft's *Rights of Woman*, portions of which were sold in cheap editions in the early nineteenth century.

SOCIAL CHANGES

Marriage, divorce and alternative unions were excitingly discussed for a few years as radical France experimented with a removal of legal restraints. In *Political Justice* William Godwin described marriage as the worst of monopolies; 'So long as I seek, by despotic and artificial means, to maintain my possession of a woman, I am guilty of the most odious selfishness . . .'[11] Paine believed relationships should last only as long as both parties wanted them to, a view that seems to have guided Mary Wollstonecraft and her lover Gilbert Imlay when they failed to marry in France. Earlier, in 1792, she had mocked 'the divine right of husbands', and her acquaintance William Blake imagined a world of free and guiltfree copulation. James Lawrence's *Empire of the Nairs* (not published until 1811 but written earlier) fantasised a world without conventional marriage, where female chastity was not a social necessity.

Yet, for all the speculation, there is not, in radical and liberal circles, much real consideration of the alternatives to traditional patriarchal marriage. Even Wollstonecraft when she treats the subject in *A Vindication of the Rights of Woman* simply opposes the sentimental emotional ideal with a chilly sort of union in which the partners are not passionate or sexually inclined and which women can enter – so long as they do so without sentimental expectations; a woman 'might as well pine married

206

as single, for she would not be a jot more unhappy with a bad husband than longing for a good one'.

By the late 1790s the agitation, far more extreme in parodies than in the reality, was largely replaced by a reassertion of traditional verities. The divine right of husbands was restated, buttressed by appeals to scripture and common sense: in 1797 Thomas Gisborne in *An Enquiry into the Duties of the Female Sex* asserted that men should exact obedience in the manner enjoined by the New Testament, although they should refrain from being tyrannical. The sympathy felt by the senti-mental novelists and the later Wollstonecraft and Mary Hays for the woman who has married an unworthy man is eschewed; if a woman marries a person without having understood his moral character, Gisborne states, 'the fault surely is her own'. The novelist Charlotte Smith or the polemicist Mary Ann Radcliffe, who knew this predicament intimately from their unwise teenage marriages, would no doubt have smiled sourly at this.

'Home must, if possible, be always rendered pleasant to its master; and a wife must ever strive to be aimiable in the eyes of her husband,' wrote Jane West in 1806.[12] Far more than male writers, women used the vocabulary of 'striving' and 'rendering' for domestic life. They advised resignation in marriage, together with a firm focus on the next world. Totally accepting subordination, writers such as Priscilla Wakefield were nonetheless realistic about what it entailed – the constant control of the self; consequently they believed that a girl 'should be impressed, from the first dawnings of reason, that she lives, not for herself alone, but to contribute to the happiness of others'.[13] Mary Hays, however, could not imagine many women rising to this challenge: 'When a man falls in with such a woman, he should cherish her as the apple of his eye when alive; and afterwards pickle or preserve her . . .'[14]

Almost all writers accepted the companionable marriage where a husband and wife should feel some affection and esteem for each other, although they also stressed financial considerations. The warnings against romantic notions continues, but less urgently than in the age of high sensibility, so that, for example, Hannah More in 1777 expatiates more fully than in 1799 on the danger of 'sentimental or romantic connexions'. As poisonous by the late 1790s is an attachment to the absurd new philosophies of equality perpetrated by Godwin and Wollstonecraft.

The required attitude is now not sentimental and romantic or entirely filial but simply prudential and commonsensical. Jane West, for example, echoes Mary Astell in pointing out that 'choice' is not usually an issue for women, as so many romantic novels suggest: 'lovers rarely appear in groups, very seldom amount to plurality.' Often conservative comment sounds decidedly pessimistic. 'The precept, that in the married state women should never *expect* too much, nor feel too *keenly*, can never be too deeply impressed on the ardent mind of youth,' insists West. Her mixed images take on the resonance of the biblical curse: 'Let all who approach the nuptial altar resolve never to withdraw the hand which they there lay upon the plough. Let them remember, that they *then* enter upon a state of enlarged duty and extended trial.'[15] Worrying about the effects of novel-reading on girls, Anna Laetitia Barbauld warns that fiction does not prepare a woman for 'the neglect and tedium of life which she is perhaps doomed to encounter'.

Despite some changes in attitude to the relationship of the partners in marriage, the legal basis of the husband's power remained pretty much intact, and the various commentators on Blackstone reassert the basic principles of patriarchal unions. Even in the thinking of quite liberal writers there is no sense of real equality.[16] The Rousseauian experiment of Thomas Day, who adopted an orphan girl to educate into a wife for himself, was eccentric but would have been unthinkable in reverse.

Divorce still required an Act of Parliament and was usually initiated by a husband following damages obtained from his wife's lover, stressing again the notion of the wife as property. Most writers during the conservative end of the century did not consider any extension of divorce but instead worried that the odd divorced woman might be free to marry her lover – perhaps a fear of the judge who refuses a petition from Wollstonecraft's heroine in *The Wrongs of Woman* – or, in William Duff's words, to enter 'a scandalous cohabitation with her seducer'.[17] But divorce was of course unlikely for women except those in the highest classes, where, in any case, adultery if not premarital sex was far more condoned than in the middle ranks. The poor could still indulge in wife-selling (existing at least in fiction as late as Thomas Hardy's *Mayor of Casterbridge*), although it had no legal status.

Some women, like Hays and Wollstonecraft, in the heady days of the early 1790s inveighed against the double standard of chastity. A thoughtful discussion of it occurs in Catherine Macaulay's *Letters on Education* (1790):

> The great difference now beheld in the external consequences which follow the deviation from chastity in the two sexes, did in all probability arise from women having been considered as the mere property of the men; . . . when the plea of property had been given up . . . [it] was still preserved in society from the unruly licentiousness of the men, who . . . continue . . . by mutual support and general opinion to use their natural freedom with impunity . . . This state of things renders the situation of females . . . very precarious . . .[18]

But on the whole the double standard was still accepted. Often the acceptance was less cynical than in the Restoration and less materialistic than in the middle years of the century; instead it could become a tribute to the moral superiority of women, who, it was thought, required higher standards than men. Feminine chastity was a kind of power in a situation of considerable powerlessness and most women thought it absurd to throw such influence away.

The sentimental concern for the fallen woman tended, as Mary Ann Radcliffe suggests, to give way in women writers to an emphasis on the economic causes of prostitution. But, although more conservative writers insisted that a fallen woman might be pitied if she were thoroughly repentant, she could not be rehabilitated – hence the alarm, even in an early review by Mary Wollstonecraft, at the adulteress in Charlotte Smith's *Emmeline* who seems to be forgiven after a period of intense humility. The later, more radical Wollstonecraft of *The Rights of Woman* thought differently, however, glossing 'ruin' as error or mistaken affection and pointing out that the vicious label is placed on many girls before 'they know the difference between virtue and vice'. Magdalens, so excitedly established in the middle years of the century, were not now 'the proper remedies for these abuses. It is justice, not charity, that is wanting in the world!'[19]

Such improper forgiveness of the fallen is termed by Hannah More 'the affectation of charity' and by Elizabeth Hamilton, the liberal novelist and poet, a fashionable 'excess of charity'. According to More in *Strictures* respectable women should not be not anxious to embrace penitents in society: 'To restore a criminal to public society, is perhaps to tempt her to repeat her crime, or to deaden her repentance for having committed it.' A mark of proper penitence for West and More was precisely a woman's lack of desire to come back into public life.

At the end of the century, as the conservative backlash strengthened, there seems to have been little middle-class sympathy for the poor unmarried mother, who simply represented a charge on the parish, although there was considerable pity for the poor wife. Simple irritation was provoked by the aristocratic woman who appeared to be escaping the bourgeois morality of female chastity, 'the prostitute of high life' as Jane West contemptuously called her.

Motherhood continued to be elaborately respected. Wet-nursing, becoming even less fashionable, but the early nineteenth-century woman was still being urged to breast-feed for medical and social reasons, so presumably the practice remained strong. Certainly children were now thought to be central to a family, and more liberal women tended to support what might be termed the companionate childhood in which mothers conversed with children, becoming, as Mary Hays suggests, both friends and monitors.[20]

In advice books and didactic novels there is a shift in tone, and the sentimental elevation tends to give way to an emphasis on rational and moral motherhood, avoiding extreme displays of affection. In *The Rights of Woman* Wollstonecraft goes so far in this direction that its absolute responsibilities seem almost an infringement of the autonomy of individuals. In the popular romantic and gothic novels that burgeoned during this time, however, the sentimental concept remained intact and Mary Hays is as likely to capitalise the 'mother' as Mrs Gunning.

Views on early child-rearing depend on a person's ideas of human nature, whether, for example, they lean towards the radical notion of essential goodness if society is not allowed to warp the character or whether they accept the Christian conservative one of imperfect beings needing constant restraint. The conservative view allowed more heroic expression than the radical-rational one; Hannah More ringingly addresses mothers: 'On YOU, depend in no small degree the principles of the whole rising generation.'

But More herself became neither a wife nor a mother and many women took a similar path of spinsterhood. According to male commentators of the 1780s it was a harsh and rather ridiculous route: 'a single woman is, particularly, defenceless. She cannot move beyond the precincts of her house without apprehensions ... As she goes down the *hill* of life, her friends *gradually* drop away from her, like the leaves in the autumn, and leave her a pining, *solitary* creature ... she wanders through a wide, bustling world, uncomfortable in herself, uninteresting to others, frequently the sport of wanton ridicule, or a proverb of reproach.' A woman's assertion that she chose to remain single was, many men thought, simply sour grapes, 'a kind of ill-constructed rampart, raised very hastily by mistaken pride, to defend an uneasy situation'.[21] Given such opinion, it is not surprising that women put considerable effort into raising the status of the single woman, and their frequent praise of the single life is a sturdy strand throughout the eighteenth century, given impetus by the sentimental ideas of solitude and contemplation and by the cult of friendship. Certainly the young Mary Wollstonecraft looked forward to an unmarried life with her beloved friend Fanny Blood (her memoirist William Godwin would describe their first meeting in terms of the romantic encounter of Charlotte and Werther in Goethe's sentimental romance *The Sorrows of Young Werther*) and the age delighted in the insistently pure friendship of Lady Eleanor Butler and Sarah Ponsonby, the Ladies of Llangollen. Many women writers would make attractive portraits of single independent women. Clara Reeve's *The School for Widows* shows a woman preferring a poor independent existence as a village schoolteacher to the dependence of a companion, while Elizabeth Hamilton's *The Cottagers of Glenburnie* (1808) depicts an exemplary old maid, old-fashioned, kindly and tolerant, who organises and reforms a whole neighbourhood.

EDUCATION

Many of the age's conflicting ideas about women are enshrined in educational writings. These form part of a general debate on education, over whether or not the gentleman's training in the classics should be reformed, whether there should be some sort of state system of instruction for everyone, whether boarding schools were better or worse than day schools and whether education should be in the hands of the church, the state or the parents.

Almost all serious women writers wanted a more rational education for women and often Hannah More can sound almost identical to Mary Wollstonecraft and Catherine Macaulay. All would have united in opposing the specifically feminine education prescribed for Sophie by Rousseau in *Emile* and in castigating what they regarded as the mistaken training in sensibility, although conservative women would have agreed with Rousseau in his assertion of gender differences.

By the 1790s the mid-century worry over whether women should have much learning at all had given way to discussion of the gendered intellect and whether or not there are masculine and feminine areas of intellectual life. Obviously one's views on education in general depended on which notion was held: if gender differences are natural, then education should stress them and intellectual advancement for women should and could go only so far; if there are no differences in intellect according to gender, then environment and education can accomplish everything. If the latter view is held, the next problem is whether, when a girl has suffered from a deficient education, the only one actually available in society, she can be reclaimed or whether she is marked or distorted for life. The rationalist and radical advice books of Mary Hays and Mary Wollstonecraft tend to concentrate on the possibilities of education and it is only in their novels and private letters that the pessimistic corollary of the absolute marking of a personality by environment is suggested. Both women, when passionately and unhappily in love, lamented a sentimental imprinting that they could not eradicate.

The great challenge of the more radical writers was the assertion that woman was created for herself and not, in Wollstonecraft's words, 'merely to be the solace of man'. There is no sex in the mind or the soul, she declared, and education should go as far as intellectual capacities will allow in arts, philosophy and science.

Throughout the period the old advice books on education were current. *The Spectator* was still read and Fordyce and Gregory from the 1760s and 1770s still consulted. Hence Mary Wollstonecraft's attack on them for their contingent views of women in *The Rights of Woman.* Accomplishments were regarded ambiguously, as both useless and necessary as domestic therapy, keeping women out of public places. They continued to be essential primarily for catching a husband, though many girls worked at music, embroidery and painting to a high level, often against family wishes. If a woman became destitute, she might make use of these skills, to heighten her attractions as a governess, but on the whole they would not have procured her a living, as many writers pointed out. In boarding schools deportment was still stressed and a number of extraordinary machines for ensuring posture were introduced so that girls could be strapped and dangled into proper erectness.

At the same time experimental science on a fairly superficial and entertaining level was introduced into the curriculum of many schools. Mary Scott in her *Female Advocate* urged women to enter scientific study, but the very few who did tended to avoid the flair and flamboyance of the Duchess of Newcastle, instead insisting on their subordination to male relatives or friends. Caroline Herschel, the sister of Sir William Herschel, astronomer to George III after 1783, discovered comets and nebulae on her own but always declared that her work depended on that of her 'immortal brother'. Hannah More for one accepted that the female mind could not attain so high a degree of perfection in science: 'It appears that the mind in each sex has some natural kind of bias, which constitutes a distinction of character, and that the happiness of both depends, in a great measure, on the preservation and observance of this distinction.'[22]

By 1800 the radical excitement about rational education was largely over, but it does seem that education had improved for some girls in the middle class. Gisborne in 1797 noted the better prose style of the average lady, as well as the increase in books on science and history written especially for girls. The question then arose over whether education should go on improving or whether it had gone quite far enough already, and whether what appeared improvements were really so. In 1799 Hannah More cautioned against the superficial knowledge that could be given by a perusal of popular introductions, abridgements and selections. Both she and Jane West stressed that no knowledge should be given without the context and function of morality, and any works of science should be scrutinised for tinctures of immorality or deism before being given to girls. Women should be morally rather than intellectually educated, they thought, for they required the constraints of Christianity more than men.

Despite the dominance of the conservative view, the serious-minded activity of women of all political persuasions meant that, by 1800, while women's subordinate social position seemed absolute, there was far less belief in female intellectual inferiority than fifty years before. The prevailing view of the thinking woman at the turn of the century seemed to exist on a kind of tightrope precariously poised between female subordination and female potential intellectual equality. An example which moved towards the latter was Maria Edgeworth's *Letters for Literary Ladies* (1795). Based on the correspondence of her father and Thomas Day (the Rousseauian educator of the perfect wife), it is a debate about female education, together with two cautionary tales that oppose the self-indulgence of sensibility with rationality. This rationality is required both for virtue and for submissiveness, for, although Edgeworth is deeply committed to female intellectual development and securely rationalistic and enlightened in her proposals for women's education, nonetheless she knows the social reality, that 'women must always see things through a veil, or cease to be women'. Moving in the other direction is Hannah More's *Coelebs in Search of a Wife*, in which the hero seeks an ideal woman who is elegant, sensible, well-bred, consistent and pious, having all these qualities at the disposal primarily of her husband and children.

IMAGES OF WOMAN

By the end of the century there was a consensus that things were right for women, or at least improving steadily. William Alexander's *The History of Women* (1779) was complacent about their status in society and under British law, and even Mary Hays, outliving the radical years in which she had played a conspicuous part, wrote in her obituary of Mary Wollstonecraft that 'the spirit of reform is silently pursuing its course'. Yet the defensiveness that increased through the years in her references to her friend suggests that this progress is not entirely towards the equality envisaged by Wollstonecraft's *Rights of Woman*, written at the height of radical euphoria.

Wollstonecraft's is the most famous expression of feminist opinion but in many ways it is close to Catherine Macaulay's more modestly entitled *Letters on Education*, published in 1790 just before her death and reviewed and praised by Wollstonecraft in the *Analytical Review*. This work still has the religious stress of, for example, the early rationalist

Mary Astell, whom Wollstonecraft appears not to have known, but it makes a feminist statement beyond even Wollstonecraft's when it asserts, in total opposition to the 'notion of a sexual difference in the human character', that the only distinction between the sexes is physical (Wollstonecraft felt that intellectual equality was still to be proved). Wollstonecraft gains, however, from her style which, despite her assertions of plainness, is often emotional, striking and personal, aiming to shock men and women into listening and changing. She wrote, for example, of 'weak beings only fit for a seraglio', of faculties 'cramped with worse than Chinese bands' (an image used by many women, including Elizabeth Griffith in the mid-century and, ironically, Hannah More) and of 'the tyranny of man'. She mocked as well as refuted, declaring facetiously, 'I have, probably, had an opportunity of observing more girls in their infancy than J. J. Rousseau,' and she linked her protest, as few before had done, to the wider political protest – in a manner Burke had dimly feared:

> Let not men then in the pride of power, use the same arguments that tyrannic kings and venal ministers have used, and fallaciously assert that woman ought to be subjected because she has always been so.[23]

Wollstonecraft's book sold well and was praised by radical journals; it had a heartening influence on women like Mary Hays who were thinking similar thoughts. If Hannah More refused to read it – 'I am sure I have as much liberty as I can make use of,' she wrote – many other women did so and there are favourable references to it in the journals and letters of several contemporaries. Some quite conservative writers approved it, while Anna Laetitia Barbauld rather surprisingly took issue with it in a poem entitled 'The Rights of Woman' – perhaps she had been provoked into poetry by Wollstonecraft's sharp rebuke of her for making the 'ignoble comparison' of women and flowers. The poem begins with the Amazonian, 'Yes injured Woman! rise, assert thy rights!' but it ends rather strangely for a Dissenter, usually opposed to the flights of feminine sensibility: 'Then, then, abandon each ambitious thought,/ ... In Nature's school, by her soft maxims taught,/ That separate rights are lost in mutual love.'[24]

The moment of Wollstonecraft was short. Several women would echo her views in the late 1790s or early 1800s but state defensively that these views had been written down long before, in the early 1790s; often they mentioned Wollstonecraft's influence but carefully dissociated themselves from what was now almost invariably termed her 'Amazonian spirit'. Even her friend Mary Hays, who in *Appeal to the Men of Great Britain in behalf of Women* (1798) saw the sexual difference in terms of usurped political power and regarded women as being forced to create a mask for themselves, insisted that she was not coming in Wollstonecraft's Amazonian garb to demand a revolution in female manners, but as a friend of man wishing for a 'gentle emancipation from error'.

Such tentativeness was inevitable, for by the late 1790s Mary Wollstonecraft had largely been discredited. This was less because of her revolutionary views than because of revelations about her irregular life published by her husband William Godwin. So the severe rationalist Wollstonecraftian feminism became synonymous with licentiousness, as the vicious attack in the *Anti-Jacobin Review* of 1801 reveals:

> Whilom this dame the Rights of Woman writ,
> This is the title to her book she places,
> Exhorting bashful womankind to quit
> All foolish modesty, and coy grimaces;
> And name their backsides as it were their faces;
> Such license loose-tongued liberty adores,
> Which adds to female speech exceeding graces;
> Lucky the maid that on her volume pores,
> A scripture, archly fram'd, for propagating w----s.[25]

Godwin's exposure of her liaison with Imlay was ridiculed and even her death in childbirth was held against her by the Reverend Polwhele:

> I cannot but think, that the Hand of Providence is visible, in her life, her death, and the Memoirs themselves. As she was given up to her 'heart's lusts', and let 'to follow her own imaginations', that the fallacy of her doctrines, and the effects of an irreligious conduct, might be manifested to the world; and as she died a death that strongly marked the distinction of the sexes, by pointing out the destiny of women, and the diseases to which they are liable; so her husband was permitted, in writing her Memoirs, to labour under a temporary infatuation, that every incident might be seen without a gloss – every fact exposed without an apology.[26]

As Wollstonecraft's death turned providential, standing in for the sexual fall she had experienced but refused to acknowledge in her life, so it became a Christian duty for all women to oppose her principles.

By the end of the century, then, few were trying to prove female intellectual equality and urge social and political rights. The stress had shifted from revolution and reform to reaction and retreat or to amelioration within social constraints. In 1798 Priscilla Wakefield in *Reflections on the Present Condition of The Female Sex, With Suggestions for Its Improvement* pleads for more intellectual opportunities for women indeed but puts greater emphasis on occupational ones. The subordination of women is perhaps not 'in the Order of Nature', as

Rousseau would have had it, but there is no Wollstonecraftian demand for equality. The superiority in feeling of the sentimental years is often mocked, but it is just as often replaced by a newer notion of women's moral superiority.

The new images are expressed more aggressively than the earlier Bluestocking ones which they resemble and they clearly form part of the political debates of the revolutionary decade. Hannah More, Jane West, Elizabeth Hamilton and Fanny Burney are as keen to murder the sentimental woman as the author of *The Rights of Woman*, but they are also eager to show sensibility colluding with rationalist feminism. Somewhat sympathetic to many of the claims of rationalism, the liberal Elizabeth Hamilton yet mocks Mary Hays because she expresses her notion of women's rights in personal emotional terms.

Although gentleness and meekness are preached again, they are severed from sensibility. Often the new meek and gentle woman is tinged with evangelical forms of Christianity, so potent during the early years of the next century; even Mary Hays in her older age came to be associated with Hannah More's brand of evangelicalism and her later works were published by More for the edification of the poor.

The new woman should be modest, practical and pragmatic. She should avoid the secrecy about her intellectual attainments enjoined on girls at the time of Lady Mary Wortley Montagu, but she must accept society as it is and not expect much gratification from her beauty or her brains. In Maria Edgeworth's *Practical Education* (1798) there is a pragmatic rather than providential need for an education in constant self-control. Equality and power are not the issues – in fact are rather vulgar as well as stupid considerations – and a little Christian humility is worth 'all the wild metaphysical discussion which has unsettled the peace of vain women'. Women must seek to be 'excellent women' not, as the Wollstonecraftian philosophy would have them, 'indifferent men'. As such they will improve society, and the old notion, so cynically expressed by Lord Chesterfield, that young men should be socialised – and sexualised – by sophisticated ladies, is replaced by the idea that men must be morally improved by the company of good women.

Conservative *male* writers expressed sentiments similar to women's, modifying the old sentimental construction and attacking political rationalism. They restated the gender difference; woman is cheerful and sprightly and man profound and intellectual, according to Gisborne. Erasmus Darwin in *A Plan for the Conduct of Female Education* (1797) gave the mild and retiring virtues to women, but in keeping with the more serious practical temper of the times he noted that there were situations in single life where women could cultivate an interest in arts and sciences and in married life where, because of the failure or death of a man, they might have to take charge of a family.

If there was much less opposition than before to intellectual development, the notion remained current among men that women who gained much learning would grow undomestic or eccentric. The term 'Bluestocking' became abusive in male vocabulary, a synonym for affectation of learning, sloppiness of dress and frustrated desire. The essayist William Hazlitt mentioned his 'utter aversion to *Bluestockings*' and the anonymous author of *The Female Jockey Club* (1794) described them letting their charms wither in time rather than submitting them 'to the *rude mercy* of that *odious monster* man'. More than women writers, men tended to stress female contingency. Women's first definition was through relationships: she was 'the sister . . . the daughter . . . the wife' according to Gisborne, echoing Addison and Steele. The notion was now welded to that of superior female morality, so that the whole became expressed in a woman's need to reform and inspire rather than please a man. Greater female sensitivity turned into a moral quality, avoiding the self-indulgence of sensibility, and women became examples of selflessness for men, rather than vessels of self-regarding feeling. Yet, according to a long line of male commentators, this female excellence needed gallant male protection, presumably because of women's mental weakness. Rousseau's sensual serviceable woman had become a moral serviceable woman and, in spite of Mary Wollstonecraft, sex remained in the soul.

12

RADICALS AND REACTIONARIES:
WOMEN WRITERS OF THE
LATE EIGHTEENTH CENTURY

Although there were still some conventional statements of uneasiness over the woman writer, the professional female author was by the late 1790s pretty much established in England and at least three to four hundred women published during the decade. Few followed Priscilla Wakefield in declaring that 'Literature affords a respectable and pleasing employment, for those who possess talents . . .' but many simply took the road she indicated and, by the end of the 1790s, whether preaching independence, duty or submission, they were assuming a remarkable authority for themselves as authors. Women had been involved in politicial controversy before and had penned much moral advice, but they had rarely done either so assertively as they would do in this unsettled time. In part the change must be ascribed to two factors: the growth in the audience for many types of literature and the politicising of all activities – even novel-writing, so peculiarly associated with women.

THE LITERARY MARKET PLACE

Commonly the author whose life is at all known was middle class. She often needed to work at literature because other avenues of employment were closed to her. More than the Victorian writer she was likely to be married, but she was often separated, her dependent children excluding her from the few career opportunities available to women. She wrote in other words possibly for enjoyment and satisfaction, certainly for money. The sorry picture the poet William Cowper drew of Charlotte Smith is extreme but perhaps not untypical of one group of novelists: 'Chained to her desk like a slave to his oar, with no other means of subsistence for herself and her numerous children . . .'[1]

Patronage had been declining throughout the eighteenth century, although it was still sought even in the 1790s in dedications and prefaces which aimed to prod the wealthy and well placed into giving support. Since it had never been a great method for women, except for a few learned ladies in the Bluestocking circles, and since it was of little use to the novelist, the decline could only be advantageous to female writers in general.

Some continued the habit of subscription, although a writer needed to have many friends or to be well established in society to make a success of the method. Fanny Burney fell into both categories, having been a great favourite with the Bluestocking hostesses as well as a lady-in-waiting at court. Less well-placed women could use the same method but it was preferable to have a group such as a church community to muster support. If a woman were publishing in a commercially unpopular area like a translation from the classics or a collection of sermons, or if she had chosen an unusual idea like popularised science, subscription might be an actual necessity.

It was certainly so for women in the lowest class, who would not have had access to publishers and would need to have relied on better-placed women to gain a subscription list for them, since inevitably the readership they sought was from the higher orders. This was the case with the poet Ann Candler, who needed wealthier friends to raise a subscription for a volume in the early 1800s; she hoped that its success would release her from the workhouse from which she was writing her doleful verses. The most famous of the working-class poets, the natural songstresses so much beloved by the eighteenth-century public, was Ann Yearsley, 'Lactilla' or the poetical milkwoman; she had to depend on the strenuous efforts of Hannah More for subscribers. The danger of such dependence became clear in the sequel: after a quarrel about the control of the money raised, Hannah More removed her support. Later, Yearsley had great difficulty in making literature pay without the help of the network of middle-class ladies on which her patron could call.

The usual procedure for the novelist rather than the poet or miscellaneous writer was to sell her copyright directly to a publisher. The late eighteenth century saw an explosion of novel-publishing to feed the ever increasing circulating libraries, although on the whole print runs remained small, usually well under 1000, and price seems to have increased. The circulating library suited the status of most women's fiction since its ownership delivered no prestige, unlike the ownership of Dr Johnson's essays or Cowper's poems. Notorious presses like William Lane's Minerva specialising in gothic sentimental novels provided the libraries with books that were hurriedly written to a formula by obscure women writers. The increase in unscrupulous publishing and the appeal to women – the class basis perhaps prevents reference to a mass market although many of the novel's themes and techniques do anticipate this nineteenth-century phenomenon – were largely responsible for the constant criticism and mockery aimed at fiction by educated people in the period who saw in it an undermining of traditional classical culture.

Lane's rise and profits were legendary: although beginning as a poulterer, he lived to see his son ride about in a carriage with two footmen in cockades, while at his death in 1814 he left the considerable estate of £17,500.[2] But subscription to a circulating library was quite expensive, between one and three guineas a year, the amounts paid to authors for run-of-the-mill fiction were fairly low, usually under ten pounds – indeed there is some evidence that women may have earned as little as a guinea for a novel.[3] To keep herself and her family respectably, then, an indifferently successful woman novelist would have had to produce as many as ten books a year. There were of course the great and famous exceptions: Ann Radcliffe and her £800 for *The Italian* or Fanny Burney's amazing £2000 for *Camilla*. The enormous sums for exceptional women suggest that, in the area of fiction publishing, the usual discrimination according to sex did not apply.

At the end of the century women writing in magazines and reviews for the general public became relatively common. Mary Wollstonecraft excitedly asserted that she was 'the first of a new genus' when she became the editorial assistant on *The Analytical Review* in 1787. Mary Hays wrote for *The Monthly Magazine*, as did Wollstonecraft and even Fanny Burney on occasion, and Elizabeth Inchbald for *The Edinburgh Review*. Women's journals of tales, recipes and letters continued, while magazines devoted to fashion spread the mode of London to the provinces. A sophisticated network of advertising was being established aided by improved transport, so that papers and magazines could be quickly distributed throughout the populous parts of the country.

A new development in which women played a significant part was the production of literature aimed at the lower orders. It was often thought by the middle-class writer that servants and the lower class in general were reading popular fiction. But in fact the price even of circulating library volumes would make this doubtful, unless servants could borrow from their employers. The new writing of the late eighteenth century was directly aimed at the poor and efficiently marketed to them.

The educational Sarah Trimmer had given impetus to the trend with her *Family Magazine* (1788–9) for 'cottagers and servants', providing moral tales and simplified sermons which preached a mixture of resignation and patriotism. It was not wildly popular at the time, but a volume of its stories appeared as *Instructive Tales* in 1810 when there was far more enthusiasm for this kind of literature. Trimmer, a mother of twelve children, was eager to give the benefit of her domestic experience to the poor, and she was quite clear that her work, including her magazine, was written to combat the disturbing effect of radical books and to improve the religion and morals of her readers.

The most successful and prolific author in the genre was of course Hannah More, who reached a very large audience indeed with her *Cheap Repository Tracts*, written in the 1790s and sold to the lower orders by hawkers and booksellers. Even more urgently than Trimmer's works, these tracts aimed in the unsettled war years to combat the political works that glamorised insubordination and revolt and made heroes of criminals. Incidentally More's experience suggests that piety directed at the poor could be quite profitable. Often the proceeds were intended for charitable use, but Hannah More managed to leave a large fortune at her death gained from writing. (Presumably not all of this derived from literature for the poor, since she seems to have had the knack of making almost all genres pay: she even managed to receive quite a handsome sum for her poems, 'Sir Eldred of the Bower' and 'The Bleeding Rock' in the 1770s.)

More was aware that her success with her didactic material was due to her unison with the moment: in 1801 she looked back on her successful literary career, remarking:

> If I have been favoured with a measure of success, which has as much exceeded my expectation as my desert, I ascribe it partly to a disposition in the public mind to encourage, in these days of alarm, attack, and agitation, any productions of which the tendency is favourable to good order and Christian morals, even though the merit of the execution by no means keeps pace with that of the principle.[4]

By 1800 Elizabeth Hamilton could make her exemplary spinster a writer of moral works, now a part of the enterprise of moral reform in which all good women should be engaged.

A sense that the lower as well as the upper orders were reading made it especially incumbent on writers to consider the moral tenor of their work. Clara Reeve put the point clearly:

> If there are more writers than formerly, there are likewise more readers: especially among the lower classes of people; this consideration should induce every writer to be particularly careful of what he offers to the public, that there be nothing contrary to religion and virtue and that through the vehicle of entertainment, moral inferences should be conveyed to the reader.[5]

Other didactic genres involved in the new urgency of morality included works on education and literature for as well as about children, all written and avidly consumed especially in the later 1790s. Ann Murry's *Mentoria* books were still popular from the 1770s, teaching girls proper and decorous subjects by the Rousseauian method of questions and answers. Wollstonecraft also wrote in this genre, a series of harsh moral tales illustrated by William Blake in the 1780s, but by the 1790s she was more concerned to preach to parents. More important for the development of the genre was Sarah Trimmer again, who wrote religious tales for children and began the vogue for stories about animals treated as humans – especially well received was her description of the robin family which in the nineteenth century, long after her death, was removed from its moral framework and repeatedly published alone. Anna Laetitia Barbauld provided poems for children as well as works on their education. The concern for education meant a market also for translations and for introductions to science. An example is Margaret Bryan's *A Compendious System of Astronomy*, published in 1797 by subscription and intended 'to be Intelligible to Those Who Have Not Studied the Mathematics'.

Women continued to write quite successfully for the theatre, and a few, like the much praised Joanna Baillie, Hannah Cowley and Elizabeth Inchbald, made considerable names for themselves. It helped to know the managers or to be an actress and so have some idea of the fare wanted. Inchbald was no great success on the stage but had acclaim in the late 1780s and 1790s for her comedies and farces; she was particularly adept at translating (and often almost rewriting) plays from German and French, forming clumsy works into dramatic fast-paced vehicles. It was one of these, a translation or adaptation from the German sensational dramatist Kotzebue entitled *Lovers' Vows* (1798), that caused such havoc in the study of Austen's Mansfield Park. In her original plays Inchbald touched on social issues like prison reform and on women's concerns; although she always came down on the side of security and marriage – as she does in her novels – she suggests that spirited behaviour might be as sensible as submissiveness and that divorce might be a useful route on occasion.

Poetry remained a popular genre and its elite status was encouraging to women, but it was not an especially paying one: some novelists like Charlotte Smith preferred to write verse but it could not feed her ten children. Women like Anna Laetitia Barbauld, Mary Robinson, Anna Seward and later Jane Taylor wrote verses of specific social criticism, fixing their poetry in the everyday world of objects and ordinary people. But on the whole it was the melancholy self-reflecting style of the earlier decades that was most appreciated and the lugubrious verses of Charlotte Smith and Mary Robinson about feeling hearts caught in the vanity and ingratitude of the world were more popular than Barbauld's occasional attempts at social criticism. The journals of the day were filled with women's effusions, complaining of discomfort in the world or generally lamenting the ills of slavery and war. What women did not write was *Romantic* poetry, giving the word all the resonance of later literary history, and, except for the extraordinary religious mystic and cult leader Joanna Southcott, they did not lay claim to the prophetic voice or to a visionary mode.

Mary Robinson had been famous as an actress for playing the role of Perdita. In this part she captivated the young Prince of Wales, whose mistress she became for a year. Robinson continued writing much distinguished poetry throughout her life – a sad one for she spent the last seventeen years paralysed – but, constantly needing money, she also wrote novels, one of which, *Vancenza; or, the Dangers of Credulity* (1792), sold out on its day of publication primarily because it was suspected to be a *roman à clef* about her liaison with the Prince. She also seems to have written a couple of works on the condition of women, radical enough for the late 1790s; her opinions, along with her association with some of the radicals, like William Godwin, entitled her to a place among Polwhele's 'Unsex'd Females'.

The cases of Robinson, Wollstonecraft, More, Smith, Trimmer, Inchbald – in fact almost all the professional women writers so far mentioned – indicate that, although the novel is the major form for women, the typical female writer crosses genres. Often she begins with poetry or an educational work in an amateur sort of way, but, as literature emerges as a method of earning a living or as circumstances begin to press on her, she turns towards the novel. Yet fiction was not the only paying genre, as Hannah More's experience testifies, and a woman could make quite a tidy living by ranging over nonfictional sorts of literature, while padding out her income with anthologies, encyclopedias, and collections of miscellaneous prose and poetry – rather like today. A few years later, Jane Austen would complain in *Northanger Abbey* that compilers and anthologisers often had more status – and probably therefore more money – than many novelists.

Few women wrote about female authors in their fiction, although there are many comments in their letters. An exception was the prolific and needy Charlotte Smith. She made her happy ending in *The Old Manor House* (1793) include the release of her hero from the exigencies of professional authorship. But in *The Banished Man* (1798) at the end of her novel career she presented a more realistic picture in Mrs Denzil, whose rent and bare cupboard force her day after day to churn out scenes of love between the most perfect of damsels and the most Richardsonian of heroes.

POLITICS

An extraordinary feature of literature of all types in the 1790s is its political nature, as Hazlitt noted when he summed up the tone of the times. Almost all genres were politicised in some way, while the choice of genre became a political statement itself and each fictional plot and literary device had some implications.

Women were of course excluded from participation in actual politics and only a very few men and women suggested that women could take part. Catherine Macaulay mentioned in passing women's lack of civic and political rights, while Wollstonecraft imagined a time when women *might* have the suffrage and compared their unenfranchised state with that of working men; Mary Hays hinted at political rights in her *Appeal*. From the fact that at different times in the century men had speculated that single propertied women might have the vote, it seems that the stumbling block was less gender than marriage, which made a single unit of the couple. In time the arbitrary nature of this would become apparent, but in the 1790s hardly anyone seriously took up the question of female suffrage – it first arose in Parliament through Charles James Fox in 1797 who argued that better-educated women might deserve the franchise more than ill-educated men, but even this was not a call for female suffrage as much as a plea for caution about male suffrage. Mostly the notion of the vote for women was used as the ultimate in absurdity by conservatives who mockingly attributed it to radicals who had never conceived of it. Even during the revolutionary decade, then, women were usually classed with infants, idiots and lunatics in political discussions.

Although Wollstonecraft had been careful to stress that marriage and motherhood were women's primary if not only functions, the 1792 *Rights of Woman* with its suggestion of public roles for women was going too far for most writers in the late 1790s; Wakefield thought public office highly improper for women, as did Elizabeth Hamilton, whose remarks can be read as typical of the post-radical years:

> By far the greater part of those who have hitherto taken upon them to stand forth as champions for sexual equality, have done it upon grounds that to me appear indefensible, if not absurd. It is not equality of moral worth for which they contend, and which is the only true object of regard, nor for an equality of rights with respect to the Divine Favour, which alone elevates the human character into dignity and importance; but for an equality of employments and avocations, founded upon the erroneous idea of a perfect similarity of powers. Infected by the prejudices which associate ideas of honour and esteem with knowledge . . . they desire for their sex an admission into the theatre of public life, and wish to qualify them for it by an education in every respect similar to that of men.[6]

224

The always forceful Hannah More expressed the common view in *Moral Sketches of Prevailing Opinion and Manners*:

> That providential economy which has clearly determined that women were born to share with men the duties of private life, has as clearly demonstrated that they were not born to divide with them in the public administration . . .

With this subordinating view most men agreed. After enumerating the dazzling routes to fame – of the soldier, the statesmen and the author – William Duff addressed his female reader: 'From all these splendid and envied spheres, (the last only excepted,) you my fair readers are debarred . . .'

It is an interesting exception, indicating the greatly improved status of authorship for women. Consequently one of the liveliest political debates in women's literature was over whether or not women should *write* overtly about political matters. Most knew nothing of or strategically ignored the contributions of women like Delarivier Manley or Catharine Trotter in what was now regarded as a distant degenerate age. Women divided on the subject along predictable ideological lines. Surprisingly, however, the conservative Jane West recommended that girls should *study* politics in a time of national emergency, such as the revolutionary 1790s appeared to be, so that they would strengthen their respect for king and country, although she firmly banished any notion of party politics.

Helen Maria Williams, a sentimental poet and novelist turned chronicler of the French Revolution, was associated in the public mind with French Jacobinism (which she detested) partly because of her friendship with English 'Jacobins' like Paine and Wollstonecraft. She wrote in a sentimental, sometimes gushing style, giving the day-to-day experience of revolution as she knew it; naturally she commented on the political scene in which she was caught up and she was free in her absolute judgements of the 'good' Madame Roland, for example, and the 'bad' Robespierre. Her books on the early Revolution were widely read and formed the basis for much British comment on French events.[7]

The unwomanly spectacle of the chronicling Miss Williams provoked irritation when enthusiasm for French events turned sour. Her former friend, the poet Anna Seward, advised her in print to fly the land of carnage, while James Boswell who had in his *Life of Johnson* recorded the Doctor's appreciation for the charming young poet and described her as 'amiable', expunged the word when he realised that she had forfeited esteem by writing 'in favour of the savage Anarchy' of France.[8] The staunchly conservative Laetitia Matilda Hawkins was inspired by the idea of Williams to declare that women should have nothing whatsoever to do with politics – she even managed to evade the assertive political nature of this statement by insisting that her idea was not original, but merely a feminine repetition of what others had said. Echoing Steele, who had attacked the political Manley, she proved that women were not created for the intense thought politics required since thinking screwed up the face and destroyed feminine beauty:

> Our Maker never designed us for anything but what he created us, a *subordinate* class of beings; a sort of noun adjective of the human species, tending greatly to the perfection of that to which it is joined, but incapable of sole-subsistence.[9]

A more thoughtful debate could be abstracted from the writings of Charlotte Smith and Fanny Burney. Smith believed that women could and should comment on politics, but she wrote defensively about their intervention, knowing that the prevailing attitude – at least after the middle of the decade – was against her. Already in *Desmond* (1792), in which she supported the early French Revolution, she had feared that she would be accused of impropriety for mixing entertainment and politics. In later years, when revolutionary support was considered far more outrageous, she referred to her success with a novel 'notwithstanding the politics' (*The Young Philosopher*, 1798), which she now anxiously asserted were not extreme or offensive.

But her political opinions *did* prove offensive and, as the public fell away from her in the increasingly conservative final years of the decade, she had to turn to children's books to make a living. Polwhele, who had admired the early, more escapist novels, which he placed beside the approved work of Ann Radcliffe and Fanny Burney, inserted the later Smith into his 'unsex'd female writers [who] instruct or confuse us and themselves, in the labyrinth of politics, or turn us wild with Gallic frenzy'. Smith was suffering from a 'disorder', an infection of 'the Gallic mania'.

The proper way to avoid the extremes of Hawkins's silence and Smith's impropriety was to follow the route of the cautious Fanny Burney. Her *Brief Reflections Relative to the French Clergy* (1793) would at first seem an example of the political concern which Charlotte Smith believed women should show but which many more conservative women opposed. Yet in fact it comes in apologetic mode and makes the point that women, or rather ladies, may comment politically – indeed *should* since they have the leisure for reflection and since the extraordinary times demand it – as long as they retain their *moral* role in the culture. In other words, women can comment if they turn the political into the moral, if they reflect and refine and remark 'feelingly, nay awefully, upon the woes they see, yet are spared!' The feeling response is essential for femininity: in women 'public affairs assume the interest of private feelings'. For Burney it is woman's axiomatic separation from the public sphere which actually allows comment on it, comment that enhances her moral status while it accepts her absolute exclusion from day-to-day politics.[10]

Whatever the theory, in practice an immense amount of political writing by women was produced during a short period when it was felt possible for people from the cultural margins to speak out. Wollstonecraft in her *Vindication of the Rights of Men* commented on Burke's parliamentary speeches and on the breakdown of authority implied by George III's madness; later she wrote a lengthy history of the first years of the French Revolution. The reactionary Hannah Cowley attacked her for this kind of activity, insisting that 'politics are *unfeminine*' (*A Day in Turkey*, 1792). Yet, although she denied any political content in her own theatrical work, she clearly attacked feminist opinion and the French Revolution. In this the device of Burney is apparent – if one held radical or liberal views, this was a political stance, but if one expressed proper conservative ones, this was a moral position. It was this notion that allowed conservative women to send a barrage of abuse at what they regarded as the political or Jacobin novel while denying in their own forthright assertive books any tincture of politics.

FICTION

By the 1790s female sentimental and romantic fiction was in disrepute. Hardly any serious person had a good word to say for it and radicals, liberals and conservatives vied with each other to hurl abuse at the escapist, self-indulgent, immoral fantasy which they believed the women's novel had become. Hence in the final years few writers with any claims to seriousness wished to be caught writing novels and a peculiar situation arose in which novelist after novelist declared with Burney and Edgeworth that she was not writing what she so obviously was. Only the gothic writers embraced the uncomfortable word 'Romance', although as early as 1785 Clara Reeve in her *A Progress of Romance* was trying to stiffen the form with educational purpose.

But it was not only the triviality of the novel that was unsettling but its power, its ability to grab and divert the mind. So in the radical years the idea gained ground that this fictional power could be harnessed for reform. A spate of novels by men like Godwin, Holcroft and Bage and women like Wollstonecraft, Hays and to some extent Helen Maria Williams, Charlotte Smith and Elizabeth Inchbald aimed to raise political consciousness and to preach the new ideas more winningly. It is probably fair to say that each of them found, like the equally didactic Samuel Richardson before them, that the power of fiction was difficult to harness for political and educational purposes. On the whole, then, their novels tended to become muddled and schematic tracts like Wollstonecraft's *The Wrongs of Woman*. Or, like Godwin's *Caleb Williams* and Mary Hays's *Memoirs of Emma Courtney*, they presented a peculiarly pessimistic picture of a world which seemed open to improvement only in the nonfictional works. In the case of Smith and Inchbald the message was more ambiguously delivered, for Charlotte Smith coupled her overt political and social statements with almost parodic exaggeration of the elements in the traditional feminine novel which for financial reasons she felt she had to write, while Elizabeth Inchbald followed a seemingly satirical first section of *A Simple Story* – almost a throwback to the Manley plot of the eroticised tie of guardian and ward – with a sentimentalised version in which the actors are familial father and daughter. With this repetition she made – but only by implication – a biting attack on authoritarian patriarchy.

Although Wollstonecraft and Hays are fascinating for their efforts to turn the novel into a vehicle of reform and for their passionate analysis of the legacy of sensibility, it is not with them that the strength of late-eighteenth-century fiction lies. Rather it is with those women who managed to insert into the novel that extraordinary authority already noticed in Hannah More, of the woman as moralist. Such women – Fanny Burney, Ann Radcliffe, Charlotte Smith, and a little later Maria Edgeworth and Jane Austen – dominated the fiction of the late eighteenth and early nineteenth centuries, unrivalled by any male writer until the rise of Walter Scott. It is worth contemplating this unique phenomenon in literary history, this conjunction of genre and gender, and setting it in a critical perspective.

Throughout the eighteenth century prose fiction was not a privileged elite genre. But the existence of the earlier male writers, especially of Richardson and Fielding, had given it some status in culture; this was not readily available to the host of sentimental women writers but it could be achieved by a well-placed writer such as Fanny Burney. In addition prose writing in general, never as privileged as poetry, had been elevated by the example of Samuel Johnson, who helped to turn the author into the man of letters. The image was predominantly male, but it was open to women to make it theirs.[11]

Towards the end of the century, however, many educated men thought that prose had been somewhat debased by the intrusion of women and uncultured men from the lower ranks. Direct political statement of the sort made by Godwin in *Caleb Williams* became increasingly inappropriate and the most imaginative male writers tended to turn towards poetry for self-expression. The Romantic poets from this period dominate literary history and, despite some interest in the speech of the common man, their concern is to move from direct political expression into a realm of the aesthetic. They take on the prophetic voice rather than the mundane commentator's and, in the piercing of surface trivialities, become indeed 'unacknowledged legislators of the world', in Shelley's resonant phrase.

It is strange, remarked the poet Samuel Rogers, that, while 'we men are modestly content to amuse by our writings, women must be didactic'. Female novelists united in their effort to use fiction for interventionist purposes, to comment on life as it was lived at the particular historical moment and to provide a moral or political critique that would help the reader to bear or change her conditions. Taking the bare bones of the sentimental romantic plot, rarely avoided by women, they became not historians or visionaries but moral commentators. They eschewed claims to original creation as an image of divine activity and chose the didactic-moral ground; it was in part the usual gesture of feminine modesty and in part a conscious boast. After her early flirtation with poetry, Hannah More found it solipsistic, too indulgent of passive feelings, and she turned to prose. Female art was resolutely *not* transcendental; ethics not aesthetics was its business. Unfortunately, established literary criticism has never taken kindly to the moral-didactic in art, nor to most of the women who profess it.[12]

The ubiquity of the moral imperative for women can be gauged from the most popular — and many thought the most debased — fiction, the gothic novel. This had emerged as the sentimental romance was sensationalised, primarily in the 1790s. It had a staple plot, deriving from Horace Walpole's *jeu d'esprit, The Castle of Otranto*, from the mid-century; relying on the theatrical props of dungeons, forests, curses and buried secrets, the gothic could deliver a potent myth of sadism and incest. Although male and female versions have much in common, there are immediate distinctions between them — for example, the male tends to allow violation, as Richardson had done within the sentimental novel, and present a far more masochistic helpless heroine. In general the female plot wrenches a pure heroine from the female space of home to enter the frightening male space of the castle, monastery, dungeon or its equivalent, where she encounters an older father or husband figure who is not her father or husband but who has authority over her and who may pose a sexual as well as social threat. The heroine's experiences will be nightmarish and unclear; consequently these novels can be interpreted by later ages in psychological terms. But female authors themselves were usually unremittingly moral and Ann Radcliffe, the acknowledged queen of the genre, certainly saw her work as improving and educating her readers. Terror is contained and the worst does not happen to girls who practise some self-control.

POLITICS IN THE NOVEL

Women writers of the mid-century clearly felt under the shadow of *Clarissa*. The shadow is still present but considerably lightened by the final years when many readers disliked the intense piety of the work and revolted against Clarissa's seeming complicity in her own death. The dominant influence now comes from an altogether more subversive and ambiguous book, itself greatly influenced by *Clarissa*, Rousseau's *La Julie ou Nouvelle Héloïse*, published in the mid-eighteenth century but makings its major impact in the late 1780s and '90s.

Many women, most notably Wollstonecraft and Macaulay, had attacked the contingent picture of the sexually alluring Sophie in *Emile*. Rousseau himself must have felt somewhat uncomfortable too because he began a sequel, *Emile et Sophie*, in which Sophie rebels and grows unfaithful. The problem of women's sexual activity rather than simply their sexual allure is squarely faced in *Héloïse*; the first part, told in passionate letters, describes the love affair of the aristocratic Julie with her tutor Saint-Preux, while the second, despite the sexual activity, makes Julie the wife of her father's old friend Wolmar, an enlightened atheist, with whom she forms an ideal community of children, friends, faithful servants and retainers until her early death. Rousseau does not differentiate letter styles in the skilful manner of Richardson but he does echo the earlier writer's psychological intensity and his influence helped to impel other novelists towards a more undramatic style of self-expression or moral opinion. For many male writers the non-Christian views of Wolmar had considerable fascination, while for others the social implications were the issue – Burke attacked the novel as undermining the proper hierarchy of class, since Saint-Preux is merely a tutor. But for women gender was far more important and the sexual act outside wedlock in the first part had the kind of unsettling fascination exerted on early decades by the rape of Clarissa. As Richardson's friend Lady Echlin had wanted to rewrite the ending of his novel, so the critic Clara Reeve wanted to alter *Héloïse* to make 'the two lovers stop short of the act that made it criminal in either party to marry another'.[13]

Rousseau himself was worried about the effect of his book, feeling it unsuitable for unmarried girls. It became unsuitable for anyone in the

1790s; his ideas had become associated with the French Revolution and the intense subjectivity – and passionate sexuality – he described seemed implicated in the social chaos of revolutionary France. Its use in a spate of novels by women writers had, then, both political and social resonance.

Early rewritings of Rousseau up to the mid-1790s avoid the heady issue of female desire and sexuality and concentrate on the psychological nuances of the various lovers' triangles. In one imitation, *Julia de Roubigné* (1777), Henry Mackenzie simplifies the story by making the lovers pure and the husband unwanted; the death at the end is even more escapist than Rousseau's. Helen Maria Williams's version, *Julia* (1790), rendered more obnoxious by an inserted poem in praise of the French Revolution, makes the triangle two women loving the same man. Everything is rigidly moral, as Wollstonecraft complained in her review; interestingly, however, it is the man rather than the woman who dies under the strain. The ending leaves the two women comfortably together raising a child. A similar ending is provided in Charlotte Lennox's late final novel *Euphemia* (1790) and in some versions of Wollstonecraft's unfinished *The Wrongs of Woman*; it is a female communal conclusion, very rarely provided by male writers.

For the few daring writers in the mid- and later 1790s Rousseau's book seemed to suggest that a woman who had had a sexual experience could be redeemed. Such a reading indicates an involvement only in Part I and indeed the novels of Mary Wollstonecraft, Mary Hays, Eliza Fenwick and Amelia Opie refer almost entirely to this section. In these works the book functions as intellectual seduction, the equivalent of Ovid and Catullus discovered in libraries by Manley's unfortunate ingenues; its reading is the prelude to sexual fall, undermining the strict notion of the double standard and bringing female desire firmly within sensibility. The result in the most radical writers is extremely ambiguous, both liberating and, because this liberation takes place in the world as it is, destructive.

The novels of Wollstonecraft, Hays, Fenwick, Smith and Williams were all suspected of having autobiographical elements. This had been assumed of women in the sentimental phase, but it was given a political tinge by the recently published autobiography of Rousseau, which had revolutionised the form by concentrating not on public life but on private sensation. Hays was most notorious in her use of her own actual letters in her fiction but all these writers call rather obviously on their own characters or experiences or on those of people they have known. Charlotte Smith, whose unseemly portraits of the feckless Mr Smith and her victimised self had been much criticised, felt impelled to justify the habit in the preface to *The Banished Man*:

231

> The History Painter gives to his figures the cast of countenance he is accustomed to see around him – the Landscape Painter derives his predominant ideas from the country in which he has been accustomed to study – a novelist, from the same causes, makes his drawing to resemble the characters he has had occasion to meet with.[14]

This was reasonable doctrine for a man – and her pronoun is necessarily male – but women's writing was not as alienable as this, as Charlotte Smith well knew, and observation could not so easily become an autonomous commodity for a woman writer.

With all these fictional traits of the radical and liberal writers, first-person or epistolary narrative and self-display, the moral reactionary novel took great exception. By the end of the century many conservative and liberal women had been urged into the novel – or rather what they regarded as the anti-novel – by the idea that the new, already waning philosophy of liberation represented by Wollstonecraft and Godwin might yet succeed. The 'Jacobin' novels were attacked as French, rather like the secret political histories of Manley and Haywood had been earlier in the century. Despite the fact that none of these works actually showed the unconventional, sexually experienced woman triumphant – although they might be sympathetic to the fallen woman and recommend divorce – the reactionary writers treated them as if they had done so and they countered the influence with a spate of moral tales taking liberated women to the traditional female end of seduction, betrayal and death. In the process they regarded themselves as striking a blow for king, country and constitution.

The most obnoxious novel was probably Hays's *Emma Courtney*. Elizabeth Hamilton mocked it for equating political revolution and sexual freedom; in *Memoirs of Modern Philosophers* she parodied its abstract sentimental language and self-righteous tone: 'She finally consented to set an example of moral rectitude, by throwing off the chains of filial duty.'[15] The ugly Bridgetina Botherim becomes the image of Emma Courtney – Mary Hays, the self-asserting dupe of Rousseau's *Héloïse*, the heroine of which is described unceremoniously by one of the male characters as 'a wanton baggage, who was got with child by her tutor'.

But, despite the opportunities afforded by the spectacle of Mary Hays publishing her own love letters, there was obviously a need for a 'novel' that wholeheartedly supported the desiring heroine *and* radical politics. This was discovered not in fiction at all but in William Godwin's *Memoirs of the Author of a Vindication of the Rights of Woman*, written in 1798, the year after his wife's death.

It was easy to attack the rigidly moral *Rights of Woman* only if, like Hannah More, one refused to read it. But the publication of the *Memoirs* and the fragment of *The Wrongs of Woman* clearly allowed more conservative readers to link the new rationalist philosophy with sensibility, already associated with sexuality, in a way difficult before. For Godwin made of his wife a heroic and romantic fallen woman and he told his tale of her passion for a married man, her betrayal, her illegitimate child, her suicide attempts and death in an admiring tone that suggested that she was in fact a model of virtue and fidelity. Such an individualistic, sentimental, antisocial and subversive portrait was a generous gift to conservatives, who made a great deal of it.

The reactionary moral novel took many devices from earlier fiction. The two heroines demanded by the epistolary form and so imaginatively used by Richardson and Rousseau became schematised into contrasting girls whose different educations propelled them towards content or destruction. But the moral novelists pulled away from Rousseau in their effort to avoid the self-centredness of sensibility and turned to the device of the authoritative and characterised narrator to control their works. The third-person method was useful for women who, like Ann Radcliffe, wanted to distance the effect of sensibility or who, like Charlotte Smith, desired to stress the social and political rather than the psychological; it was serviceable to all writers who wished to stress the moral over the personal and present their views, not themselves. (Fittingly, later ages know infinitely more about the short life of Mary Wollstonecraft than about the doubly long one of Jane West.) West invented Prudentia Homespun to deliver her tales with 'the stamp of truth', so avoiding any taint of improper self-assertiveness. Homespun and other named and unnamed narrators often tended to be spinsters or widows – in opposition to the image of the sexually available Wollstonecraft – detached from the hurly-burly in which the heroines were enmeshed, advocating a marriage that should be endured but hinting that one might do worse than join the 'fraternity' of old maids.

The moral reactionary novel preached domesticity and resignation with an absolute certainty that had been lost by the more radical writers. Jane West announced bluntly that *A Gossip's Story* (1798) was designed 'to illustrate the Advantages of CONSISTENCY, and the DOMESTIC VIRTUES; and to expose to ridicule, CAPRICE, AFFECTED SENSIBILITY, and an IDLE, CENSORIOUS HUMOUR . . .' Like all her novels, it attacked the new philosophy of liberation and took badly brought-up girls to ruin, often through a feminist desire for adultery or simply some initiating activity, seen as defiance of omnipotence since the divine scheme dictated subordination and passivity for women. The new philosophy was invariably tried out through male sexual seduction, and invariably found ruinous to domestic (and national) peace and moderate happiness. The particular feminine trajectory stood in for the trajectory of the nation.

233

Although the moral writers were as strong in their opposition to the female romantic novel as they were to 'Jacobin' ideas, their plots suggest that they could not escape the influence of feminine romantic and sentimental fiction, even though they sometimes banished the classic feminine plot to the margins – as Jane Austen would do in *Sense and Sensibility*. In the hands of the less skilful exponents this influence gave the novels a curiously fragmented quality very similar to that caused by the ideological difficulties in Hays and Wollstonecraft. West and More and many others insisted on the mundane unromantic nature of the experience they described against the high-flown rhapsodies of the radical novel or the sensational exoticism of the gothic; yet their cautionary tales revolved endlessly around melodramatic destruction and death.

With all the differences and modifications, there is some unity to the fiction of the end of the century. All the women writers continued to employ some sentimental elements within their novels and all stayed largely within the confines of the feminine romantic plot. Ageing though the authors might be, none made the central character an older woman with feckless dependants or a lonely governess of intellectual taste but without physical charms – although these characters could appear as subsidiaries in fiction and could become central in autobiographical writings such as Mary Ann Radcliffe's *Memoirs*. The revolt against sensibility became a restatement of art's need to involve itself in life, a reaction to the tendency of late sentimental literature to stray too far from the moral.

The new novel did not take its stand on verisimilitude, but it did intend to be psychologically 'true' and it allowed the readers to learn, despite its plot, the difference between real life and the sentimental romances on which they had probably been nurtured. Although they differ in resignation or anger, all the writers accept the power of words to define reality and stifle and control desire in a way quite foreign to the liberated visions of Romantic poetry. So Wollstonecraft and Hays describe the magic circle of languge that circumscribes female longing and ambition and prevents political action, and Burney and West show the power of reputation, the loss of self involved in another's speech, the fear of being named and known. All seem to suggest that the discourse of certain kinds of subjectivity is dangerous for women – and, if women try to appropriate it, as Wollstonecraft and Hays seem to do, they will arrive at a self-destroying impasse. All equate sexual and political struggle and place the former within the social, so that sex does not stand for some intellectual union or transcendental experience, as so often in Romantic art, but simply runs its course into pregnancy and lost reputation.

All the serious writers believe in the educational purpose of fiction. All see themselves in some way as moral commentators, charting and investigating their specific times, speaking not like the Romantic poets for posterity or the chosen few of all ages but for ordinary people of their own day. All deny the autonomy of the aesthetic realm and refuse a division between Romantic and realistic, avoiding both vision and seemingly neutral reportage. All are self-conscious about the novel form and claim for it an authority through the techniques of traditional feminine modesty and authenticity. In short, whatever their persuasion, all these writers are political; as Jane West remarked in *Letters to a Young Lady* – prosaically anticipating to very different effect Shelley's poetic notion – 'Although we are not entitled to a place in the senate, we become *legislators* in the most important sense of the word, by impressing on the minds of all around us the obligation which gives force to the statute.'

13

'THE UNSEX'D FEMALES':

MARY WOLLSTONECRAFT AND MARY HAYS

About this time last year I closed my poor Fanny's eyes – I have been reviewing my past life – and the ghost of my former joys, and vanished hopes, haunted me continually – pity me – and excuse my silence – do not reproach me – for at this time I require the most friendly treatment . . . sick and low spirited I may sometimes long for the bosom of a friend – and fondly dwell on scenes which will obtrude themselves on my bitter recollections wound my poor heart which cannot be filled by mere common placed affections . . . This warfare will in time be over –and my soul will not vainly pant after happiness – or doubt in what it consists – I have fostered too great a refinement of mind, and given a keener edge to the sensibility nature gave me – so that I do not relish the pleasures most people pursue – nor am I disturbed by their trifling cares – yet it would be well if I had any hope to gild my prospect – any thing to animate me in my race besides the desire of reaching the goal . . .[1]

Mary Wollstonecraft wrote this self-pitying letter to George Blood, the brother of her dead friend Fanny, when she was a resentful governess to the aristocratic Kingsboroughs in Ireland. It is a good example of the female posture of sensibility in the late eighteenth century.

About the same time as she was lamenting to George Blood, she was writing her first novel, *Mary, A Fiction*, in which she anatomised the friendship with Fanny, complacently finding most pathos in the fact that the living woman had in the end disappointed her generous and benevolent friend (although her death had been more gratifying). The fictional heroine Mary has much of her real-life creator's characteristics of self-centredness, self-satisfaction and genuine good will. It was perhaps inevitable that she should, since the Wollstonecraft who wrote the letters was as much under the influence of the late-eighteenth-century conception of feminine sensibility as the character she created. The style of writing in both genres is typical of the sentimental novel of the 1780s and 1790s.

236

Already in the 1780s, the heroic sentimental story of virtuous distress and triumph appeared threadbare to some and the Wollstonecraft of this period was influenced less by sentimental fiction than by nonfictional versions of sensibility – by Rousseau in *Emile*, whom she called in her letters 'a strange inconsistent unhappy clever creature' with 'an uncommon portion of sensibility . . .', and by Charlotte Smith's grumbling and melancholic sonnets, at times very similar in tone to the outpourings of *Mary, A Fiction*.[2] The problem was that such nonfictional and poetic works provided rather a mood and a predicament than a plot, and it was difficult to translate them into a story or to make them suggest any progress for the heroine. Undoubtedly a sense of sentimental superiority could comfort the educated, poor and unappreciated woman, but it did not indicate a future or make much material difference to her situation.

Yet there is an effort being made in *Mary, A Fiction*, an effort typical of a few serious but seriously flawed novels of this period. For in them women were trying, through self-pitying contemplation, to move from the dream of spiritual power caught in *Clarissa* and from the fantasy of social power through attractive impotence caught in the sentimental novel of Frances Brooke and Mrs Gunning, to a new notion of female signficance based merely on self-consciousness, desire (not yet overtly sexual in an early novel like *Mary, A Fiction*) and self-expressiveness. In this effort sensibility is unsettled but not in the end opposed and the route is not out of it but into its excess.

It is in Mary Hays and Mary Wollstonecraft that the literary nature of the feminine ideology of sensibility is clearest and in whom autobiography and fiction are most scandalously entwined. In both *Mary, A Fiction* and *The Memoirs of Emma Courtney* the loud message is that of Wollstonecraft's letter, 'pity me'. The demand is for a childish significance which the culture has too quickly demanded that women surrender. This significance may be delivered both in pity and in fulfilment of active sexual or emotional desire. For a brief moment, then, it seemed that women could, through the indulgence rather than the repression of sensibility, break out of the 'magic circle' of constructed impotence.

The Rights of Woman and *Appeal to the Men of Great Britain* both testify to the fact that at moments in their lives Hays and Wollstonecraft saw a rationalist hope for their sex and understood the imprisoning cultural construction of female sensibility. But at other times they were trapped in the ideology of femininity and in the myths of the sentimental novel, a comfort against the cold winds of contempt endured by both. Different genres expressed the different facets of their personalities; in their polemical nonfiction both wrote of a world that ought to be, a rational one in which women would pierce through the ideology that ensnared them, but in fiction they both tried to bend the sentimental ideology to their own purpose, creating unstable stories that proclaimed and castigated women's peculiar sensibility, the emotional vulnerability of the superior feeling heart that twists and turns to irritate and wound itself. Wollstonecraft's fictional treatments of sensibility flank *A Vindication of the Rights of Woman*. *Mary, A Fiction* was written in 1787 and published in 1788, *The Wrongs of Woman or Maria* exactly a decade later in 1797 and published posthumously in 1798. Hays's *Memoirs of Emma Courtney* appeared between her friend's two novels in 1796, after she claims to have written the *Appeal to the Men of Great Britain* and before its anonymous publication in 1798.

Mary, A Fiction was composed when Wollstonecraft was a governess in Ireland.[3] A reader of her letters may well feel some wicked sympathy for Lady Kingsborough, who offered her prickly insubordinate employee her used gowns only to have them thrown back at her, and who included her in parties only to find her despising the noble guests. As Wollstonecraft repeatedly asserted, she was not cut out for subservience or contingency. As a teenager she had already declared that she had to be first in friendship and as an employee she simply could not be pleased. Before she arrived at the Kingsboroughs' she had left her inadequate family of feckless father, subordinate mother and many siblings to be a companion and then the organiser of a school. She sacrificed the school for Fanny Blood, the poor but accomplished friend whose desire for marriage to a merchant in Portugal had been a sore test of Wollstonecraft's affection. Yet, when the ailing Fanny was near her confinement, Wollstonecraft abandoned her school and arrived just in time to see her friend die. She returned home to find, as she no doubt expected, that her school was in ruins. She had little choice but to sell herself as governess, knowing full well the social horrors of the position for such a woman as herself. She took refuge in the only obvious role open, that of sentimental lady, and her letters, like the one to George Blood, are full of the cries of superior feeling in a desert of social trivia. *Mary, A Fiction,* which both expresses and unkindly anatomises the friendship with Fanny, is likewise one immense cry for sympathy and it is often unclear whether this sympathy is demanded for author or character.[4]

Both the plot and the comment within the novel loudly declare the need for belief in sensibility and its total inadequacy as a social philosophy. As a child of a trivial woman, the heroine Mary, like her creator, lives through the reclusive individualistic poetry of sensibility with its emphasis on the finer feelings, not, it is stressed, through trivial sentimental fiction. So Wollstonecraft, writing a novel, indulges in the conventional, almost obligatory sniping at the form she is using. The friendship of Mary and 'Ann' avoids the appealing equality of previous sentimental female friendship, as well as the exciting inequality of relationships based on devotion and patronage so popular in the 1760s (and due for a resurrection in the gothic romance). Yet there seems no other vocabulary for relationship besides the sentimental, and it is almost a relief when the rather disappointing Ann enters the proper sentimental plot of dying heroine, when language and situation, sentiment and plot, can coalesce.

The sentimental language is equally suitable for the next relationship, of Mary and the hero Henry, denied the role of threatening sexual male by a confirmed invalidism and an early failure in love. He becomes interested in Mary when he sees her in a tableau of sensibility, a ministering angel to her dying friend. In him the feminised man of feminine romantic fantasy is both taken to its extreme and taken apart: he is powerless to serve the heroine and instead co-opts the moment of death; it is he not she who dies surrounded by tearful onlookers.

From the start the authorial investment in the portrait of Mary is apparent. She is the 'little blushing girl' who gives all her possessions away to the poor, the solitary sufferer whose only joy is in her suffering, 'the slave of compassion'. Philanthropy which should be the social expression of sensibility becomes merely desire for love, never gratified. The fault is always outside the self: the world is 'ever hostile and armed against the feeling heart'. There is no social and active route for this sensibility, termed 'the most exquisite feeling of which the human soul is susceptible' and it simply vacillates, now seeming a kind of hint of immortality on earth, now a fictional construction: 'One moment she was a heroine, half determined to bear whatever fate should inflict; the next, her mind would recoil – and tenderness possessed her whole soul.'[5] In a letter of the time Wollstonecraft, who came later to repudiate her embarrassingly revelatory first novel, considered that it showed how 'a genius will educate itself'. In fact, however, the heroine has little education and makes no forward progress. Her sensibility has nothing to do in the world, nothing to create or achieve, and it simply consumes itself. Without the sustaining myth of male desire, it shrivels up and Mary is left looking to an afterworld in which she seems hardly to believe. The God of *Mary, A Fiction* is not the Father of Clarissa and he provides no substitute for the earthly lovers that have eluded her. She achieves no autonomy and it is not suggested that this might be her aim. In *David Simple* after an appalling life progress, the death hunger of sensibility had become clear. It is once again starkly apparent here, but without much Christian justification.

The story of *Mary, A Fiction* is close in essence to Wollstonecraft's life – despite a wish-fulfilling movement of the central character from the middle class into the nobility and from the margins into the centre of the lives of her family and of her friend who, unlike Fanny Blood, dies unmarried. In her 'Advertisement' Wollstonecraft stressed how intimately she was concerned with her suffering heroine. Scorning derivative and artificial writers, she included herself among the 'chosen few' who 'wish to speak for themselves', to write without masks, and she praised only works 'where the soul of the author is exhibited, and animates the hidden springs'. At the end of the preface she reinforced the connection of character and creator when she wrote that in her tale 'the mind of a woman, who has thinking power is displayed'.

Within the novel Mary reaches absolute impasse as she comes up against the various problems inherent in the notion of sensibility for women. She loses the sense of gratification through sentimental benevolence when the objects of largesse become ungrateful and she faces an afterlife that is simply the negation of the fearful married state of the world, a place *'where there is neither marrying*, nor giving in marriage'; meanwhile the death she hopes for will be completely without audience and so without significance. The sensibility in the novel has eschewed such female sentimental power by defining itself not through feminine romance, in which there is always some eroticising, but through asexual and individual sentimental poetry; consequently sensibility cannot empower or redeem. But it cannot be dismissed either:

> Surely life is a dream, a frightful one! and after those rude, disjointed images are fled, will light ever break in? Shall I ever feel joy? Do all suffer like me; or am I framed so as to be particularly susceptible of misery? It is true, I have experienced the most rapturous emotions – short-lived delight! – ethereal beam, which only serves to shew my present misery – yet lie still, my throbbing heart, or burst; and my brain – why dost thou whirl about at such a terrifying rate? Why do thoughts so rapidly rush into my mind, and yet when they disappear leave such deep traces? I could almost wish for the madman's happiness, and in a strong imagination lose a sense of woe ... I am now the prey of apathy – I could wish for the former storms! a ray of hope sometimes illumined my path; I had a pursuit; but now *it visits not my haunts forlorn.* Too well have I loved my fellow creatures! I have been wounded by ingratitude ... When overwhelmed by sorrow, I have met unkindness; I looked for some one to have pity on me; but found none! – The healing balm, of sympathy is denied; I weep, a solitary wretch, and the hot tears scald my cheeks.[6]

In many ways the passage is appalling in its total self-regard expressed in the hackneyed language of sensibility. But it is undeniably modern, quite distinct from the grand laments of the victims of the early women writers or indeed from the sorrowings of such sentimental heroines as Clarissa or Sidney Bidulph. Quoting from Charlotte Smith's sonnets, it suggests the use of writing by women for a kind of therapy, an outlet for what would otherwise be intolerable and maddening pressure. What it fails to suggest is any detachment and mode of release from the pathos of the predicament.

Yet, in the event, there *was* a clear distinction between life and literature, for Wollstonecraft herself broke through the complainings and the fantasy of easeful death conveyed in the letter to George Blood by turning her self-expression into a profession and becoming a writer for the radical publisher Joseph Johnson. A few years later she tried in *A Vindication of the Rights of Woman* to mount a large-scale attack on the sensibility of *Mary, A Fiction* that was entrapping her and her heroine. In this work women's seeming intellectual inferiority became due to men's oppression, but also to a mistaken ideology of sensibility that formed part of that oppression and in which women themselves were involved. Sexuality and passion, the hidden synonyms of sensibility, were traps for women and the correct way forward was not through excess of self-contemplating sensibility but through reason.

The Rights of Woman was greatly admired by Mary Hays, also a friend of Joseph Johnson; she had had the assurance in the heady days of the early Revolution to write a pamphlet supporting public worship, the kind of subject usually reserved for men. While Wollstonecraft was working out her sad infatuation with Gilbert Imlay, the American mercantile adventurer whom she had met in revolutionary France, Hays was falling in love with the Unitarian thinker and leader William Frend, who may have initially encouraged her advances though the public sensationally liked to regard them as entirely unrequited. She described her emotional odyssey to Wollstonecraft's future husband, William Godwin, who sent letters urging her to control herself and understand the historical female predicament of sensibility. But understanding was not enough, and in 1796 Hays eased her feelings by publishing her thinly disguised account of the affair using the letters of herself and Godwin to form the body of her novel. In doing so she arrived by a lengthier route at something close to the impasse of *Mary, A Fiction*.

Like *Mary, A Fiction*, *Emma Courtney* is a vivid expression of the problem of the sentimental ideology for women, its simultaneously liberating and stultifying effect, allowing the route of excess and yet giving a conventional trajectory of misery and death to that excess. Until the sensational end, its plot is simple. Emma is brought up in snatches by a cynical rationalist father, by a sentimental aunt who peruses old romances, and finally by vulgar relatives. She finds refuge with a benevolent widow whose image of her son Harley strongly attracts the heroine despite the advances from a physically present suitor, Mr Montague. With the self-confidence that individualistic sensibility can create, she throws off the mask of feminine coyness and firmly announces her affection for Harley, who repulses her. Through most of the remainder of the novel she relentlessly pursues him with reproaches and arguments, rationally demanding that her emotions be attended to.

The denouement briefly aligns the novel with the conventional romantic plot and provides the wish-fulfilment Wollstonecraft had likewise not denied herself – it is revealed that Harley had some years earlier made an imprudent marriage. The disclosure allows Emma to become a sentimental fictional heroine. She falls ill and suffers a brain fever which is terminated by her marriage to the convenient Mr Montague. Harley is fatally wounded and dies in Emma's arms. But again the novel veers from convention. Gnawed by jealousy of a love that his new wife has taken no trouble to hide, Montague contracts a liaison with a servant. His bizarre reaction is to save the servant from scandal by killing her baby and then himself. Emma is left with her own child, Emma, and the son of her dead love. Years later the daughter dies and she has only the comfort of the loving couple across generations. It is for Harley's son that the memoir is written.

This tangled ending of infidelity and suicide, together with the union of mother and child so common in the female fiction of this period, will recur in the final work, *The Wrongs of Woman*; so it becomes ironic that Wollstonecraft lost sympathy with *Emma Courtney* after the removal of Harley, when the novel becomes, in her view, a succession of brutalities and deaths.[7]

The ambiguous messages of the book, like those of *Mary, A Fiction*, are delivered in the contradictions between the novel and the preface, in which the author tries to make the work cautionary: 'the errors of my heroine were the offspring of sensibility; and ... the result of her hazardous experiment is calculated to operate as a warning, rather than as an example.' The heroine will love virtue but be ensnared by passion and be 'liable to the mistakes and weaknesses of our fragile nature'. By 1796 it is a usual aim, worthy of any conservative writer, and indeed Hays states that her subject is 'a sentiment hackneyed in this species of composition'. Yet the effect of the book is far from cautionary. Emma's errors certainly deserve that name if the reader attends to the plot, but the perspective throughout is dangerously the heroine's and she is as likely to glory in as to denigrate her sensibility. The reader is allowed to identify with her, indeed is encouraged to do so – as she has been in most of the novels of high sensibility. Concerning the repression of the hero and his more rationalist point of view, the author tartly remarks, 'It was not his memoirs I professed to write.'

The debate of reason and the varieties of sensibility takes up much of the book. The characterisation of Emma is made primarily by herself in terms of the dichotomous psychology of her time which she both criticises and exemplifies. Not wanting to be an essentialist and associate women biologically with sensibility, a position from which no feminist future could be envisaged, yet desiring to hold to some of the psychological advantages of the association, Emma argues for a strict environmentalist position. People are the creation of education and education, which includes all aspects of upbringing, is a matter of chance, with literature forming the single most influential element. Emma's reading becomes a kind of history of fiction and her progress a summary of the progress of constructed femininity allied to this fiction. Because she has not remained like Wollstonecraft's Mary with sentimental and reclusive poetry, but ventured into the world of female romance and even in time the sexual fantasy of *Héloïse*, she is in far more social if not pyschological danger than her predecessor.

Her earliest reading was in marvellous tales and the result is a period of quixotism like that of Lennox's heroine, a yearning for what the world cannot provide:

> Stories were still my passion,.and I sighed for a romance that would never end. In my sports with my companions, I acted over what I had read, I was alternately the valiant knight – the gentle damsel – the adventurous mariner, the daring robber . . .[8]

By adolescence she is reading modern romance, which leads her to inhabit a dream world destructible only through disillusion in real life. Both sets of reading have nurtured her sensibility, as has her first female mentor, her aunt: 'the tendencies of this worthy woman generated in my infant disposition that susceptibility, that lively propensity to attachment to which I have through life been a martyr.'[9]

But it is in fact solipsistic not benevolent sensibility that is encouraged, a development in the woman of some of the characteristics accepted in men – vanity, impetuosity and self-will – stemming from stress on feelings uncurbed by the usual feminine goals of sexual involvement, surrender or resistance, to a man. Again, as in *Mary, A Fiction*, there is a definite sense of modernity – the woman as heroine of her own inner life, woman expressing her unnarrated identity or woman caught in the prison-house of feeling.

One of Emma's problems is gender confusion exaggerated through her reading. It is already clear in her reception of old romance; this provides only the role of the damsel for the girl, but Emma thinks she can play the parts of either sex. In modern sentimental romance too she believes that male and female roles are open to her and even with Plutarch she manages to identify with the classical heroes. In the midst of this heroic identification she is asked a question by a man that immediately reduces her to the feminine position of passive mistress. The reality of woman's social status clashes with the free mental space of literature and Emma is reduced to silence in a confusion of worlds.

The great indelible influence is, however, not ancient and classical but seductively modern, Rousseau's infamous *La Nouvelle Héloïse*. Emma quotes from the radical works of the 1790s such as *A Vindication of the Rights of Woman* and Godwin's *Caleb Williams*, as well as from the great sentimental writers Richardson and Sterne, but it is in *Héloïse* alone that she seems to find the mixture of radical liberation and sentimental endorsement that she craves. As usual, it is the first part of *Héloïse* that moves her; Julie's consummated love affair with the hero Saint-Preux becomes her Bible, the Old Testament fall rather than the New Testament redemption through marriage and motherhood.

Paradoxically Emma first meets the potent book in her father's library. It provides an instantly acceptable pattern and calls forth all the enthusiasm she usually reserves for her own sensibility: 'With what transport, with what enthusiasm, did I peruse this dangerous, enchanting, work! – the pleasure I experienced approached the limits of pain – it was tumult – and all the ardour of my character was excited.' In this almost sexual encounter with a book she becomes (again) both hero and heroine and even when she associates the still unseen Harley with Rousseau's hero, he is an extension of self, a fantasy of self-love: 'He was the St Preux, the Emilius, of my sleeping and waking reveries.' It is only in the second volume when Emma has been completely entangled in her obsession with Harley that she associates herself firmly with the feminine.

The passion is clearly sexual as Mary's for Ann and the invalid Henry was not, but it is also imaginary, fulfilling all the urgent needs of the self. Under its influence Emma admits those desires that Mary Wollstonecraft would later admit to her lover Imlay a few years after the fierce independence of *The Rights of Woman*, that she wanted to cling and depend: 'That I require protection and assistance, is, I confess, a proof of weakness, but it is nevertheless true.'[10] Emma is not asking for the gallant knight of romance but for something far more difficult to find, a man who will be her equal *and* adore her, love *and* respect her. She admits that 'the customs of society . . . have enslaved, enervated, and degraded woman' but she will not accept her own progress as an example of this degradation or site her own impossible needs on the muddle of sensibility.

When she comes to her unconventional act of declaring herself first, she is confounding roles and yet fulfilling them. Her sensibility convinces her that, if her passion is true, the object of it must be so too (Wollstonecraft would let her misguided final heroine make a similar point, while Jane Austen would firmly oppose it in the portrait of the impulsive Marianne in *Sense and Sensibility*.) Emma slips from caution to justification. Like Rousseau, she believes that 'energy of sentiment is the characteristic of a noble soul'; passions should not be controlled but vindicated. Seeing herself as triumphantly female, as acting in a male way for a female reason, she argues, 'the Being who gave to the mind its reason, gave also to the heart its sensibility.'

It is a radical point that cannot, however, be sustained in the patriarchal world in which Emma is acting. In the face of this, she can only progress from struggle for her own balance to acceptance of female imbalance. Self-command and equanimity will not come through reason but from passionate need. Sensibility, once denigrated, becomes no longer the constructed opposition to reason but the natural mode refined by reason, 'when mind has given dignity to natural affections; when reason, culture, taste and delicacy, have combined to chasten, to refine, to exalt (shall I say) to sanctify them'.

But, although the character of Emma may refuse the confusion of sensibility, this confusion remains apparent to the reader. After all, what the heroine wants is the conventional romantic ending albeit brought about by unromantic means: marriage to Harley proposed by herself. The selfishness of desire is not disguised, and development in the individualistic sensibility results in an impossible social presence as Emma becomes rude, harsh and assertive. Another response is the one so much indulged in by Wollstonecraft's Mary, self-pity. Emma is moved by her own self-image and calls herself 'a deserted outcast from society'. At times she comes close to suggesting that women are cut off from psychological wholeness by cultural assumptions; at others it seems that their passions are powers and the turmoil within the thinking woman a sign of superiority. Self-pity turns to smugness: 'I had yet to learn, that those who have courage to act upon advanced principles, must be content to suffer moral martyrdom.'

Two people try to halt Emma's progress in sensibility and act as the mentor figures of female fiction. The first is her rationalist father who, speaking the language of *The Rights of Woman*, opposes the notion of contingent femininity, woman as 'half-being', the 'soft solace of man', a 'sheet of white paper' on which, as Laetitia Matilda Hawkins had declared, lines of thinking should never appear. He also dislikes the woman of exaggerated sensibility, concerned with her own emotions and needs, believing it would 'be more judicious to prepare and strengthen my mind to encounter, with fortitude, some hardships and rude shocks, to which I might be exposed, than to foster a sensibility which he already perceived, with regret, was but too acute'. Emma is excited by the notion of exclusion and repression of women but she expresses her father's reasonable view in the patterned emotional style of sensibility:

> Why was I not educated for commerce, for a profession, for labour? Why have I been rendered feeble and delicate by bodily constraint and fastidious by artificial refinement? Why are we bound, by habits of society, as with an adamantine chain? Why do we suffer ourselves to be confined within a magic circle without claiming, by a magnanimous effort, to dissolve the barbarous spell?[11]

The main rationalist response comes from a second man, Mr Francis, the writer of Godwin's real-life letters and an echo of the cautionary Mr Francis in Haywood's *Betsy Thoughtless*. The similarity of names emphasises how far this book has travelled from the tradition of moral sentiment. Mr Francis wages an all-out war against sensibility, 'a fastidious delicacy', which he sees overwhelming Emma. He views her as a sentimental dupe and dismisses her woes as the result of 'indolence'. The sentimental woman is an historical victim, an embodiment of repressive and nostalgic ideology; Emma's sensibility is 'the unnatural and odious invention of a distempered civilization' and her conduct 'moon-struck madness, hunting after torture'.[12] She has not understood that independence is the first necessity for any person, man or woman. This Enlightenment view is articulated in Hays's book mainly by men; it demands a change but is helpless if one does not occur.

Emma is clearly not the rationalist ideal, the woman of sense from *The Rights of Woman*, but a woman wanting passion on her own terms, emotional, introspective and demanding. Implicitly she seems to be qualifying the Wollstonecraftian feminist ideal, urging a place for the affections within radical discourse and encouraging an ideal based less on the predominance of male reason over female sensibility within one androgynous pysche than on the apotheosis of female sensibility. So when she reiterates the image of the 'magic circle' of femininity, used first in an emotional but clearly Wollstonecraftian feminist context (and, incidentally, echoing the 'enchanted Circle' of Mary Astell), she does so with no suggestion of social development:

Hemmed in on every side by the constitutions of society, and not less so, it may be, by my own prejudices – I perceive indignantly perceive, the magic circle, without knowing how to dissolve the powerful spell. While men pursue interest, honour, pleasure, as accords with their several dispositions, women, who have too much delicacy, sense, and spirit, to degrade themselves by the vilest of all interchanges, remain insulted beings, and must be content tamely to look on, without taking any part in the great, though often absurd and tragical, drama of life. Hence the eccentricities of conduct, with which women of superior minds have been accused – the struggles, the despairing though generous struggles, of an ardent spirit, denied a scope for its exertions! The strong feelings, and strong energies, which properly directed, in a field sufficiently wide, might – ah! what might they not have aided? forced back, and pent up, ravage and destroy the mind which gave them birth![13]

It is both heroic and self-indulgent, a wallowing in self-analysis. Personal failings are excused in terms of a wider societal struggle and yet there is no desire for struggle on behalf of anyone else, for the moral is founded in the self. The protest seems rationalist but the language and punctuation are of high sensibility. The trap is complete and the magic circle is closed. It is no surprise for the reader soon to come upon such a passage as this:

Hapless woman – crushed by the iron hand of barbarous despotism, pampered with weakness, and trained the slave of meretricious folly – what wonder, that, shrinking from the chill blasts of penury . . . thou listenest to the honied accents of the spoiler.

Emma is not a fallen woman but she needs the conventional stance of social martyrdom to express her moral state. Rejecting Enlightenment language, as well as the decorous feminine language of silence, she holds to the shifting feminine sentimental discourse even if it brings with it incoherence. The only closure of this sort of book has to be death and, as in Wollstonecraft's two novels, this is suggested at the end. But there is no longer any way to describe it.[14] There can be no real voice outside the heroine's and her death cannot be assumed into a now threadbare myth.

Although Emma does not 'fall', the sexual nature of her demands is never in doubt; it is clearest when she rails against chastity as simply a social demand and when she describes her response to the notorious *Héloïse*. A similar rescuing of female sexual desire after the anti-sexual stance of *The Rights of Woman* occurs in Wollstonecraft's final novel, *The Wrongs of Woman*, which becomes, in its confused unfinished state, a kind of summary of the route of sentimental excess followed by the unconventional novels of the 1790s. At the same time it joins *Emma Courtney* in trying to personalise the political, allow room in the radical system for the

247

affections. But far more than either *Emma Courtney* or *Mary, A Fiction*, it participates in the more respectable struggle of women writers to move the female novel back into the world as guide and teacher.

Like *Emma Courtney*, *The Wrongs of Woman* is in dialogue with *La Nouvelle Héloïse* in whose margins – literally, for the heroine's fascination is fuelled by the hero's marginalia – the prison romance takes place. Wollstonecraft had answered *Mary, A Fiction* with her *Rights of Woman* which attacked sensibility and the Rousseau of *Emile*; here she modifies *The Rights of Woman* with the Rousseau of *Héloïse*, itself in turn the subject of her criticism. Sensibility is not repudiated as in *The Rights of Woman* and its excess is allowed a certain grandeur as in the claustrophobic and obsessive *Emma Courtney*. But it is also consciously shown as an impasse.

Hays's novel anticipates Wollstonecraft's in many respects. But the similarities as well as the dates do not suggest derivation as much as a coincidence of response to the same social and fictional stimuli.[15] Emma and Wollstonecraft's heroine Maria have the same feminine education in dangerous sensibility and yet their creators will not take sympathy from them by entirely condemning their excess. Both heroines romantically progress in much the same way, love occurring through imaginative anticipation and through identification of the object with a fictional character. Both heroines break down when they miss the meetings with the heroes and both pride themselves on the strength of their emotion. In both, the passions are socially and culturally conditioned.

In *The Wrongs of Woman* Hays's 'magic circle' has become a physical madhouse in which the heroine has been imprisoned (without her baby) by her wicked and avaricious husband bent on keeping her inheritance. Maria has a tendency to extend physical into metaphoric and see the whole world as a vast prison for women who inevitably have 'the aggravated ills of life', but her extreme situation expressing the female legal and social status anchors her protest in the material world of marriage and laws.

In the novel Maria, who, like many heroines of this period recounts her own story for the benefit of her lost child – though significantly she delivers it to the unfaithful lover – briefly tries the usual female routes of her predecessors: Christian resignation – 'misery endured, and proudly termed patience' – philanthropy and, more lengthily, the dramatisation of the self as self-conscious and superior sentimental heroine. But in a book that has an intermittently detached narrator rather than the completely partisan one of *Mary, A Fiction* all these routes are judged and found wanting. Less conventionally she also tries the Rousseauian route of sentimental sexual fulfilment which Emma Courtney had craved.

When this too fails, Maria in several alternative endings retreats into the death that Emma and Mary had contemplated. And yet the route is only partially condemned.

The plot of suffering indicates, as in *Emma Courtney*, an attack on sensibility that has resulted in Maria's belief in the validity of all feelings, including the sexual, and a consequent blindness in love and marriage. Maria's early childhood 'in one of the most romantic parts of England' which develops in her 'an enthusiastic fondness for the varying charms of nature', as well as her attachment to a kindly but melancholic uncle (the providing uncle of sentimental fiction), suggest her erroneous route from the start. Yet the book as a whole neither glorifies nor condemns emotion, although it shows its inadequacy in situations where reason might have helped. When Maria first arrives in the asylum she is overwhelmed by the magnitude of her grief, which 'seemed to have suspended her faculties'. The result is that, when she meets the keeper, she has lost her battle for composure and she 'raved of injustice in accents that would have justified his treatment'. Nothing in her previous education has taught her the need for careful argument. At a later stage she discerns that sorrow indulged blunts or sharpens the faculties, producing either the stupidity of indolence or 'the restless activity of a disturbed imagination'. Yet, when she thinks of the past, she still finds 'the agonising emotions' returning to paralyse her mind and she is predictably unsuccessful in her efforts at self-control. So by the time the gentleman-annotator Darnford is mentioned, the reader is prepared for the inevitable 'romantic' continuation of Maria's story.

Under the influence of *La Nouvelle Héloïse* and her isolation in the madhouse, which exaggerates the usually confined situation of women, Maria falls in love with her fellow prisoner. The narrator comments on the inevitable outcome, without clearly placing it: 'Fancy, treacherous fancy, began to sketch a character congenial with her own.' On his personality, Maria judges from the heart – as she had done when she made her disastrous marriage, although the narrator fails to stress the parallel – revealing as she does so the self-centredness at the core of her sensibility. Yet she is not entirely blind to her mental predicament; disappointed on one occasion by Darnford's failure to appear in the courtyard, she 'began to reflect, as an excuse to herself, on the little objects which attract attention when there is nothing to divert the mind; and how difficult it was for women to avoid growing romantic, who have no active duties or pursuits'.[16]

When the two actually meet, he mouths the proper Rousseauian sentiments; she is enraptured, and soon admits him 'as her husband'. An idyll follows in which Maria forgets her lost baby, her ravening husband outside and her own imprisonment. When she is freed, her lover proves unfaithful and she either kills herself or, at the last minute, suffers a rescue by the faithful asylum servant and prostitute Jemima who, in one of the several suggestions for an ending, persuades her to live for her child – newly discovered, like so many relatives in endings of romance.

The immense difference from *Mary, A Fiction*, apart from the less collusive relation of character and narrator, is the actual sexual activity. This is described in the sentimental language of religiosity that alone appears available to women writers touching on this explosive subject, language which at times seems to suggest the constructed nature of the sexual experience and at others seems dimly to be trying to convey a feeling for which there is no appropriate vocabulary: 'So much of heaven did they enjoy, that paradise bloomed around them; or they, by a powerful spell, had been transported into Armida's garden.' Love, the grand enchanter, 'lapt them in Elysium', and every sense was 'harmonised to joy and social extacy'.

But this is not the whole of the treatment and elsewhere sexuality is described far more in terms of society. In the inset lives of the various classes of women, female sexual activity results in disaster every time, as it does in the end for Maria; yet there is a new realism in the acceptance that sexual activity will occur and might as well be enjoyed, even though in a debased patriarchal world it must come with some fantasy. In *Mary, A Fiction* sexuality has been severed from sensibility, which had been firmly associated with chastity, while the austere *Rights of Woman* had recommended coldness as part of the feminist struggle. Here sexuality is a pleasing illusion inside the dreary cell of life and, in its temporary untranscending way, worthwhile. In this acceptance Wollstonecraft shows herself a child of her time, locating the erotic in the imagination, and some of her vocabulary serves to modify the mechanistic notion of inevitable lust which had always made her uneasy.

The main new development in *The Wrongs of Woman* is the character and tale of Jemima, a lower-class 'fallen' woman intended in many ways as a contrast both in status and type to Maria. Although to speak in a novel she must be able to manipulate middle-class language, her style is nonetheless distinctively unsentimental and plain. At her introduction her step is firm and deliberate and she counters Maria's sentimental notion of starving herself in the manner of Clarissa with the observation that most people eat as they recover their senses.

The narrator stresses her coldness and her constant focus on her own self-interest. Prolonged misery has taught her calculation and selfishness and she has escaped all nurturing in feminine sensibility. So she is entirely without fantasies about sex, which she does not enjoy. Her tale is indeed a sorry one. If the sentimental middle-class woman is perhaps always a child, she was always an adult, born into no family, rather like Mary Shelley's monster created by Frankenstein, probably influenced by her mother's portrait of Jemima. Illegitimate, put to work when she was scarcely more than a baby, she already 'looked like a little old woman, or a hag shrivelling into nothing' with 'furrows of reflection and care' destroying the appearance of youth. She spent time as a beggar, as a whore, in the workhouse, and with a 'worn-out votary of voluptuousness' who allowed her some literary development through books and conversation – the Restoration writers had noted that the 'experienced' woman could have the benefit of association with sophisticated men, denied to the virtuous girl. Other episodes were more harrowing. Jemima once had to abort a baby to protect her own life although she had felt some tenderness for the unborn child, and it is Maria's story of the loss of her baby that moves her to sympathy, despite the fact that she had been 'long estranged from *feminine* emotions' (my italics).

Yet, although it is a remarkable performance for the time, one should not make too much of Jemima, whose tale is far shorter than the corresponding one of Maria. In one of the fragmentary endings, there is the by now conventional suggestion of a female community in which Jemima and Maria live together for Maria's daughter – it would be a more radical statement if either decided to live for herself. And it is Jemima who is integrated into the still sentimental world of Maria, not the reverse. There is no question of her romantic activity and nothing is really made of her relationship with Maria. The bulk of the endings with their suicide so reminiscent of Wollstonecraft's own attempts suggest that both heroine and narrator have turned away from Jemima and the possible stylistic and political route she might have opened up.

The reader is left with a variety of effects: with ambiguity rather than irony since no proper connections are made between the narratives of the two women, with a fairly conventional attack on the power of sentimental fiction – along with sentimental imagination and projection – and with a potentially powerful but still muddled analysis of female sexuality as both part of the sentimental trap and as self-fulfilling comfort. The overwhelming effect is, however, of sensibility that cannot be abandoned and of the female need to tell and tell again her own melancholy story; it is close to the effect described for Maria's supposed writings within the novel: 'She lived again in the revived emotions of youth, and forgot her present in the retrospect of sorrows.'[17]

But the final voice is not Maria's, Jemima's, the narrator's or Wollstonecraft's, but William Godwin's. In *Emma Courtney* the voice of reason and control was given to Mr Francis-Godwin; without the author's intention, he functions in similar fashion in *The Wrongs of Woman*, of which he is the ultimate controller and editor. His position is strengthened by the sentimental convention that often pretended that a male author like Richardson or Defoe was the editor of a female text which he had himself actually created. The endings of the posthumous novel were arranged by Godwin, and the language with which he binds and organises the text is judicious and rational, clearly in opposition to the sentimental outpourings which he nonetheless endorses. Although he insists that it is his 'most earnest desire, to intrude nothing of himself into the work', he yet comes forward to tell readers when the manuscript appears imperfect, and indeed to urge them to become sentimental responders to the sentimental text instead of 'fastidious and cold-hearted critic[s]' repelled by the incoherent form.[18] Since the former are like the author, the latter closer to himself, it sounds as though Godwin is in some measure restating the gender distinction and forcing the ambivalent and struggling Wollstonecraft and her readers back into the safe but imprisoning sentimental mould.

The Wrongs of Woman is in some ways a rewriting of *Mary, A Fiction* and *The Memoirs of Emma Courtney*. In none of the books is there any exit from the political impasse of sensibility; women will cling to the fantasy of romantic love simply because the world is indeed a prison and a magic circle. Yet the three novels modernise women's association with sensibility. In doing so they have a legacy in one strand of self-obsessive female writing which, for nearly two centuries, has been condemned to transforming the world inwards and to valuing feminine feeling even when it marginalises into madness and makes subjectivity subject. As the closeness of the novels to the lives of the authors and to the often self-pitying grumblings of their letters suggests, there is here an acceptance of fiction as autobiography, the tradition of literature as therapy which would become so dominant in the women's novel of the twentieth century.

14

'THE GREAT ENCHANTRESS':
ANN RADCLIFFE

In Jane Austen's *Northanger Abbey*, the heroine, Catherine Morland, follows the novels of Ann Radcliffe into social embarrassment. Later she recants and concludes that Radcliffean Italy, with its pines and vices, is no guide to life in the Midland counties of England.

Austen mocks the overwhelming effect on feeble intellects of the Radcliffe formula of suspense and wicked deeds. Yet her mockery does not encompass Radcliffe as an author; the witty hero, Henry Tilney, is allowed to read her novels through with his hair standing on end and receive no lasting damage. Nor does the Austen mockery really diminish the gothic mode; it simply indicates what it is not, a real picture of real life, a forerunner of Jane Austen herself and her social subject. Indeed *Northanger Abbey* is in a way a tribute to Radcliffe. While the heroine is presented with many horrid novels, it is *The Mysteries of Udolpho* that is most compelling and that keeps her from the sights of Bath. In her own slightly earlier time too Radcliffe was distinguished from her numerous followers partly by her sheer mastery of suspense and partly by the obvious seriousness of her enterprise.

Mrs Radcliffe came into the public consciousness with her third novel, *The Romance of the Forest*, in 1791. This was followed in 1794 by *The Mysteries of Udolpho* and in 1797 by *The Italian*. The three novels span the 1790s, the years of liberal welcome for the early moderate phase of the French Revolution and the later comprehensive reaction in an England now at war. They also surround the publication of the two most notorious works of Wollstonecraft and Hays, and the sensational gothic novel *The Monk* of Matthew Lewis.

Ann Radcliffe was read by those who now form part of the literary heritage of England: Coleridge, Shelley, Keats and Byron, all of whom show her distinctive influence. She was also read by women, serving-men and apprentices. Her popularity was extraordinary. Walter Scott described how the volumes flew from person to person and were sometimes torn from a reader's hand, and she was accepted as 'at the head of a class' according to Mrs Barbauld in her *British Novelists* of 1810. Whatever their considered attitude might have been, many educated women made it clear that the books were a felt presence in their lives. Mrs Piozzi wrote to her daughter in 1794 that she was compared to Radcliffe's Emily in her habit of versifying at odd moments, a comparison also made to flatter the Lichfield poet Anna Seward. When reviewed alone, Radcliffe was considered as a serious historical writer, coupled on the odd occasion with the securely great like Shakespeare.

But, as imitators proliferated and the romantic gothic became firmly associated with women and with pap literature, the carping grew. Along with Jane Austen, E. S. Barrett in *The Heroine* mocked the effect on his ludicrous heroine of the 'inebriating stimulants' of Radcliffe. He also managed to associate her 'extreme of vicious refinement' with the malign destabilising influence of Rousseau.[1] Mrs Radcliffe would not have liked a connection either with inebriation or with revolutionary France. Indeed there is evidence that she would rather have avoided entirely this public discussion of herself and the mode which she so successfully dominated.

Unlike Wollstonecraft and Hays, whose lives became public property, Mrs Radcliffe guarded her privacy. Despite her stature in the women's fictional tradition and in Romantic literature generally, there are remarkably few biographies and Christina Rossetti abandoned the notion of writing her life for lack of material. Indeed in her later years she was so secluded that many contemporaries thought that she had died long before she had or that she was confined in a lunatic asylum, driven mad by her own terrors. It was typical of her extreme value of privacy that she did not write to the newspaper to refute the rumour. The situation was made the more ridiculous and confusing by the weird proliferation of her image, brought about by unscrupulous publishing houses like the Minerva Press. Late into the nineteenth century, books by the far less versatile gothic novelist Mary Anne Radcliffe were still said to be by the author of *The Romance of the Forest*, while the publisher of the polemical *The Female Advocate* by Mary Ann Radcliffe, who had wanted to remain anonymous, also wished to profit from a confusion of names.

The little that is known of Radcliffe concerns mainly her context. She came from lower-middle-class stock, had some connections with Dissenters and some reassuring ties with the gentry. Her husband William was a political journalist with Whig views, a supporter of the early Revolution, but later, once war was declared and the Revolution had entered its violent phase, an upholder of national unity. As they can be gauged from her novels, Ann Radcliffe's own political views responded to the stirring events of the times but did not change with them. Holding to a Whiggish line, she nostalgically valued the sentimental notion of community above individualistic effort and believed with Edmund Burke in the commonsensical English way of slow constitutional reform rather than outright revolution. But she also held the liberal's abhorrence of secretive power, dangerous both to the individual and to the state, whether it was embodied in a person or in an institution like the Catholic Inquisition, and there may be muted references in her novels to the contemporary forms of institutional power in the *ancien régime*, the French revolutionary tribunals, and indeed the repressive war government of England itself.

An an Anglican, Radcliffe opposed religious extremes of all kinds. She disliked Catholic celibacy because it worked against the sense of community and family, on which foundation she placed her values. She accepted divine providence but opposed superstition. In her novels no supernatural explanation is given and the dead do not return to haunt the living, although providence may be working in her plots and many coincidences. Indeed at the end of *The Romance of the Forest* she draws attention to this force, which is not chance but 'a Power whose designs are great and just'.[2]

With such conservative, sentimental values, it is not surprising that Mrs Radcliffe should also hold to the conventional image of the woman writer, the genteel domestic lady who happens to write and whose writing, in the absence of superior duties – the Radcliffes had no children – could serve as an extension of her domestic social role. Her sign as author was clearly that of the lady, who, like her heroines, fell into verse on many occasions but did not set up primarily for artistry and, while heavily marked by sentimental qualities, entirely avoided the route of individualistic emotion and excess followed by the heroines of Wollstonecraft and Hays. Her obituary by her husband catches the image; it reveals his wife's 'natural repugnance to authorship' although her genius directed her towards it and declares her refusal to 'sink for a moment, the gentlewoman in the novelist'.[3] Unlike Monk Lewis, who dined out on his novel for the rest of his life, she did not desire fame or publicly enjoy success.

Despite her discreet image, Radcliffe was most associated in the popular mind with horror and sensation, a manipulation of menace and terror. Taking the archetypal sentimental story of fatherly male menacing a weak but virtuous female who in the end triumphs over him or neutralises his power, she heightens the elements, obscures and magnifies, making a moody menacing patriarch whose immense shadowy outlines suggest incest, rape and murder. She does so, however, with control. Terror is tamed and her endings see the light switched on in the murky places. Ordinary justice deals with extraordinary guilt.

Consequently the sentimental gothic novel was for Radcliffe and many other women writers a genre suitable for a lady, dealing in the possible but improbable, facing fears in an ultimately decorous because oblique and displaced way. When Matthew Lewis broke through the veil of decorum with his sadistic fantasy, *The Monk*, and made explicit the implicit, not only describing a rape but making the rapist a monk, the victim his sister and blaming male sexual arousal on women, Radcliffe must have felt rather like Lady Echlin contemplating the appalling fate of Clarissa or Clara Reeve coming upon the sexual act in Rousseau's *Héloïse*. She must have considered herself rather more implicated, since Lewis openly claimed to have been inspired by the work of Mrs Radcliffe.

As she aims to use the fearful gothic elements with care, she also aims to use with control the powerful legacy of female sensibility, by this time a potentially dangerous self-indulgent and socially disruptive quality. Unlike so many writers at the end of the decade, she seems not to want to abandon sentimental values altogether, but she clearly does wish to stiffen them. Principle is added to feeling as a guide to action, and fortitude is stressed to combat self-indulgence. Unregulated sensibility creates victims of feeling, sensualists like Laurentini of *The Mysteries of Udolpho* who acts like 'a fiend'. Without regulation sensibility can degenerate into sexuality in an individual and anarchy within a community, but without sensibility at all there can be only selfishness, coldness and cruelty.

In form she seems to have aimed at a judicious mix. The gothic must remain within the sentimental romance or else it can become sensational and horrific like Lewis's *Monk*. But the sentimental must also be contained in the gothic, the obscure, the slightly distanced. In the early *Romance of the Forest* she seems momentarily to have forgotten this in her treatment of the hero when in prison awaiting execution with his father: the scene is so sentimentally realised that it can be halted only by bizarre anticlimax. She does not make a mistake like this in her last two novels.

Because she insists on moral clarity, Radcliffe's gothic romance can become a novel of ideas, harking back to the early novel of sentiment. In *The Romance of the Forest*, for example, the villain puts forward the Hobbesian notion, being revitalised at the time by the Marquis de Sade, that self-preservation is the first law of nature, that the world must be apprehended dialectically and that morality is relative: 'It is the first proof of a superior mind to liberate itself from prejudices of country, or of education,' he insists, echoing the seducers of Delarivier Manley, who also relied on the argument of varying cultures to relieve their victims of their principles. But the sentimentalist knows that all this philosophy ends in the defiling of a woman or of the community she embodies, and their argument has the last word through its expression in conversation and plot.

Holding to the image of the lady writer, then, Radcliffe withdraws from the extremes of sentimental fiction as it had developed in the 1770s and 1780s and as it was being exemplified in the scandalous works of Wollstonecraft and Hays. Her books are launched with a definite and morally reliable storyteller or narrator, who expects to share her values with her readers. As in most earlier female fiction, the narrator does not assume the importance of a main character, as happens in Fielding's novels, since this would suggest for Mrs Radcliffe an unfeminine assumption of authority, but, unlike the characters, this narrator is in control – hence the annoyance of some readers at what seems a wilful refusal to tell all the facts – and any exclamatory writing to the moment in the manner of high sensibility occurs only in interpolated manuscripts. The narrator endorses the heroines but also judges them when inadequate, and the verdicts on lesser characters are absolute. There is none of the conflicting or modifying impressions of Hays and Wollstonecraft, heirs of the epistolary fiction that always had a tendency towards solipsism and relativity.

As in the novel of sentiment, readers are organised in their responses; they are co-opted into the judgements of the narrator and also allowed into the suspense of the characters whose 'thrilling curiosity', paranoia and superstitious terror they are sometimes reproved for sharing too whole-heartedly. The need for control as well as sensitivity is stressed when readers are drawn to follow events as they appear to the protagonists rather than heeding the narrator's admonishments. 'Pleasing dread' is expected for characters and readers, but should not be taken to paralysing excess. The disappointment many male readers, including Hazlitt and Coleridge, felt at the rational explanations and final morals was in a way a proper punishment for too great indulgence in the simple delight of suspense. Only horrors could begin to fulfil the expectations and Mrs Radcliffe unlike Monk Lewis will not provide these; horror, she considers, contracts the soul where terror humbles and opens it. A woman reader might welcome the experience of female powerlessness removed and vulnerability protected by firm narrative, and might dissent from the (still current) male response to Lewis's explicit sexual writing as liberating.

257

As was suggested by Wollstonecraft and Hays, fiction in the late eighteenth century was often concerned with sensibility as self-expression, with a solipsistic world in which alone the individual feminine sensibility could be pre-eminent. Mrs Radcliffe will have none of this, and readers and characters are taught responsibility through idyllic pictures of sentimental community, through narrative comments and through anecdotes designed for edification. In *The Romance of the Forest* a girl learns that artistic longings must give place to domestic duties for women in an incident that is solely displayed for the improvement of readers. Elsewhere in the same novel they are encouraged to judge what they might indulgently have approved or to be indulgent where they might have mocked: 'If this sensibility was . . . a weakness, it was at least an amiable one, and as such deserves to be reverenced.'[4] In *The Mysteries of Udolpho* readers are taught to temper sensibility with common sense and 'beware of the first indulgence of the passions'.[5] Certainly there is no self-indulgent reference to the author's life – although even Radcliffe could not resist publishing a poem separately under the pseudonym Adeline, the name of the heroine in *The Romance of the Forest*.

Her aim was to harness the sentimental novel once again for serious purpose, to return it to the moral ethical aim of the earlier novel of sentiment while greatly extending its range. With her sure narrative voice and moral purpose, she wanted to pull such fiction out of its self-indulgent morass and ensure its continuing commitment to a conservative vision of harmonious and loving community. At the same time she knew herself to be a writer of romance and a dealer in magic, and she was not prepared to follow the route of the tract-writing Hannah More.

Radcliffe's gothic romances each have similar patterns. In *The Romance of the Forest* the heroine, Adeline, is forced by her captors on the moody La Motte, who is escaping from justice in Paris. The ruin in the forest where they hide belongs to the wicked Marquis Montalt, who first aims to seduce the beautiful Adeline and then to murder her when he discovers in her his dispossessed niece. She is helped in her escape by the hero, Theodore, with whose idyllic family, La Luc, she unknowingly takes refuge in the mountains; it is to this retreat that hero and heroine return once Adeline has been ennobled and enriched by discovery of her birth. In *The Mysteries of Udolpho* the idyllic patriarchal family community of La Vallée begins the novel and it is broken up by the forces of selfishness and materialism when the father of Emily, the heroine, dies. She comes under the guardianship of a rich and trivial aunt, Madame Cheron, whose ill-judged marriage makes the threatening Italian, Montoni, into her uncle. In his enormous and remote castle of Udolpho, parody or reverse of the ideal La Vallée, Emily experiences the terror both of the supernatural and of the natural as she confronts the castle's bloody past and the present possibility of rape and assault. The ending re-establishes the idyllic community of hero and heroine and, as in *The Romance of the Forest*, this is again set in a rural Eden away from aristocratic power.

Perhaps in response to *The Monk*, published nine months before Radcliffe's novel was advertised, her last novel, *The Italian*, is more sombre. Opening with an assassin in an Italian church, it is less about the internal terrors of the mind than about real ones, about human cruelty and material oppression rather than ghostly fears. The heroine, Ellena, is loved by the noble Vivaldi, whose ferocious mother is helped in her persecution of innocence by the mysterious and gloomy monk Schedoni, the most developed of Radcliffe's villains. Idyllic and familial communities are even more threatened than in the earlier novels and the place of imprisonment, the prison of the Inquisition, is made more terrible through its association with religion and state power. The ending resettles the good characters in the social world of emotional personal ties, away from aristocratic cruelty and mercantile greed.

An obvious appeal in all three novels is the gothic interior – castles, monasteries, prisons, dungeons and remote huts – site of the heroine's encounter with the evil guardian. Such places suggest the power of others and yet to the imaginative mind, both of the characters and of the reader, they are strangely ambiguous, in one view oppressive in their force and in another liberating to the mind in their obscurity, rather like the visionary prisons and castles of Piranesi's drawings. They have as comparison the great prison of the Bastille, recently destroyed but still fascinating to a Europe in political turmoil. They are associated with the powerful villains, who are certainly horrific in their potential cruelty but also, in a way, noble beside the other weak and debased men.

In all the Radcliffe endings, as obscure and shifting identity is finally made clear, there is a flight from the shadowy aristocratic edifices, although the legacy of the castle in the shape of the heroine's inheritance is usually accepted when tamed and clarified to benevolent purposes. Despite Adeline's newfound nobility and wealth, she and the more middle-class hero Theodore flee the castles and estates of aristocracy to set up as the new guardians of the rural community with La Luc, aristocrats of sentiment rather than of rank.

This is a nostalgic paternalistic grouping mixing the sentimental visions of Richardsonian service and Rousseauian bonding, in which hierarchy is softened by affection and familial love. Avoiding the potentially disruptive and excessive ties of female friendship, Radcliffe concentrates on the affectionate relationship of husband and wife and of father and daughter, and she socialises the reclusive obsessive tendency of individual sentiment by describing the melancholy moods feeding back into social action, not into exaggerating self-absorption. La Luc, the exemplary father of Theodore, derives strength for benevolence through his solitary contemplation of his wife's grave.

The benevolent person dominates the community; the philanthropy, described as 'divine', was 'diffused through the whole village, and united the inhabitants in the sweet and firm bonds of social compact', while the happiness of Adeline and Theodore was 'diffused to all who came within the sphere of their influence'.[6] The open community of La Luc contrasts with aristocratic power in the shadowy forest and with the debased society of Nice where arbitrary government has rendered the peasants discontented. It is a sentimental replacement, not by force or forceful revolution but by providential means through the established institutions of the law – even the Inquisition finally delivers justice – or through the activities of individual benevolent men and women. The guardians are not tainted with capitalist competition like city people or with aristocratic privilege, but they have effortlessly the power to do good. The books are full of veils that in the end are understood rather than torn off, suggesting that the 'decent drapery' so appreciated by Burke need not be ripped away but may, if necessary, be slowly removed.

Servants figured both in the gothic extravaganza of Walpole and in the sentimental novel, but it was left to Mrs Radcliffe to raise the tie of master and servant to its affective height. Against the background of middle-class grumbling about uppish domestics and the perennial worry, no doubt exacerbated by the Revolution in France, that servants would form a class antagonistic to the interests of their employers, Radcliffe created a series of comic and devoted retainers, who ministered to the age's desire for an image of selfless service outside the capitalist reality of cash and wages. The most striking of her creations is Paulo in *The Italian*.

Paulo stays with his master when his friends desert him. He tries to cheer him even when it appears that Vivaldi has brought them both to certain death. Indeed he seems to have no life of his own that is not at the service of his master, although it is stressed that he is in fact a lively, gregarious fellow. Given the peculiarly decorous nature of the heroine in *The Italian*, his emotional attachment to Vivaldi very much moves the tie of master and servant into the centre of the stage, and the last section of the novel, which takes Paulo to the dungeons of the Inquisition solely to be with his master and then finds him exulting throughout the town at the final escape, is very much a male love affair excluding any woman. It has all the emotionality of the tableaux of high sensibility:

'It is my master! it is my dear master!' cried Paulo, and, sending off a nobleman with each elbow, as he made his way between them, he hugged Vivaldi in his arms, repeating, 'O, my master! my master!' till joy and affection overcame his voice, and he fell at his master's feet and wept.[7]

The chaste caress of Ellena is no match for this and Paulo with his noisy love dominates the ending with a joy that 'has rendered him delirious'. When asked to name a reward, his only demand is that no money be given to him to make him independent of his master.

Paulo represents a fantasy of service, an exaggeration of the component in the sentimental novel. Thrilled by their tie to their masters – it is more a male than a female image, although there *are* devoted female servants – these unmercenary men become as passionate in their devotion as any lovers. When the tie is between man and maid as in Richardson's *Pamela*, a sado-masochism is latent in the relationship, as Mr B amply shows in the numerous scenes he stages for Pamela to sob at his feet (the Marquis de Sade with his rewritings of Richardson and Rousseau in brutal sexual mode made it difficult for any of his readers to see these exploits as completely innocent again); at the same time there is a threat to the social hierarchy since inappropriate marriage can after all occur, as it does in *Pamela*. When master and servant share the same sex there is less sexual and social threat, and the proper working of the relationship becomes part of the proper working of harmonious community. La Motte alienates his faithful manservant and cannot function as the patriarch of his family and friends.

In its use of obscure interiors and veiled terrors, the world of Radcliffe's novels exemplifies the Burkean sublime. In his *Philosophical Enquiry into the Origin of our Ideas of the Sublime and Beautiful*, Burke had discussed the human fascination with what should repel, for the forbiddingly grand, for the half known and the hidden. Art is not a photographic copy but, in its reference to the sublime, deals with the obscure and the secret. For Radcliffe suspense is in the mind's response to the hidden, in fearful dreams and in faulty perceptions that fashion the supernatural, and in the doubling of character that obscures the proper barrier of inner and outer worlds. Her works show the etiology of illusion and fear, knowing that, as she expressed it, reason may not impose her laws on all the obscurities of the imagination. Terror is sophisticated and it exists in the veil, the curtain or the mist. In *The Mysteries of Udolpho* a black veil becomes a famous symbol of gothic suspense; it conceals the wax image of a corpse from which the heroine flees in unnecessary fear.[8] Readers share the fear – including the most famous reader, Catherine Morland of *Northanger Abbey*, who never seems to get beyond the veil with her reading. Had she done so she would have learned that real fear should be reserved for what is not at all obscure or sublime, the passion of the violent uncontrolled woman with whom the veil and the image are associated.

Fear is an appropriate response in a world where women have property or at least the opportunity of transmitting it, but where they have little power to control it. Mrs Radcliffe does not bring into sharp focus what is so apparent to the modern reader of her books, the financial as well as sexual threat to the heroines, but she does present it. Adeline was to be seduced or raped when she was innocent, but killed when she might be rich; Emily is pursued by Montoni for her money not her body, and even the would-be rapist in *The Mysteries of Udolpho* is a man 'of ruined fortunes' who craves Emily's estates as well as her virginity. Sexual energy turns quickly into capitalist energy, the individualistic enterprising desire of the entrepreneur of sex and money. Where her dying father warns Emily against excessive feeling, her dying aunt talks of the estates in France which, because she has refused to sign them over to her husband, she can leave to her niece.

The villains are uncles. In the sentimental novel the uncle figure, divorced from patriarchal authority but still close kin to the heroine, has often been an influence for good, the giver of sound advice and perhaps the provider of fortune – the experience of Maria in Wollstonecraft's *Wrongs of Woman*. But he could also hark back to Manley and express a threatening desire for the heroine, either directly or through a younger man, often his son. The desire might well be sexual but it is just as likely to be economic as well; usually the uncle has usurped the status and wealth of the heroine's father and the defiling of the daughter becomes a final triumph in a process of wickedness or a horrific act that displaces the economic one not represented. Certainly for Radcliffe the sexual and economic are mingled, but it is not really an equal association; perhaps it might better be said that the economic is sexualised, given the erotic power of sexuality, but that sex itself is played down.

Actual sexual lust appears rather absurd; it tends to motivate the young and uncontrolled. These are no match for the controlled and single-minded older men who crave the always obscurer power of status and money. Despite his wife's fears and despite eroticised descriptions of his encounters with the heroine – he is described as towering over the weeping girl in dishabille – La Motte in *The Romance of the Forest* is not interested in Adeline sexually; Montoni in *The Mysteries of Udolpho* wants Emily's money and arrays her seductively to be bought by others; Schedoni in *The Italian* is concerned with manipulation and control; leaning over to kill Ellena, worrying unnecessarily that her clothes will impede his knife, he is stopped only by a portrait that seems to represent himself. All these men are vigorous and middle-aged; their threat is physical, economic and social but not primarily sexual, although the female fear of violation, rape or incest lends power and vocabulary to their menace, especially for the fearful reader. They do not commit rape and incest, at least not on the body of the heroine, and often they rescue her from sexual assault. Sexuality in Radcliffe suggests lack of self-control and the most obvious feature of her later villains is their icy self-possession.

The exception would seem to be Montalt, the uncle villain of *The Romance of the Forest* who tries to buy Adeline. But even in him the desire is more for the submission of a woman than for sexual pleasure – he would have agreed with Burke's quintessentially masculine statement that 'we submit to what we admire, but we love what submits to us'. Yet he plays a less conspicuous part than the other uncle villains and does not dominate the book as much as the mediocre villain La Motte. After *The Romance of the Forest* Radcliffe does not repeat her overt use of the sexual threat in the uncle villain and her later creations are never motivated by a desire of violation at whatever social and spiritual cost, unlike the wicked Ambrosio of Lewis's *Monk* – nor would she ever have muddied the clear issue of female victimisation by making the victimised woman a seducing devil, as Lewis did.

Ambiguity is not allowed to Radcliffe's heroines and the collusion of heroine and villain which the twentieth-century, psychoanalytical reader insists in finding in the Clarissa myth and in the gothic novel is not the most important feature in the ties of Emily and Ellena with Montoni and Schedoni.[9] Again in Radcliffe there is the spectacle of the female novel pulling away from any founding of villainy on the ultimate fact of rape, perhaps because of the fear that rape as defined in the eighteenth century always might implicate the woman. The threat of rape in Radcliffe is usually embodied in far less terrifying and fascinating men than the uncle villains. Never could a Radcliffe heroine follow Richardson's Pamela into disliking the actions and attitudes of a man but admiring 'his Person'.

But of course it is precisely the unknowable motivation, the brooding sense of menace that does not quite seem contained in the economic motives, that make Radcliffe's villains so fascinating to the reader, caught up in their plots quite as much as the young heroines. When at the end the past is revealed, it is always disappointing, for it is delivered without description of those passions that have etched deep lines on the interesting faces of the villains. Byron's moody heroes in *Childe Harold* and his oriental tales, who descend from Radcliffe's gothic Italians, have usually loved and lost as explanation for their harsh isolation, but they have a similar excess of energy.

263

The Byronic hero, although influenced by Radcliffe, is not a Radcliffean creation and the distinction between the types is significant. Sympathy may be granted momentarily to a villain in his loneliness or wavering, but Radcliffe will not allow the reader to take the amoral stance of Byron and find these men the centres of interest. They remain like Milton's Satan evil, not energetically admirable in the manner of Blake's Romantic version. All are ultimately bad and their crimes are real, even if, as in Montoni's case, they may not be as numerous as the imaginative heroine had supposed. All are denied an heroic death that might give them centrality and undermine the re-establishment of the idyllic community which they have menaced. Montalt and Schedoni are simply and banally condemned by the law and they kill themselves; La Motte, only a semi-villain, is tamed into a pensioner of the heroine, and Montoni is killed off as a brigand in one clause of a sentence. The radical notion that villainy can be explained and excused by knowledge of the circumstances and constraints of a life is eschewed in favour of the sentimental idea that there are good and evil; the evil may suddenly and absolutely reform or they may not.

In complete contrast to the villains are the young heroes, whose faces are entirely unlined. Like Radcliffe's other main character types they are taken from the sentimental novel and they function according to type whatever the suspense of the action; as the faithful servant will not prove faithless to the virtuous characters, as the heroine will never lose her virginity, and as the villain may engage the reader but cannot flourish, so the hero may be passive and inept, but the heroine will in the end marry him. As in the earlier sentimental novel he is a refined feminised man, well born but not excessively privileged in his social position. He expresses the sentimental fantasy that unaggressive feminine sentiment can be extended to men. If the villain has an exaggerated menace, the hero has absolutely none – except perhaps the worry that his weakness may lead him into vice – and indeed he is frequently inept in his necessary function of rescuing or saving the heroine. He is often absent during the heroine's ordeals and he is given to moaning and complaining about his own situation as much as pitying hers. Rarely does he encounter the villain directly and there is never the straight battle of romance for the lady. In the end she herself usually takes charge through her superior firmness – or her money and status. In some ways the hero functions as an inferior version of the charming and benevolent heroine, weaker or perhaps less well born and often less perfect.

In Radcliffe's gothic romances there are touches of psychological realism which lure the reader into belief in their world. Whole characters like La Motte in *The Romance of the Forest*, the irascible selfish husband whose moods must be attended to by all his women, and Madame Cheron in *The Mysteries of Udolpho*, the heroine's selfish and trivial aunt who is humanised only in the end by her understanding of the common female predicament, have a realism beyond the schematic needs of romance; in their arbitrary power over the fates of the heroines they must have seemed a pretty convincing threat to young female readers. The heroines too have touches of human complexity; Adeline is too self-pitying, Emily too indulgent of her imaginative susceptibility, and Ellena almost obsessive in her concern for propriety.

Yet there is no real inner life of the kind being investigated by Wollstonecraft and Hays. Terror and anxiety are rendered through fear of doubling images of the self – 'There was a glass before her upon the table, and she feared to raise her looks towards it, lest some other face than her own should meet her eyes'[10] – and through dreams recounted in a style that stresses their archetypal nonspecific quality and inevitably brings them close in appearance if not in purpose to the analysed dreams of Freud. Adeline, for example, obsessed with her lack of a conventional loving parent, dreams of herself bleeding and wounded, the situation of the father she will later discover. She dreams again of a dying man, subsequently revealed as her father; like a lover he tries to hold her, but she pulls away from him. Pursuer and pursued are mixed, lover and father, safety and menace. These dreams differ from the simply monitory dreams of, for instance, Fanny Burney, in their use again of the terror of doubled characters, simultaneous existence in and outside the dream, but they are not really allowed psychological import. They function primarily as gothic supernatural without the supernatural being invoked, rather like the phantasmagoria about to become popular in England, which paradoxically made spectres absurd and at the same time 'real' since they were actually to be seen. Radcliffe, famous for explaining the non-natural, does not explain the possible revelations of dreams. But neither does she insist that the truth exists in the unconscious.

As in Sarah Fielding's novel of sentiment, inner drama is often rendered generally and epigrammatically through abstractions: 'Terror was softened into anxiety, and despair into grief.'[11] Or it is given through theatrical soliloquies of the characters that avoid the problem of gradual disclosure. The mind is not clearly individualised, but in the virtuous characters has a generalised, aesthetically pleasing quality. In all it is aptly imaged through the phantasmagoria or magic mirror: 'His mind resembled the glass of a magician, on which the apparitions of long buried events arise, and as they fleet away, point portentously to shapes half hid in the duskiness of futurity.' A kind of fantastic psychology replaces both the supernatural and the earlier mechanistic notion of the mind.[12]

Radcliffe's novels are not really tending to realism of surface and character. She is not trying to recuperate the recent past and display it in all its specificity and detail, as Sir Walter Scott will soon begin to do in his historical novels. Indeed her anachronistic descriptions are closer in effect to the poetic use of the past in the sentimental poets, who, like Gray and Macpherson with Ossian, create an obscure and romantic ancient Britain, still potent in the verse of the 1790s. She is not aiming at 'life' or insisting with a nineteenth-century novelist like George Eliot that what she writes is inevitably the reflection of surface truth. Ultimately for her the novel, although it must powerfully engage the reader, must also be useful in a way the male gothic of Monk Lewis clearly was not. So her characters stop to display feminine propriety, often to the amazement of a modern reader – as when Emily at a moment of extreme danger worries that she is leaving in undress without a hat or when Ellena is concerned about being alone with her fiancé on whose help her life depends.

The heroines of Radcliffean romance are virtue in distress, although passivity alone is not as potent as in earlier sentimental fiction.[13] The beauty of their role is unquestioned and is often expressed in poetry that demands complete assent. In *The Romance of the Forest*, Adeline is introduced with the very sound of feminine sensibility: 'sobs and moanings'. Her first action is worthy of Richardson's Pamela: 'She sunk at his feet, and with supplicating eyes, that streamed with tears, implored him to have pity on her.'[14] She has the spontaneity and authenticity of sensibility; her expressions are artless and simple. 'Mild, persecuted', pale and timid, she is constantly reacting with her body; she goes white, totters, and faints, to the extent that she almost involves the hero in death, since he attacks his commander while trying to support her on one of the many occasions when she is insensible.

The expressive body of sentimental fiction is again clearly the mark of the sincere heroine, but it must also be controlled for it may express more than is proper for the conscious woman. The body may be abducted, stolen and imprisoned, taken out of its own control, but the heroines must not collude in these acts.[15] In uncontrollable situations, unconsciousness or domination, desire may be expressed, but decorum must quickly halt the expression.

As Edmund Burke had noted to Wollstonecraft's irritation and as the Marquis de Sade would exemplify, the affecting pathetic beauty is best calculated to move a man. But, although Radcliffe touches on the sexual attractiveness of the distressed beauty of Adeline and Emily, she refuses to accept this sexuality overtly. She simply will not know and she rejects the escape of irony. In a way she here exemplifies the route of the heroines themselves, who display and yet must efface their own sexuality. 'The languor of sorrow threw a melancholy grace upon her features, that appealed immediately to the heart,' the narrator declares of Adeline, and 'her beauty, touched with the languid delicacy of illness, gained from sentiment what it lost in bloom. The negligence of her dress, loosened for the purpose of free respiration, discovered those glowing charms, which her auburn tresses, that fell in profusion over her bosom, shaded, but could not conceal.' Emily had 'the *contour* of a Madonna with the sensibility of a Magdalen'. It is a watcher's view, for Mrs Radcliffe is always aware of the gaze on and of the woman. Yet she insists, despite these descriptions, so reminiscent of the romances of Haywood or Behn, on the reader's decorous response. (The heroines also avoid sexual involvement and, when Emily watches for Montoni out of the castle window, she is fascinated by his power but inspired less by sexual attraction than by moral amazement, sentimentally disappointed that a fair exterior should clothe inner evil.)[16]

After the publication of *The Monk*, in which the passionate sexual woman *is* the madonna – she has modelled for the picture – and uses the identification to seduce the monk, Radcliffe pulls away from any risqué physical depictions of the heroine. Ellena in *The Italian* is by far the most passive of the three heroines, the most concerned with propriety, the most anxious to refuse sexual allure. Her face is only unveiled for the first time when she stoops to do a kind deed, in complete contrast to the first sensational appearance of Adeline, and, as she faints less, she is less available for scenes of erotic gazing. In addition she divides the book with the hero who is himself often placed in the helpless position of a woman; the possibility of sadistic description is lessened when it is a man who is dominated and tortured.

Because sexual love is the 'selfish passion' and because sensual beauty divorced from sensibility is an economic commodity in these novels, scenes of love between hero and heroine must avoid the erotic. So courtship is conveyed through conversations on 'elegant literature', through appreciation and interpretation in music, and through shared raptures over scenery, in sum through similar sensibility, controlled and refined away from self-indulgence and existing as a kind of surplus in the economic framework of the novel. The quality is essential in both partners, an innate one nurtured by a good home and by nature, and it forms the basis of choice in relationships; if virtue is active sensibility, then such a method of finding a husband is probably preferable to the usual method of following sexual desire. This sensibility opposes both the unprincipled insensibility of the aristocracy and the crude insensibility of the lower orders.

For all their famous fainting, the heroines, unlike Monk Lewis's, are strong and educated, although not in the threatening Wollstonecraftian way. Their accomplishments have a surprising value – in their dungeons and turrets they can strengthen their self-composure by sketching and writing verses – but their first identification is always as lady. Adeline with her facility in poetry never thinks of actually following Priscilla Wakefield's advice into authorship when she lives awkwardly with the impoverished La Mottes. The only earning heroine is Ellena in *The Italian*, who secretly makes money from needlework to support herself and her aunt. She sells her work anonymously to greedy aristocrats who despise her supposed rank. When her noble birth is discovered and her noble marriage assured, no more is made of this accomplishment.

It is as lady that they have most economic value for themselves rather than simply for other people who would use them, and the discovery of noble birth is often an assertion of their intrinsic worth. Adeline who neither works nor hunts to help the community in the forest has a high precise value put on her chastity and beauty; when she is ennobled she acquires economic and social power to such an extent that she can herself determine the time of her marriage.

Yet, for all the generalised moral and social commentary on women that can be squeezed from the heroines, Radcliffe accepts as well their literary nature and she draws attention to the fulfilment of literary expectations in the reader. Undressed distress she knows is a cliché. So Adeline is described as 'like a romance of imagination' and her lamentable situation becomes 'one of those improbable fictions that sometimes are exhibited in a romance'. The habit is taken to an extreme in *The Mysteries of Udolpho*, where Emily is ridiculed by Montoni for playing the heroine. His nakedly pragmatic rhetoric of power easily overtops her sentimental heroic speeches. When Emily urges her fine abstract qualities, her strength of mind and fortitude against oppression, Montoni taunts her, 'You speak like a heroine . . . we shall see if you can suffer like one,' and he later mocks her fearful trembling as ill-becoming her role.[17] Her romantic assumptions that she will be rescued by the hero prove entirely false. The veil that should, romantically, conceal desire and love, as in a bride, conceals a corpse, and a false one at that.

Ann Radcliffe was famous as a creator of fictional scenery or imaginative topography. In this habit she seems to be making a subtle claim for distinction with her genre. She inserted poetry as well as history into her books – a habit for which she was criticised by Leigh Hunt – but more significantly, in her passages of natural description, she edged her prose towards the condition of poetry. In his 1818 lecture on the English novelists Hazlitt depicts her 'describing the indefinable . . . she has all the poetry of romance', while Scott calls her 'the first poetess of romantic fiction' for passages such as this:

> The vessel cut its way through the liquid glass. The water was so transparent that she saw the sun-beams playing at a considerable depth, and fish of various colours glance athwart the current.[18]

Poetic natural description is most associated with the heroines. In this Radcliffe is stressing their sensibility and virtue, both almost seen as products of landscape, but she may also be asserting a kind of female response to the growing Romantic conception of nature and the artist. On the whole, where the male poet sees himself within the sublimity of nature and makes response heroic, the female novelist's stance is more modest, and nature itself remains the sole seat of the sublime. True Romantic poetry with its self-assertion is a mode as inappropriate for the lady writer's image as 'Amazonian' political protest.

The novels liberally quote from sentimental English poetry in which nature is often depicted as an expression of God. In Radcliffe, it is a kind of undoctrinal immanence and spirit, both test of and comfort to the protagonists, working in the world almost in the manner of divine grace. It can provide a code of values and act as 'a talisman' to expel 'all the poison of temporary evils'.[19] Characters reflect nature and their ideas become simple and sublime with the scenes they contemplate. Like the heroines and the gothic edifices, however, nature is also a cultural construction, a mingling of poetry and painting, especially of the dark Salvator Rosa and the idyllic Claude whom Radcliffe so much admired. With the help of poetry and painting nature achieves a pictorial and narrative coherence and the reader progresses through a world that is framed and organised.[20]

The scenery of the novels is operatic and grand, full of contrasts of pinnacles and abysses, flowery rivulets and infinite chasms, representing and inspiring the human mind that perceives it. The contrasts, often clichéd, often wonderfully suggestive, reflect contrasts in the mind as well as in human society and even in gender. Trees are masculine, with their gigantic arms aloft, and Alpine landscape becomes 'beauty sleeping in the lap of horror'. 'Deep valleys, that, winding into obscurity, seemed to invite curiosity to explore the scene below' resemble the veiled elusive heroines and are described in female aesthetic vocabulary as beautiful, sweet, elegant and charming, blushing in the rising sun; mountains are grand and awful guardians of their charms.

The frequent poetic descriptions of nature stop the action and hold suspense. They have no interest in moving the plot along or in explaining and clarifying human action and motive. Mostly landscapes are seen in obscurity through distance or atmospherics of storm, dusk or dawn. The obscurity signifies religious obscurity, as the scenery itself expresses God and as the watcher's reverential response expresses the proper attitude to God. The natural sublime is the nearest people can come to the supernatural on earth; only when contemplating it can they properly imagine what is naturally beyond the world and supernaturally beyond everything. In *The Mysteries of Udolpho*, Emily, looking at the landscape, imagines 'vast regions of space, glowing with worlds beyond the reach of human thought'.

Nature, changing but repeating, obscure and revealing, intensifies religious emotion, and ultimately human virtue. Those who are most responsive to landscape are most responsive to God and so most virtuous in inclination:

> The first tender tints of morning now appeared on the verge of the horizon, stealing upon the darkness; – so pure, so fine, so aetherial it seemed as if Heaven was opening to the view. The dark mists were seen to roll off to the west, as the tints of light grew stronger, deepening the obscurity of that part of the hemisphere, and involving the features of the country below; meanwhile, in the east, the hues became more vivid, darting a trembling lustre far around, till a ruddy glow, which fired all that part of the Heavens, announced the rising sun. At first, a small line of inconceivable splendour emerged on the horizon, which, quickly expanding, the sun appeared in all his glory, unveiling the whole face of nature, vivifying every colour of the landscape, and sprinkling the dewy earth with glittering light. The low and gentle responses of birds, awakened by the morning ray, now broke the silence of the hour; the soft warbling rising by degrees till they swelled the chorus of universal gladness. Adeline's heart swelled too with gratitude and adoration.
>
> The scene before her soothed her mind, and exalted her thoughts to the great Author of Nature; she uttered an involuntary prayer: 'Father of good, who made this glorious scene! I resign myself to thine hands: thou wilt support me under my present sorrows, and protect me from future evil.'
>
> Thus confiding in the benevolence of God, she wiped the tears from her eyes, while the sweet union of conscience and reflection rewarded her trust; and her mind, losing the feelings which had lately oppressed it, became tranquil and composed.[21]

At other times the effect is less overtly religious and more simply poetic but the movement from outer to inner as the world moves from one state to another is repeated. Although the hero and heroine might discover their kinship in their rapt contemplation of nature, in general the natural passages do not express individual character as much as the sensibility of the novel as a whole. Hence their repetitiveness, their incantatory unspecific effect. Radcliffe was aware of the repetition: 'It is difficult to spread varied pictures of such scenes before the imagination,' she wrote.

> A repetition of the same images of rock, wood and water, and the same epithets of grand, vast and sublime, which necessarily occur, must appear tautologous, on paper, though their archetypes in nature, ever varying in outline, or arrangement, exhibit new visions to the eye, and produce new shades of effect upon the mind.[22]

Nature and the sentimental poetry of nature, associated with the English poets and with women, function in opposition to sensuality. It is almost nature as real transcendental art against materialistic mundane culture. The luxurious interior of the aristocratic seducer in *The Romance of the Forest* is outside nature, loudly expressing artifice. It is a 'magnificent saloon, splendidly illuminated, and fitted up in the most airy and elegant taste' with silver Etruscan lamps, music and perfumed flowers. It is like a palace of seductive male culture, full of literary references. The heroine warned by nature's darkness and storm is Persephone in this Hades – like the goddess she takes only a single fruit – and she is almost seduced by the display. But soon she understands that sensual art is ranged with masculine vice and should be closed to women. Later she looks from outside through a window and sees the wicked Marquis 'reclining on a sofa, near which stood a table covered with fruit and wine ... alone and his countenance was flushed with drinking'.[23] The art and artifice simply exaggerate the man's sensual threat; a lady can allow herself to be inebriated only with natural scenery and the 'higher kinds of poetry' that express it.

Yet of course nothing is entirely untinged by its contrast. As the lighted sensuous interiors imply the dark austerity outside, as the landscapes have required light and darkness, obscurity and clarity, as dread has come with desire, so in a way the open valleys of La Luc demand the forests of Montalt or La Vallée the dark castle of Udolpho. The identity so strenuously supported by the heroines is based on the fear of its destruction, the doubling seems to imply dissolution, and enlightenment always suggests a flickering out into night. Consequently a later age, withdrawing from the absolute, sentimental allegorising of Mrs Radcliffe's endings, found, against all her expressed intentions, an ambiguous, subversive, voluptuous quality that linked the novels quite clearly with the excesses of *The Monk* and of the French. It was perhaps such a response that pushed Radcliffe into relative silence for many years after the publication of *The Italian*, fearing that her books like the sentimental body might speak beyond conscious control, that they might escape decorum and suffer misinterpretation, and that sentimental values might not in the end be unpolitical in a political age.[24] She would have been even more horrified by the twentieth century that rescued her gothic fantasies from the oblivion into which they had fallen by making of them dark and explicit images of female claustrophobia and sexual desire, while it made her genre which, despite Catherine Morland's Midlands experience, she intended as a 'guide to life', into a vehicle for escape and lurid sensationalism.

15

MORAL AUTHORSHIP AND AUTHORITY:
FANNY BURNEY

In Radcliffe the mask of the lady novelist is firmly in place. But a question about the ethical and aesthetic implications is posed discreetly between the work and the writer – a writer who stopped writing at the height of her powers to let herself be re-masked as domestic woman and wife. With Fanny Burney, the most esteemed woman novelist of the period, the questions are again posed with discretion. They never come directly from the author and artist who wrote the novels, the exemplary daughter, wife and lady-in-waiting to the Queen. Yet they are nonetheless raised and to a large extent answered for those readers who reached the end of the obsessive and increasingly repetitive books, written after the detested French Revolution had emphasised what was at stake in allowing fantasy and solipsistic feeling to triumph.[1]

Burney moved in more exalted circles than Radcliffe, Wollstonecraft or Hays, attached by family inclination to an older conservatism than the middle-class variety of Radcliffe, idealising the settled provincial life in England, domestic hierarchy and a moderate clergy and gentry without modish Rousseauian overtones. Like the radical Hays and Wollstonecraft, of whom she heartily disapproved, Burney wanted to urge the novel back into life and make it again an interventionist genre, but, like them, she too was writing in the shadow of the sentimental female novel, the expectations of the genre and the proper imagination of the woman writer. Horrified at the self-indulgence that sensibility had become, she avoided the route of excess that more emotionally adventurous women like Wollstonecraft and Hays had tried to follow. At the same time she could not believe with Radcliffe or even the later Wollstonecraft that sensibility and the sentimental image should be rescued. Although inevitably (and strangely) compromised by the conventions and strategies of sentiment, her books make an open assault on sensibility and feminine romance in much the same way as Hannah More's tracts or as Jane

Austen's novels would later do. Indeed for the younger novelist Burney represented the *pre-eminent* woman writer, a female Spectator rather than a Tatler, who could, as *Northanger Abbey* asserts, edify with more purity than the coarse pages of Addison and Steele.

And yet Burney is *not* Austen, as the very form and style of her lengthy and unironic novels immediately shows. Far less secure in authorship, she allows her books to provoke those questions of inner and outer, public and private, author and novel, authority and femininity that Austen deftly stifles. The questions are posed too by the famous diaries – private works but with a sense of audience, even if this audience is only an aspect of herself, named 'Nobody' – which are full of the excitement and anxiety of disguise, stratagems and manipulation, and which were in the end muted, excised and clarified by the older Fanny Burney, the famous novelist, who wished to express herself and yet preserve her privacy and propriety.[2] Not known at the start as the author of the successful *Evelina* (1778), the story of a shy girl entering society with trepidation but also great éclat, the Burney of the diaries goes where she will hear herself spoken of in speculation and praise, where her anonymously published novel can act in disguise to receive the public compliments that a lady author should never openly allow, and where she can masquerade as what she insists she is, a modest young daughter who knows when to be silent, not a garrulous author.

In the preface to *Evelina* she shows herself uneasy over the popularity and non-elite status of the novel:

> In the republic of letters, there is no member of such inferior rank, or who is so much disdained by his brethren of the quill, as the humble Novelist, nor is his fate less hard in the world at large, since, among the whole class of writers, perhaps not one can be named, of whom the votaries are more numerous, but less respectable.[3]

Yet the insistent masculine pronoun undercuts the complaint, for it is not on the whole the *male* novelist who is humble, and indeed she allies herself as novelist precisely with those male fictional writers who eschew humility and *do* have an elite or semi-elite reputation: Rousseau, Johnson, Fielding, Richardson and Smollett. Only in her diary does she call herself an 'Authoress', a title that brings no authority of authorship, but instead enters the social world with a flippant, assuming quality which above all she wishes to avoid. So, since her sex prevents her from joining the group of Rousseau and Richardson, she will take anonymity. The posture continues inside the novel as well, in the letter form which, like the diaries and journal letters (letters written over a long time in the form of a journal), discloses the characters but leaves their author undisclosed.

The worry of authorship is not ended in the three later novels but the strategy changes. Burney, the exemplary lady admired by such eminent men as Dr Johnson, becomes in a way the heir of Aphra Behn and Delarivier Manley in her assertion of herself as a gendered writer and yet her claim to a male tradition. Like Radcliffe she takes the route of the woman author as moralist, rather lost in the headiness of introverted sensibility. The unease, the anxiety, the strategies and the complicities of gender and genre are well illustrated in each of the novels but especially in *Camilla* (1796), the work in which the obsessiveness of authorship, together with the theme of public and private with which it is so intimately connected, is only just held in check. 'A fear of doing wrong has always been the leading principle of my internal guidance,' she declared. In *Camilla* to avoid 'doing wrong' is not a passive but a herculean ambition for a woman – and for her female author. The theme is the young girl's entry into society; in a way the novel also depicts the older woman's entry into repressing moral art.

In 1786 Dr Burney, pleased with the fame of his daughter's authorship – which she had so fearfully kept from him – was even more delighted to learn that she had been invited to become second keeper of the robes to Queen Charlotte. She herself dreaded the exactions of the position but accepted it nonetheless. She remained with the Queen for five wearying years. At court she needed to disguise and control with a vengeance. All spontaneous physical activity was to be suppressed. Wryly she described the rules:

> In the first place, you must not cough. If you find a cough tickling in your throat, you must arrest it from making any sound; if you find yourself choking with the forbearance, you must choke – but not cough.
> In the second place, you must not sneeze. If you have a vehement cold, you must take no notice of it; if your nose membranes feel a great irritation, you must hold your breath; if a sneeze still insists upon making its way, you must oppose it, by keeping your teeth grinding together; if the violence of the repulse breaks some blood-vessel, you must break the blood-vessel – but not sneeze.[4]

(The uncharacteristic humour here is possible because the passage was written *before* she took up the dreaded position at court.) No wonder she formed the plan 'to wean myself from myself – to lessen all my affections – to curb all my wishes – to deaden all my sensation', a plan devised on 'the first day my dear father accepted my offered appointment'. Later she referred to it as a kind of patriarchal arranged marriage: 'I am *married*... I look upon it in that light – I was averse to forming the union, and I endeavoured to escape it; but my friends interfered – they prevailed –

and the knot is tied. What, then, now remains but to make the best wife in my power?'[5]

The position at court was a grotesque exaggeration of the female position in middle- and upper-class society. Liking, even loving her quietly exacting mistress the Queen, but debilitated by the contingency, the dependence, the inferiority, the exclusion from all spontaneity of response, Burney felt herself stifled and buried alive – rather as Wollstonecraft felt when she filled the unsuitable subordinate roles of companion and governess. Like so many of her heroines, Burney halted her seemingly relentless decline by falling ill. She recovered only after she had left the Palace in 1791 after months of fearful apprehension of disapproval exaggerated into royal displeasure. Her third fictional heroine, Camilla, whose 'skeleton' was created during these isolated, repressing years, would be much taken to task for nervously willing herself into disease to escape from her otherwise overwhelming troubles. Much later, after she had really married, when the King asked her how long she had taken to write the book she replied, '*All* my time, sir! – from the period I planned publishing it, I devoted myself to it wholly; – I had no Episode – but a little baby! – My subject grew upon me.'[6]

As her reply to the King suggests, Burney was writing out of 'devotion' as well as need for money, the most obvious impetus for the book. Possibly obsession would be a more adequate word now. Certainly both *Camilla* and *The Wanderer* (1814) suggest the term in their extraordinary repetitiveness – beyond the need to make a large expensive book – that relentlessly takes the heroines towards but not quite to destruction again and again. Despite their financial success, these enormous works turned Burney from the popular novelist of the prerevolutionary *Evelina* and *Cecilia* (1782) into a post-revolutionary unpopular one, both with a general contemporary readership and with critics. By *The Wanderer* her disquiet over the novel's place in culture, expressed in the preface to *Evelina*, had become fear of its 'degradation'.

It was not 'novels' or 'a mere love story' that the older Fanny Burney was choosing to write. She was not supplying wish fulfilment, a fantasy that might take over from life; no novel could or should have that function. Nor was it a straight conduct book in the manner of Hannah More. As she wrote at the beginning of *Camilla*, only suffering directly reforms conduct:

> The experience which teaches the lesson of truth, and the blessings of tranquility, comes not in the shape of warning nor of wisdom; from such they turn aside, defying or disbelieving. 'Tis on the bitterness of personal proof alone, in suffering and in feeling, in erring and repeating, that experience comes home with conviction, or impresses to any use.[7]

What she was providing were 'morals put in action'. She wished to make money certainly but she wished even more to write what she deeply felt she ought.

To get a sense of the context of Burney's fictional devotion one has to look into the life she displayed in her letters and novels. At every turn after *Evelina*, the first spontaneous theatrical fiction in letter form, her novels seem associated with paternal authority, either with her 'dear father' or with his various substitutes, who act in her fiction-writing life like extreme patriarchal versions of the loving guardians of the sentimental novel.[8] The Burneys were concerned about respectability – there was much they had to hide with crimes, peccadilloes and even an incestuous elopement in the immediate family – and Dr Burney, a musician, had achieved a position in London society only with diligence and constant care.[9] His daughter's authorship was at first kept from him, but when he knew of its success, he clearly saw it as part of the family's status and he urged her to stop working on a play (her natural bent was probably theatrical – her father's was not although he craved success in the theatre) which imprudently satirised the Bluestockings and instead write another novel, *Cecilia*. Into this he prodded and pushed Fanny until she actually fell ill from the pressure to please, as her friend Mrs Thrale noted. That she was writing against the grain is evident from her violent statements about the work – she was afraid to see her father when it did not go well and, but for him, she declared she would have thrown it behind the fire. (The reason for all the haste seems to have been Dr Burney's desire to publish his volume on the history of music simultaneously with his famous daughter.) 'The Family of the Burneys are a very surprising Set of People,' wrote Mrs Thrale, 'their Esteem & fondness for the Dr. seems to inspire them all with a Desire not to disgrace him; & so every individual of it must write and read & be literary.'[10] Fanny's appointment to court was seen by many as a consolation to Dr Burney for his failure to receive a royal appointment; perhaps it was for this reason that she left the momentous decision of whether or not to accept to him and then went tottering and fainting to court, not telling her misery for several years until it seemed to many that, as Dr Burney himself finally put it, he was like Agamemnon sacrificing his daughter to the state.[11] Later Fanny Burney would marry against the wishes, but not without the consent, of her father, an unthreatening unpatriarchal man, but by then the pattern of authorship and authority was established.

The world of Burney's late novels is still the familiar one of eighteenth-century women's fiction. Women differ severely from men and fall more heavily; rape hides round a corner and ruin results from a chance encounter. But, although the progress of the young girl through illness and misery to marriage is usual, it is not given the heroic status of earlier pilgrimages, and the entry into 'life', because it is defined through eighteenth-century social and public entertainments, can more easily be seen as prelude only to a (finally) longed-for exit. Male villainy (and incompetence), though plentiful, is simply a component in the suffering and 'difficulties' of women, attractive because they are young and, because they are young, unwise. The fables are not unlike those of high sentiment; the main ingredients are still the romantic courtship and marriage of a young girl, left unprepared and undefended in society. But the tone is quite distinct. Even more than in Wollstonecraft and Radcliffe, it is clear that money – and the control of it – is the issue, while the gloom of the proceedings is hardly lifted by the cruel farce that passes for humour.

The heroine's progress towards maturity, here a sort of mental and physical passivity, makes even active female philanthropy a problem, for, like Wollstonecraft's Mary, Camilla finds benevolence far from simple in a world that does not conform to sentimental expectations, where the kind spontaneous act is not always the wisest, and good deeds may corrupt as often as reform. She is kind to a needy family beyond her ability, and the harsh remark of the narrator in the earlier novel about the heiress Cecilia who is taxed by insatiable friends could well be applied to her: 'The ardour of her benevolence which taught her to value her riches merely as they enabled her to do good and generous actions was here of no avail to console or reward her.' Sentimental notions prove expensive.

In her later novels Burney reveals the gap between sentimental expectation and sober reality, between surface expression and unknowable deep feeling, and between the impassive exterior and the ferocious unexpressed desire to sneeze. In the earlier diary, there is a picture of Miss Sophy Streatfild, learned in Greek but more famous for her sentimental manifestations, 'her softness, her caressing manners, her tearful eyes'. Mrs Thrale exhibits her as both a curiosity and as an expression of femininity when she insists that Miss Streatfeild has 'the power of crying herself into any of your hearts she pleased'. To prove the point, Mrs Thrale pleads with her to cry for her guests and, while they are still laughing, 'two crystal tears came into the soft eyes of the S.S., and rolled gently down her cheeks!' The tears are decorous and her face remains 'smooth and elegant' throughout the exercise – indeed she 'was smiling all the time'. After much laughter, Mrs Thrale ends the proceedings by saying, 'There now . . . she looks for all the world as if nothing had happened; for, you know, nothing *has* happened.'[12] The pretty girl is in the end unknowable, giving the emotional response wanted, provoking contemptuous admiration, and arrogantly interpreted by onlookers.

'The S.S.' is a caricatured version of what the Burney heroine, little characterised beyond a few sketchy remarks, is and also should not be. She is unknowable to the people with whom she associates precisely because she must be on display. But, despite all pressures, she must be careful not to become like Sophy Streatfeild a *spectacle*. Surrounded by objects that can corrupt, money that might mean inappropriate power or improper dependence, people who might lay claim to her or a claim on her, she must avoid the contamination of being known and of receiving labels at all costs. To owe money is somehow to owe herself, to accept a locket or a bank cheque is to have given the surety of herself, to speak much is to lose the delicacy of silence. In another entry, Burney wrote of a female acquaintance, 'She is too sincere: she pays too little regard to the world.' A young girl should cry, but only when sure of her audience.

Inevitably reputation, the sign of woman, comes to the fore. As the mentor figure Mr Villars had written in *Evelina*, 'Remember, nothing is so delicate as the reputation of a woman: it is, at once, the most beautiful and most brittle of all human things.' In Burney's work it is not enough for the heroine to be spotless herself: her excellence must be 'fearful' and 'exemption from actual blemish could only be a negative recommendation'. Any activity in her behalf by another or any talk about her may stain as well. The message of the woman must be carefully attended to in all its forms.

She is read partly through the constraints and expressiveness of dress, which as the sign of femininity appears to control romance and status for the girl but which, as packaging, must be paid for with money owned by men. Disguise is deeply improper. The masquerade threatens because it allows a woman to be what she is not or to uncover under cover what she might be. In everyday life the middle-aged and lower-class Mrs Mittin of the often snobbish *Camilla* simply dresses as 'a mere commonperson' and renders herself invisible to people of a higher class; she is then as free to walk the streets 'ever so late' as the young men who saunter where they wish, taking up attitudes and costumes at will. But a *young* girl without the props of decently fashionable dress and company cannot walk abroad without being taken for a shoplifter or a whore – in *The Wanderer* the heroine, dressed as a peasant, avoids the harassment of gentility only to suffer sexual harassment. Yet, if she openly endeavours to be fashionable, the young girl risks becoming noticeable; 'unfeminine popularity' ensues and she may become a woman 'easy of access', the improper centre of a crowd of flatterers and lookers, available to all meanings. She has not kept control of her sign or hidden herself in preparation for her revelation to one man only, her husband. Censorious men as well as libertines lie in wait for such girls, in much the way that

Winterbourne does in Henry James's *Daisy Miller*, to brand them with the dismissive sign of coquette or flirt.

In the world of Burney's novels, coquetry is seen within male ideology not as female freedom of activity but as its reverse. A woman who engages in it can no longer be a free agent because her identity resides not in herself, but in her reputation and that has been compromised. Real femininity must have no manipulative desires and take none of the verbal initiative that marks the coquette. Indeed the proper young girl shrinks back, hides, refuses, is silent or speaks only in very restricted codes, never, for example, seeing parents in the jolly way of young men as 'hunks' and 'bores'.

Such girls should live for family duty. Eugenia, the ugly sister in *Camilla* whose deformities have been caused by her uncle's negligence, must yet desire to do whatever 'will most conduce to [her uncle's] tranquility and recovery' even though some of the demands seem 'almost too severe a trial of the duty and fortitude'. The highest praise comes for the moments of noble self-sacrifice, when a woman reveals herself as perfectly free from self and perfectly free from guile, every species of scheme, of art. Art becomes the word in women for coquetry, for manipulation not of words or paint but of people.

A problem associated with the fear of art and artfulness in women is education. Stupid girls are mocked and Eugenia's facility with classical languages is presented attractively. But her ability seems of no use whatsoever in ordinary life and, although the remark that Latin is a great 'disadvantage' to the prospects of a pretty girl is made by a trivial woman, the plot shows it to be no advantage. The main heroines are not scholarly or artistic themselves. Far more important are quickness and common sense, and an ability to understand and conform to the social codes, qualities which are not especially promoted in the home. In fact girls in society are required to have precisely the qualities that experience could give, but to have them spontaneously. In this formulation Burney is only partly in tune with Hannah More and Mary Wollstonecraft, who both stress the need for an education in conscious and active virtue.

Burney's most bizarre discussion of education occurs in *Camilla* regarding the upbringing of Eugenia. A part of this has been an acceptance of the truism that moral beauty is of more value than physical. But like Lennox's Female Quixote who is persuaded to take French romances seriously or Opie's Adeline Mowbray who espouses Wollstonecraft's feminist views – or indeed Manley's heroines brought up on a diet of literary virtue – it seems disastrous to accept in life ideas culled from books, even if these express the culture's overt beliefs and even if, as in Burney's case, the narrative voice seems to validate them.

The family colludes in Eugenia's belief that her appearance is unimportant; consequently when she unexpectedly becomes the butt of the lower orders who have no literature to tamper with the message of their eyes and of young men who have no such refined belief, she rounds on her education as an upbringing in 'worldy darkness', a simple unhelpful knowledge of dead books and languages. But her pedagogic family will not leave her alone and her father insists on reconciling her to her deformed state by shock tactics: showing her the greater horror of 'intellectual darkness'. By this he means not a pretty girl without Latin but a pretty maniac, conveniently to hand like the maniacs of high sentimental literature. But, despite the manipulations of plot and despite her acceptance of the duty of 'filial gratitude', Eugenia's agonised question is never answered within the ideology of femininity that allows no social route but marriage:

> Can you expect to reconcile to existence a poor young creature who sees herself an object of derision and disgust? Who, without committing any crime, without offending any human being, finds she cannot appear but to be pointed at, scoffed and insulted![13]

So too with book learning. Her grounding in Latin simply adds to her freakishness. The only salvation seems to be through a homiletic father and an innately pliant disposition. Wollstonecraft would have been appalled at so deterministic a conclusion.

Female friendship like education is also problematic for the young girl out of her father's house. In their rejected predicaments the heroines receive it less as a comfort than as a test and trial. In sentimental fiction from the later Haywood to Wollstonecraft and Hays, friendship had been the great support and defence against male social and sexual depradations. But in earlier writers such as Manley and Behn, it often represented a state of warfare. If Burney seems to return to the unflattering pictures of the early female authors, she does so moralistically, not cynically. The heroines are in danger from villains but it is usually an external danger, whereas manipulative female friendship is insidiously threatening. Frequently it is built not on equality but on a hierarchy that relationships of sensibility had abjured. This allows its danger to be more apparent.

The worldly women – and they exist in most of Burney's novels – reveal themselves in wit, that self-wounding female sword that Mrs Montagu had deplored in Laetitia Pilkington. Wit like art suggests a kind of trickery. It overwhelms judgement. Yet the situation is complicated by the fact that the witty older woman often gives out truths that are never quite contained in the novel, showing a worldly wisdom that would probably prove fairly accurate in its assessments, if the romantic fantasy plot did not in the end take over. They resemble the successful women of Haywood and Manley, able to see the sexual game, and play it well, but never themselves enslaved either by sexual or sentimental passion. They see the struggle between the sexes and assert that the social and emotional constraints under which women must operate are not innate but cultivated. As Mrs Arlbery in *Camilla* remarks;

> Every damsel, as she enters the world, has some picture ready painted upon her imagination, of an object worthy to enslave her, in the firm persuasion of her ductile fancy, that he is just the model it had previously created.[14]

In reality entry into society should be treated as entry into a game: 'Know your own power more truly,' Mrs Arlbery tells her young friend, 'and use it better. Men, my dear, are all spoilt by humility, and all conquered by gaiety.' For all the undercutting she suffers from the narrative voice, her view of the hero sticks:

> He is a watcher; and a watcher, restless and perturbed himself, infests all he pursues with uneasiness. He is without trust, and therefore without either courage or consistency. To-day he may be persuaded you will make all his happiness; to-morrow, he may fear you will give him nothing but misery. Yet it is not that he is jealous of any other; 'tis of the object of his choice he is jealous, lest she should not prove good enough to merit it.[15]

It is not the sentiment of the narrator and it has the tight language of homily.

The line of seductive female friends who mouth wrong doctrine culminates in the extraordinary Elinor of *The Wanderer*, the most anxious of the novels; she like Emma Courtney (both love a man called Harley or Harleigh) believes she can force her love on a man. She is given the politics of Hays and the Wollstonecraft of 1792 but these Enlightenment views are embedded in a context of eccentricity and hysteria – alternately she threatens murder and suicide in reference to the now notorious suicide attempt of Wollstonecraft. Yet, like the wit of the witty woman, her tirades are not entirely contained. As the witty woman's knowledge would not have been disadvantageous to the heroine had the sentimental plot not triumphed, so the feminism of Elinor provides an apt diagnosis of the miseries of the unprotected and ultimately impotent heroine, prevented from any strenuous and effective effort by her laudable femininity:

> Must every thing that she does be prescribed by rule? Must every thing that she says, be limited to what has been said before? Must nothing that is spontaneous, generous, intuitive, spring from her soul to her lips?[16]

The answer is yes, as it was in *Emma Courtney*. For it is not she who wins the prized man.

In the end there is no one so safe as sisters, as Christina Rossetti would say fifty years later at the conclusion of that great paean to sisterly relations, 'Goblin Market', even if, as in *The Wanderer*, the girls do not immediately know of the blood relationship. And it is the gentle Aurora, possessed of an 'excess of sensibility' – not the mad Elinor, whose antics come to resemble those of the shrieking heroines of Aphra Behn and Manley, rending clothes and hair in the most unfeminine fashion – to whom the heroine's heart and tears are given in feminine friendship not feminist alliance. Camilla ends by promising that, during 'her present season of inexperience', she will allow herself no independence of choice in friends outside her family.

When the heroine marries, the control of her social being will devolve on her husband and indeed in *Camilla* the hero has largely anticipated this role. The feminised hero of the sentimental novel had often revealed a certain impotence – as younger son, poorer man or invalid. In Burney's novels, however, the hero is usually more in charge, closer to the commanding father figures of Jane Austen, though deeply flawed as a romantic actor. As the sentimental components of plot and character are lessened, the patriarchal scheme comes to the fore, with men inevitably at the apex of the hierarchy. The hero is inflexible, mentor and judge as well as lover of a woman whose femininity no longer effortlessly signifies superior virtue. He functions as a kind of spoiler of the heroine's naughty social pleasure, a superego in dress suit.

Camilla loves Edgar who loves her back but will not marry her until she proves her character utterly worthy – of him, presumably. 'I will watch by her unceasingly!' he declares early in the novel, echoing the many guardian figures of female fiction. But Burney's Edgar is a dark version of the loving guardian, readier to censor than to save, his character subordinated to his role as promoter of ideological femininity. Consequently Camilla's fear is less of male predatory sexuality, as in most sentimental novels, than of herself revealed to a man through her actions and friendships. It is no accident that in the end Edgar appears to her disguised as a priest (artlessness is not a necessity in men, it seeems). In Radcliffe's works the heroine ended the novel and entered marriage equal or superior in character or possessions; the Burney heroine must give up any advantage to be married. Indeed most of Burney's novels end with the heroine, once potentially or actually an heiress, 'owned' by father or surrogate and husband, any independent 'fortune' that might have been hers abjured, her loss symbolised by marriage and the semi-death that is almost invariably its prelude.[17]

In Burney's fiction, there is less stress on the inner life than in the sentimental novel; yet the focus is not primarily on society either, but on some interaction of it with the inner life. At times seemingly plotless, the almost thousand-paged *Camilla* appears like the transcript of some interminable psychological case study, with events repeating themselves and guilt and innocence wildly fluctuating. Ultimately the effect is of the precariousness of life, not the exhilaration of either the external picaresque or the internal sentimental, the need for close and closed middle-class family existence against the danger outside, of control rather than expansion of the self. At the end of most of the novels happiness could well be defined for the much tried heroine as never having to go off in a coach alone again.

It was a truism of the time that pathos paid more than humour and Burney was a professional writer. This is a cynical view of the sudden immersion in sentiment in each of the novels. Perhaps it is fairer to see the author as ambivalent about the expressive sentimental language, attacking its self-indulgent aims and yet desiring, like the later Wollstonecraft and Radcliffe, to take on some of its power, giving the sentimental scene and yet withholding total assent. Although Mrs Thrale cried herself blind over the pathetic conclusion of *Cecilia*, Burney insisted on the moderation of her ending, distinct from absolutes, the usual 'farce' of feminine romance.

The extreme expressive behaviour that the novel of sensibility had normalised comes as a shock in a Burney work, partly because of the sheer length of the unsentimental and commonplace preparation. With no sexual fall but with almost all the consequences of one – indeed it is notable how little difference a sexual slip would make, not to the ending indeed, but to the preceding horrors – the heroine is rescued into the sentimental scene of familial bliss, as in this episode from *Camilla*:

Her Mother, leaning over her, was watching her breathe, with hands uplifted for her preservation, and looks of fondness which seemed to mark that her happiness depended upon its being granted; but as she raised herself, to throw her arms around the loved maternal neck, the shadow of another form, quickly, yet gently receding, struck her sight; . . .

'Ah, Heaven!' she exclaimed, 'who is that?'

'Will you be good,' said Mrs Tyrold, gently, 'be tranquil, be composed, and earn that I should tell you who has been watching by you this hour?'

Camilla could not answer; certain, now, who it must be, her emotions became again uncontrollable; her horror, her remorse, her self-abhorrence revived, and agonizingly exclaiming, 'Tis my Father! – O, where can I hide my head?' She strove again to envelop herself with the bed-curtains from all view.

'Here – in his own arms – upon his own breast you shall hide it,' said
Mr Tyrold, returning to the bed-side, 'and all now shall be forgotten, but
thankfulness that our afflictions seem finding their period.'

'O my Father! my Father!' cried Camilla.[18]

Ignoring the 'earn' of the indelibly monitory mother, a reader would be
forgiven for ascribing this scene to a thoroughgoing sentimental writer.

Yet the impression does not remain and the scene is gently distanced
with a variety of devices, ranging from moral maxims and commonsensical remarks to stress on the literary nature of reaction and response.
The especial suffering of the heroine, almost justified by the imprisonment of a father, the loss of a lover, and the torment of a sister, is
nonetheless judged adolescent; she wishes for death, says the narrator,
'in common with every youthful mourner'. Meanwhile the suffering itself
is interrupted by remarks on the 'tardy prudence of a rash character'.
Camilla learns that female illness is often self-inflicted; in an implied
criticism of *Clarissa* and a host of female novels immediately presenting
sickness from sorrow, her illness is portrayed as self-indulgent and
histrionic, robbed of its feminine power, described harshly as the
'cruelty of . . . egotism'. Had she died she would have been 'self-
murdered through wilful self-neglect'. Clearly she must get out of the
Richardsonian plot.

Sentiment has burgeoned in the presence of the father, but it is not his
language that expresses it. Opposing the feminine language of sensibility,
both bombastic and colloquial, is the rotund Johnsonian male discourse
of common sense and morality used by fathers, guardians and proper
lovers. In *Evelina*, the grandfatherly figure gives advice so aptly, generally
and often that his letters could be removed from the novel to form a
conduct book for young ladies – as in fact happened with the advice of
the father to his daughter in *Camilla*. No wonder then that the heroine's
progress is measured in her learning of the discourse of the patriarchs and
that her last letters resemble her father's in style. The proper message is
her unworthiness and humility. For when in her nightmares she had
dreamed of her hand grasping a 'pen of Iron' she found that it deeply and
speedily wrote her guilt but would not write her worth.

It is not only her father's style that the heroine comes to echo but also
that of the narrator. Burney's narrator is the one woman in the novel
who possesses the moral authority of men, the only woman who can be
self-confident and assertive with impunity and who can be associated
with art – although not with wit. It is the narrator who provides the
main characteristic of Burney's novels after the youthful *Evelina*.

Omnipresent and morally secure, the woman writer here comes
forward as maternal teacher far beyond the tentative role adumbrated so

long before by Aphra Behn. She is smug at times, complacent and genteel. Her control is most apparent in the abstract, sometimes pompous style that distances or prevents an emotional response, functioning to stop enactment and to silence the plot. 'The changeful tide of mental spirits from misery to enjoyment, is not more rapid than the transition from personal danger to safety, in the elastic period of youth,' she declares sententiously, putting a dampener on the rapturous familial scene quoted above.[19]

Burney's narrator differs from the Fielding narrator, the omnipotent puppeteer who manipulates plot and characters as he will. She also differs from the narrator of the novel of sentiment who addresses maxims to all humanity from an impersonal general standpoint; instead she gives advice and moral and social comment like a stern mother or aunt, directed to the characters in the story and to the girls outside. So when Camilla worries whether she should speak and to whom, the narrator, unfortunately barred from acting within the novel, states baldly, 'A moment's reflection would have told her, that quietness alone . . . could do justice to the purity of her intentions.' Elsewhere the narrator interferes to support the good and criticise the trivial, to put the experienced middle-aged view, expecting after all only so much of youth, annoyed, like the narrator of George Eliot's *Adam Bede*, at the propensity of young men to approve conventional feminine beauty in a vapid selfish girl, insisting on naming its use as coquetry and pitting her views against the wit of the dubious older women in the text. Although some aspects of sensibility are supported in the characterisation of the young heroines, the narrators are firm in their mockery of sensibility in general, judged to be spurious in its external modes and gestures. Always on the side of authenticity and spontaneity in youth when these are in the service of virtue, the narrators yet constantly and sourly contextualise: 'the artlessness of unadorned truth, however sure in theory of extorting admiration, rarely, in practice, fails inflicting pain or mortification.'[20]

The rather smug superiority of the Burney narrator does not make her entirely unattractive. Certainly it gives her a definable character even beyond that of Radcliffe's storyteller. She comes across as an older experienced woman who has lived, suffered and overcome, a kind of Prudentia Homespun for the genteel classes, the old maid of women's fiction, standing in for Burney, who did not marry until she was over forty. She is usually predictable like a person of settled character, but occasionally she surprises with her bitterness. At the end of *Camilla*, having presented impartially, even favourably, the testing of Camilla by Edgar, supported in his caution by an older misogynist male mentor, the narrator rounds on this figure whose own disappointment in love determines his advice, declaring 'its injustice, its narrowness and its arrogance'. In such touches the narrator obtrudes her own older personality, the personality of a female author who creates moral art, an involved commentator of real life, similar to, although less cynical than, the voyeurs of Delarivier Manley, avoiding both amoral verisimilitude and the escapism of sentimental romance, presiding with a mingling of involvement and world-weariness over the darkening path of the tortured heroine. Perhaps she might appear transgressive in her freedom but she overcomes this appearance in the end by the way she normalises nightmare.

Although the plot of the female novel with its obligatory ending in happy marriages rescues the various young women from the horrors they have entered, the narrator seems uninvolved in the rescue, allowing romance only as a sop to the weary reader and more implicated in repetition than in resolution. This repetition, here avoiding the self-indulgent appearance of the sentimental novel and the obsessive fiction of Wollstonecraft and Hays, works against the closure of romance. The heroines after Evelina have simply suffered too much, have been too embarrassed, too often interrupted, too watched and misinterpreted, and they enter marriage like invalids entering an asylum. Only the pedagogic, garrulous and moralistic Burney narrator remains outside, wrapping herself in her own rhetoric.

In the end it is the narrator and the impasse of female life which she repetitively exhibits that stay with the reader and it is she, the internalised parental authority transmuted into female author, who most clearly represents the future of culturally approved fiction by women. In this tradition there is no sense of the aesthetic salvation of Romanticism or any stress on verisimilitude for its own sake, but there is insistence that it is the province of the woman writer to investigate the 'human heart', understand desire but make morality clear. As Burney wrote at the outset of *Camilla*:

> The historian of human life finds less of difficulty and of intricacy to develop, in its accidents and adventures, than the investigator of the human heart ... that amazing assemblage of all possible contrarieties, in which one thing alone is steady – the perverseness of spirit which grafts desire on what is denied. Its qualities are indefinable, its resources unfathomable, its weaknesses indefensible ... In one grand and general view, who can display such a portrait? Fairly, however faintly, to delineate some of its features, is the sole and discriminate province of the pen which would trace nature, yet blot out personality.[21]

NOTES

INTRODUCTION

1. Aphra Behn, *The Rover*, ed. Frederick Link (London: Arnold, 1967). In *The Rover*, second part (London, 1681) the hero chooses again between the virgin and the whore and this time chooses the latter.

2. Ian Watt's *The Rise of the Novel* (Berkeley and Los Angeles: University of California Press, 1957) is an immensely influential study of the early novel that connects the rise of the novel with developing capitalism, the increasing dominance of the middle class, the spread of secularised Protestantism and the growth of the reading public. It privileges a certain sort of formal realism to which it sees the novel tending or rising and it tells its story in terms of the five great male writers: Defoe, Fielding, Richardson, Sterne and Smollett. The major competitor to Watt is Michael McKeon's intricate intellectual study *The Origins of the English Novel 1600–1740* (Baltimore: Johns Hopkins Press, 1987), which again takes the social and literary together, although it modifies the model by seeing ideas as productive. It locates the beginnings of the modern English novel in the dialectical movements on the one hand of romance and naive empiricism and on the other of aristocratic and progressive ideology. It is a more rigorously argued work than Watt's in a currently fashionable critical mode that interweaves historical trends and philosophical notions intending to destabilise the categories of both society and literature. But its brilliance cannot obscure what is largely left out of its systematic analysis: adequate treatment of women as writers and readers. After the general argument, the book settles down to trace the novel through Cervantes, Bunyan, Defoe, Swift, Richardson and Fielding. Such powerful, provocative and indeed seminal studies as those of Watt and McKeon demand the compensatory activity of Jane Spencer in *The Rise of the Woman Novelist from Aphra Behn to Jane Austen* (Oxford: Basil Blackwell, 1986) and Dale Spender in *Mothers of the Novel* (London: Pandora, 1986).

3. Mary Wollstonecraft, *Letters Written ... in Sweden* (1796; Lincoln: University of Nebraska Press, 1976), pp. 180–81.

4. Mary Brunton, *Emmeline with some other pieces* (Edinburgh, 1819), p. xxxvi.

CHAPTER 1: THE RESTORATION AND EARLY EIGHTEENTH CENTURY

1. The effect is similar to that described in Michel Foucault's *The Order of Things* (London: Tavistock, 1970) when he imagines Western bemusement in front of a seemingly impossible Chinese catalogue.

288

2. *The Spectator* (London, 1747), vol. 5, no. 342.
3. See Patricia Crawford, 'Women's Published Writings 1600–1700' in *Women in English Society 1500–1800*, ed. Mary Prior (London: Methuen, 1985), p. 213.
4. Although there is an increase in female literacy, it should always be remembered that female literacy lagged far behind male and that female publications were only a small fraction of men's. See David Cressy, *Literacy and the Social Order* (Cambridge: Cambridge University Press, 1980).
5. Mary Astell, *Some Reflections upon Marriage* (Dublin, 1730), p. 20.
6. John Locke, *Two Treatises of Government*, ed. P. Laslett (Cambridge: Cambridge University Press, 1963), I, 5, sec. 48, pp. 11–16.
7. For a summary of the political history of the period, see David Ogg, *England in the Reign of Charles II* (1934; Oxford: Oxford University Press, 1984).
8. For short descriptions of the women writers see the entries in *A Dictionary of British and American Women Writers 1660–1800* (London: Methuen, 1985).
9. For the famous idea of the causal relation between the Protestant ethic and the spirit of capitalism, see Max Weber, *The Protestant Ethic and the Spirit of Capitalism*, trans. Talcott Parsons (1904–5; New York: Charles Scribner's Sons, 1958). For a later discussion, see McKeon, *The Origins of the English Novel* and Peter Stallybrass and Allon White, *The Politics and Poetics of Transgression* (London: Methuen, 1986).
10. For the economic position of women see Alice Clark, *Working Life of Women in the Seventeenth Century* (London: Routledge & Sons, 1919) and Roger Thompson, *Women in Stuart England and America* (London: Routledge and Kegan Paul, 1974).
11. For accounts of the midwifery books see Robert A. Erickson, '"The books of generation": some observations on the style of the English midwife books, 1671–1764' in *Sexuality in Eighteenth-Century Britain*, ed. Paul-Gabriel Boucé (Manchester: Manchester University Press, 1982), pp. 74–94.
12. An account of this occurs in Ruth Perry, *The Celebrated Mary Astell* (Chicago: University of Chicago Press, 1986), p. 226.
13. For an account of fashion in the Restoration and eighteenth century see Ludmilla Kybalova, Olga Herbeneova and Mileria Claudia Roson, *The Pictorial Encyclopedia of Fashion* (New York: Crown Publishers, 1968).
14. *Memoir of Lady Warwick: also Her Diary from AD 1666 to 1667, now first published, to which are added Extracts from her other Writings* (London: The Religious Tract Society, 1847); *Autobiography of Mary Countess of Warwick*, ed. T. C. Croker (London: Percy Society, 1848).
15. Quoted in Perry, *Mary Astell*, p. 513. I am indebted to Marilyn Butler for bringing this passage to my attention.
16. Quoted in Perry, *Mary Astell*, p. 74.
17. For an account of this altercation see Sara Heller Mendelson, *The Mental World of Stuart Women* (Brighton: Harvester Press, 1987), p. 44.
18. See James Miller, *The Humours of Oxford* (London, 1730), p. 79.
19. Barbara J. Todd, 'The remarrying widow: a stereotype reconsidered' in *Women in English Society 1500–1800*, ed. Prior, pp. 54–92. See also in passing Antonia Fraser, *The Weaker Vessel* (London: Weidenfeld and Nicolson, 1984).
20. Lawrence Stone in *The Family, Sex and Marriage in England 1500–1800* (1977; Harmondsworth: Penguin, 1982) holds a progressive view of the family and he sees society moving towards the companionate marriage and greater equality between the sexes. His thesis is criticised by Christopher Hill in 'Sex, Marriage and the Family in England' in *Economic History Review* xxxi, 1978, pp. 450–63, and opposed by Peter Laslett in *Family Life and Illicit Love in Earlier Generations* (Cambridge:

Cambridge University Press, 1977). Of course it is not always clear what the 'family' is in the past, nuclear or extended kin and friends; in addition, many of the accounts fit only the middle class and are based on the art and documentation of the middle and upper orders.

21. *The Ladies Calling* (London, 1673), Part II, sec. II, par. 2.
22. Mary Astell, *The Christian Religion, As Profess'd by a Daughter of the Church of England* (London, 1705), p. 113.
23. Astell, *Reflections upon Marriage*, p. 20.
24. Mary, Lady Chudleigh, 'To the Ladies' in *Poems on Several Occasions* (London, 1703). Some of Lady Chudleigh's poetry is reprinted in *First Feminists*, ed. Moira Ferguson (Bloomington: Indiana University Press, 1985).
25. Warwick, *Diary*, and Mendelson, *Stuart Women*, p. 103.
26. Perry, *Mary Astell*, p. 156.
27. Jane Barker, *Poetical Recreations* (London, 1688), pp. 91 and 12.
28. Margaret, Duchess of Newcastle, *The Convent of Pleasure, Plays, Never Before Printed* (London, 1668); repr. in *First Feminists*, ed. Ferguson, p. 89.
29. Aphra Behn, 'To the Fair Clarinda' in *Lycidus: Or, The Lover in Fashion* (London, 1688).
30. *Short Remarks upon the Original and Pernicious Consequences of Masquerades* (London, 1721). See Terry Castle, *Masquerade and Civilization* (Stanford: Stanford University Press, 1986).
31. *The Life and Death of Mrs Mary Frith* (1662). See Paul Salzman, *English Prose Fiction 1558–1700* (Oxford: Oxford University Press, 1985), p. 213.
32. Bathsua Makin, *An Essay to Revive the Ancient Education of Gentlewomen, in Religion, Arts & Tongues* (1673; Los Angeles: Clark Memorial Library, 1980). The work has a male persona, which has led to speculation that Makin may have commissioned the work from a man. For an account of Makin, see Mitzi Myers, 'Domesticating Minerva: Bathsua Makin's "curious" argument for women's education' in *Studies in Eighteenth-Century Culture*, ed. O. M. Brack, 14 (1985), pp. 173–92.
33. The banal purpose of such training was satirised in Thomas D'Urfey's *Love for Money, or The Boarding School* (1691) in which the girls exist mainly to eat and flirt.
34. For a discussion of Astell's educational views, see Perry's *Mary Astell*.
35. See Robert Adams Day, 'Aphra Behn and the works of the intellect' in *Fetter'd or Free? British Women Novelists 1670–1815*, ed. Mary Anne Schofield and Cecilia Macheski (Athens: Ohio University Press, 1986), pp. 372–82.
36. Quoted in Perry, *Mary Astell*, p. 229. *The Tatler* article mocks Delarivier Manley and Elizabeth Elstob as well as Astell.
37. See Felicity Nussbaum, *The Brink of All We Hate: English Satires on Women, 1660–1750* (Lexington: University Press of Kentucky, 1984).
38. The great satiric influence was Juvenal, especially in his sixth satire against women from *Sixteen Satires Upon the Ancient Harlot*. It is possible to trace the softening of misogynistic satire through the various translations of Juvenal. For pornography see David Foxon, *Libertine Literature in England 1660–1745* (New York: University Books Inc., 1965).
39. R. Gould, *Love given O're: or, A Satyr Against . . . Woman* in *Satires on Women* (Los Angeles: Augustan Reprint Society, 1976), and *Poems* (London, 1689).
40. See Ellen Pollak, *The Poetics of Sexual Myth: Gender and Ideology in the Verse of Swift and Pope* (Chicago: Chicago University Press, 1985).
41. Sarah Fyge (Egerton), *The Female Advocate* (1686; second edn. repr. Los Angeles: Clark Memorial Library, 1976).

42. *The Ladies Calling*, Part II, sec. 1, par. 5.
43. *The Tatler*, no. 172, 16 May 1710.

CHAPTER 2: WOMEN WRITERS OF THE RESTORATION AND EARLY EIGHTEENTH CENTURY

1. Samuel Pepys, *The Diary of Samuel Pepys*, ed. R. Latham and W. Matthews (London: Bell & Hyman, 1970–83), IV, p. 9.
2. For a discussion of female political writing in general see Elaine Hobby, *Virtue of Necessity* (London: Virago, 1988).
3. 'The Introduction' in *The Poems of Anne, Countess of Winchilsea* (Chicago: University of Chicago Press, 1903).
4. Lady Sarah Piers's prefatory poem to *The Unhappy Penitent* (London, 1701).
5. 'To my Excellent Lucasia' in *Poems by the most deservedly Admired Mrs Katherine Philips* . . . (London, 1667). Philips wrote not only about friendship but also about political matters; in 'To Antenor, on a Paper of mine which J.J. threatens to publish' she defended her husband in verse when he had been attacked because of her poetry.
6. Countess of Winchilsea, 'Ephelia to Ardelia' in *The Poems of Anne, Countess of Winchilsea*. The sentiment was not confined to poetry and Mary Astell, a great admirer of Katherine Philips, wrote of 'this happy Society' as 'one Body, whose Soul is love, animating and informing it, and perpetually breathing forth it self in flames of holy desires after GOD, and acts of Benevolence to each other' in *A Serious Proposal to the Ladies* (London, 1694) pp. 97–8.
7. For further discussion of Polwhele, see the introduction by Judith Milhous and Robert D. Hume to *The Frolicks* (Ithaca: Cornell University Press, 1977).
8. Mary Pix, Prologue to *The False Friend: or, The Fate of Disobedience* (London, 1699).
9. See Thomas Birch, 'An Account of the Life of the Author' in *The Works of Mrs Catharine Cockburn* (London, 1751).
10. For short accounts of these dramatists and examples of their works see Fidelis Morgan, *The Female Wits: Women Playwrights of the Restoration* (London: Virago, 1981).
11. For a description of Elizabethan prose fiction see Salzman, *English Prose Fiction*.
12. See Madelon Gohlke, 'Reading "Euphues"' in *Criticism*, 19, 1977, for the idea that deceit is central to *Euphues*.
13. Salzman, *English Prose Fiction*, p. 142.
14. Salzman, *English Prose Fiction*, pp. 139 and 144. See also G. F. Waller, introduction to Lady Mary Wroth's *Pamphilia to Amphilanthus* (Salzburg: Studies in English Literature, 1977).
15. For accounts of this work, see Salzman, *English Prose Fiction*, pp. 130–31, and B. G. MacCarthy, *Women Writers: Their Contribution to the English Novel 1621–1744* (Cork: Cork University Press, 1944).
16. *The Letters of Dorothy Osborne to Sir William Temple*, ed. Kingsley Hart (London: Folio Society, 1968).
17. Ian Maclean, *Woman Triumphant: Feminism in French Literature 1610–1652* (Oxford: Oxford University Press, 1977); Domna Stanton, 'The Fiction of *Preciosity* and the fear of women' in *Yale French Studies*, 62, 1981, pp. 107–34.
18. For an account of this process see Rosalind Ballaster's unpublished dissertation 'Seductive Forms: Women's Amatory Fiction 1680–1740'.
19. William Congreve, preface to *Incognita* (1692; Menston: Scolar Press, 1971). See

Lennard J. Davis, *Factual Fictions* (New York: Columbia University Press, 1983) for a discussion of various real-life genres.

20. Preface to *Queen Zarah, Novels of Mary Delariviere Manley*, ed. Patricia Koster (Gainesville: Scholars' Facsmiles & Reprints, 1971).

CHAPTER 3: 'WERE I EMPRESS OF THE WORLD': THE 'GERMAN PRINCESS' AND THE DUCHESS OF NEWCASTLE

1. Ernest Bernbaum in *The Mary Carleton Narratives* (Cambridge, Mass.: Harvard University Press, 1914) claims that she inspired more written accounts than anyone in the period. See also C. F. Main, 'The German Princess, or, Mary Carleton in fact and fiction' in *Harvard Library Bulletin*, 10, 1956, pp. 166–85.

2. Mary Carleton, *The Case of Madam Mary Carleton* (London, 1663), p. 30. (This is an expansion of the earlier, *An Historical Narrative of the German Princess*.)

3. Carleton, *The Case*, p. 69.

4. Carleton, *The Case*, p. 73.

5. She does not present herself as a deluded rogue, an image given in more moralistic narratives including Francis Kirkman's *The Counterfeit Lady Unveiled* (London, 1679) which sees her as fooled by heroic romance and caught in a fantasy world, unable to distinguish between true and false. The play in which she is supposed to have acted herself is Thomas Parker's *A Witty Combat*.

6. Pepys, *Diary*, 18 March 1668, vol. 9, p. 123.

7. Osborne, *Letters*, p. 58.

8. Pepys, *Diary*, 26 April 1667, vol. 8, pp. 186–7.

9. Osborne, *Letters*, p. 53.

10. Margaret, Duchess of Newcastle, dedication 'To all Noble, and Worthy Ladies' in *Poems and Fancies* (1653; Menston: Scolar Press, 1972).

11. Margaret, Duchess of Newcastle, *Sociable Letters* (1664; Menston: Scolar Press, 1969).

12. Margaret, Duchess of Newcastle, *Poems and Fancies*, p. 105.

13. 'The Description of a New World, Called the Blazing-World', *Observations Upon Experimental Philosophy* (London, 1668).

14. Margaret, Duchess of Newcastle, 'A True Relation of my Birth, Breeding, and Life', written in 1649 and published in 1656 in *Natures Pictures Drawn by Fancies Pencil to the Life* (London, 1656), p. 387. The autobiography was dropped from the second edition of 1671.

15. For additional information on the Duchess, see Mendelson, *Stuart Women*, and William D. B. Grant, *Margaret the First: a Biography of Margaret Cavendish, Duchess of Newcastle* (London, 1957).

16. Margaret, Duchess of Newcastle, *Plays, Never before Printed* (London, 1668) p. 96.

17. Edward, Earl of Clarendon, *History of the Great Rebellion and Civil Wars in England Begun in the Year 1641* (Oxford: Clarendon Press, 1888), III, pp. 382–3.

18. William, Duke of Newcastle, 'To the Lady Newcastle, On her Booke of Poems' in *Poems and Fancies*.

19. Margaret, Duchess of Newcastle, 'To His Excellency the Lord Marquess of Newcastle' in *Sociable Letters*.

20. Margaret, Duchess of Newcastle, 'To all Noble, and Worthy Ladies' in *Poems and Fancies*.

21. Margaret, Duchess of Newcastle, 'To the Reader' in *Natures Pictures*.

22. Margaret, Duchess of Newcastle, 'Female Orations' in *Orations of Divers Sorts* (London, 1662), p. 226.

23. *Diary and Correspondence of John Evelyn*, ed. W. Bray (London: Henry Coburn, 1850–1852), IV, pp. 8–9.
24. Margaret, Duchess of Newcastle, *Wits Cabal, Playes* (London, 1662), p. 254. In *Virtue of Necessity*, Hobby speculates that the Duchess's final silent years might have been influenced by her presentation of herself as a submissive wife in her life of her husband, which emphasised the contradiction between fame and female honour.
25. Margaret, Duchess of Newcastle, 'The Discreet Virgin' in *Natures Pictures*, pp. 109–113.
26. Margaret, Duchess of Newcastle, 'To the Two Universities' in *The Philosophical and Physical Opinions* (London, 1655).
27. Margaret, Duchess of Newcastle, 'Female Orations' in *Orations of Divers Sorts*, p. 228.
28. Margaret, Duchess of Newcastle, 'The Discreet Virgin' in *Natures Pictures*, pp. 112–13.
29. See Sandra Gilbert and Susan Gubar, *The Madwoman in the Attic* (New Haven: Yale University Press, 1979), pp. 62–3, for the idea that the contradictions did in a way make the Duchess 'mad'.
30. See McKeon, *The Origins of the English Novel*, pp. 101–17 for discussion of travel literature. Frank and Fritzie Manuel in *Utopian Thought in the Western World* (Cambridge, Mass.: Harvard University Press, 1979) dismiss 'The Blazing-World' as bordering on the schizophrenic, p. 7, and even the Duchess's biographer, W. D. B. Grant, regards it as confused and ridiculous, see *Margaret the First*, p. 208. 'Assaulted and Pursued Chastity' is in *Natures Pictures*.
31. Pepys, *Diary*, 11 April 1667, vol. 8, p. 163.

CHAPTER 4: 'AN HONOUR AND GLORY TO OUR SEX': APHRA BEHN

1. Virginia Woolf, *A Room of One's Own and Three Guineas* (London: Chatto & Windus, 1984), p. 61.
2. Recent accounts include Maureen Duffy, *The Passionate Shepherdess: Aphra Behn 1640–89* (London: Cape, 1977), which pays little attention to literary qualities, and Angeline Goreau's *Reconstructing Aphra: A Social Biography of Aphra Behn* (New York: Dial Press, 1980).
3. The suggestion that she did not visit Surinam was made by Ernest Bernbaum, who argued that she took her descriptions from previous accounts. See 'Mrs Behn's biography, a fiction' in *PMLA*, 28 (1913), pp. 432–53.
4. 'Love-Letters to a Gentleman' in *The Plays, Histories and Novels of the Ingenious Mrs Aphra Behn* (1696, repr. London: John Pearson, 1871), V, p. 66.
5. Behn, 'Love-Letters to a Gentleman' in *The Plays, Histories and Novels*, V, p. 59.
6. 'History of the Life and Memoirs of Mrs Behn' by 'One of the Fair Sex', reprinted in *Plays, Histories and Novels*.
7. See G. Guffey in *Two English Novelists: Aphra Behn and Anthony Trollope* (Los Angeles: Clark Memorial Library, 1975).
8. Dedication to *The Fair Jilt* in *The Works of Aphra Behn*, ed. Montague Summers (London: Heinemann, 1915), p. 70.
9. See Mendelson, *Stuart Women*, p. 176.
10. See Gerald Duchovnay, 'Aphra Behn's Religion' in *Notes & Queries* 221, May–June 1976, pp. 235–7. See Mendelson, *Stuart Women*, pp. 117–18 for the speculation that she may have been a Roman Catholic.
11. Ernest Baker in his introduction to *The Novels of Aphra Behn* (London, 1905) calls it 'coarseness'.

12. For a historical account of events see Maureen Duffy's introduction to *Love Letters Between a Nobleman and His Sister* (London: Virago, 1987).
13. Behn, *Love Letters Between a Nobleman and His Sister*, p. 52.

CHAPTER 5: LIFE AFTER SEX: DELARIVIER MANLEY

1. The various fictions are printed together as if they were an actual autobiography by Fidelis Morgan in *A Woman of No Character: An Autobiography of Mrs Manley* (London: Faber, 1986). Owing possibly to a confusion of sources, it was common until recently to refer to Mrs Manley as 'Mary', although her signed works, private letters, will and tombstone bear the name 'Delarivière' or 'Delarivier'; for a discussion of the matter see Patricia Köster's introduction to *The Novels of Mary Delarivier Manley*, I, pp. v–vi.
2. Manley, *The Novels*, II, p. 203. See vol. II for a key to *The New Atalantis*.
3. Manley, *The Novels*, II, pp. 41 and 58–9.
4. Manley, *The Novels*, II, p. 111.
5. Manley, *The Novels*, I, pp. 33–4. For a rather different interpretation of the erotic content see John J. Richetti, *Popular Fiction before Richardson: Narrative Patterns, 1700–1739* (Oxford: Clarendon Press, 1969).
6. Manley, *The Novels*, II, p. 192.
7. Manley, *The Novels*, II, p. 57.
8. Manley, *The Novels*, II, pp. 57–8.
9. Manley, *The Novels*, I, p. 55.
10. Manley, *The Novels*, I, p. 72.
11. Manley, *The Novels*, I, p. 88.
12. Manley, *The Novels*, II, p. 191. (Köster, I, 723).
13. Manley, *The Novels*, II, 15.
14. Manley, *The Novels*, II, 16.
15. Manley, *The Novels*, II, 17.

CHAPTER 6: THE MID-EIGHTEENTH CENTURY: SENTIMENT AND SINCERITY

1. William Alexander, *The History of Women, From the Earliest Antiquity to the Present Time* (London, 1779), II, p. 317.
2. See Marilyn Butler, *Romantics, Rebels & Reactionaries* (Oxford: Oxford University Press, 1981), for a description of the phenomenon.
3. Mariana Starke, *The Sword of Peace; or, the Voyage of Love*, performed in 1788, and *The Poor Soldier; An American Tale* (London, 1789).
4. For an account of the political importance of Macaulay see Natalie Zemon Davis, 'Gender and genre: women as historical writers 1400–1820' in *Beyond Their Sex: Learned Women of the European Past*, ed. Patricia Labalme (New York: New York University Press, 1980).
5. For a summary of the politics of the age see J. Steven Watson, *The Reign of George III* (1960; Oxford: Clarendon Press, 1981).
6. *The Complete Letters of Lady Mary Wortley Montagu*, ed. Robert Halsband (Oxford: Clarendon Press, 1965), March 1739. See also Robert Halsband, *The Life of Lady Mary Wortley Montagu* (Oxford: Clarendon Press, 1956).
7. See *The Life and Times of Selina, Countess of Huntingdon* (London, 1844), especially I, pp. 78 and 193.
8. For discussions of the effect of the economic changes on women see the essays in *Women in English Society 1500–1800*, ed. Prior.

9. There was much grumbling at the increased importance and economic independence of the manservant; see, for example, the work of Jonas Hanway, especially *Virtue in Humble Life, containing Reflections on the Reciprocal Duties of the Wealthy and the Indigent* (London, 1774), and John Shebbeare, *Letters on the English Nation* (London, 1755).

10. Pat Rogers, 'The breeches part' in *Sexuality in Eighteenth-Century Britain*, ed. Paul-Gabriel Boucé (Manchester University Press, 1982), p. 250.

11. Stone, *Family, Sex and Marriage*, p. 521.

12. For a fuller account see Pat Rogers, *Literature and Popular Culture in Eighteenth Century England* (Brighton: Harvester, 1985), p. 12.

13. See Roy Porter, 'Mixed feelings: the Enlightenment and sexuality in eighteenth-century Britain' in *Sexuality in Eighteenth-Century Britain*, p. 9, and Castle, *Masquerade and Civilization*, p. 64.

14. Lawrence Stone finds in this period the beginning of the replacement of the close domesticated family of the upper-middle and upper orders by the modern family. But see Note 20, Chapter One, for the disputes concerning the social history of this period. See also Peter Laslett and Richard Wall, ed., *Household and Family in Past Times* (Cambridge: Cambridge University Press, 1973), and E. A. Wrigley, 'Family limitation in preindustrial England' in *Economic History Review*, 2nd series, 19, 1966, pp. 82–109.

15. J. Steven Watson, *The Reign of George III*, p. 7. A measure of the change was the imposition of duty on spirits in the 1750s so that the more innocuous tea-drinking became more popular.

16. *Critical Remarks on Sir Charles Grandison, Clarissa and Pamela* (London, 1754).

17. John Gregory, *A Father's Legacy to His Daughters* (Dublin, 1790), pp. 33–4.

18. See Barbara B. Schnorrenberg with Jean E. Hunter, 'The eighteenth-century Englishwoman' in *The Women of England from Anglo-Saxon Times to the Present*, ed. Barbara Kanner (London: Mansell, 1980), p. 193.

19. *The Commentaries on the Laws of England of Sir William Blackstone* (1765–9; London: Reeves and Turner, 1896). See Christopher Hill, 'Clarissa Harlowe and her times' in *Essays in Criticism 5*, October 1955, pp. 315–40.

20. Blackstone, *Commentaries*, p. 97.

21. Hester Mulso Chapone, *Works and Life* (London, 1807), II, p. 149.

22. Sarah, Lady Pennington, *An Unfortunate Mother's Advice to her Absent Daughters, The Young Lady's Pocket Library, or Parental Monitor* (Dublin, 1790), p. 103.

23. Blackstone, *Commentaries*, p. 99.

24. See Dorothy McLaren, 'Marital fertility and lactation 1570–1720' in *Women in English Society 1500–1800*, ed. Prior, pp. 22–53, for a discussion of upper-class fecundity and wet-nursing.

25. Arthur H. Cash, 'The birth of Tristram Shandy: Sterne and Dr Burton' in *Sexuality in Eighteenth-Century Britain*, p. 207.

26. Opponents could not avoid sexualising even this image and 'Mr Town' attacked Mary Singleton as a frustrated old woman in the *Connoisseur 95*, 20 November 1755.

27. *The proceedings at the sessions of the Peace . . . upon a bill of indictment found against Francis Charteris, for committing a rape on the body of Anne Bond . . .* (London, 1730).

28. A further discussion occurs in L. Schwartz, 'Madame d'Epinay's *Emilia*: a woman's answer to Rousseau's *Emile*', paper given at the 7th International Congress on Enlightenment, Budapest, July–August 1987.

29. Hester Mulso Chapone, *Essays . . . for Young Ladies* (London, 1777).
30. See Schnorrenberg, 'The Eighteenth-Century Englishwoman' in *The Women of England*, p. 186.
31. Gregory, *A Father's Legacy*, p. 31.
32. William Kenrick, *The Whole Duty of Woman, by a Lady, Written at the Desire of a Noble Lord* (London, 1753).
33. *Letters on the Improvement of the Mind, The Works of Mrs Chapone* (Dublin, 1786), p. 119.
34. Pennington, *An Unfortunate Mother's Advice, The Young Lady's Pocket Library*, p. 78.
35. Sarah Fielding, *The Adventures of David Simple* (London: Oxford University Press, 1969), p. 101.
36. Lady Mary Wortley Montagu, *The Complete Letters of Lady Mary Wortley Montagu*, I, 44.
37. See Ch. Battersby, '"Genius" and "The Female Sex" in the eighteenth century', paper given at the 7th International Congress on Enlightenment, Budapest, July–August 1987.
38. *The Nonsense of Common-Sense*, 27 December 1737; repr. in *Lady Mary Wortley Montagu: Essays and Poems*, ed. Robert Halsband and Isobel Grundy (Oxford: Clarendon Press, 1977), p. 109.
39. James Fordyce, *Sermons to Young Women* (London, 1766), II, p. 261.
40. Thomas Marriott, *Female Conduct* (London, 1759).
41. Fordyce, *Sermons*, I, 208 and Mary Wollstonecraft, *A Vindication of the Rights of Woman* (Harmondsworth: Penguin, 1985), ch. 5, sec. 2.
42. Edmund Burke, *A Philosophical Enquiry into the Origin of our ideas of the Sublime and Beautiful* (Menston: Scolar Press, 1970), p. 219.
43. *Mrs Montagu 'Queen of the Blues': Her Letters and Friendships from 1762 to 1800*, ed. Reginald Blunt (London: Constable n.d.) II, 119.

CHAPTER 7: THE MODEST MUSE: WOMEN WRITERS OF THE
MID-EIGHTEENTH CENTURY

1. Preface to *The Cry* (London, 1754).
2. *A Series of Letters between Mrs Elizabeth Carter and Miss Catherine Talbot, from the year 1741 to 1770* (London, 1809), 12 August 1752.
3. *The Complete Letters of Lady Mary Wortley Montagu*, 16 February 1752.
4. Laetitia Pilkington, *The Memoirs* (London, 1748–54), p. 350.
5. Pilkington, *Memoirs*, p. 345.
6. *The Letters of Mrs Elizabeth Montagu*, p. 97.
7. Samuel Richardson, *Selected Letters of Samuel Richardson*, ed. John Carroll (Oxford: Clarendon Press, 1964), p. 173.
8. See *The Poems of Mary Collier . . . to which is prefaced her life, drawn by herself* (Petersfield, 1765?).
9. Ann Candler, *Poetical Attempts* (Ipswich, 1803).
10. For an account of the growth of magazines see Alison Adburgham, *Women in Print: Writing Women and Women's Magazines from the Restoration to the Accession of Victoria* (London: Allen & Unwin, 1972).
11. Mary Tonkin, *The Female Spy: or Mrs Tonkin's Account of her Journey through France* (London, 1783).
12. Mary Collier, *The Woman's Labour, an epistle to Mr Stephen Duck* (London, 1739).

13. Frances Greville, 'A Prayer for Indifference' repr. in *The New Oxford Book of Eighteenth Century Verse*, ed. R. Lonsdale (Oxford: Oxford University Press, 1984); Helen Maria Williams, 'To Sensibility' in *Poems* (London, 1786).

14. Hannah More, 'Sensibility: An Epistle to the Honourable Mrs Boscawen' (1782), *The Works of Hannah More* (London, 1834),V, pp. 329–340.

15. *Correspondence between Frances, Countess of Hertford (afterwards Duchess of Somerset) and Henrietta Louisa, Countess of Pomfret, between 1738 and 1741*, ed. W. Bingley (London, 1805), I, p. 20.

16. Lady Mary Coke, *Letters and Journals, 1756–74* (Bath: Kingsmead Reprints, 1970), I, p. 18.

17. Miss Talbot to Mrs Carter, *A Series of Letters*, 27 June 1744.

18. For further discussion of sensibility and its contradictions, see R. F. Brissenden, *Virtue in Distress: Studies in the Novel of Sentiment* (New York: Barnes & Noble, 1974) and Janet Todd, *Sensibility: An Introduction* (London: Methuen, 1986).

19. See, for example, Robert Whytt, *Observations on the Nature, Causes and Cure of those Diseases which are commonly called Nervous, Hypochondriac or Hysteric* (London, 1764), which describes sympathy as physiological.

20. For the cult of Richardson, see T. C. Duncan Eaves and B. D. Kimpel, *Samuel Richardson: A Biography* (Oxford: Oxford University Press, 1971). For the discussion of justice see Richardson, *Selected Letters*, p. 108, and [Sarah Fielding] *Remarks on Clarissa Addressed to the Author* (London, 1749), p. 48.

21. See Lady Echlin, *An Alternative Ending to Richardson's 'Clarissa'*, ed. Dimiter Daphinoff (Bern: Francke Verlag, 1982).

22. The motif was much mocked by anti-sentimentalists, for example, by Fanny Burney, Jane Austen and the author of the *Anti-Jacobin*'s review of Mary Robinson's *Walsingham* (1797).

23. Review of *Louis and Nina*, probably by Wollstonecraft, *Analytical Review*, IV, May–August 1789; quoted in *A Wollstonecraft Anthology*, ed. Janet Todd (Bloomington: Indiana University Press, 1977), p. 222.

24. Quoted from the *Gazette salutaire*, 6 October 1768, by Michel Foucault in *Madness and Civilization* (London: Tavistock, 1967).

25. George Colman, Prologue to *Polly Honeycombe, A Dramatick Novel of One Act* (London, 1760).

CHAPTER 8: RE-FORMERS: ELIZA HAYWOOD AND CHARLOTTE LENNOX

1. Clara Reeve, *The Progress of Romance* (Colchester, 1785), I, pp. 120–21.

2. *Monthly Review*, quoted in Margaret Dalziel's introduction to Lennox's *The Female Quixote* (London: Oxford University Press, 1970).

3. See Spencer, *The Rise of the Woman Novelist*, p. 141.

4. Quoted in Ioan Williams, *Novel and Romance 1700–1800: A Documentary Record* (New York: Barnes & Noble, 1970), p. 103.

5. For a fuller account of Haywood see George Frisbie Whicher, *The Life and Romances of Mrs Eliza Haywood* (New York: Columbia University Press, 1915).

6. Eliza Haywood, *The History of Miss Betsy Thoughtless* (London: Pandora Press, 1986), p. 68.

7. Haywood, *Betsy Thoughtless*, p. 352.

8. Haywood, *Betsy Thoughtless*, p. 98.

9. Haywood, *Betsy Thoughtless*, p. 291.

10. Haywood, *Betsy Thoughtless*, pp. 468–9.

11. Haywood, *Betsy Thoughtless*, p. 519.
12. James Boswell, *The Life of Samuel Johnson*, ed. George Birkbeck Hill and L. F. Powell (Oxford: Clarendon Press, 1934–50), IV, 274.
13. Charlotte Lennox, *The Female Quixote* (London: Pandora, 1986), p. 365.
14. Lennox, *The Female Quixote*, pp. 8–9.
15. Lennox, *The Female Quixote*, pp. 135–36.
16. Lennox, *The Female Quixote*, p. 68.
17. Lennox, *The Female Quixote*, pp. 420–21.

CHAPTER 9: NOVELISTS OF SENTIMENT:
SARAH FIELDING AND FRANCES SHERIDAN

1. Samuel Richardson, *Selected Letters*, p. 330.
2. See Spender, *Mothers of the Novel*, pp. 184–5.
3. *Complete Letters of Lady Mary Wortley Montagu*, 23 July 1754.
4. Alicia Lefanu, *Memoirs of the Life and Writings of Mrs Frances Sheridan* (London, 1824), pp. 2, 87 and 97.
5. Lefanu, *Memoirs*, p. 306.
6. Lefanu, *Memoirs*, p. 111.
7. McKeon's dialectical view in *The Origins of the English Novel*, which takes into account categorical instability, also tends in the end to privilege the sceptical and empirical.
8. See Henry Fielding's preface to the second edition of *David Simple*. For a description of *David Simple* as a novel of sensibility see Gerald A. Barker, '*David Simple*: the novel of sensibility in embryo' in *Modern Language Studies* 12, no. 2, 1982, pp. 69–80, and Todd, *Sensibility*, pp. 88–105.
9. This is true so long as one discounts the rather unfortunate sequel, *Conclusion of the Memoirs of Miss Sidney Bidulph*, published posthumously in 1767.
10. Frances Sheridan, *Memoirs of Miss Sidney Bidulph* (London, 1761), II, 239.
11. Sheridan, *Sidney Bidulph*, II, p. 40.
12. Sarah Fielding, *The Adventures of David Simple* (London, 1744), p. 412.
13. Sheridan, *Sidney Bidulph*, II, pp. 96–7.
14. Fielding, *David Simple*, p. 109.
15. In *Sidney Bidulph* too there is some satire and a sense of other ways of looking at events. This is especially suggested through Faulkland's letters, which display, rather like Lovelace's in *Clarissa*, a masculine, flippant and in this case passionate attitude that Sidney denies and must deny in herself.
16. See David Hume, *Treatise on Human Nature* (Oxford: Clarendon Press, 1888).
17. Sheridan, *Sidney Bidulph*, I, p. 121.
18. Fielding, *David Simple*, p. 71.
19. Fielding, *David Simple*, pp. 430–31.
20. Boswell, *Life of Johnson*, I, p. 390.
21. Sheridan, *Sidney Bidulph*, II, 226.
22. Sheridan, *Sidney Bidulph*, II, p. 247.
23. *The Complete Letters of Lady Mary Wortley Montagu*, 23 July 1754.
24. Sheridan, *Sidney Bidulph*, II, p. 247.
25. Sheridan, *Sidney Bidulph*, II, p. 254.

CHAPTER 10: THE FANTASY OF SENSIBILITY:
FRANCES BROOKE AND SUSANNAH GUNNING

1. Review of *The Mental Triumph, Analytical Review* V, September–December 1789, in *A Wollstonecraft Anthology*, p. 223.
2. *Monthly Review* 14, 1756, p. 560.
3. For the life of Frances Brooke, see Lorraine McMullen, *An Odd Attempt in a Woman* (Vancouver: University of British Columbia Press, 1983).
4. Frances Brooke, *The History of Lady Julia Mandeville* (London: 1763), p. 64.
5. Susannah Gunning, *Coombe Wood* (London, 1783), p. 12.
6. Brooke, *Lady Julia Mandeville*, p. 42.
7. Frances Brooke, *The History of Emily Montague* (London, 1769), II, p. 103.
8. Susannah and Margaret Minifie, *Histories of Lady Frances S— and Lady Caroline S—* (1763), p. 16.
9. Gunning, *Coombe Wood*, p. 98.
10. Brooke, *Lady Julia Mandeville*, p. 213.
11. Minifie, *Lady Frances S—*, II, p. 106.
12. Gunning, *Coombe Wood*, p. 116.
13. Gunning, *Coombe Wood*, pp. 15–20.
14. Gunning, *Coombe Wood*, p. 233.
15. *A Narrative of the Incidents which form the mystery in the family of General Gunning* (London, 1791), p. 1.
16. Susannah Gunning, *A Letter from Mrs Gunning addressed to His Grace, the Duke of Argyll* (London, 1791), p. 55.
17. Gunning, *A Letter*, p. 102.
18. For a discussion of female romance, see Tania Modleski, *Loving with a Vengeance* (1982; London: Methuen, 1984), and Janice A. Radway, *Reading the Romance: Women, Patriarchy and Popular Literature* (Chapel Hill: University of North Carolina Press, 1984).

CHAPTER 11: THE LATE EIGHTEENTH CENTURY:
THE DECADES OF REVOLUTION

1. Hannah More, *Strictures on the Modern System of Education* (London, 1799), I, 2, pp. 66–8.
2. Edmund Burke, *Reflections on the Revolution in France* (London, 1790), p. 114.
3. *Anti-Jacobin Review*, 9 July 1798, pp. 283–4.
4. For the economic history of the time, see T. S. Ashton, *An Economic History of England: the Eighteenth Century* (London: Methuen, 1955), and Neil McKendrick, 'Home demand and economic growth: a new view of the role of women and children in the Industrial Revolution' in *Historical Perspectives: Studies in English Thought and Society in Honour of J. H. Plumb*, ed. Neil McKendrick (London, 1974).
5. See L. Davidoff and C. Hall, *Family Fortunes: Men and Women of the English Middle Class 1780–1850* (London: Hutchinson, 1987).
6. See Castle, *Masquerade and Civilization*, p. 98.
7. Mary Wollstonecraft, *An Historical and Moral View of the Origin and Progress of the French Revolution* (1794; New York: Scholars' Facsimiles & Reprints, 1975), Book 5, ch. 4.
8. Mary Wollstonecraft, *Thoughts on the Education of Daughters: with Reflections on Female Conduct* (1787); repr. in *A Wollstonecraft Anthology*, p. 33.
9. Mary Ann Radcliffe, *The Female Advocate; or, an Attempt to Recover the Rights of*

Women from Male Usurpation (London, 1799), and Priscilla Wakefield, *Reflections on the Present Condition of the Female Sex, With Suggestions for Its Improvement* (1798).

10. Quoted in Alice Browne, *The Eighteenth Century Feminist Mind*, (Brighton: Harvester, 1987), p. 137.
11. See William Godwin on marriage, in *An Enquiry concerning Political Justice* (London, 1793), II, pp. 850–2.
12. Jane West, *Letters to a Young Lady* (London, 1806), III, 12, p. 143.
13. Wakefield, *Reflections*, III, p. 42.
14. Mary Hays, *Appeal to the Men of Great Britain in Behalf of Women* (New York: Garland, 1974), p. 273.
15. West, *Letters*, III, 12, p. 101; II, 4, pp. 279–80, and III, 12, p. 133.
16. See Browne, *The Eighteenth Century Feminist Mind*, pp. 158–9, for a discussion of liberal writers on marriage.
17. See William Duff, *Letters on the Intellectual and Moral Character of Women* (London, 1807), XXXI, pp. 172–3.
18. Catherine Macaulay, *Letters on Education* (London, 1790), I. Letter xxiii, pp. 220–21.
19. Wollstonecraft, *The Rights of Woman*, p. 165.
20. See Mary Hays, *Letters and Essays, Moral and Miscellaneous* (London, 1793).
21. John Bennett, *Letters to a Young Lady on Useful and Interesting Subjects* (Dublin, 1789), II, pp. 94–5; William Hayley, *A Philosophical, Historical and Moral Essay on Old Maids* (London, 1785), I, 1, p. 12.
22. Hannah More, *Essays . . . for Young Ladies* 5th ed. (London, 1791), p. 6.
23. Wollstonecraft, *The Rights of Woman*, p. 132.
24. Anna Laetitia Barbauld, 'The Rights of Woman' in *The Works of Anna Laetitia Barbauld* (London, 1825), I, pp. 185–7.
25. *Anti-Jacobin Review*, 1801, p. ix.
26. Richard Polwhele, *The Unsex'd Females* (London, 1798), pp. 29–30.

CHAPTER 12: RADICALS AND REACTIONARIES:
WOMEN WRITERS OF THE LATE EIGHTEENTH CENTURY

1. William Cowper, *The Correspondence of William Cowper*, ed. Thomas Wright (London: Hodder & Stoughton, 1904), IV, p. 367.
2. For a full description of the Minerva Press see Dorothy Blakey, *The Minerva Press 1790–1820* (London: Bibliographical Society, 1939).
3. See James Lackington, *Memoirs of the Forty-Five First Years of the Life of James Lackington*, 13th edn. (London, [1791]), p. 222.
4. For the life of Hannah More, see *Memoirs of the Life and Correspondence of Hannah More*, ed. William Roberts, and for a discussion of her popularity see Mitzi Myers, 'Hannah More's tracts for the times: social fiction and female ideology' in *Fetter'd or Free?*, ed. Schofield and Macheski, pp. 264–84.
5. Clara Reeve, *The Exiles* (London, 1788), I, p. xiii.
6. Elizabeth Hamilton, *Letters on Education* (London, 1801), I, ii, p. 243.
7. Helen Maria Williams, *Letters from France* (New York: Scholars' Facsimiles & Reprints, 1975).
8. Boswell, *Life of Johnson*, II, p. 542, note 2.
9. Laetitia Matilda Hawkins, *Letters on the Female Mind* (London, 1793), 2, p. 197.
10. For further discussion of this work see William R. Ede, unpublished PhD

dissertation, 'The gentlewoman as artist in the life and romances of Ann Radcliffe: 1764–1823', Swansea, 1986.

11. Betty Rizzo, 'Johnson's efforts on behalf of authorship in *The Rambler*', paper given at the 7th International Congress on the Enlightenment, Budapest, July–August 1987.

12. Even some women critics who read the fiction seem to dislike this element; in the introduction to the Pandora edition of *Adeline Mowbray*, Jeanette Winterson makes Amelia Opie's moral attack on Wollstonecraftian feminism into a dramatic celebration of female individuality which makes 'no moral judgements'.

13. Clara Reeve, *Progress of Romance*, II, pp. 17–18.

14. Charlotte Smith, preface to *The Banished Man* (London, 1794).

15. Elizabeth Hamilton, *Memoirs of Modern Philosophers* (London, 1800), II, p. 283.

CHAPTER 13: 'THE UNSEX'D FEMALES': MARY WOLLSTONECRAFT AND MARY HAYS

1. 'To George Blood', 1786, *Collected Letters of Mary Wollstonecraft*, ed. Ralph M. Wardle (Ithaca: Cornell University Press, 1979), p. 128.

2. Wollstonecraft, *Collected Letters*, p. 145; Charlotte Smith, *Elegiac Sonnets* (London, 1784).

3. For the life of Wollstonecraft see Ralph M. Wardle, *Mary Wollstonecraft* (Lawrence: University of Kansas Press, 1951); Eleanor Flexner, *Mary Wollstonecraft* (New York: Coward, McCann & Geoghegan, 1972); Emily Sunstein, *A Different Face* (New York: Harper & Row, 1975), and Claire Tomalin, *The Life and Death of Mary Wollstonecraft* (New York: Harcourt, Brace, Jovanovich, 1974).

4. For a fuller description of fictional friendships see Janet Todd, *Women's Friendship in Literature* (New York: Columbia University Press, 1980).

5. Mary Wollstonecraft, *Mary, A Fiction* and *The Wrongs of Woman* (Oxford: Oxford University Press, 1976), p. 59.

6. Wollstonecraft, *Mary, A Fiction*, pp. 51–2.

7. Wollstonecraft, *Collected Letters*, p. 376.

8. *Mary Hays, The Memoirs of Emma Courtney* (1796; New York: Garland Publishing, 1974), I, p. 18.

9. Hays, *Emma Courtney*, I, pp. 15–16.

10. Hays, *Emma Courtney*, I, p. 70.

11. Hays, *Emma Courtney*, I, p. 55.

12. Hays, *Emma Courtney*, II, p. 99.

13. Hays, *Emma Courtney*, I, pp. 168–9. Wollstonecraft herself expresses the ambiguity and irony of the phrase when, in *Letters from Sweden* (1796), she begs 'Phantoms of bliss' to enclose her again in 'the magic circle' of her belief in romantic love.

14. Hays resisted Godwin's comforting suggestion of changing the novel to make the love reciprocal.

15. In a similar way Charlotte Smith treated sensibility in an asylum setting in *The Young Philosopher* (1798) and in her preface she insisted that she was not plagiarising.

16. Mary Wollstonecraft, *Mary, A Fiction* and *The Wrongs of Woman*, p. 87.

17. Wollstonecraft, *The Wrongs of Woman*, p. 82.

18. Wollstonecraft, *The Wrongs of Woman*, p. 186.

CHAPTER 14: 'THE GREAT ENCHANTRESS': ANN RADCLIFFE

1. E. S. Barrett, *The Heroine, or Adventures of Cherubina* (London: H. Coburn, 1814), III, p. 253.

2. Ann Radcliffe, *The Romance of the Forest* (Oxford: Oxford University Press, 1986), p. 346.

p. 3. For Ann Radcliffe as domestic lady see 'Mrs Ann Radcliffe' in *Lives of Eminent Novelists and Dramatists* (London: Frederick Warne, n.d.), pp. 551–78.

4. Radcliffe, *The Romance of the Forest*, p. 347.

5. Ann Radcliffe, *The Mysteries of Udolpho* (London: Oxford University Press, 1970), p. 646.

6. Radcliffe, *The Romance of the Forest*, p. 363.

7. Ann Radcliffe, *The Italian* (Oxford: Oxford University Press, 1981), p. 405.

8. For a discussion of veils in Radcliffe, see Eve Kosovsky Sedgwick, *The Coherence of Gothic Conventions* (London: Methuen, 1986).

9. See Masao Miyoshi, *The Divided Self* (New York: New York University Press, 1969), and Lowry Nelson, 'Night Thoughts on the Gothic Novel' in *Yale Review*, 1963.

10. Radcliffe, *The Romance of the Forest*, p. 134.

11. Radcliffe, *The Romance of the Forest*, p. 8.

12. For a discussion of transformations in Radcliffe's novels, see Robert Kiely, *The Romantic Novel in England* (Cambridge: Harvard University Press, 1972), pp. 75–6. See also Terry Castle, 'Phantasmagoria', *Critical Inquiry*, Fall, 1989, for the idea that supernatural language is displaced onto psychology, so that Emily is in fact 'haunted' by the image of Valancourt.

13. See Mary Poovey, 'Ideology and "The Mysteries of Udolpho"' in *Criticism*, 1979, pp. 307–30.

14. Radcliffe, *The Romance of the Forest*, p. 5.

15. See Daniel Cottom, *The Civilized Imagination* (Cambridge, Mass.: Cambridge University Press, 1985), p. 54.

16. Marilyn Butler notes this watching as a motif in women's fiction in the period, 'The woman at the window' in *Gender and Literary Voice*, ed. Janet Todd (New York: Holmes & Meier, 1980), pp. 128–48.

17. Radcliffe, *The Mysteries of Udolpho*, p. 381.

18. Radcliffe, *The Romance of the Forest*, p. 292.

19. See Cottom, *The Civilized Imagination*; for the importance of landscape in morality see David S. Durant, 'Aesthetic heroism in *The Mysteries of Udolpho*' in *The Eighteenth Century*, 22, 1981, pp. 75–88.

20. Rhoda L. Flaxman in 'Radcliffe's dual modes of vision' in *Fetter'd or Free?*, ed. Schofield and Macheski, p. 128, sees Radcliffe in cinematic terms as framing a landscape and as trying to write movement into description.

21. Radcliffe, *The Romance of the Forest*, p. 22.

22. Ann Radcliffe, *A Journey Made in the Summer of 1794, through Holland and the Western Frontier of Germany* (London, 1795), p. 419.

23. *The Romance of the Forest*, p. 165.

24. Only in the posthumous *Gaston de Blondeville*, not intended for publication, did she appear to be allowing herself an indulgence in the unnaturalised supernatural.

CHAPTER 15: MORAL AUTHORSHIP AND AUTHORITY: FANNY BURNEY

1. For the life of Fanny Burney see Joyce Hemlow, *History of Fanny Burney* (Oxford: Oxford University Press, 1958), and *The Journals and Letters of Fanny Burney*, ed. Joyce Hemlow et al. (Oxford: Clarendon Press, 1972–84).

2. See Patricia M. Spacks, *Imagining a Self: Autobiography and the Novel in Eighteenth-*

Century England (Cambridge, Mass.: Harvard University Press, 1976).

3. Preface to *Evelina* (New York: Norton, 1965), n.p.

p. 4. *Diary and Letters of Madame d'Arblay*, ed. Charlotte Barrett (London: George Bell and Sons, 1891), II, 345–6.

5. Burney, *Diary and Letters*, II, 76.

6. Burney, *Diary and Letters*, II, 54.

7. Fanny Burney, *Camilla; or A Picture of Youth* (Oxford: Oxford University Press, 1983), p. 8.

8. A similar pattern of father and daughter occurs in the lives of Maria Edgeworth and Jane Austen.

9. For the life of Dr Burney, see Roger Lonsdale, *Dr Charles Burney* (Oxford: Clarendon Press, 1965).

10. See *Thraliana: The Diary of Mrs Hester Lynch Thrale (later Mrs Piozzi) 1770–1809*, ed. Katharine C. Balderston, 2nd edn. (Oxford, 1951), I, p. 399.

11. See Lonsdale, *Dr Charles Burney*, p. 357.

12. *Diary and Letters*, I, 154–5.

13. Burney, *Camilla*, p. 302.

14. Burney, *Camilla*, p. 366.

15. Burney, *Camilla*, p. 482.

16. Fanny Burney, *The Wanderer; or, Female Difficulties* (London, 1814), I, pp. 404–405.

17. See Martha G. Brown, 'Fanny Burney's "feminism": gender or genre' in *Fetter'd or Free?*, ed. Schofield and Macheski, pp. 29–39, and Judith Lowder Newton, *Women, Power, and Subversion: Social Strategies in British Fiction 1778–1860* (Athens, Georgia: University of Georgia Press, 1981), who argues that Burney endorses the patriarchal authority of ruling-class men but also reveals the contradictions of the situation for women.

18. Burney, *Camilla*, p. 884.

19. Burney, *Camilla*, p. 889.

20. Burney, *Camilla*, p. 563.

21. Burney, *Camilla*, p. 7.

BIBLIOGRAPHY

PRIMARY WORKS

The Adventures of Lindamira. London, 1702.

Alexander, William, *The History of Women From the Earliest Antiquity to the Present Time*. London, 1779.

[Allestree, R.], *The Ladies Calling*. London, 1673.

Astell, Mary, *The Christian Religion, as Profess'd by a Daughter of the Church of England*. London, 1705.

    A Serious Proposal to the Ladies For the Advancement of their True and Greatest Interest. London, 1694.

    Some Reflections Upon Marriage. Dublin, 1730.

Baillie, Joanna, *Metrical Legends of Exalted Characters*. London, 1821.

Ballard, George, *Memoirs of Several Ladies of Great Britain*. Oxford, 1752.

Barbauld, Anna Laetitia, *The Works of Anna Laetitia Barbauld*. London, 1825.

Barker, Jane, *The Lining to the Patch-Work Screen*. London, 1726.

    A Patch-Work Screen for the Ladies. London, 1723.

    Poetical Recreations. London, 1688.

Barrell, Maria, *British Liberty Vindicated*. London, 1788.

    The Captive. London, 1790.

Barrett, E.S., *The Heroine, or Adventures of Cherubina*. London, 1814.

Beaumont, Agnes, *The Narrative of the Persecution of Agnes Beaumont in 1674*. London: Constable's Miscellany, 1929.

Behn, Aphra, *A Congratulatory Poem . . . on the happy birth of the Prince of Wales*. London, 1688.

    A Discovery of New Worlds, Transl. from Bernard de Fontanelle. 1688.

    The Emperor of the Moon, ed. Leo Hughes and A.H. Scouten, *Ten English Farces*. Austin: University of Texas Press, 1948.

    Love Letters Between a Nobleman and his Sister. London: Virago, 1987.

    Lycidus; Or The Lover in Fashion . . . From the French. London, 1688.

    The Plays, Histories and Novels of the Ingenious Mrs Aphra Behn. London: John Pearson, 1871.

    The Rover, ed. Frederick M. Link. London: Arnold, 1967.

The Second Part of the Rover. London, 1681.

The Novels of Aphra Behn, ed. Ernest Baker. London: Library of Early Novelists, 1905.

The Works of Aphra Behn, ed. Montague Summers. London: William Heinemann, 1915.

Bennett, John, *Letters to a Young Lady on Useful and Interesting Subjects*. Dublin, 1789.

Blackstone, William, *Commentaries on the Laws of England*. London: Reeves and Turner, 1896.

Boswell, James, *The Life of Samuel Johnson*, ed. George Birkbeck Hill and L.F. Powell. Oxford: Clarendon Press, 1934–50.

Brooke, Frances, *The History of Emily Montague*. London, 1769.

The History of Lady Julia Mandeville. London, 1763.

Brunton, Mary, *Emmeline, with some other pieces*. Edinburgh, 1819.

Burke, Edmund, *A Philosophical Enquiry into the Origin of our ideas of the Sublime and Beautiful*. Menston: Scolar Press, 1970.

Reflections on the Revolution in France. London, 1790.

Burney, Fanny, *Camilla; or A Picture of Youth*. Oxford: Oxford University Press, 1983.

Cecilia; or Memoirs of an Heiress. London: Virago, 1986.

Diary and Letters of Madame d'Arblay, ed. Charlotte Barrett. London, 1854.

The Early Diary of Frances Burney 1768–1778, with a Selection from her Correspondence, ed. Annie Raine Ellis. London: Bell, 1913.

Evelina; or The History of a Young Lady's Entrance into the World. New York: Norton, 1965.

The Journals and Letters of Fanny Burney, ed. Joyce Hemlow et al. Oxford: Clarendon Press, 1972–84.

Fanny Burney: Selected Letters and Journals. Oxford: Clarendon Press, 1986.

The Wanderer; or Female Difficulties. London, 1814.

Candler, Ann, *Poetical Attempts*. Ipswich, 1803.

[Carleton, Mary] *The Case of Madam Mary Carleton*. London, 1663.

An historical narrative of the German princess . . . Written by herself. London, 1663.

Carter, Elizabeth, *All the Works of Epictetus*. London, 1758.

Memoirs of the Life . . . to which are added some miscellaneous essays by M. Dennington. London, 1807.

A Series of Letters between Mrs Elizabeth Carter and Miss Catherine Talbot from the year 1741 to 1770. London, 1809.

Centlivre, Susanna, *The Basset Table*. London, 1705. *Letters of Wit, Politicks, and Morality*. London, 1701.

Chapone, Hester Mulso, *Essays . . . for Young Ladies*. London, 1777.

Works and Life. London, 1807.

The Works of Mrs Chapone. Dublin, 1786.

Chesterfield, Philip Dormer Stanhope, Earl of, *Letters Written . . . to his Son*. London, 1774.

Chudleigh, Mary, Lady, *Poems on Several Occasions*. London, 1703.

Clarendon, Edward Hyde, Earl of, *The History of the Great Rebellion and Civil Wars in England*, ed. W.D. Macray. Oxford: Clarendon Press, 1888.

Coke, Lady Mary, *Letters and Journals of Lady Mary Coke 1756–74*. Bath: Kingsmead Reprints, 1970.

Collier, Jeremy, *A Short View of the Immorality and Profaneness of the English Stage*. Menston: Scolar Press, 1971.

Collier, Mary, *The Woman's Labour, an epistle to Mr Stephen Duck*. London, 1739.

The Poems of Mary Collier . . . to which is prefixed her life, drawn by herself. Petersfield, 1765?

Colman, George, *Polly Honeycombe, A Dramatick Novel of One Act*. London, 1760.

Congreve, William, *Incognita*. Menston: Scolar Press, 1971.

Conway, Anne Finch, Viscountess, *Conway Letters*, ed. M.H. Nicholson. New Haven: Yale University Press, 1930.

Cowper, William, *The Correspondence of William Cowper*, ed. Thomas Wright. London: Hodder & Stoughton, 1904.

Critical Remarks on Sir Charles Grandison, Clarissa and Pamela. London, 1754.

Darwin, Erasmus, *A Plan for the Conduct of Female Education in Boarding Schools*. London, 1797.

D'Aulnoy, Marie Catherine La Mothe, Countess, *Memoirs of the Court of England*. London, 1707.

The Present Court of Spain. London, 1693.

Davys, Mary, *Familiar Letters Betwixt a Gentleman and a Lady*, ed. Robert Adams Day. Los Angeles: Augustan Reprint Society, 1955.

The Reform'd Coquet; a novel. London, 1724.

Defoe, Daniel, *Moll Flanders*, ed. J. Sutherland. Boston: Houghton Mifflin, 1959.

Delany, Mary, *Autobiography and Correspondence of Mary Granville, Mrs Delany*, ed. Lady Llanover. London: Richard Bentley, 1861.

Duff, William, *Letters on the Intellectual and Moral Character of Women*. Aberdeen, 1807.

Duncombe, John, *Feminiad*. London, 1754.

Echlin, Lady, *An Alternative Ending to Richardson's 'Clarissa'*, ed. Dimiter Daphinoff. Bern: Francke Verlag, 1982.

Edgeworth, Maria, *Letters for Literary Ladies*. London, 1795.

Ephelia, *Female Poems on Several Occasions*. London, 1679.

Evelyn, John, *Diary and Correspondence of John Evelyn*, ed. W. Bray. London: Henry Coburn, 1850–1852.

Fanshawe, Ann, Lady, *The Memoirs of Anne, Lady Halkett and Ann, Lady Fanshawe*, ed. John Loftis. Oxford: Oxford University Press, 1979.

Fell, Margaret (Fox), *Womens Speaking Justified*. Los Angeles: Clark Memorial Library, 1979.

Fenwick, Eliza, *Secresy, or, the ruin on the rock*. London: Pandora, 1988.

Fielding, Sarah, *The Adventures of David Simple*. London: Oxford University Press, 1969.

The Countess of Dellwyn. London, 1759.

and Jane Collier, *The Cry*. London, 1754.

Remarks on Clarissa Addressed to the Author. London, 1749.

Filmer, Robert, *Patriarcha; or the natural power of kings*, ed. P. Laslett. Oxford: Blackwell's Political Texts, 1949.

Fordyce, John, *The Character and Conduct of the Female Sex*. London, 1776.

Sermons to Young Women. London, 1766.

Fyge, Sarah (Egerton), *The Female Advocate*. Los Angeles: Clark Memorial Library, 1976.

The Gentlewoman's Companion. London, 1673.

Gisborne, Thomas, *An Enquiry into the Duties of the Female Sex*. London, 1797.

Glasse, Hannah, *The Art of Cookery Made Plain and Easy*. London, 1747.

Godwin, William, *An Enquiry concerning Political Justice*. Oxford: Clarendon Press, 1971.

Memoirs of Mary Wollstonecraft. London: Constable, 1927.

Gould, Robert, *Love given o're . . . Satyr against . . . woman, Satires on Women*. Los Angeles: Augustan Reprint Society, 1976.

Poems. London, 1689.

Gregory, John, *A Father's Legacy to his Daughters*. Dublin, 1790.

Greville, Frances, 'A Prayer for Indifference', *The New Oxford Book of Eighteenth Century Verse*, ed. R. Lonsdale. Oxford: Oxford University Press, 1984.

Griffith, Elizabeth, *The History of Lady Barton*. London, 1771.

A Series of Genuine Letters between Henry and Frances. London, 1753.

Gunning, Susannah, *Coombe Wood*. London, 1783.

A Letter from Mrs Gunning addressed to His Grace, the Duke of Argyll. London, 1791.

Halifax, George Savile, Marquess of, *The Lady's New-Years Gift; or Advice to a Daughter*. London, 1688.

Hamilton, Elizabeth, *Letters on Education*. London, 1801.

Memoirs of Modern Philosophers. London, 1800.

Hawkins, Laetitia Matilda, *Letters on the Female Mind*. London, 1793.

Hayley, William, *A Philosophical, Historical and Moral Essay on Old Maids*. London, 1785.

Hays, Mary, *Appeal to the Men of Great Britain in Behalf of Women*. New York: Garland, 1974.

Letters and Essays, Moral and Miscellaneous. London, 1793.

The Memoirs of Emma Courtney. New York: Garland Publishing, 1974.

Haywood, Eliza, *The British Recluse*. London, 1722.

The History of Miss Betsy Thoughtless. London: Pandora, 1986.

Love in Excess; or The Fatal Enquiry. London, 1719.

Memoirs of a Certain Island. London, 1725.

Hertford, Countess of, *Correspondence between Frances, Countess of Hertford (afterwards Duchess of Somerset) and Henrietta Louisa, Countess of Pomfret, between 1738 and 1741*, ed. W. Bingley. London, 1805.

Hume, David, *A Treatise on Human Nature*, ed. L.A. Selby-Bigge. Oxford: Clarendon Press, 1888.

Enquiries concerning the Human Understandings and concerning the Principles of Morals, ed. L.A. Selby-Bigge. Oxford: Clarendon Press, 1966.

Hutchinson, Lucy, *Memoirs of the Life of Colonel Hutchinson*, ed. J. Sutherland. London: Oxford University Press, 1973.

Inchbald, Elizabeth, *A Simple Story*. London: Pandora, 1987.

James, Elinor, *An injur'd prince vindicated*. London, 1688.

Most dear Sovereign. London, 1689.

Johnson, Samuel, *The Rambler*. New York: Garland, 1978.

Kenrick, William, *The Whole Duty of Woman*. London, 1753.

Killigrew, Anne, *Poems*. Gainesville: Scholars' Facsimiles & Reprints, 1967.

Kirkman, Francis, *The Counterfeit Lady Unveiled*. London, 1679.

Lennox, Charlotte, *The Female Quixote*. London: Pandora, 1986.

Locke, John, *Two Treatises of Government*, ed. P. Laslett. Cambridge: Cambridge University Press, 1963.

Macaulay, Catherine, *Letters on Education*. London, 1790.

[Makin, Bathsua], *An Essay to Revive the Antient Education of Gentlewomen* 1673; Los Angeles: Clark Memorial Library, 1980.

Manley, Delarivier [Mary], *A Lady's Packet of Letters Broke Open*. London, 1707.

The Novels of Mary Delarivier Manley, ed. P. Köster. Gainesville: Scholars' Facsimiles & Reprints, 1971.

Marriott, Thomas, *Female Conduct, being an essay in the art of pleasing to be practised by the Fair Sex, before and after marriage*. London, 1759.

Miller, James, *The Humours of Oxford*. London, 1730.

Minifie, Susannah and Margaret, *Histories of Lady Frances S— and Lady Caroline S—*. London, 1763.

Montagu, Elizabeth, *The Letters of Mrs Elizabeth Montagu*, ed. Matthew Montagu. London, 1809–13.

Mrs Montagu 'Queen of the Blues': Her Letters and Friendships from 1762 to 1800, ed. Reginald Blunt. London: Constable, n.d.

Montagu, Lady Mary Wortley, *The Complete Letters of Lady Mary Wortley Montagu*, ed. Robert Halsband. Oxford: Clarendon Press, 1965–7.

Lady Mary Wortley Montagu: Essays and Poems, ed. Robert Halsband and Isobel Grundy. Oxford: Clarendon Press, 1977.

More, Hannah, *Coelebs in Search of a Wife*. London, 1809.

Essays . . . for Young Ladies. London, 1777.

Memoirs of the Life and Correspondence of Hannah More, ed. William Roberts. London, 1834.

Strictures on the Modern System of Education. London, 1799.

The Works of Hannah More. London, 1834.

Murry, Ann, *Mentoria; or, The Young Ladies Instructor*. London, 1776.

Narrative of the Incidents which form the mystery in the family of General Gunning. London, 1791.

Newcastle, Margaret Cavendish, Duchess of, *The Life of . . . William Cavendish, Duke . . . of Newcastle.* London, 1667.
Natures Pictures Drawn by Fancies Pencil to the Life. London, 1656.
Observations upon Experimental Philosophy. London, 1666.
Orations of Divers Sorts. London, 1662.
Philosophical and Physical Opinions. London, 1655.
Playes. London, 1662.
Plays, Never Before Printed. London, 1668.
Poems and Fancies. Menston: Scolar Press, 1972.
Sociable Letters. Menston: Scolar Press, 1972.
The Worlds Olio. London, 1655.
Newcastle, William Cavendish, Duke of, *The Phanseys of William Cavendish Marquis of Newcastle,* ed. D. Grant (London: Nonesuch Press, 1956).
Osborne, Dorothy, *Letters from Dorothy Osborne to Sir William Temple,* ed. Kingsley Hart. London: Folio Society, 1968.
Pennington, Lady, *An Unfortunate Mother's Advice to her Absent Daughters, The Young Lady's Pocket Library or Parental Monitor,* Dublin, 1790. See p. 295, note 22.
Pepys, Samuel, *The Diary of Samuel Pepys,* ed. R. Latham and W. Matthews. London: Bell & Hyman, 1970–83.
Philips, Katherine, *Letters from Orinda to Poliarchus.* London, 1705.
Poems By the most deservedly Admired Mrs Katherine Philips. London, 1667.
Phillips, Teresia Constantia [Con], *An Apology for the Conduct of Mrs Teresia Constantia Phillips. . . .* London, 1748.
Piers, Lady Sarah, prefatory poem to *The Unhappy Penitent.* London, 1701.
Pilkington, Laetitia, *The Memoirs.* London, 1748–54.
Pix, Mary, *The False Friend; or, The Fate of Disobedience.* London, 1699.
Polwhele, Elizabeth, *The Frolicks,* ed. Judith Milhous and Robert Hume. Ithaca: Cornell University Press, 1977.
Polwhele, Richard, *The Unsex'd Females.* London, 1798.
The proceedings at the sessions of the Peace . . . upon a bill of indictment found against Francis Charteris, for committing a rape on the body of Anne Bond. London, 1730.
Pope, Alexander, *Poetical Works,* ed. H. Davis. Oxford: Oxford University Press, 1978.
Radcliffe, Ann, *The Italian.* Oxford: Oxford University Press, 1981.
A Journey Made in the Summer of 1794 through Holland and the Western Frontier of Germany. London, 1795.
The Mysteries of Udolpho. Oxford: Oxford University Press, 1970.
The Romance of the Forest. Oxford: Oxford University Press, 1986.
Radcliffe, Mary Ann, *The Female Advocate; or, an Attempt to Recover the Rights of Women from Male Usurpation.* London, 1799.
Reeve, Clara, *The Exiles.* London, 1788.
Plans of Education, with Remarks on the System of Other Writers. New York: Garland, 1974.
The Progress of Romance. Colchester, 1785.

Richardson, Samuel, *Clarissa, or the History of a Young Lady*. Harmondsworth: Penguin, 1985.
The History of Sir Charles Grandison. Oxford: Oxford University Press, 1986.
Pamela, or Virtue Rewarded. Boston: Houghton Mifflin, 1971.
Selected Letters of Samuel Richardson, ed. John Carroll. Oxford: Clarendon Press, 1964.
Rochester, Earl of, John Wilmot, *Poems on several occasions*. London, 1680.
Rousseau, Jean-Jacques, *Emile*, Transl. B. Foxley. London: Dent, 1974.
Julia; or, The new Eloisa. Edinburgh, 1773.
Scott, Sara, *Millenium Hall*. London: Virago, 1986.
Scott, Sir Walter, *The Lives of the Novelists*. London: J.M. Dent & Sons, 1910.
Scudéry, Madeleine de, *Clelia, An excellent new romance*. Transl. J. Davies. London, 1656–61.
Sharp, Jane, *The Midwives Book or the Whole Art of Midwifery discovered*. London, 1671.
Sheridan, Frances, *The History of Nourjahad*. n.p.; Norwood Editions, 1977.
Memoirs of Miss Sidney Bidulph. London, 1761.
Short Remarks upon the Original and Pernicious Consquences of Masquerades. London, 1721.
Smith, Charlotte, *The Banished Man*. London, 1794.
Elegiac Sonnets. London, 1784.
Emmeline: The Orphan of the Castle. London: Oxford University Press, 1971.
The Old Manor House. London: Pandora, 1987.
The Young Philosopher. London, 1798.
The Spectator. London, 1747.
Stark, Mariana, *The Poor Soldier; an American Tale*. London, 1789.
The Sword of Peace; or, the Voyage of Love.
Swift, Jonathan, *Satires and Personal Writings*, ed. William Alfred Eddy. London: Oxford University Press, 1932.
The Poems of Jonathan Swift, ed. H. Williams. Oxford: Clarendon Press, 1958.
The Tatler. London, 1803.
Thrale, Hester, *Thraliana: The Diary of Mrs Hester Lynch Thrale [later Mrs Piozzi] 1770–1809*, ed. Katherine C. Balderston, 2nd edn. Oxford: Oxford University Press, 1951.
Tonkin, Mary, *The Female Spy; or Mrs Tonkin's Account of her Journey through France*. London, 1783.
Trimmer, Sarah, *The Oeconomy of Charity*. London, 1787.
Fabulous Histories, designed for the Instruction of Children, respecting their treatment of animals. London, 1786.
Trotter, Catharine, *Olinda's Adventures: Or, The Amours of a Young Lady*, 1693, ed. Robert Adams Day. Los Angeles: Augustan Reprint Society, 1969.
The Works of Mrs Catharine Cockburn. London, 1751.
Wakefield, Priscilla, *Reflections on the Present Condition of the Female Sex, With Suggestions for Its Improvement*. London, 1798.

Warwick, Mary Rich, Countess of, *Autobiography of Mary Countess of Warwick*, ed. T.C. Croker. London: Percy Society, 1848.

Memoir of Lady Warwick: also Her Diary from AD *1666 to 1667.* London: The Religious Tracts Society, 1847.

Weamys, Anne, *A Continuation of Sir Philip Sidney's Arcadia.* London, 1651.

West, Jane, *Letters to a Young Lady.* London, 1806.

Whytt, Robert, *Observations on the Nature, Causes and Cure of those Diseases which are commonly called Nervous, Hypochondriac or Hysteric.* London, 1764.

Williams, Helen Maria, *Julia.* London, 1790.

Letters from France. New York: Scholars' Facsimiles & Reprints, 1975.

Poems. London, 1786.

Winchilsea, Anne Finch, Countess of, *The Poems of Anne, Countess of Winchilsea.* Chicago: University of Chicago Press, 1903.

Wolley, Hannah, *The Accomplish'd Lady's Delight.* London, 1677.

Wollstonecraft, Mary, *Collected Letters of Mary Wollstonecraft*, ed. Ralph M. Wardle. Ithaca: Cornell University Press, 1979.

An Historical and Moral View of the Origin and Progress of the French Revolution. New York: Scholars' Facsimiles & Reprints, 1975.

Letters Written . . . in Sweden 1796; Lincoln: University of Nebraska Press, 1976.

Mary, A Fiction and *The Wrongs of Woman.* Oxford: Oxford University Press, 1976.

A Vindication of the Rights of Woman. Harmondsworth: Penguin, 1985.

A Wollstonecraft Anthology. Bloomington: Indiana University Press, 1977.

Wright, Thomas, *Female Vertuoso's.* London, 1693.

Wroth, Lady Mary, *Pamphilia to Amphilanthus.* Salzburg: Studies in English Literature, 1977.

SECONDARY WORKS

Adburgham, Alison, *Women in Print: Writing Women and Women's Magazines From the Restoration to the Accession of Victoria.* London: George Allen and Unwin, 1972.

Amussen, S., 'Gender, Family and the Social Order, 1560–1725', *Order and Disorder in Early Modern England*, ed. A. Fletcher and J. Stevenson. Cambridge: Cambridge University Press, 1985, pp. 196–217.

Ashton, T.S., *An Economic History of England: the Eighteenth Century.* London: Methuen, 1955.

Auty, Susan G., *The Comic Spirit of Eighteenth-Century Novels.* Port Washington: Kennikat, 1975.

Avery, Emmett, 'The Restoration Audience', *Philological Quarterly* 65, 1966.

Backscheider, Paula R., 'Woman's Influence', *Studies in the Novel*, 11, 1979, pp. 3–22.

Bernbaum, Ernest, *The Mary Carleton Narratives.* Cambridge, Mass.: Harvard University Press, 1914.

'Mrs Behn's biography, a fiction', *PMLA*, 28, 1913, 432–53.

Bernikow, Louise, ed., *The World Split Open: four centuries of women poets . . . 1552–1950*. London: The Women's Press, 1979.

Blakey, Dorothy, *The Minerva Press 1790–1820*. London: Bibliographical Society, 1939.

Bloom, A. and Lillian D., 'Fanny Burney's Novels: The Retreat from Wonder', *Novel*, 12, 1979, 215–35.

Brailsford, Mabel, *Quaker Women 1650–1690*. London: Duckworth & Co., 1915.

Brink, Jeanie, ed., *Female Scholars: A Tradition of Learned Women Before 1800*. Montreal, 1980.

Brissenden, R.F., *Virtue in Distress: Studies in the Novel of Sentiment*. New York: Barnes & Noble, 1974.

Browne, Alice, *The Eighteenth Century Feminist Mind*. Brighton: Harvester, 1987.

Butler, Marilyn, *Jane Austen and the War of Ideas*. Oxford: Oxford University Press, 1975.

Romantics, Rebels & Reactionaries. Oxford: Oxford University Press, 1981.

'The woman at the window', *Gender and Literary Voice*, ed. Janet Todd. New York: Holmes & Meier, 1980.

Cash, Arthur H., 'The birth of Tristram Shandy: Sterne and Dr Burton', *Sexuality in Eighteenth-Century Britain*, ed. Paul-Gabriel Boucé. Manchester: Manchester University Press, 1982.

Castle, Terry, *Masquerade and Civilization*. Stanford: Stanford University Press, 1986.

'The spectralization of the other in *The Mysteries of Udelpho*', *The New Eighteenth Century: Theory, Politics, English Literature*. New York: Methuen, 1987.

Clark, Alice, *Working Life of Women in the Seventeenth Century*. London: G. Routledge & Sons, 1919.

Cottom, Daniel, *The Civilized Imagination*. Cambridge, Mass.: Cambridge University Press, 1985.

Cotton, Nancy, *Women Playwrights in England ca. 1363–1750*. Lewisburg: Bucknell University Press, 1980.

Crawford, P., 'Women's Published Writings 1600–1700', *Women in English Society 1500–1800*, ed. M. Prior. London: Methuen, 1985, pp. 211–82.

Cressy, David, *Literacy and the Social Order*. Cambridge: Cambridge University Press, 1980.

Davidoff, L. and C. Hall, *Family Fortunes: Men and Women of the English Middle Class 1780–1850*. London: Hutchinson, 1987.

Davis, Lennard J., *Factual Fictions*. New York: Columbia University Press, 1983.

Davis, Natalie Zemon, 'Gender and genre: women as historical writers 1400–1820', *Beyond Their Sex: Learned Women of the European Past*, ed. Patricia Labalme. New York: New York University Press, 1980.

Day, Robert Adams, 'Aphra Behn and the works of the intellect', *Fetter'd or Free? British Women Novelists 1670–1815*, ed. Mary Anne Schofield and Cecilia Macheski. Athens: Ohio University Press, 1986.

'Aphra Behn's First Biographer', *Studies in Bibliography*, xxii, 1969, pp. 227–40.

Told in Letters: Epistolary Fiction before Richardson. Ann Arbor: University of Michigan Press, 1966.

Delany, Paul, *British Autobiography in the Seventeenth Century*. London: Routledge and Kegan Paul, 1969.

Devlin, D.D., *The Novels and Journals of Fanny Burney*. London: Macmillan, 1986.

Doody, Margaret, 'Deserts, Ruins and Troubled Waters: Female Dreams in Fiction and the Development of the Gothic Novel', *Genre*, 10, 1977, pp. 529–72.

Duchovnay, G., 'Aphra Behn's Religion', *Notes & Queries*, ccxxi, May–June, 1976, pp. 235–7.

Duffy, Maureen, *The Passionate Shepherdess: Aphra Behn 1640–89*. London: Jonathan Cape, 1977.

Durant, David S., 'Aesthetic heroism in *The Mysteries of Udolpho*', *The Eighteenth Century*, 22, 1981, 175–88.

Eaves, T.C.D. and B.D. Kimpel, *Samuel Richardson: A Biography*. Oxford: Oxford University Press, 1971.

Flaxman, Rhoda L., 'Radcliffe's dual modes of vision', *Fetter'd or Free?*, ed. Mary Anne Schofield and Cecilia Macheski. Athens, Ohio: Ohio University Press, 1986.

Foxon, David, *Libertine Literature in England 1660–1745*. New York: University Books, 1965.

Foucault, Michel, *Madness and Civilization*. London: Tavistock, 1967.

The Order of Things. London: Tavistock, 1970.

Fraser, Antonia, *The Weaker Vessel*. London: Weidenfeld and Nicolson, 1984.

Gagen, Jean, 'Honor and Fame in the Works of the Duchess of Newcastle', *Studies in Philology*, 56, 1959.

Gardiner, Dorothy, *English Girlhood at School: A Study of Women's Education through Twelve Centuries*. Oxford: Oxford University Press, 1929.

Gardiner, Judith Kegan, 'Aphra Behn: Sexuality and Self-Respect', *Women's Studies*, 7, nos. 1 and 2, 1980, 67–78.

George, Dorothy, *London Life in the Eighteenth Century*. Harmondsworth: Penguin, 1966.

Gilbert, Sandra and Susan Gubar, *The Madwoman in the Attic: the Woman Writer and the Nineteenth-Century Literary Imagination*. New Haven: Yale University Press, 1979.

Gohlke, Madelon, 'Reading "Euphues"', *Criticism*, 19, 1977.

Goreau, Angeline, *Reconstructing Aphra: A Social Biography of Aphra Behn*. New York: Dial Press, 1980.

Grant, W.D.B., *Margaret the First: A Biography of Margaret Cavendish, Duchess of Newcastle 1623–1673*. London: Rupert Hart-Davis, 1957.

Guffy, G., *Two English Novelists: Aphra Behn and Anthony Trollope*. Los Angeles: Clark Memorial Library, 1975.

Habbakkuk, H.J., 'Marriage Settlements in the eighteenth century', *Transactions* of the Royal Society, XXXII, 1950, pp. 15–30.

Halsband, Robert, *The Life of Lady Mary Wortley Montagu*. Oxford: Clarendon Press, 1956.

Hellmann, John, *Fables of Fact: The New Journalism as New Fiction*. Urbana: University of Illinois Press, 1981.

Hemlow, Joyce, 'Fanny Burney and the Courtesy Books', *PMLA*, 65, 1950, pp. 732–61.

History of Fanny Burney. Oxford: Oxford University Press, 1965.

Hill, Christopher, *The world turned upside down: radical ideas during the English Revolution*. London: Maurice Temple Smith, 1972.

'Sex, Marriage and the Family in England', *Economic History Review*, xxxi, 1978, pp. 450–463.

Hobby, Elaine, *Virtue of Necessity*. London: Virago, 1988.

Horner, Joyce M., *The English Women Novelists and Their Connection with the Feminist Movement (1699–1797)*. Smith College Studies in Modern Languages. Northampton: The Collegiate Press, 1929–30.

Hull, Suzanne W., *Chaste, Silent, and Obedient: English Books for Women, 1475–1640*. San Marino: Huntington Library, 1982.

Hume, Robert, *The Development of English Drama in the Late Seventeenth Century*. Oxford: Clarendon Press, 1976.

Isles, Duncan, 'Johnson and Charlotte Lennox', *New Rambler* 19, 1967, 34–38.

Jordanova, L.J., 'Natural Facts: a historical perspective on science and sexuality', *Nature, culture and gender*, eds. Carol P. MacCormack and Marilyn Strathern. Cambridge: Cambridge University Press, 1980.

Kamm, Josephine, *Hope Deferred: Girls' Education in English History*. London: Methuen, 1965.

Kavanagh, Julia, *English Women of Letters*. London, 1862.

Kelly, Gary, *The English Jacobin Novel*. Oxford: Clarendon Press, 1976.

Kelsall, Malcolm, Introduction to Sarah Fielding's *David Simple*. London: Oxford University Press, 1969.

Kiely, Robert, *The Romantic novel in England*. Cambridge, Mass.: Harvard University Press, 1972.

Kinnaird, Joan, 'Mary Astell and the Conservative Contribution to English Feminism', *Journal of British Studies*, 19, 1979.

Koon, Helene, 'Eliza Haywood and *The Female Spectator*', *Huntington Library Quarterly*, 42, 1978–9, 43–55.

Laslett, Peter, *Family Life and Illicit Love in Earlier Generations*. Cambridge: Cambridge University Press, 1977.

and Richard Wall, eds., *Household and Family in Past Times*. Cambridge: Cambridge University Press, 1973.

The World We Have Lost. New York: Charles Scribner's Sons, 1965.

Lefanu, Alicia, *Memoirs of the Life and Writings of Mrs Frances Sheridan*. London, 1824.

London, April, 'Placing the Female: The Metonymic Garden in Amatory and Pious Narrative, 1700–1740', *Fetter'd or Free?*, ed. Mary Anne Schofield and Cecilia Macheski. Athens, Ohio: Ohio University Press, 1986.

Lonsdale, Roger, *Dr Charles Burney*. Oxford: Clarendon Press, 1966.

MacCarthy, B.G., *The Female Pen*. 2 vols: *Women Writers: Their Contribution to the English Novel 1621–1744* and *The Later Women Novelists 1744–1818*. Cork: Cork University Press, 1944 and 1947.

McKeon, Michael, *The Origins of the English Novel 1600–1740*. Baltimore: Johns Hopkins Press, 1987.

McLaren, Dorothy, 'Marital fertility and lactation 1570–1720', *Women in English Society 1500–1800*, ed. M. Prior. London: Methuen, 1985.

Maclean, Ian, *Woman Triumphant: Feminism in French Literature 1610–1652*. Oxford: Oxford University Press, 1977.

McMullan, Lorraine, *An Odd Attempt in a Woman*. Vancouver: University of British Columbia Press, 1983.

Main, C., 'The German Princess: or, Mary Carleton in Fact and Fiction', *Harvard Library Bulletin*, 10, 1956.

Mattes, Eleanor, 'The "Female Virtuoso" in Early Eighteenth Century English Drama', *Women & Lieature*, 3, Fall 1975, 3–10.

Mayo, Robert, *The English Novel in the Magazines 1740–1815*. Evanston: Northwestern University Press, 1962.

Mendelson, Sara Heler, *The Mental World of Stuart Women*. Brighton: Harvester Press, 1987.

Miyoshi, Masao, *The Divided Self*. New York: New York University Press, 1969.

Modleski, Tania, *Loving with a Vengeance*. London: Methuen, 1984.

Morgan, Fidelis, *The Female Wits: Women Playwrights of the Restoration*. London: Virago, 1981.

A Woman of No Character: an autobiography of Mrs Manley. London: Faber, 1986.

Myers, Mitzi, 'Domesticating Minerva: Bathsua Makin's curious argument for women's education', *Studies in Eighteenth-Century Culture*, ed. O.M. Brack, 14, 1985, 173–92.

'Hannah More's tracts for the times: social fiction and female ideology', *Fetter'd or Free?*, ed. Mary Anne Schofield and Cecilia Macheski. Athens, Ohio: Ohio University Press, 1986.

'Unfinished Business: Wollstonecraft's *Maria*', *Wordsworth Circle*, 11, 1980, 107–114.

Nelson, Lowry, 'Night Thoughts on the Gothic Novel', *Yale Review*, 1963.

Newton, Judith, '*Evelina*; or, The History of a Young Lady's Entrance into the Marriage Market', *Modern Language Studies*, 6, 1, 1976, 48–56.

Women, Power, and Subversion: Social Strategies in British Fiction 1778–1860. Athens, Georgia: University of Georgia Press, 1981.

Nussbaum, Felicity, *The Brink of All We Hate: English Satires on Women 1660–1750*. Lexington: University Press of Kentucky, 1984.

Ogg, David, *England in the Reign of Charles II*. Oxford: Oxford University Press, 1984.

Perry, Ruth, *The Celebrated Mary Astell*. Chicago: University of Chicago Press, 1986.

Women, Letters and the Novel. New York: AMS Press, 1980.

Pierce, Robert B., 'Moral Education in the Novel of the 1750s', *Philological Quarterly*, 44, 1965, 73–87.

Plant, Marjorie, *The English Book Trade*. London: George Allen and Unwin, 1965.

Plumb, J.H., *The commercialization of leisure in eighteenth-century England*. Reading: University of Reading, 1973.

Pollak, Ellen, *The Poetics of Sexual Myth: Gender and Ideology in the Verse of Swift and Pope*. Chicago: Chicago University Press, 1985.

Poovey, Mary, 'Fathers and Daughters: The Trauma of Growing Up Female', *Men by Women*, ed. Janet Todd. New York: Holmes & Meier, 1982, 39–57.

'Ideology and *The Mysteries of Udolpho*', *Criticism*, 1979, 307–30.

Porter, Roy, 'Mixed feelings: the Enlightenment and sexuality in eighteenth-century Britain', *Sexuality in Eighteenth-Century Britain*, ed. Paul-Gabriel Boucé. Manchester: Manchester University Press, 1982.

Radway, Janice A., *Reading the Romance: Women, Patriarchy and Popular Literature*. Chapel Hill: University of North Carolina Press, 1984.

Rendall, Jane, *The Origins of Modern Feminism: Women in Britain, France and the US, 1780–1860*. London: Macmillan, 1985.

Reynolds, Myra, *The Learned Lady in England, 1650–1760*. Boston: Houghton Mifflin, 1920.

Richetti, John J., *Popular Fiction Before Richardson: Narrative Patterns, 1700–1739*. Oxford: Clarendon Press, 1969.

Rivers, Isabel, ed., *Books and their Readers in Eighteenth-Century England*. Leicester: University of Leicester Press, 1982.

Rogers, Katharine, *Feminism in Eighteenth-Century England*. Urbana: University of Illinois Press, 1982.

Rogers, Pat, 'The breeches part', *Sexuality in Eighteenth-Century Britain*, ed. Paul-Gabriel Boucé. Manchester: Manchester University Press, 1982.

Literature and Popular Culture in Eighteenth Century England. Brighton: Harvester, 1985.

Salzman, Paul, *English Prose Fiction 1558–1700*. Oxford: Oxford University Press, 1985.

Schilz, D., '"Novel", "Romance", and Popular Fiction in the First Half of the Eighteenth Century', *Studies in Philology*, 70, 1973, 77–91.

Schnorrenberg, Barbara B. with Jean E. Hunter, 'The eighteenth-century Englishwoman', *The Women of England from Anglo-Saxon Times to the Present*, ed. Barbara Kanner. London: Mansell, 1980.

Schofield, Mary Anne, *Quiet Rebellion: The Fictional Heroines of Eliza Fowler Haywood*. Washington: University Press of America, 1982.

Sedgwick, Eve Kosofsky, *The Coherence of Gothic Conventions*. London: Methuen, 1986.

Smith, Hilda L., *Reason's Disciples: Seventeenth-Century English Feminists*. Urbana: University of Illinois Press, 1982.

Spacks, Patricia M., *The Adolescent Idea: Myths of Youth and Adult Imagination*. London: Faber and Faber, 1982.

'Every Woman is at Heart a Rake', *Eighteenth-Century Studies*, 8, 1974–5, pp. 27–46.

Imagining a Self: Autobiography and the Novel in Eighteenth-Century England, Cambridge: Harvard University Press, 1976.

Spencer, Jane, *The Rise of the Woman Novelist*. Oxford: Basil Blackwell, 1986.

Spender, Dale, *Mothers of the Novel*. London: Pandora, 1986.

Spufford, Margaret, *Small Books and Pleasant Histories: Popular Fiction and its Readership in the Seventeenth Century*. London: Methuen, 1981.

Stafford, Barbara M., *Voyage into substance: art, science, nature, and the illustrated travel account, 1760–1840*. Cambridge: MIT Press, 1984.

Stallybrass, Peter and Allon White, *The Politics and Poetics of Transgression*. London: Methuen, 1986.

Stanton, Domna, 'The fiction of *Preciosity* and the fear of women', *Yale French Studies*, 62, 1981, 107–34.

Starr, G.A., 'Only a Boy: Notes on Sentimental Novels', *Genre*, 10, 1977, 501–27.

Staves, Susan, *Players' Scepters: Fictions of Authority in the Restoration*. Lincoln: University of Nebraska Press, 1978.

Stenton, Doris M., *The English Woman in History*. London: Allen and Unwin, 1957.

Stone, Lawrence, *The Family, Sex and Marriage in England, 1500–1800*. Harmondsworth: Penguin, 1982.

Straub, Kristina, *Fanny Burney and Feminine Strategy*. Lexington: University Press of Kentucky, 1987.

Thompson, Roger, *Women in Stuart England and America*. London: Routledge and Kegan Paul, 1974.

Unfit for Modest Ears: A Study of Pornographic, Obscene and Bawdy Works ... in the Second Half of the Seventeenth Century. London: Macmillan, 1979.

Todd, Barbara J., 'The remarrying widow: a stereotype reconsidered', *Women in English Society 1500–1800*, ed. M. Prior. London: Methuen, 1985.

Todd, Janet, ed., *A Dictionary of British and American Women Writers 1660–1800*. London: Methuen, 1985.

Sensibility: An Introduction. London: Methuen, 1986.

Women's Friendship in Literature. New York: Columbia University Press, 1980.

Tompkins, J.M.S., *The Popular Novel in England 1770–1800*. Lincoln: University of Nebraska Press, 1961.

Wardle, Ralph M., *Mary Wollstonecraft*. Lawrence: University of Kansas Press, 1951.

Watson, J. Steven, *The Reign of George III*. Oxford: Clarendon Press, 1981.

Watt, Ian, *The Rise of the Novel*. Berkeley: University of California Press, 1957.

Webber, Joan, *The Eloquent 'I': Style and Self in Seventeenth-Century Prose*. Madison: University of Wisconsin Press, 1968.

Weber, Max, *The Protestant Ethic and the Spirit of Capitalism*. New York: Charles Scribner's Sons, 1958.

Whicher, George F., *The Life and Romances of Eliza Haywood*. New York:

Columbia University Press, 1915.

Williams, Ioan, *Novel and Romance 1700–1800: A Documentary Record*. New York: Barnes & Noble, 1970.

Woodcock, G., 'Mary Manley and Eliza Haywood', *Room of One's Own*, 2, 4, 1977, 549–65.

Woolf, Virginia, *The Common Reader*. London: The Hogarth Press, 1984.

A Room of One's Own and Three Guineas. London: Chatto & Windus, 1984.

Wrigley, E.A., 'Family limitation in preindustrial England', *Economic History Review*, 2nd series, 19, 1966, 82–109.

INDEX

Act of Toleration (1689), 21
actresses, 44, 133
Addison, Joseph, 17, 23, 32, 33, 35, 40,
  106, 109, 133, 177, 217, 274
adultery, 112
Adventures of Lindamira, 49
advice books, 110, 118, 122, 134, 138,
  210, 211–12
*Advice to the Women and Maidens of
  London*, 20
Alexander, William, *The History of
  Women*, 213
Amazons, 33, 125
The Analytical Review, 213, 220
Anne, Queen, 17, 18, 104
Anti-Jacobin, 199, 215
Antwerp, 70
'Ariadne', *She Ventures and He Wins*, 45
Astell, Mary, 9, 29, 41, 62, 122, 214, 246;
  background, 39; and celibacy, 63, 115;
  The Christian Religion, 37; and the
  Dissenters, 22; and education, 21,
  31–2, 39; interest in philosophy, 23–4,
  38; pamphleteering, 18, 19; proposes
  all-female college, 29, 39, 92, 115, 119;
  religion, 22–3; *Some Reflections upon
  Marriage*, 27–8; royalism, 15, 16, 17;
  and the South Sea Bubble, 20
Aubin, Penelope, 50, 87, 142, 147
Aulnoy, Marie d', 85
Austen, Jane, 2, 76, 160, 168, 191, 200,
  273–4; *Emma*, 171, 182; and the
  gothic novel, 147, 253, 254, 261–2;
  male mentors as reforming agents, 147,
  283; *Mansfield Park*, 182, 201, 222;
  Northanger Abbey, 8, 110, 147, 223,
  253, 261–2, 274; *Persuasion*, 33; *Pride
  and Prejudice*, 118; satire, 92; *Sense and
  Sensibility*, 234, 245; woman as
  moralist, 228
autobiography, 43, 252; Delarivier Manley,
  96–8; Duchess of Newcastle, 43,
  57–9, 60–1, 62–3, 66

Bacon, Francis, 23; *The New Atlantis*, 24, 90
Bage, 227–8
Baillie, Lady Grizel, 102
Baillie, Joanna, 222; *Metrical Legends of
  Exalted Characters*, 102
Ballard, George, *Memoirs of Several Ladies
  of Great Britain*, 122
Bank of England, 19
Barbauld, Anna Laetitia, 2, 196, 197, 208,
  22–3; *British Novelists*, 254; 'The
  Rights of Woman', 214
Barber, John, 85
Barker, Jane, 62, 139, 142; background,
  39; education, 32; *Exilius*, 50; interest
  in medicine, 24; *A Patch-Work Screen*,
  50, 51; royalism, 15, 16, 17; and the
  South Sea Bubble, 20; spinsterhood, 29,
  42
Barrell, Maria, 205–6
Barrett, E.S., *The Heroine*, 254
Barry, Elizabeth, 44
Bath, 135
Beaumont, Agnes, 43
Behn, Aphra, 29, 37, 47, 69–83, 97, 126,
  139; *Abdelazar*, 44; 'The Adventures of
  the Black Lady', 76, 77, 78; 'Agnes de
  Castro', 40, 77, 78; background, 38, 39,
  70, 132; biography, 70–2; construction
  of femininity, 4, 5; 'The Court of the
  King of Bantam', 76–7, 78; 'The
  Disappointment', 81; and the
  Dissenters, 22; *The Dutch Lover*, 69,

319